B. Rotman
10.2.71

SEMANTICS

An Introduction to

THE SCIENCE OF MEANING

SEMANTICS

An Introduction to

THE SCIENCE OF MEANING

BY

STEPHEN ULLMANN

Ph.D., D.Litt.

Professor of the Romance Languages in the University of Oxford

OXFORD
BASIL BLACKWELL
1970

First Edition 1962
Reprinted 1964, 1967, 1970

631 07120 2

Reprinted by offset in Great Britain by Alden & Mowbray Ltd
at the Alden Press, Oxford
and bound at Kemp Hall Bindery

TO MY WIFE

PREFACE

During the last decade there has been a considerable quickening of interest in semantics. A number of scholars have re-examined the principles on which this branch of linguistics is based; others have explored specific aspects of meaning; others again have focused their attention on the semantics of particular languages. Research in this field has been revitalized by the great revolution which has taken place in modern linguistics: the new vision of language as a highly organized structure made up of interdependent elements, and the realization that words play a crucial part in moulding our thoughts and directing them into certain channels. Recent advances in philosophy, psychology, anthropology, communication engineering and other spheres have also had important repercussions in the study of meaning. It is the main purpose of this book to provide an interim progress report on semantics: an account of past achievements, current research, and future tasks.

The present volume differs in several respects from my *Principles of Semantics* which was first published in 1951 (2nd edition, 1957; reprinted with additional material in 1959). It is more empirical in approach and deals with questions of theory only in so far as these help us to understand how language is built up, how it works, and how it changes. The previous book was addressed mainly to philologists; in the present one, the needs of specialists have not been forgotten, but it is also intended for other readers interested in meaning, including undergraduate and postgraduate students who are increasingly attracted by these problems.

During the ten years which have passed since the publication of the *Principles*, there have been many significant developments in semantics and general linguistics, and my own views have changed on some fundamental points. These changes, which could merely be touched upon in the new edition of the previous book, have been fully integrated into the structure of the present one. I have also introduced many new examples from literature and have in general paid more attention to the stylistic side of semantic phenomena such as synonymy, ambiguity and metaphor. Semantics is one of those modern disciplines which lie astride the borderline between linguistic and literary studies and thus help to emphasize the essential unity of the humanities.

I am indebted to a great many colleagues for offprints and other information. My special thanks are due to the following for kindly show-ing me their works before they appeared in print: Mr. T. E. Hope (University of Manchester), Dr. W. Rothwell (University of Leeds), and Dr. N. C. W. Spence (The Queen's University, Belfast).

LEEDS, 1961.   STEPHEN ULLMANN

CONTENTS

CHAPTER   PAGE

Introductory   I

1. How Language is Built Up   11

2. The Nature of Words   36

3. Meaning   54

4. Transparent and Opaque Words   80

5. Logical and Emotive Factors in Meaning   116

6. Synonymy   141

7. Ambiguity   156

8. Change of Meaning   193

9. The Structure of the Vocabulary   236

Conclusion   259

Select Bibliography   264

Subject Index   273

Note on Abbreviations

Few special abbreviations have been used in this book. An asterisk before a title or a quotation means that it has been taken from *The Oxford Dictionary of Quotations* (2nd impression, revised, 1942). Before a word, an asterisk indicates that the form is a reconstructed one. The symbol > signifies that one form has changed into another, as for example in Old English *brid* > Modern English *bird*. *NED* stands for *A New English Dictionary on Historical Principles*, commonly known as *The Oxford English Dictionary*, and *Shorter OED* for *The Shorter Oxford English Dictionary on Historical Principles* (3rd ed., reprinted with corrections, 1952). Other dictionaries frequently referred to: Bloch-Wartburg: O. Bloch-W. von Wartburg, *Dictionnaire étymologique de la langue française* (3rd ed., revised, 1960); Lewis and Short: C. T. Lewis-C. Short, *A Latin Dictionary* (1951 impression); Liddell and Scott: *An Intermediate Greek-English Lexicon founded upon the Seventh Edition of Liddell and Scott's Greek-English Lexicon* (1955 impression).

INTRODUCTORY

Two major branches of linguistics are specially concerned with words: etymology, the study of word-origins, and semantics, the study of word-meanings. Of the two, etymology is an old-established discipline whereas semantics is comparatively new. Speculation on the origin of words was prominent in early Greek philosophy, as every reader of Plato's *Cratylus* will remember.[1] There were two rival schools of thought: the naturalists, who believed that there was an intrinsic connexion between sound and sense, and the conventionalists, who held that the connexion was purely arbitrary. When, in the first century B.C., Varro codified Latin grammar, he set up etymology as one of the three main divisions of linguistic study, alongside of morphology and syntax. Etymological methods remained unscientific until the nineteenth century, but the etymological approach itself always held a key-position in the study of language. The need for an independent science of meaning was not felt till much later: it was not till the nineteenth century that semantics emerged as an important division of linguistics and received its modern name.

This does not mean, however, that the Ancients were indifferent to problems of meaning. They made many penetrating observations on the sense and use of words, and noticed several fundamental aspects of semantic change. Indeed it is hardly an exaggeration to say that most of the principal themes of modern semantics are adumbrated in the stray remarks of Greek and Latin writers.[2] One problem which interested them was that of changes in meaning reflecting changes in public mentality. In a famous passage about the lowering of ethical standards during the Peloponnesian War, Thucydides detected a symptom of this general trend in the depreciation of certain words denoting moral values:

> The ordinary acceptation of words in their relation to things was changed as men thought fit. Reckless audacity came to be regarded as courageous loyalty to party, prudent hesitation as specious cowardice, moderation as a cloak for unmanly weakness, and to be clever in everything was to do nought in anything (Book III, lxxxii).

[1] On the history of etymology see recently P. Zumthor, 'Fr. *Étymologie*. Essai d'histoire sémantique', *Etymologica. W. v. Wartburg zum 70. Geburtstag*, Tübingen, 1958, pp. 873-93.
[2] On these and other remarks of semantic interest in Greek and Latin authors, see R. H. Robins, *Ancient and Mediaeval Grammatical Theory in Europe*, London, 1951, and H. Kronasser, *Handbuch der Semasiologie*, Heidelberg, 1952, pp. 25 ff. and 70 f.

There is an echo of this passage in Sallust's *War with Catiline* where he says, through the mouthpiece of Marcus Porcius Cato:

> But in very truth we have long since lost the true names for things. It is precisely because squandering the goods of others is called generosity, and recklessness in wrong doing is called courage, that the republic is reduced to extremities (ch. lii).

It is impossible for the modern reader not to think of similar cases of depreciation in our own days: the vicissitudes of terms like *democracy*, and the semantic nightmare of Orwellian double-speak where peace means war and love means hate.

In a less sinister key, Cicero traced, in *De Officiis*, Book I, xii, the history of an interesting euphemism and also showed how, in the course of time, it lost its euphemistic value and came to be directly applied to the unpleasant idea which it was designed to veil:

> This also I observe — that he who would properly have been called a 'fighting enemy' (*perduellis*) was called 'a guest' (*hostis*), thus relieving the ugliness of the fact by a softened expression; for *hostis* meant to our ancestors what we now call 'stranger' (*peregrinus*) ... What can exceed such charity, when he with whom one is at war is called by so gentle a name? And yet long lapse of time has given that word a harsher meaning; for it has lost its signification of 'stranger' and has taken on the technical connotation of 'an enemy under arms'.

In a more general way, Horace summed up the rise and fall of words in a terse formula which reflects a surprisingly broad-minded attitude to the vexed question of correctness in language:

> Multa renascentur quae iam cecidere, cadentque
> Quae nunc sunt in honore vocabula, si volet usus,
> Quem penes arbitrium est et ius et norma loquendi.
> *Ars Poetica*, ll. 70 ff.[1]

In the fifth century of our era, the Neo-Platonic philosopher Proclus surveyed the whole field of semantic changes and distinguished a number of basic types — cultural change, metaphor, widening and narrowing of meaning, etc. — which are still part of our modern stock-in-trade.

The Ancients' interest in words was by no means confined to changes in their meanings; they also made some pertinent observations on their

---

[1] 'Many a term which has fallen from use shall have a second birth, and those shall fall that are now in high honour, if so Usage shall will it, in whose hands is the arbitrament, the right and rule of speech' (*The Oxford Dictionary of Quotations*, p. 541).

behaviour in actual speech. The vagueness of words and the diversity of their uses is already remarked upon in the *Iliad*: 'Glib is the tongue of mortals, and words there be therein many and manyfold, and of speech the range is wide on this side and on that' (XX, ll. 248-9). Democritus clearly saw that there are two distinct kinds of multiple meaning: the same word may have more than one sense, and conversely, more than one word may stand for the same idea. At a more systematic level, Aristotle made several important statements on word-meanings. He was the first to define the word as the smallest significant unit of speech — a definition which held sway until quite recently and which is still valid in a somewhat modified form. Aristotle also established a fruitful distinction between two kinds of words: those which have meaning in isolation and those which are mere grammatical tools. This division is still widely accepted by linguists and philosophers alike. Finally, we owe to Aristotle a classification of metaphors which, developed and refined by subsequent writers, notably by Quintilian, played a crucial part in the rhetorical tradition and was taken over into semantics by the pioneers of the new science.

Graeco-Roman ideas on words and their uses have thus exercised a strong, if not always beneficial, influence on modern semantics, but the impetus for the creation of a science of meaning came from elsewhere. Two factors in particular played a decisive part in its emergence in the first half of the nineteenth century. One was the rise of comparative philology and, more generally, of scientific linguistics in the modern sense. The term *linguistics* itself was formed at this time: it appeared in French in 1826 (*la linguistique*) and in English eleven years later (at first without an *s*).[1] Although attention was mainly focused on phonetic and grammatical changes, it soon became necessary to explore also the semantic side of language. The other factor was the influence of the Romantic Movement in literature. The Romantics had an intense and catholic interest in words, ranging from the archaic to the exotic, and including the dialects of the countryside and the slang of the underworld.[2] Even more important, they were fascinated by the strange and mysterious potencies of words. Many poets of the period gave expression to this new attitude. For Wordsworth,

[1] See the *NED* and Bloch-Wartburg's French etymological dictionary (3rd ed., Paris, 1960). Cf. J. Perrot, *La Linguistique*, Paris, 1957, p. 14, n. i.

[2] On the Romantic attitude to words, see my *Style in the French Novel*, Cambridge, 1957, ch. I: 'Some Romantic Experiments in Local Colour'. Cf. also H. Temple Patterson, *Poetic Genesis: Sébastien Mercier into Victor Hugo; Studies on Voltaire and the Eighteenth Century*, XI, Geneva, 1960.

Visionary power
Attends the motions of the viewless winds,
Embodied in the mystery of words.
The Prelude, Book V.

To Shelley, 'words are like a cloud of winged snakes' (*Prometheus Unbound*, I), but language is also a

perpetual Orphic song
Which rules with Daedal harmony a throng
Of thoughts and forms, which else senseless and shapeless were.
(*ibid., IV)

Victor Hugo goes even further; in a famous poem of the *Contemplations*, a sequence of terrifying images describing the word and its workings leads up to a climax which echoes the opening verse of the Gospel according to St. John:

Il est vie, esprit, germe, ouragan, vertu, feu;
Car le mot, c'est le Verbe, et le Verbe, c'est Dieu.[1]

Intrigued by the strange properties of the words they were using, the Romantic writers looked to the philologists for enlightenment. In France, Charles Nodier, an imaginative rather than a scholarly student of language, became their chief authority on things linguistic. The need was felt, however, for a special science dealing with the meanings of words. This need was eloquently argued by Balzac on the opening pages of his philosophical novel *Louis Lambert*. The passage is worth quoting in some detail since it is symptomatic of the climate of opinion in which modern semantics took shape:

Quel beau livre ne composerait-on pas en racontant la vie et let aventures d'un mot? Sans doute il a reçu diverses impressions des événements auxquels il a servi; selon les lieux, il a réveillé des idées différentes ... Tous sont empreints d'un vivant pouvoir qu'ils tiennens de l'âme, et qu'ils lui restituent par les mystères d'une action et d'une réaction merveilleuse entre la parole et la pensée ... Par leur seule physionomie, les mots raniment dans notre cerveau les créatures auxquelles ils servent de vêtement ... Mais ce sujet comporte peut-être une science tout entière![2]

---

[1] 'It is life, spirit, germ, hurricane, virtue, fire; for the name is the Word, and the Word is God' (*Réponse à un acte d'accusation. Suite*).
[2] 'What a fine book one could write by relating the life and adventures of a word! It has no doubt received various impressions from the events in which it has been used; it has evoked different ideas in different places ... All words are impressed with a living power which

Louis Lambert was published in 1832, and it is certainly more than a coincidence that the new science foreshadowed by Balzac had actually been founded a few years earlier, though he was of course unaware of it. Since about 1825, the classical scholar C. Chr. Reisig had begun to evolve a new conception of grammar. In his university lectures at Halle on Latin philology, he set up 'semasiology', the study of meaning, as one of the three main divisions of grammar, the other two being etymology and syntax. He regarded 'semasiology' as a historical discipline which would seek to establish 'the principles governing the development of meaning'. As his tentative classification of semantic changes shows, he had as yet no very clear ideas about the subject-matter of 'semasiology'; nevertheless he had taken the decisive step by giving it its own niche among linguistic studies.

The subsequent history of the subject falls into three distinct phases.[1] The first, which covers roughly half a century, has been aptly described as the 'underground period' of semantics.[2] Reisig's initiative was welcomed by some of his German colleagues who saw in it a healthy reaction against the excessive preoccupation with form in philological studies. But the diffusion of the new ideas was at first strictly limited: it was confined, in the main, to classical scholarship in Germany. The first two works on the subject, those of Reisig himself and his disciple F. Haase, were both published posthumously, which suggests that there was as yet no widespread interest in these matters. It is not surprising therefore that when, several decades later, Michel Bréal began to think on the same lines he was under the impression that he was starting an entirely new science which did not even possess a name.

The second phase in the history of semantics began in the early 1880s and lasted once more for almost exactly half a century. It was ushered in by an article published by Bréal in 1883 in a classical journal, in which he outlined the programme of the 'new' science and gave it the name by which it is still best known:

> L'étude où nous invitons le lecteur à nous suivre est d'espèce si nouvelle qu'elle n'a même pas encore reçu de nom. En effet, c'est sur

they derive from the mind and which they return to it through the mysteries of a miraculous action and reaction between speech and thought. ... By their very appearance, words reawaken in our minds the creatures whose garments they are ... But this subject would perhaps require an entire science to itself!'

[1] See esp. Kronasser, op. cit., pp. 29 ff., and K. Baldinger, *Die Semasiologie. Versuch eines Überblicks*, Berlin, 1957, pp. 4 ff.
[2] Baldinger, op. cit., p. 5.

le corps et sur la forme des mots que la plupart des linguistes ont exercé leur sagacité: les lois qui président à la transformation des sens, au choix d'expressions nouvelles, à la naissance et à la mort des locutions, ont été laissées dans l'ombre ou n'ont été indiquées qu'en passant. Comme cette étude, aussi bien que la phonétique et la morphologie, mérite d'avoir son nom, nous l'appellerons la sémantique (du verbe σημαίνειν), c'est-à-dire la science des significations.[1]

It is clear from this passage that Bréal, like Reisig before him, regarded semantics as a purely historical study. This orientation remained characteristic of the subject throughout this second phase: most semanticists took it for granted that their prime task was to study changes of meaning, to explore their causes, to classify them according to logical, psychological or other criteria, and, if possible, to formulate the general 'laws' and tendencies underlying them.

The last two decades of the nineteenth century brought a quickening of interest in the subject. In Germany, a number of specialized studies began to appear, and semantic questions were given some prominence in the most influential general treatise of the period, Hermann Paul's *Prinzipien der Sprachgeschichte*, which was first translated and then adapted into English.[2] In France, two important and readable books acquainted the general public with semantic problems: Arsène Darmesteter's *La Vie des mots étudiée dans leurs significations* (1887) and, ten years later, Bréal's *Essai de sémantique*. These two works were the earliest classics of the new science: they ran into a large number of editions and were also made promptly available in English.[3] It is interesting to note that one of the most language-conscious and linguistically sophisticated poets of our time, Paul Valéry, read Bréal's book as a young

[1] 'The study where we invite the reader to follow us is of such a new kind that it has not even yet been given a name. Indeed, it is on the body and the form of words that most linguists have exercised their acumen: the laws governing changes in meaning, the choice of new expressions, the birth and death of idioms, have been left in the dark or have only been casually indicated. Since this study, no less than phonetics and morphology, deserves to have a name, we shall call it semantics (from the verb σημαίνειν), i.e. the science of meaning' (from an article on 'Les Lois intellectuelles du langage', published in *L'Annuaire de l'Association pour l'encouragement des études grecques en France*). On the history of the term *semantics*, see A. W. Read, 'An Account of the Word *Semantics*', *Word*, iv (1948), pp. 78-97.

[2] 1880; 5th ed., Halle, 1920. It is especially from the second edition (1886) onwards that semantic matters occupy a prominent place in the book. The second edition was translated into English by H. A. Strong in 1889, and an English adaptation was published in 1891 by H. A. Strong, W. S. Logeman and B. I. Wheeler under the title, *Introduction to the Study of the History of Language*.

[3] An English version of Darmesteter's work was published already in 1886. An English translation of Bréal's book, by Mrs. H. Cust, appeared in 1900 under the title *Semantics*.

man of seventeen and published an enthusiastic review of it in the *Mercure de France* (1898).[1]

In the first three decades of the twentieth century, considerable progress was made in the study of changes of meaning. Semanticists gradually emancipated themselves from the antiquated categories inherited from rhetoric, and turned instead to neighbouring disciplines — philosophy, psychology, sociology, history of civilization — for a fuller understanding of semantic processes. An interesting experiment was made by the Danish linguist K. Nyrop when, in 1913, he included a volume on semantics in his widely used *Grammaire historique de la langue française*. The attempt was, however, premature: semantics did not yet possess the necessary techniques for identifying the distinctive tendencies of a particular language. The crowning achievement of this period was a monumental synthesis published in 1931 by the Swedish philologist Gustaf Stern under the title: *Meaning and Change of Meaning, with Special Reference to the English Language*, where a new, purely empirical classification of semantic changes, based on the author's own extensive researches, was put forward and an attempt was also made to bring semantics into line with recent advances in other fields, including the study of aphasia and other disorders of speech.

The same year in which Stern's treatise appeared saw the publication of another work which opened a new phase in the history of semantics: Jost Trier's monograph on terms of knowledge and intelligence in German.[2] To understand the nature of the new phase, it will be necessary to mention briefly some fundamental changes which had taken place in general linguistics since the turn of the century. These changes, which have been described as a 'Copernican revolution' in our ideas about language, had originated in the teaching of the Swiss scholar Ferdinand de Saussure whose lectures on linguistics in the University of Geneva were published posthumously in 1916 under the title *Cours de linguistique générale*.[3] In this book, extraordinarily rich in bold and original conceptions, there were two points in particular which revolutionized the theory and practice of linguistic studies. Firstly, Saussure broke with the historical orientation of nineteenth-century linguistics and cogently argued that there are two basically different and equally legitimate approaches to language: one descriptive or 'synchronic',[4] recording it as it exists at a

---

[1] See F. Scarfe, *The Art of Paul Valéry*, London, 1954, pp. 56 f.
[2] *Der deutsche Wortschatz im Sinnbezirk des Verstandes. Die Geschichte eines sprachlichen Feldes I*, Heidelberg, 1931.
[3] 5th ed., Paris, 1955. (English transl. by Wade Baskin, London, 1960.)
[4] From Greek *syn* 'together' + *chronos* 'time'.

B

given moment and ignoring its antecedents, the other historical or 'diachronic',[1] tracing the evolution of its various elements. The two approaches are complementary but must under no circumstances be confused; to pursue the two concurrently would mean, as one of Saussure's disciples wittily put it, to paint a portrait from photographs taken at different times, combining the mouth of an infant with the beard of an adult and the wrinkles of an old man. Secondly, Saussure visualized language as an organized totality or *Gestalt* in which the various elements are interdependent and derive their significance from the system as a whole. He compared language to a game of chess where no unit can be added, removed or displaced without altering the entire system of relations on the chessboard. This vision of language as a system of interdependent elements lies at the root of what has come to be known as '*structural linguistics*'. Under Saussure's influence, a number of structuralist schools — in Geneva, Prague, Copenhagen, London and elsewhere — came into being, and though there are vast differences between them they all agree on this fundamental principle. The structuralist current in Europe has been powerfully reinforced by the American school of linguistics founded by Leonard Bloomfield, which, starting from different premises, has arrived at very similar results.

Professor Trier's work on terms of knowledge in German was the first serious attempt to introduce Saussure's principles into semantics. His doctrine, the so-called 'theory of semantic fields', had some immediate repercussions and was followed up by a few disciples and like-minded fellow-linguists. The diffusion of his ideas was, however, retarded by the war, and it was not till about 1950 that the new semantics got into its stride. True to its Saussurean background, the main trend in contemporary semantics differs from the older school in two vital respects. It has abandoned the one-sidedly historical orientation of earlier days, and although changes of meaning continue to receive a great deal of attention, there has been an unmistakable shift of emphasis towards descriptive semantics. Secondly, a number of attempts have been made in recent years to study the inner structure of the vocabulary. The importance attached to these problems can be seen from the fact that 'structural semantics' was on the agenda of the Eighth International Congress of Linguists, held in Oslo in August 1957, and appears again on that of the Ninth Congress, to be held at Cambridge, Mass., in 1962.

In some other respects too, the new semantics differs markedly from the traditional approach. The appearance, since the early years of this

---

[1] From Greek *dia* 'through'+*chronos*.

century, of a new science of *stylistics* has had a profound influence on semantic studies. Broadly speaking, stylistics is concerned with the expressive and evocative values of language. The new discipline has made great strides forward in recent years,[1] and has developed particularly close connexions with semantics. It is now clear that every major problem of semantics has stylistic implications, and in some cases, as for example in the study of emotive overtones, the two approaches are inextricably intertwined.

Another distinctive feature of the new semantics is a shift of interest from general principles to the study of particular languages. During the last few years, attempts have been made to explore the semantic tendencies peculiar to a given idiom,[2] and the outlines of a new classification of languages on purely semantic grounds have begun to take shape.

Contemporary semantics is also characterized by an absorbing interest in relations between language and thinking. Language is no longer regarded as a mere instrument for expressing our thoughts, but as an influence in its own right, which shapes and predetermines them and directs them into specific channels. These ideas, which were already prominent in the theory of 'semantic fields', have gained fresh impetus from the late Benjamin Lee Whorf's writings on the subject, which have aroused considerable interest in America. Whorf's studies were concerned with grammar rather than vocabulary, but it is in semantics that the impact of language on thought can be seen most clearly, and some promising results have already been achieved in this sphere.

One may also note, as an indication of the shape of things to come, the introduction of mathematical and even electronic methods into semantics. The use of such methods is likely to be rather restricted, but some important problems may well be approached this way with greater precision than has been possible so far, and even though the linguist may not be able to follow every detail of the operations involved, he cannot afford to disinterest himself in the results.

Finally, there has been a remarkable change of late in relations between linguistics and philosophy. Liaison between the two disciplines is no new

---

[1] A survey of recent developments in stylistics will be found in the introductory chapter of my book, *Style in the French Novel*. See also more recently R. F. Retamar, *Idea de la Estilística*, Havana, 1958, and M. Riffaterre, 'Criteria for Style Analysis', *Word*, xv (1959), pp. 154-74.
[2] On Greek and Latin see E. Struck, *Bedeutungslehre. Grundzüge einer lateinischen und griechischen Semasiologie*, 2nd ed., Stuttgart, 1954; on English, E. Leisi, *Das heutige Englisch. Wesenszüge und Probleme*, 2nd ed., Heidelberg, 1960; on French, E. Gamillscheg, *Französische Bedeutungslehre*, Tübingen, 1951, and my *Précis de sémantique française*, 2nd ed., Berne, 1959; on German, L. Weisgerber, *Vom Weltbild der deutschen Sprache I-II*, 2nd ed., Düsseldorf, 1953-54.

thing; what is, however, significant is that contemporary philosophers are so preoccupied with problems of meaning that they have evolved their own particular brand, or brands, of semantics. For the more esoteric, philosophical semantics is a branch of symbolic logic or, more specifically, of the 'theory of signs'.[1] For the more practical, it is a technique for correcting certain abuses of language such as the uncritical use of ill-defined abstractions.[2] Connexions between linguistic and philosophical semantics have so far been rather tenuous, but in a more general way there can be no doubt that philosophers and linguists can help each other greatly and that they have many problems in common, even though they tend to approach them from different angles.

On the pages that follow, I shall try to present, in brief outline, a survey of the contemporary scene in semantic studies. Naturally, traditional problems such as changes of meaning will not be neglected, but they will be fitted into the general pattern of present-day research. The first three chapters will discuss fundamental principles, starting with the structure of language as a whole, and then narrowing the circle to words and more specifically to their meanings. These will be followed by four chapters on descriptive semantics, one on semantic change, and a final chapter on the general structure of the vocabulary. It will be my endeavour to give a reasonably up-to-date and representative account of a fast-moving science without discarding the valuable results of earlier research and also without trying to put new wine into old bottles.

[1] See especially R. Carnap, *Introduction to Semantics*, Cambridge, Mass., 1942, and Ch. Morris, *Signs, Language and Behavior*, New York, 1946. Cf. also L. Linsky (ed.), *Semantics and the Philosophy of Language*, Urbana, 1952, and P. Ziff, *Semantic Analysis*, Ithaca, 1960.

[2] See especially A. Korzybski, *Science and Sanity. An Introduction to Non-Aristotelian Systems and General Semantics*, 3rd ed., Lakeville, 1948; H. R. Walpole, *Semantics. The Nature of Words and their Meanings*, New York, 1941, and the writings of S. Chase, S. Hayakawa, and other scholars connected with the review, *Etc.*

CHAPTER I

HOW LANGUAGE IS BUILT UP

The Act of Speech

LANGUAGE in the abstract is not directly accessible to the observer, except through the artificial medium of the dictionary and the grammar book. In actual experience, it always appears in the form of individual acts of speech. Any analysis of the structure of language is therefore bound to start with an examination of such acts.

The most penetrating analysis of an act of speech is that given by L. Bloomfield in his book *Language*[1] where it is described in 'behaviourist' terms, as a sequence of stimuli and responses. A concrete example will help to bring out the basic differences between linguistic and non-linguistic behaviour. Suppose that, sitting in my study, I suddenly feel thirsty. I shall go to the nearest tap, fill a glass with water, and drink it. In Bloomfield's terminology, I shall have experienced a 'practical', i.e. non-linguistic stimulus (S), a sensation of thirst, and this will have prompted me to a practical reaction (R), a series of movements leading to the drinking of a glass of water. In this sequence of events no speech has occurred, and the practical reaction was performed by the same person who had received the original stimulus. The whole process may be symbolized in the formula:

$$S \longrightarrow R$$

where the capital letters signify that both the stimulus and the reaction were of a non-linguistic nature.

Suppose, now, that I have a sudden sensation of thirst not in my own home but during a meal in a restaurant. Instead of getting the water myself I shall signal to the waiter and say something like this: 'May I have a glass of water?' The waiter, having understood my request if it was spoken in comprehensible English, will perform the necessary actions and fetch a glass of water. This chain of events differs from the previous one in two respects. Firstly, the pattern is complicated by the introduction of linguistic processes between the original stimulus and the final response.

---

[1] L. Bloomfield, *Language*, New York, 1933, pp. 22 ff. For an analysis of the act of speech on somewhat different lines, see Sir Alan Gardiner, *The Theory of Speech and Language*, 2nd ed., Oxford, 1951, ch. II; cf. also the Retrospect to the second edition.

The practical stimulus of thirst will elicit from me a linguistic reaction (r) in the form of an utterance. The sound-waves generated by the utterance will cross the space between speaker and hearer and will act on the latter as a linguistic stimulus (s) prompting him (possibly after some further linguistic exchanges) to a practical reaction (R): he will go and get a glass of water. We thus have two linguistic events, (r) and (s), intercalated between the two non-linguistic ones. Symbolically:

$$S \longrightarrow r \ldots \ldots s \longrightarrow R$$

The other difference between the two situations is that in the first case only one person is involved whereas in the second there are two: the person who receives the original stimulus and the one who performs the final response. As Professor Bloomfield rightly emphasizes, 'the division of labour, and, with it, the whole working of human society, is due to language' (op. cit., p. 24).

The above scheme may be further complicated in two ways. The communication may be 'relayed' by the listener passing on the message to some third person instead of acting on it himself. This third person may proceed likewise, and the communication may be relayed several times until some positive action ensues. On the other hand, more than one person may be listening to the same message. There will normally be one speaker only, but under modern conditions millions of people may be tuned in to the same radio or television broadcast and may be influenced by it.

If we go beyond a strictly behaviouristic analysis of an act of speech, we may draw some further conclusions from the situation just discussed. It is clear, first of all, that there are three elements involved: the speaker, the hearer or hearers, and the communication that passes between them. A well-known psychologist has summed up this threefold aspect of language in a neat formula: from the speaker's point of view, the act of speech is a *symptom*, an indication of what is in his mind; from the hearer's point of view it is a *signal*, calling on him to take some kind of action; from the point of view of the communication itself it is a *symbol*, a sign standing for whatever the speaker intends to convey.[1] The first two of these, speech as a symptom and a signal, are easy to see, but the third aspect, the symbolic nature of the utterance, requires some further comment.

When, in the example just quoted, I said to the waiter in the restaurant: 'May I have a glass of water?', his reaction to my request showed that he

---

[1] K. Bühler, *Sprachtheorie*, Jena, 1934, pp. 24-33.

had understood what I meant. How had this understanding come about? To narrow down the question to the operative term, how is it that both he and I automatically attached the same meaning to the word *water*? It is obvious that there exists no intrinsic necessity why this particular substance should be denoted by this particular sequence of sounds, nor is it so denoted in other languages: the French call it *eau*, the Spaniards *agua*, the Finns *vesi*, the ancient Greeks ὕδωρ (*hydōr*), etc. All these forms are totally different from one another, yet they all mean 'water' in their respective languages because people have been accustomed from early childhood to use them as a conventional and generally accepted sign for water. As Bacon wrote in the *Advancement of Learning*, 'words are the tokens current and accepted for conceits, as moneys are for values'. To use different analogies, one could say that the word *water* stands for the substance in the same way as black colour symbolizes mourning, a flag at half-mast indicates death, or a nod of the head signifies assent.

The fact that language is made up of signs makes it necessary to consider it within the wider context of symbolic processes. The next step in the analysis of language must therefore be a brief examination of the general properties of signs and of the features which distinguish linguistic from other symbols.[1]

SIGNS AND SYMBOLS

Since the Romantic Movement, European thought and art has been greatly concerned with symbols and was at times almost obsessed with them. As Emerson tersely put it, 'we are symbols, and inhabit symbols' (*Essays XIII*). The poets' imagination began to people nature with symbols of metaphysical significance. Wordsworth saw in the Alpine landscape

> Characters of the great Apocalypse,
> The types and *symbols* of Eternity,
> Of first, and last, and midst, and without end.
> *The Prelude*, Book VI,

[1] An attempt to differentiate between signs and symbols was made by Ogden and Richards (*The Meaning of Meaning*, 4th ed., London, 1936, p. 23) when they defined symbols as 'those signs which men use to communicate one with another and as instruments of thought'. This distinction, though useful in principle, is not consistent with the meaning of the term *symbol* in general usage, as some of the quotations in the next section will show. The same may be said of Saussure's suggestion (op. cit., 4th ed., Paris, 1949, p. 101) that symbols are never completely arbitrary: there is always some kind of natural connexion between them and the things they stand for. In the present book I have made no systematic distinction between signs and symbols. On the difference between signal and symbol, cf. Morris, op. cit., pp. 23 ff.

while Keats discovered

> upon the night's starr'd face,
> Huge cloudy *symbols* of a high romance.
>> *When I have fears ...*

Baudelaire had a haunting vision of man wandering among forests of symbols watching him with a familiar gaze:

> L'homme y passe à travers des forêts de *symboles*
> Qui l'observent avec des regards familiers.
>> *Correspondances*,

and the Symbolist poets took their cue from Baudelaire.[1]

On an entirely different plane, preoccupation with signs and symbols has left its mark on many branches of scientific thought; it looms large, to mention but a few, in anthropology, psychoanalysis, aesthetic theory[2] and in various other fields. It has also made a direct impact on philosophy. Foreshadowed by the late Greek philosopher Aenesidemus,[3] pioneered in the last century by the American logician C. S. Peirce,[4] the theory of signs has come into its own, during the last few decades, as an autonomous and highly complex discipline. One of its earliest and most influential products was Ogden and Richards's *The Meaning of Meaning* which first appeared in 1923,[5] the same year which saw the publication of another important book on the subject, the first part of E. Cassirer's *Philosophy of Symbolic Forms*. As the movement gathered momentum, the theory of signs — or 'semiotic', as some of its practitioners

---

[1] For some later pronouncements on the symbol, see Ch. Bruneau, *Petite Histoire de la langue française II*, Paris, 1958, p. 194.

[2] For example in the writings of Susanne K. Langer. An interesting discussion of these matters will be found in chs. 8 and 9 of P. Henle (ed.), *Language, Thought, and Culture*, Ann Arbor, 1958.

[3] See Ogden-Richards, op. cit., Appendix C.

[4] See ibid., Appendix D, § 6, and Morris, op. cit., pp. 287 ff.

[5] In H. G. Wells's *The Shape of Things to Come*, there is an entertaining but unduly pessimistic account of the Ogden-Richards experiment: 'An interesting and valuable group of investigators, whose work still goes on, appeared first in a rudimentary form in the nineteenth century. The leader of this group was a certain Lady Welby (1837-1912), who was frankly considered by most of her contemporaries as an unintelligible bore. She corresponded copiously with all who would attend to her, harping perpetually on the idea that language could be made more exactly expressive, that there should be a "Science of Significs". C. K. Ogden and a fellow Fellow of Magdalene College, I. A. Richards, were among the few who took her seriously. The two produced a book, *The Meaning of Meaning*, in 1923, which counts as one of the earliest attempts to improve the language mechanism. Basic English was a by-product of these inquiries. The new science was practically unendowed, it attracted few workers, and it was lost sight of during the decades of disaster. It was revived only in the early twenty-first century.'

prefer to call it — was divided into three branches: 'semantics'[1] deals with the meaning of signs, 'syntactics' with combinations of signs, and 'pragmatics' with their 'origin, uses and effects within the behaviour in which they occur'.[2]

Summarized in this way, the theory of signs sounds highly abstract and even abstruse, but in fact it is not, or need not be, anything of the kind. It is concerned with a wide variety of phenomena encountered in everyday life, which have only one thing in common: they are all signs standing for something else, pointing to something other than themselves. Some of them arise spontaneously and become signs only when interpreted as such: clouds on the sky, which we take as an indication of impending rain, or the flights of birds construed as an omen by the augurs of ancient Rome. Then there are the signs used by animals to communicate with each other or with humans — signs ranging from simple sounds and movements, such as the dog's scraping at the door, to the incredibly complex and delicate system of signalling used by bees and discovered in von Frisch's famous experiments. Finally, there is the vast multiplicity of signs employed in human communication. These fall roughly into two groups. On the one hand we have non-linguistic symbols such as expressive gestures, signals of various kinds, traffic lights, road signs, flags, emblems and many more; on the other hand there is language itself, spoken as well as written, and all its derivatives: shorthand, morse and other codes, the deaf and dumb and braille alphabets, the symbols of mathematics and logic, etc. Since language is by far the most important and most articulate form of symbolic expression, it is bound to hold a key-position in any theory of signs. The linguist on his part is keenly interested in these studies as he hopes that a deeper understanding of symbolism in general may throw valuable light on purely linguistic problems. This was already clear to Saussure when he wrote, many years before an independent theory of signs came into being in modern philosophy:

> On peut concevoir une science qui étudie la vie des signes au sein de la vie sociale; elle formerait une partie de la psychologie sociale, et par conséquent de la psychologie générale; nous la nommerons *sémiologie* (du grec *sēmeion*, 'signe'). Elle nous apprendrait en quoi consistent les signes, quelles lois les régissent.[3]

[1] See above, p. 10.   [2] Morris, op. cit., pp. 217 ff.

[3] 'One may conceive of a science which would study the life of signs in society; it would form part of social psychology and, therefore, of general psychology; we shall call it *semiology* (from the Greek *sēmeion* "sign"). It would show us what signs are and by what laws they are governed' (op. cit., p. 33). Among linguistic approaches to the problem, see

Signs can be classified in a variety of ways.[1] One may, for example, distinguish between an intentional and an unintentional type. The signs we encounter in inanimate nature are unintentional except for the superstitious who may see in them portents or warnings addressed to them by some supernatural agency. Symptoms of expectancy shown by an animal are also unintentional: in Pavlov's well-known experiments with conditioned reflexes, the dog used to salivate when hearing the sound which usually accompanied his food. In the human sphere, blushing as a mark of embarrassment is unintentional, though with human beings one can never be quite sure whether an apparently spontaneous sign has not been deliberately contrived: we may, like Iago, 'show out a flag and sign of love, which is indeed but sign'.[2] As distinct from these unintentional signs, those used by animals and men for purposes of communication — including language and its substitutes — obviously belong to the intentional type.

A second and highly important difference is that between systematic and non-systematic signs. Some signs, such as for instance gestures, form no coherent system while others are organized into a pattern. Within the systematic type there are again numerous possibilities. The system may consist of a very small number of elements alternating in a fixed order, as in the case of traffic lights. Elsewhere, as for example in musical scores, the number of elements is still limited but they can enter into all kinds of combinations. At the other end of the scale we have the vocabulary of a living language, whose resources are so vast and fluid as to be virtually unlimited, though even here the human mind will tend to introduce some kind of pattern and organization, as will be seen in the last chapter of this book.

Signs can also be classified according to the sense on which they are based. There are some cases where more than one sense is simultaneously involved: an operatic performance is addressed to the eye as well as to the ear. Most signs, however, are limited to one sense only. Unintentional signs may belong to any sense: impressions of heat, taste, smell or touch may have just as much symptomatic value — for example to the physician making a diagnosis — as visual and acoustic sensations. Intentional signs

especially E. Buyssens, *Les Langages et le discours*, Brussels, 1943; Id., 'Le Signe linguistique', *Revue Belge de Philologie et d'Histoire*, xxxviii (1960), pp. 705-17; J. Kurylowicz, 'Linguistique et théorie du signe', *Journal de Psychologie*, xlii (1949), pp. 170-80; H. Spang-Hannsen, *Recent Theories on the Nature of the Language Sign*, 'Travaux du Cercle Linguistique de Copenhague', ix (1954).

[1] See esp. Buyssens, op. cit., and P. Guiraud, *La Sémantique*, Paris, 1955, pp. 13 ff.
[2] *Othello*, Act I, scene 1.

are usually confined to the spheres of sound and sight, the most differentiated among our senses. While language itself is acoustic most of its derivative forms — writing, mathematical symbols, the deaf and dumb alphabet, etc. — are visual. In braille we have the rare case of a symbolic system based exclusively on the sense of touch.

An even more fundamental distinction is that between two types of signs: those which are similar to what they denote, and those which are not. The former are sometimes called 'iconic' (from Greek *eikōn* 'image'), while the latter are known as 'conventional'. The difference between the two types is often one of degree rather than of kind. 'Photographs, portraits, maps, roadmarkers, models are iconic to a high degree; dreams, paintings other than portraits, musical scores, moving pictures, the theatre, rituals, pageants, the dance, dress, play, and architecture, are iconic in varying degrees.'[1] On the other hand there are many signs with purely conventional meanings: codes, various kinds of signals, the dots and dashes of morse, and others. The alphabet is a clear example of a conventional sign-system: the shape of the letters bears no relation to the sounds which they transcribe.

Is ordinary spoken language iconic or conventional? Obviously this question cannot be answered by a simple yes or no. Many of the words we use are conventional, arbitrary symbols, whereas others, onomatopoeic terms like *sniff* or *hiccup*, are undoubtedly iconic. This problem, which raises many issues of far-reaching importance, will be fully discussed in the fourth chapter; here it is sufficient to note that in many respects language behaves as if it were a system of conventional symbols.

From yet another point of view, one may distinguish between two kinds of signs: those which are directly representative of the things they stand for, and those which are derived from other signs. Writing in its present form is a derivative system: it translates the sounds of the spoken language into visual symbols. The position was quite different in the early stages of our alphabet; the Egyptian hieroglyphs, for example, were pictures representing objects and not their names. Gradually, however, the written symbols acquired phonetic values and came to stand for the spoken word or some part of it: a syllable or even a single sound. Modern writing has also given rise to some subsidiary systems which are derivative in the second degree: braille, for example, derives from writing which, in its turn, derives from spoken language. There are also more unorthodox substitutes for the spoken word, such as the whistle language

[1] Morris, op. cit., p. 192.

of the island of Gomera in the Canaries, which is not a conventional code but an ingenious transposition of the phonetics of the local Spanish dialect.[1]

The realization that language ought to be viewed against the background of a general theory of signs has brought linguists into contact with a variety of disciplines, ranging from electrical engineering to aesthetic theory. Two of these contacts promise to be particularly fruitful. Interest in signs has focused attention on conditioned reflexes and other learning processes observed in animals. Pavlov's classic experiments made a profound impression on linguists, and more recent developments in this field may well throw fresh light on the workings of language.[2] Even more important perhaps are contacts between linguistics and 'information' theory. There is a voluminous literature on the subject, mostly by mathematicians and communication engineers,[3] but also by a few mathematically-minded linguists.[4] Inevitably, the rise of these studies has itself created serious problems in communication. Though the linguists are intensely interested and may have a valuable contribution to make, they are often handicapped by lack of the necessary mathematical equipment. There is also a danger that these manifold contacts, added to those he had always had with neighbouring disciplines, will make it increasingly difficult for the linguist to survey the entire subject in all its ramifications. The solution obviously lies in symposia and research projects bringing together workers from different fields, and such ventures are in fact becoming more and more frequent on both sides of the Atlantic.

---

[1] See A. Classe, 'Phonetics of the Silbo Gomero', *Archivum Linguisticum*, ix (1957), pp. 44-61.

[2] See recently R. W. Brown-D. E. Dulaney, 'A Stimulus-Response Analysis of Language and Meaning', *Language, Thought, and Culture*, pp. 49-95.

[3] See, e.g., C. Cherry (ed.), *Information Theory*, London, 1956; Id., *On Human Communication*, New York — London, 1957; G. Herdan, *Language as Choice and Chance*, Groningen, 1956; G. A. Miller, *Language and Communication*, New York — Toronto — London, 1951; L. Apostel, B. Mandelbrot, A. Morf, *Logique, langage et théorie de l'information*, Paris, 1957.

[4] See especially the works of J. Whatmough ('Statistics and Semantics', *Sprachgeschichte und Wortbedeutung. Festschrift A. Debrunner*, Berne, 1954, pp. 441-6; *Language. A Modern Synthesis*, London ed., 1956) and P. Guiraud (*Les Caractères statistiques du vocabulaire*, Paris, 1954; 'Langage, connaissance et information', *Journal de Psychologie*, lv (1958), pp. 302-18; *Problèmes et méthodes de la statistique linguistique*, Paris, 1959); cf. also the proceedings of the Seventh and the Eighth International Congress of Linguists (London, 1956, and Oslo, 1958). For a brief survey, see R. Jakobson, 'Linguistics and Communication Theory', in *Structure of Language and its Mathematical Aspects* (Proceedings of Symposia in Applied Mathematics, vol. XII, 1961), pp. 245-52.

LANGUAGE AND SPEECH

Having outlined the place of language within a general theory of signs, we can now confine our attention to linguistic symbols. Modern linguists have found it expedient to define language by contrasting it with speech. This fundamental distinction goes back to Saussure who consistently and systematically opposed *la langue* 'language' to *la parole* 'speech' and saw in them two complementary aspects of a wider entity, *le langage*.[1] No other part of Saussure's doctrine has given rise to so much discussion and exegesis; even after half a century, the debate continues, which is a tribute to the vitality of the original theory.[2]

If we accept the distinction between language and speech, we shall find a number of fundamental differences between the two phenomena:

(1) Language is a vehicle of communication, and speech is the use of that vehicle by a given individual on a given occasion. To put it more pointedly: language is a *code*, whereas speech is the encoding of a particular message which will then be decoded by the hearer or hearers.

(2) Language exists in a *potential* state: it is a system of signs stored away in our memories, ready to be actualized, translated into physical sound, in the process of speech. Language, then, does not consist of sounds in the physical sense, but of sound-impressions left behind by the actual sounds we have ourselves pronounced or heard from others. These sound-impressions are made up of acoustic and motor elements: we remember the quality of the sound and the articulatory movements we performed when pronouncing it, and with these impressions is combined a disposition to repeat the same movements. The difficulty some people experience in pronouncing a foreign sound shows that the process of innervation has not been completely successful. Other elements of the linguistic system — words, grammatical forms, syntactical constructions, etc. — are likewise deposited in our memories as impressions, patterns and

---

[1] *Le langage* has no exact equivalent in English; it embraces the faculty of language in all its various forms and manifestations. See Saussure, op. cit., pp. 25 f. and 112; in the latter passage he states quite clearly: 'La langue est pour nous le langage moins la parole. — Language is for us *le langage* less speech.' The history of these terms has recently been investigated by H. G. Koll, *Die französischen Wörter 'langue' und 'langage' im Mittelalter*, Geneva — Paris, 1958.

[2] The main themes of the debate are surveyed in Dr. N. C. W. Spence's useful article: 'A Hardy Perennial: the Problem of *la Langue* and *la Parole*', *Archivum Linguisticum*, ix (1957), pp. 1-27. Another critical re-examination of the whole problem will be found in E. Coseriu, *Sistema, Norma y Habla*, Montevideo, 1952. On the relevance of the distinction to semantic studies, cf. A. Gill, 'La Distinction entre *langue* et *parole* en sémantique historique', *Studies in Romance Philology and French Literature Presented to John Orr*, Manchester, 1953, pp. 90-101.

dispositions. The precise psychological nature of these impressions is not directly relevant here, though the behaviouristically minded could regard them as 'engrams': 'residual traces of an adaptation made by the organism to a stimulus'.[1] Be that as it may, the essential point is that language is potential whereas speech is actualized.

(3) Speech is the use of language by one person in a specific situation; it is an individual act.[2] Language, on the other hand, transcends the individual: it is the property of society at large. It can serve as a means of communication only if it is substantially the same for all speakers; it is, as Saussure puts it, a *'social institution'* (op. cit., p. 33). In other words, language is the sum total of the linguistic systems which individual members of the community carry in their memories. To quote again Saussure: 'Si nous pouvions embrasser la somme des images verbales emmagasinées chez tous les individus, nous toucherions le lien social qui constitue la langue.'[3]

(4) Another important difference concerns the attitude of the individual speaker to language and to speech. He is the sovereign master of his speech; it depends on him alone what he will say, how he will say it, and even whether he will say it at all. He may, if he so desires, deviate from ordinary usage and even evolve a private language of his own, as James Joyce did in *Finnegans Wake*, though by so doing he will run the risk of ridicule or unintelligibility. But while the individual is in sole control over speech, he is no more than a passive recipient in matters of language; he assimilates it in early childhood and can do nothing, or very little, to alter it. It is true that a few privileged individuals — a politician, a scientist, a writer, a lexicographer, a grammarian — or a group of individuals such as the French Academy, may exercise some influence on the language, but even they will hardly affect its basic texture; and the ordinary run of men will be quite powerless towards it: they will, in Saussure's words, 'register it passively' (op. cit., p. 30).

(5) Speech, as Saussure saw it, is a single act strictly limited in time. Even if one regards a lengthy oration as one act of speech it will seldom exceed an hour or two, whereas the vast majority of utterances are over in a matter of minutes or even seconds. Speech is fleeting, ephemeral and irretrievable; in Horace's famous image, 'et semel emissum volat irrevocabile verbum — a word once let out of the cage cannot be whistled back

---

[1] Ogden-Richards, op. cit., p. 53.

[2] 'La parole est un acte individuel de volonté et d'intelligence. — Speech is an individual act of will and intelligence' (Saussure, op. cit., p. 30).

[3] 'If we could encompass the sum total of verbal images stored away in each individual we could touch the social link which forms language' (ibid.).

again'.[1] In contrast to this evanescent nature of speech, language moves so slowly that at times it seems almost at a standstill. Minor adjustments in vocabulary are going on all the while, but few people will be aware of any major alteration in their mother tongue during their own lifetime; it usually takes several generations or even centuries for a phonetic or grammatical change to run its course. As an American linguist pictures-quely put it, 'Language is probably the most self-contained, the most massively resistant of all social phenomena. It is easier to kill it off than to disintegrate its individual form.'[2]

(6) Speech has two different aspects, one physical, the other psycho-logical. The actual sounds are physical occurrences, whereas the meanings they convey are psychological phenomena. Language, however, is purely psychological: it is made up of impressions of sounds, words and grammatical features deposited in our memories where they remain constantly at our disposal, in much the same way as money paid into a bank account is available to the depositor.[3]

By tabulating the main differences between language and speech we obtain the following picture:

Language	Speech
Code	Encoding of a message
Potential	Actualized
Social	Individual
Fixed	Free
Slow-moving	Ephemeral
Psychological	Psycho-physical

If we look more closely at this set of differences we notice that they are basically variations on two themes: the contrast between actual and potential and that between individual and social. This has made some linguists wonder whether it would not be better to separate the two criteria.[4] To this end it has been suggested that a middle term should be

[1] *Epistles*, I, xviii, l. 71.
[2] E. Sapir, *Language. An Introduction to the Study of Speech*, New York, 1921, repr. 1949, p. 206. Cf. Saussure, op. cit., pp. 107 f.: 'La langue est de toutes les institutions sociales celle qui offre le moins de prise aux initiatives. Elle fait corps avec la vie de la masse sociale, et celle-ci, étant naturellement inerte, apparaît avant tout comme un facteur de conservation. – Of all social institutions, language is the one which gives least scope to initiative. It is an integral part of the life of society, and the latter, being inert by nature, acts first and foremost as a conservative factor'.
[3] Cf. Saussure, op. cit., p. 32.
[4] See already O. Jespersen, *Mankind, Nation and Individual from a Linguistic Point of View*, Oslo, etc., 1925, ch. I. The whole problem has been re-examined in Spence, loc. cit.

inserted between the two extremes posited by Saussure. This middle term would be 'individual language' or, as some American linguists have called it, 'idiolect': 'the totality of the speech-habits of a single person at a given time'.[1] It is easy to see that this new term stands midway between the two Saussurean poles: it is individual like speech, as distinct from the social character of language; at the same time it is potential like language, as distinct from speech which is by definition actualized. From another point of view too, it represents a half-way house: the linguistic system as it exists in the memory of one individual is less concrete, less readily accessible to the observer than are particular acts of speech, but it is more concrete and easier of access than the language of a whole community. The question arises, however, whether anything is gained by introducing a third term and thus blunting the edge of the Saussurean distinction. One is reminded of Occam's Razor: 'entities must not be multiplied beyond necessity.'

The answer to this question will depend on the point of view from which one looks at the problem. The linguist will seldom be interested in the language of a single individual for its own sake.[2] He may have to rely on it extensively as a source of information; field workers exploring an unrecorded language will often derive most of their material from a close study of the speech-habits of a small number of informants. But even then they will not stop at this stage but will try to establish the wider norm on which these 'idiolects' are based, the linguistic system of the whole community.[3] In such cases the study of 'idiolects' will be a means to an end, an intermediate phase in research, and under more favourable circumstances there will be no need for that phase at all.

The concept of 'idiolect' will, however, be very useful in psychological and stylistic inquiries. It has been proved by experimental data that there is a definite connexion between language and personality; one psychologist has even found a statistical correlation between the ratio of verbs and adjectives and the emotional stability of a person.[4] In stylistic studies, one of the most popular methods is to investigate the usage of a particular writer in order to determine what is unique and idiosyncratic in his

[1] C. F. Hockett, *A Course in Modern Linguistics*, New York, 1958, p. 321; cf. also R. A. Hall, Jr., 'Idiolect and Linguistic Super-ego', *Studia Linguistica*, v (1951), pp. 21-7. *Idiolect* comes from Greek *idios* 'own, private'+the Greek element *-lect* 'speech', as in *dialect*.

[2] Such studies do exist, however, as, e.g., the Abbé Rousselot's classic treatise, *Modifications phonétiques du langage étudiées dans le patois d'une famille de Cellefrouin (Charente)*, 1891.

[3] Cf. H. Hoijer, 'Native Reaction as Criterion in Linguistic Analysis', in the *Proceedings of the Eighth International Congress of Linguists*.

[4] Cf. my article, 'Psychologie et stylistique', *Journal de Psychologie*, xlvi (1955), pp. 133-56: pp. 149 f.

handling of the language.[1] Echoing Buffon's famous formula, 'Le style, c'est l'homme même', Schopenhauer defined style as 'the physiognomy of the mind', and this physiognomy can best be grasped by examining the author's 'idiolect' as deposited in his writings in a more or less stylized form.

It would seem, then, that the concept of 'idiolect' may render valuable services to the psychologist and the student of style, and may have its place in certain types of linguistic inquiry, but that, in the wider sphere of general linguistics, there would be little point in blurring the distinction between language and speech by introducing a third term between the two.

THE UNITS OF LANGUAGE

Language, as we have seen, can be reached only through speech; it is therefore by analysing specific utterances that we may hope to identify the units of which language is made up.[2] In view of the mixed, psychophysical nature of speech, two ways are open to us: we can analyse a piece of connected discourse from the physical point of view, as a string of sounds, and from the psychological point of view, as a carrier of meaning. Since most utterances consist of more than one meaningful element, we shall also need a third criterion: we shall have to study the relations which exist between the various units.

1. *Units of Sound*

A purely phonetic analysis of connected speech will distinguish various acoustic segments which can be further broken down into single sounds. These sounds are the minimum physical units of speech and, as we already know, they exist in language as potential sounds, stored away in our memories as acoustic and motor impressions which can be actualized whenever necessary.

This, however, is by no means the whole story. If we consider sounds not from the phonetician's point of view but as units of language endowed with a specific function, we soon notice an essential difference between two types of sounds. Take the following pairs of words:

kill	*coal*
kin	*cone*
kit	*coat*

[1] See my *Style in the French Novel*, pp. 25 ff. and p. 35. Cf. also T. A. Sebeok (ed.), *Style in Language*, New York — London, 1960, pp. 378 and 427.
[2] On this whole question see now C. L. Ebeling, *Linguistic Units*, The Hague, 1960.

C

To the phonetician, the |k| in the first column is not identical with that in the second since its point of articulation is different: it is a forward |k| whereas the other is a backward |k| . To the linguist, this difference is of secondary importance since it is entirely mechanical: it is caused purely and simply by the fact that in the first column, the |k| is followed by a front vowel and in the second by a back vowel. The contrast between the two |k| -s can therefore have no distinctive function; there are no pairs of words in English which are distinguished solely by this contrast and would become homonymous without it. *Kill* with a backward |k| or *coal* with a forward |k| are impossible in English.

Consider now the following pairs:

cap	*gap*
came	*game*
coal	*goal*

Here again we have a purely phonetic difference: that between a voiced and a voiceless plosive articulated at the same point. But this time the contrast is of vital importance since it enables us to distinguish between words which would otherwise become identical. The sounds |k| and |g| may thus be said to form a 'distinctive opposition' in English, and they themselves are distinctive sounds, '*phonemes*'. The contrast between the two varieties of |k| , on the other hand, is not a distinctive one since it does not help to differentiate between meanings; consequently, they are not separate phonemes but so-called 'allophones'[1] of the |k| phoneme.

There is no need here to go into the intricacies of the phoneme theory which, during the last three decades, has proved of immense value to general linguistics.[2] The following points must, however, be mentioned since they are of direct relevance to the main theme of this book. Firstly, not all distinctive oppositions are based on single sounds.[3] In languages with a free accent, for example, the place of the latter may suffice to distinguish between words: English '*invalid — in'valid*, Russian '*muka* 'torment' — *mu'ka* 'flour'. Secondly, grammatical forms may be differentiated in the same way as words: the same contrast between |æ| and |e| which

---

[1] From Greek *allos* 'other'+*phōnē* 'voice, sound'.

[2] Among the numerous works on the phoneme and allied problems, mention may be made in particular of N. S. Trubetzkoy, *Principes de phonologie*, French transl., Paris, 1949; D. Jones, *The Phoneme: Its Nature and Use*, 2nd ed., Cambridge, 1961; B. Bloch, 'A Set of Postulates for Phonemic Analysis', *Language*, xxiv (1948), pp. 3-46. An up-to-date account will be found in Hockett, op. cit., chs. 2-13. For applications of the phoneme theory to historical problems, see esp. A. Martinet, *Economie des changements phonétiques*, Berne, 1955; cf. also his *Eléments de linguistique générale*, Paris, 1960, ch. 6.

[3] Distinctive features transcending the limits of single sounds are sometimes referred to as suprasegmental' or 'prosodio' phonemes.

distinguishes *bat* from *bet*, *pan* from *pen*, etc., marks the difference between singular and plural in *man* — *men*. Thirdly, the phonemes of each language form a pattern which differs from one system to another and may even vary within the history of the same idiom. Thus the opposition between voiced and voiceless consonants in English, which we found distinctive in the case of |g| and |k|, recurs in pairs like *bear* — *pear*, *down* — *town*, *wet* — *whet*, *vat* — *fat*, *joke* — *choke*, etc.

One of the most significant consequences of the phoneme theory has been the introduction of semantic viewpoints into the study of sounds. The latter have, of course, no independent meaning of their own except in the rare case of words consisting of one sound only, such as French *eau* |o| or Latin *i*, imperative of *ire* 'to go'. But this does not mean that sounds have nothing to do with meaning; the whole distinction between phonemes and allophones is dictated by semantic considerations. As one of the architects of the phoneme theory, Professor Jakobson, once said, 'the phoneme participates in the signification, yet having no meaning of its own'.[1] The semantic function of phonemes is essentially negative: they enable words and other elements to have meaning by making them phonetically different and distinguishable from each other. This is what Saussure meant when he described phonemes as 'oppositive, relative and negative' units (p. 164) and when, in a more general way, he stated: 'Dans la langue il n'y a que des différences.'[2]

It would be going too far, however, to assert, as does a recent textbook, that 'sounds and differences between them have one and only one function in language: *to keep utterances apart*'.[3] In addition to this negative function they also have a less important but by no means negligible positive role: in onomatopoeic words they are directly related to the meaning and give an 'iconic' representation of it.[4] The same may be said of phonetic features transcending single sounds, such as accent and tone. In some languages, accent will have a purely distinctive role, whereas in others it will provide a vehicle for expressing emotions; in French, for example, there is a so-called 'emotive accent', a heavy expiratory stress which falls on the first syllable of words beginning with a consonant and on the second syllable of those beginning with a vowel: '*misérable*! — *a'bominable*! The semantic functions of sounds and other phonetic features are of direct

---

[1] *Actes du VIᵉ Congrès International des Linguistes*, Paris, 1949, p. 8.
[2] 'In language, there are only differences' (op. cit., p. 166). A critique of this conception will be found in H. Galton, 'Is the Phonological System a Reality?', *Archivum Linguisticum*, vi (1954), pp. 20-30.
[3] Hockett, op. cit., p. 15 (author's italics).
[4] See above, p. 17.

interest to the student of meaning and will have their place in the semantic description of particular languages.[1]

From the point of view of linguistic method, the emergence of the phoneme theory means that we now have two disciplines dealing with sounds: phonetics and *phonology* (or 'phonemics'). Phonetics studies the acoustic and articulatory aspects of sounds, whereas phonology investigates their purely linguistic functions. The difference between the two approaches is precisely that the phonologist operates with semantic criteria and the phonetician does not. Nevertheless, the two are of necessity interdependent, and phonetics remains an essential part of the equipment of every linguist.

2. *Units of Meaning*

Aristotle, it will be remembered, defined words as the smallest significant units of speech.[2] This definition was accepted by linguists for a very long time, and it is only quite recently that modern methods of analysis, emulating the procedures (and sometimes the terminology) of nuclear physics, have discovered semantic units below the word level. A new term is therefore needed to denote the smallest significant elements of speech: in contemporary linguistic theory, they are known as '*morphemes*'.[3] In the sentence: 'John treats his older sisters very nicely', the latest standard book on structural linguistics[4] distinguishes no less than thirteen morphemes: (1) *John*; (2) *treat*; (3) *-s*; (4) *hi-*; (5) *-s*; (6) *old*; (7) *-er*; (8) *sister*; (9) *-s*; (10) *very*; (11) *nice*; (12) *-ly*; (13) the intonation of the sentence. It will be seen that — with the solitary exception of the form *his*[5] — the details of the analysis are anything but revolutionary; what is new is the inclusion of all these diverse elements within a single category.

If we look more closely at the analysis of the above sentence we find that it contains five different types of morphemes: independent words (*John, treat, old, sister, very, nice*); a stem which is not an independent word (*hi-*); a derivational suffix (*-ly*); inflexional suffixes which are themselves of three different kinds: verbal (the *-s* in *treats*), nominal and

---

[1] Cf. my *Précis de sémantique française*, ch. 2: 'Fonctions sémantiques des sons français' see also ibid., pp. 104-15.

[2] See above, p. 3.

[3] 'Morphemes are the smallest individually meaningful elements in the utterances of a language' (Hockett, op. cit., p. 123). From Greek *morphē* 'form' + the same ending as in *phoneme*. In Professor Martinet's terminology, these units are called *monemes* (*Eléments*, p. 20).

[4] Hockett, op. cit., pp. 123-6.

[5] *His* is divided into two components: a non-independent stem *hi-*, which also occurs in *him* though nowhere else, and the possessive suffix *-s* (cf. 'Paul's book, the king's horses').

pronominal (the possessive -s in his and the plural -s in sisters), adjectival
(the -er in older); finally, intonation. Nor does this list exhaust all the
possibilities; in a verb like induce, for example, there is a derivational
prefix in- plus a form which never occurs either as a word or even as a
non-independent stem, but which is found in the same position and with
roughly the same meaning in other verbs: deduce, produce, reduce.[1] While
no one would dispute the value of the morpheme in the analysis of
language,[2] one may legitimately wonder whether it should be regarded
as one of the key-elements of linguistic structure. It is an extremely mixed
category made up of forms totally different in function and in status and
held together by the sole criterion that they cannot be split up into
smaller significant units. It seems more than doubtful that a homogeneous
branch of linguistics could be built on such a basis.

The heterogeneity of the morpheme is, however, more apparent than
real. On closer inspection it is found that there are two classes of
morphemes. In the first class belong those which are either independent
words or constituents of words: non-independent stems and roots like
hi- in his and -duce in induce; derivational prefixes and suffixes, etc. The
second class comprises intonation and inflexional elements of various
kinds, which concern not single words but grammatical relations and the
structure of the sentence as a whole. This gives the word a key-position
in the hierarchy of linguistic structure.

What, then, is a word? The question seems rather futile since, in
everyday life, one usually has no difficulty whatever in recognizing words,
and as I type this page I am separating them from each other without the
slightest hesitation. But it is one thing to identify words and another to
state the criteria by which one identifies them. In fact, there is a bewildering multiplicity of rival definitions.[3] Many of the older ones were directly

[1] Cf. Hockett, op. cit., pp. 173 and 241.

[2] It would transcend the scope of this book to go into the details of morphemic analysis,
developed with much finesse and ingenuity by structuralists like Z. S. Harris, E. A. Nida,
K. Togeby and others. Some linguists have found it necessary to have a special term,
semanteme or sememe, to denote the meaning of a morpheme (cf. Bloomfield, Language,
p. 162). On this concept see recently C. E. Bazell, 'The Sememe', Litera, 1 (1954), pp.
17-31, and J. Vendryes, 'Sémantème et morphème', Archivio Glottologico Italiano, xxxix
(1954), pp. 48-55.

[3] See especially the monographs of A. J. B. N. Reichling (Het Woord, Nijmegen, 1935) and
A. Rosetti (Le Mot, 2nd ed., Copenhagen — Bucharest, 1947), as well as the following
articles: J. H. Greenberg, 'The Definition of Linguistic Units', Essays in Linguistics, Chicago
— London, 1957, ch. 2; W. Haas, 'On Defining Linguistic Units', Transactions of the
Philological Society, 1954, pp. 54-84; F. Hiorth, 'On Defining "Word" ', Studia Linguistica,
xii (1958), pp. 1-26; W. Porzig, 'Die Einheit des Wortes', Sprache — Schlüssel zur Welt.
Festschrift für Leo Weisgerber, Düsseldorf, 1959, pp. 158-67; K. Togeby, 'Qu'est-ce qu'un
mot?', Travaux du Cercle Linguistique de Copenhague, v (1949), pp. 97-111. Cf. also the
earlier definitions discussed in my Principles of Semantics, pp. 43 ff.

or indirectly based on the Aristotelian conception of words as the smallest
significant units of speech; they sought therefore to define the word in
purely or at least predominantly semantic terms.[1] We now know that the
smallest significant unit is not the word but the morpheme; we must
therefore try to approach the whole problem from a different angle.

The most successful attempt so far to define the word by formal rather
than semantic criteria was that made by Leonard Bloomfield more than
thirty years ago.[2] The pivot of his argument is the relation of the word
to the sentence. He distinguishes between two types of linguistic forms:
those which are never used as sentences are *bound forms*, whereas those
which occur as sentences are termed *free forms*. Words are obviously
free forms since they can — in replies, exclamations, etc. — stand by
themselves and yet act as a complete utterance. What distinguishes them
from other free forms is that they cannot be split up without a residue
into lesser free forms. In our previous example, the word *nicely* contains
the free form *nice*, but also the suffix *-ly* which is not a free form, since it
cannot stand by itself. This is the meaning of Bloomfield's often-quoted
formula that a word is a *minimum free form*. It should be added straight-
away that there is one class of words to which this formula does not
apply: compounds made up of two independent words such as *penknife*, *candlestick* and the like. These may be regarded as border-line
cases between words and phrases.[3] Apart from this one exception, the
formula seems to be generally valid. A glance at the sentence discussed
above will show that the six morphemes which were put down as independent words (*John, treat, old, sister, very, nice*) are all capable of acting as a
complete utterance ('What is his name? — *John*'; 'Are you happy? —
Very', etc.), whereas none of the others can stand by itself. Four of the
seven words in the sentence (*treats, older, sisters, nicely*) can be broken
down into another word plus a bound form (*-s, -er, -s, -ly*); two words
are unanalysable (*John, very*); the seventh, *his*, ranks as an independent
word in spite of its purely grammatical function ('Whose fault is it, his
or hers? — *His*'), and can be divided, as we have seen, into two morphemes,
hi- and *-s*, neither of which is a free form. It is clear that the formula holds
good and can in most cases be applied with the utmost ease.

---

[1] As, e.g., in Antoine Meillet's famous formula: 'Un mot est défini par l'association d'un
sens donné à un ensemble donné de sons susceptible d'un emploi grammatical donné. —
A word is defined by the association of a given sense with a given group of sounds capable
of a given grammatical use' (*Linguistique historique et linguistique générale*, 2 vols., Paris,
new ed., 1948-52: vol. I, p. 30).

[2] In his article, 'A Set of Postulates for the Science of Language', *Language*, ii (1926),
pp. 153-64; cf. op. cit., pp. 177 ff.

[3] Bloomfield, *Language*, pp. 180 f.

The word plays such a crucial part in the structure of language that we need a special branch of linguistics to examine it in all its aspects. This branch is called *lexicology*,[1] and it forms, next to phonology, the second basic division of linguistic science. Lexicology will deal not only with words but with all types of morphemes entering into the composition of words. Some of these have already been mentioned: non-independent stems, derivational prefixes and suffixes, etc. Other processes of word-formation will also fall within the province of lexicology: blends or 'portmanteau' words such as Lewis Carroll's *chortle*, a mixture of *chuckle* and *snort*, or some of James Joyce's ingenious coinages: *bespectable*, *beehiviour*, and others; 'back-formations', as for example the verb *laze*, extracted from the adjective *lazy*, or *burgle* from *burglar*; abbreviations of various types, etc. In some languages new terms can be formed by reduplication or by introducing a so-called 'infix' into the body of a word: in Tagalog, a language spoken in the Philippines, *'su:lat* 'a writing' gives by reduplication *su:-'su:lat* 'one who will write', and by infix *su'mu:lat* 'one who wrote'.[2] In Semitic, words are formed from consonantal roots by the insertion of different vowels: from the root |k-t-b|, modern Egyptian Arabic derives *katab* 'he wrote', *ka:tib* 'writing (person)', *kita:b* 'book' and other words.[3]

Lexicology will also have to tackle the one great exception to the Bloomfield formula: compounds formed of independent words. It will have to explore the criteria — phonetic, semantic and grammatical — which enable us to distinguish between genuine phrases and such compounds. In some cases the difference is clearly marked, as in the compound animal names *lady-bird*, *bluebottle* and *grasshopper*, or, at a more advanced stage of coalescence, in words like *breakfast*, *boatswain* and *blackguard*, whose phonetic substance has been reduced in the process. There are, however, many border-line cases, and the boundary between the two categories is often very fluid.

Lexicology deals by definition with words and word-forming morphemes, that is to say with significant units. It follows that these elements must be investigated both in their form and in their meaning. Lexicology will therefore have two subdivisions: *morphology*, the study of the forms of words and their components, and *semantics*, the study of their meanings. This, then, is the place of semantics, in the strict sense of the term, within the system of linguistic disciplines. When one speaks of semantics without any qualification, one usually refers to the study of

---

[1] From Greek *lexis* 'word', *lexikos* 'of or for words'; cf. *lexicon*.
[2] Bloomfield, *Language*, p. 218.   [3] Ibid., pp. 243 f.

word-meanings proper; but it is perfectly normal and in fact very common to explore the semantics of other elements, a suffix, a prefix, etc.

Lexicology must not be confused with *lexicography*, the writing or compilation of dictionaries, which is a special technique rather than a branch of linguistics. In recent years, a good deal of thought has been given to the semantic problems facing the lexicographer, and the matter was on the agenda of the last linguistic congress.[1] A really great lexicographer will have his own semantic theory and philosophy of language; as Dr. Johnson wrote in the preface to his dictionary: 'I am not yet so lost in lexicography, as to forget that words are the daughters of earth, and that things are the sons of heaven.'

Another discipline which finds its place within the framework of lexicological studies is *etymology* which, as already noted (p. 1), is one of the most old-established branches of linguistics. Etymology in the traditional sense is the study of the origins of words. This narrow conception of etymology is still adhered to in many of the shorter dictionaries which merely give the starting-point and the modern form of a word, and also in some branches of comparative linguistics where there is so little evidence about the earlier stages that all one can do is to reconstruct a hypothetical common root. In recent years, a broader and more ambitious conception of etymology has been evolved, which differs from the older methods on two essential points: it does not confine itself to origins but seeks to trace in detail the whole history of the word; even more important, it does not treat words in isolation but as parts of wider groups. This twofold revolution has been well summed up by one of the foremost etymologists of our time:

> L'étymologie ... ne doit plus se contenter du trait insipide qui unit le point de départ au point d'arrivée ... Elle doit au contraire nous dépeindre la vaste fresque des vicissitudes que le mot a traversées ... La recherche de la racine d'un mot ou d'un groupe de mots n'est plus aujourd'hui l'unique tâche de l'étymologie. Elle doit suivre le groupe à

---

[1] See the *Proceedings of the Eighth International Congress of Linguists*, pp. 92 ff. Among recent contributions cf. esp. J. Casares, *Introducción a la lexicografía moderna*, Madrid, 1950, Part 2, chs. 2-4, and the following articles: F. Hiorth, *Lingua*, iv (1955), pp. 413-24; Id., *Studia Linguistica*, ix (1955), pp. 57-65, and xi (1957), pp. 8-27; J. E. Iannucci, *Modern Language Journal*, xli (1957), pp. 272-81, with a reply by O. Hietsch, ibid., xlii (1958), pp. 232-4; E. A. Nida, *International Journal of American Linguistics*, xxiv (1958), pp. 279-92; A. Sommerfelt, *Norsk Tidsskrift for Sprogvidenskap*, xvii (1954), pp. 485-9; M. Wheeler, *Studia Linguistica*, xi (1957), pp. 65-9. On lexicography in general see also Y. Malkiel's useful survey: 'Distinctive Features in Lexicography. A Typological Approach to Dictionaries Exemplified with Spanish', *Romance Philology*, xii (1959), pp. 366-99, and xiii (1959), pp. 111-55. Cf. also section VI of the volume *Mélanges linguistiques publiés à l'occasion du VIIIe Congrès International des Linguistes*, Bucharest, 1957.

considérer pendant tout le temps où il appartient à une langue, dans toutes ses ramifications et tous ses rapports avec d'autres groupes.[1]

Liaison between semantics and etymology has become increasingly close and fruitful in recent years.[2] The older school of etymologists relied mainly on phonological criteria in the reconstruction of extinct words and roots, though they tried to make the result more plausible by citing semantic parallels from other languages. There were some dissentient voices,[3] but, on the whole, semantics remained a mere adjunct of etymology. Latterly, however, more attention has been paid to the semantic side of reconstruction,[4] and in a more general way, etymology has been deeply affected by the progress of semantic studies, as will be seen in the last chapter of this book.

3. Units of Relation

Words, as we have seen, are the smallest units of language capable of acting as a complete utterance. There are some languages, such as Eskimo, where an entire sentence, expressing a number of different ideas, will consist of a single complex word. In the Koryat language of Siberia, the English sentence: 'They are always lying to us', would be rendered by the following word-monster:

nakomajn'ytamjun'n'ybolamyk

[1] 'Etymology ... must no longer be satisfied with the uninteresting line connecting the starting-point with the terminal point ... It should rather paint for us a vast canvas of the vicissitudes through which the word has passed ... To trace the root of a word or a group of words is no longer the only task of etymology. It must follow the group in question throughout the period when it belonged to the language, in all its ramifications and all its relations with other groups' (W. v. Wartburg, *Problèmes et méthodes de la linguistique*, Paris, 1946, pp. 109 f.). On etymology, see recently A. S. C. Ross, *Etymology, with Especial Reference to English*, London, 1958; K. Baldinger, 'L'Etymologie hier et aujourd'hui', *Cahiers de l'Association Internationale des Etudes Françaises*, xi (1959), pp. 233-64; and a series of important articles by Y. Malkiel, especially: 'The Place of Etymology in Linguistic Research', *Bulletin of Hispanic Studies*, xxxi (1954), pp. 78-90, and 'A Tentative Typology of Etymological Studies', *International Journal of American Linguistics*, xxiii (1957), pp. 1-17.

[2] Cf. my article, 'Sémantique et étymologie', *Cahiers de l'Association Internationale des Etudes Françaises*, xi (1959), pp. 323-35.

[3] Cf. E. Tappolet, 'Phonetik und Semantik in der etymologischen Forschung', *Archiv für das Studium der Neueren Sprachen*, cxv (1905), pp. 101-23.

[4] See especially E. Benveniste, 'Problèmes sémantiques de la reconstruction', *Word*, x (1954), pp. 251-64. Cf. also the following: W. S. Allen, 'Relationship in Comparative Linguistics', *Transactions of the Philological Society*, 1953, pp. 52-108; G. Bonfante, 'On Reconstruction and Linguistic Method', *Word*, i (1945), pp. 132-61; J. Ellis, 'General Linguistics and Comparative Philology', *Lingua*, vii (1958), pp. 134-74; N. M. Holmer, 'Comparative Semantics: a New Aspect of Linguistics', *International Anthropological and Linguistic Review*, i (1953), pp. 97-106; E. Reifler, 'Linguistic Analysis, Meaning and Comparative Semantics', *Lingua*, iii (1952-53), pp. 371-90. See also the *Proceedings of the Seventh International Congress of Linguists*, pp. 103-11 and 401-23.

which literally means: 'they now greatly deceive continuously us'.[1] In
European languages, word-sentences, though not infrequent, are mostly
elliptical: they have to be supplemented either by the verbal context or
the 'context of situation'.[2] When, walking in the street, I suddenly hear
someone shouting 'Careful!', only the situation will tell me whether he is
warning me against being run over by a car or against being hit by a
falling tile.

In a language like English, words are not normally used in isolation
but combine into units expressing a certain relationship: 'John writes'
posits a relation between subject and predicate, 'red rose' a relation
between qualifier and qualified, etc. Such combinations are called '*phrases*'.
A phrase may be defined as 'a free form which consists entirely of two or
more lesser free forms'.[3] The difference between a word and a phrase is,
then, that a word cannot be split up without residue into lesser free forms
whereas a phrase can. This is why compounds like *penknife* are astride
the boundary between words and phrases (see above, pp. 28 f.): they are
phrases because they are made up entirely of lesser free forms, in this
case *pen+knife*; at the same time the stress-pattern |'pennaif| shows that
the two elements are more closely linked than in an ordinary phrase and
must therefore be treated as one word.

A phrase, like any other free form, is capable of acting as a sentence. It
will depend on the nature of the phrase whether the sentence it forms is
complete in itself ('Spring has arrived') or whether it is elliptical and has
to be supplemented by the context ('Very interesting'). On the other
hand, two or more phrases may combine in various ways to form a sentence. The study of phrases and their combinations constitutes the third
great division of linguistics, *syntax*. Since phrases and their combinations
have both form and meaning, syntax, like lexicology, will have a morphological and a semantic subdivision. The former will deal with inflexion,
word-order, concord (agreement), government[4] and other devices available for the expression of relations, whereas the semantic part of syntax
will investigate the meanings and functions of syntactical elements. In
many cases, form and meaning will be inseparable, but in others it will be
perfectly possible to concentrate on one or the other: one may study the
formation of tenses and moods with no more than a passing reference to

[1] W. J. Entwistle, *Aspects of Language*, London, 1953, p. 171. Languages of this type are
known as 'polysynthetic' or 'incorporating', and the word-sentences themselves as 'holo-
phrases' (from Greek *holos* 'whole'+*phrasis* 'speech').
[2] On this concept see ch. 2, section (3).
[3] Bloomfield, *Language*, p. 178.
[4] E.g. the Latin preposition *ante* is said to 'govern' the accusative, the verb *fruitur* the
ablative, etc.

their meaning, and one may also limit one's attention to their meanings and functions independently of their form.[1]

To recapitulate: the four basic units of language are the phoneme, the morpheme, the word and the phrase. Of these, the morpheme is too heterogeneous to form the subject-matter of a special part of linguistics. Each of the other three has a separate branch of linguistic science set aside for its study:

phoneme	phonology
word	lexicology
phrase	syntax

Both lexicology and syntax have a morphological and a semantic sub-division. It is understood, of course, that lexicology deals not only with words but also with components of words, and that syntax studies not only phrases but also the combinations into which they enter.

It is hardly necessary to emphasize that this scheme is only one of various possible ways of dividing up the field of linguistics. A great deal of thought has been given in recent years to the structure of linguistic science, and the matter has been examined from all angles at international congresses and in specialized publications, without arriving at a system acceptable to all.[2] The present arrangement, which has been tried out in research as well as in teaching, has at least the advantage of simplicity; it also has the negative advantage of doing away with the customary distinction between morphology and syntax, which involved a great many anomalies and border-line cases. In the scheme suggested, the problem does not arise since morphology, the study of forms, is opposed to semantics, the study of meanings, and both have their place in syntax as well as in lexicology. But if this particular difficulty has been avoided, there are others which are inherent in the present scheme. One of these concerns alternations in the stem of certain words. Should such alternations

[1] Since the term 'semantics' *tout court* has become specialized as the name of the science of word-meanings, the study of meaning in syntax should be referred to explicitly as 'syntactical semantics'. Cf. N. Chomsky, *Syntactic Structures*, The Hague, 1957, ch. 9.

[2] The present scheme has its origins in J. Ries's monograph, *Was ist Syntax?* (2nd ed., Prague, 1927). For recent discussions on the structure of linguistics see especially the *Proceedings of the Sixth* (pp. 19 ff. and 261 ff.) and of the *Eighth International Congress of Linguists* (pp. 363 ff.). Cf. also G. Devoto, 'Sémantique et syntaxe', *Conférences de l'Institut de Linguistique de l'Université de Paris*, xi (1952-53), pp. 51-62; O. Funke, 'On the System of Grammar', *Archivum Linguisticum*, vi (1954), pp. 1-19; P. Guiraud, *La Grammaire*, Paris, 1958, pp. 35 ff.; J. Perrot, 'Morphologie, syntaxe, lexique', *Conférences de l'Institut de Linguistique de l'Université de Paris*, xi (1952-53), pp. 63-74; R. H. Robins, 'Some Considerations on the Status of Grammar in Linguistics', *Archivum Linguisticum*, xi (1959), pp. 91-114; I. Seidel-Slotty, 'Syntax und Semantik', *Bulletin Linguistique*, xi (1943), pp. 23-32.

belong in lexicology or in syntax? The answer will depend on the nature of the alternation itself. In the pair *leaf* — *leaves*, the voicing of the *f* before the *-s* of the plural has no syntactical function; the form with *v* is a mere variant of the other, and thus obviously belongs in lexicology.[1] Other alternations have a definite syntactical function, as for example the modification of the vowel in the series *sing* — *sang* — *sung*, which marks the difference between three verbal categories; such alternations will clearly have to be accommodated in syntax.[2]

A second and more serious difficulty arises over the position of certain grammatical categories. Most of these categories fall quite naturally within syntax. The distinction between subject, object, predicate and other parts of the sentence is by definition syntactical. Case and number in nouns, adjectives and pronouns, degrees of comparison in adjectives and adverbs, tense, mood, voice and other categories of the verb are also part of syntax since it is in the sentence, in the context of a concrete utterance, that a noun will be in the singular or the plural, a verb in the present or past tense, etc.; these grammatical features do not belong to the word as such, but will come into play only at the syntactical level. There are, however, two categories whose position is somewhat different: gender and word-classes. Many languages, such as Finnish or Hungarian, have no gender at all; but where it does exist, even if grammaticalized and divorced from any connexion with sex and any distinction between animate and inanimate,[3] it is part of the constitution of each noun; even an isolated noun, torn out of all context, will have its gender, and this will be duly recorded in the dictionaries. In principle, then, one might be tempted to include gender in lexicology. On the other hand it is closely associated with other grammatical categories such as number and case, and plays an important role, through concord, in the structure of the sentence, so that it will be more expedient, on the whole, to treat it in syntax.

Word-classes, or parts of speech, are also difficult to fit into the scheme. It is an essential characteristic of each word that it belongs to a specific word-class, and where the same form appears in more than one class, as frequently happens in English, we regard them as so many separate words (for example *to run*, verb, as distinct from *a run*, noun). One linguist has even suggested that a word is defined by two factors: its

[1] As some structuralists would say, the form with *v* is an 'allomorph' of the morpheme *leaf* (cf. Hockett, op. cit., p. 272). An 'allomorph' would thus stand in the same relation to a morpheme as an 'allophone' does to a phoneme (cf. above, p. 24).

[2] For a different analysis, see Hockett, ibid.

[3] See L. Hjelmslev, 'Animé et inanimé, personne et non-personne', *Travaux de l'Institut de Linguistique de l'Université de Paris*, i (1956), pp. 155-99; reprinted in *Essais linguistiques*, Copenhagen, 1959, pp. 211-49.

semantic 'nucleus' and the class to which it belongs.[1] It might therefore seem logical to treat word-classes as a lexical category. But there are two arguments in favour of placing them within syntax: the close connexion which exists between parts of speech and parts of the sentence (noun — subject and object, verb — predicate, adjective — qualifier, etc.), and the fact that word-classes are differentiated by syntactical means such as inflexion and word-order. Once again, the weight of evidence would seem to justify their allocation to syntax.

Yet another problem is the status of pronouns, articles, prepositions and other 'minor parts of speech', which are words in some respects and mere 'grammatical tools' in others. This matter will be discussed in the next chapter as part of the wider problem of the independence of our words.

A final objection to the present scheme is that it makes no provision for *grammar* as such. Actually, it is easy to fit grammar into the system once one realizes that it will lie astride the boundary between lexicology and syntax. It is customary for linguists to distinguish between the phonology, grammar and lexicon of a language.[2] The essential difference between grammar and lexicon is that the former deals with the 'general facts of language' and the latter with 'special facts'.[3] It is in the main a question of general versus particular. There are, as always, border-line cases, but on the whole the distinction is fairly clear. On this reading, grammar would include the whole of syntax plus those parts of lexicology concerned with 'general facts', such as the formation of derivatives, but not the study of individual words. Grammar would thus be competent to deal with the meanings of prefixes and suffixes as well as with the numerous semantic problems arising in syntax, but semantics in the narrower sense, the study of word-meanings proper, would lie outside its orbit.

---

[1] V. Brøndal, 'La Constitution du mot', *Essais de linguistique générale*, Copenhagen, 1943, ch. 13. Cf. also J. v. Laziczius, 'La Définition du mot', *Cahiers Ferdinand de Saussure,* v (1945), pp. 32-7.
[2] Cf. for instance, Bloomfield, *Language,* p. 138; Guiraud, *La Grammaire,* p. 6; O. Jespersen, *The Philosophy of Grammar,* London, repr. 1929, pp. 31-5. Cf. Saussure's remarks in op. cit. pp. 186 f.
[3] Jespersen, op. cit., p. 32, echoing H. Sweet, *Collected Papers* (ed. H. C. Wyld), Oxford, 1913, pp. 40 ff. On the status of grammar in contemporary linguistics, see R. H. Robins's recent article mentioned on p. 33, n. 2 above.

CHAPTER 2

THE NATURE OF WORDS

And so the Word had breath, and wrought
With human hands the creed of creeds
In loveliness of perfect deeds,
More strong than all poetic thought.

THIS passage from Tennyson's *In Memoriam* is a typical example of the numerous attempts made by poets to crystallize, in the form of an image, their inner vision of the word. Many of these images are of biblical origin; their main source of inspiration is the opening chapter of the Gospel according to St. John. Others echo some of the stock metaphors of classical antiquity. The comparison between words and money, which we have encountered in Bacon[1] and which reappears in several modern writers, was already current in late Greek and Roman authors;[2] Horace, for instance, speaks of issuing new words marked with the stamp impression of the year's coinage.[3] Some of the images are rooted in a timeless and universally valid analogy, others reflect changing fashions, others again spring from a highly personal mode of perception. In this rich and varied imagery centred on the word, one or two persistent themes stand out clearly. Thus it is customary to picture words as sharp weapons. This notion is not confined to our civilization; the Kwakiutl Indians of Vancouver Island have the remarkable simile: 'the words of speech strike the guests, as a spear strikes the game or the rays of the sun strike the earth'.[4] In *Much Ado About Nothing*, Benedick says of Beatrice: 'She speaks poniards, and every word stabs' (Act II, scene 1), and Oscar Wilde talks of words which cut the air like a dagger (*Dorian Grey*, ch. 5). We have a variation on the weapon theme when Swift speaks of the 'artillery of words' (*Ode to Sancroft*), or Emerson of 'words as hard as cannon-balls' (*Essays II*), and an even more modern version in current expressions like a 'barrage' or a 'smoke-screen' of words.

Another favourite metaphorical theme is the picture of the word as a

---

[1] See above, p. 13.
[2] See H. Weinrich, 'Münze und Wort, Untersuchungen an einem Bildfeld', *Romanica. Festschrift für Gerhard Rohlfs*, Halle a.S., 1958, pp. 508-21.
[3] ' ... licuit semperque licebit Signatum praesente nota producere nomen' (*Ars Poetica*, ll. 58 f.).
[4] F. Boas, 'Metaphorical Expressions in the Language of the Kwakiutl Indians', in *Donum Natalicium Schrijnen*, Nijmegen – Utrecht, 1929, pp. 147-53.

chemical agent or substance. We find this in a simple form in Thomas Gray's *Progress of Poesy*:

> Bright-eyed Fancy, hovering o'er,
> Scatters from her pictured urn
> Thoughts, that breathe, and words, that burn,

and in a very elaborate form in the famous episode of frozen words in Rabelais:

> Lors nous jecta sus le tillac pleines mains de paroles gelées, et sembloient dragée perlée de diverses couleurs. Nous y vismes des mots de gueule, des mots de sinople, des mots d'azur, des mots dorés. Lesquels estre quelque peu eschauffés entre nos mains fondoient comme neiges, et les oyons réalement.[1]

Proust speaks repeatedly of words which form a crust and block the channels of our inner life, while others, 'light, fluid and respirable', circulate freely in our system.[2] From this strange chemistry of the word there is but a step to what Rimbaud called its 'alchemy'.[3] This writer cherished the hope that he could 'invent a poetic word which would one day be accessible to all the senses'. Maupassant has spoken of the light which some words emit when in contact with others, and in our own day the novelist Jean Giono has described the word as something that appeals to all our senses, something that has a weight, a light and a taste of its own.[4]

The fascination which words hold for the creative writer explains the habit of personifying them and visualizing them as animals or human beings. We have already seen that Horace likened them to birds and Shelley, in a more sinister vein, to a cloud of winged snakes (pp. 4 and 20 f.). To Milton they appeared as 'nimble and airy servitors tripping about us at command' (*Apology for Smectymnus*), and in *David Copperfield*

---

[1] 'Then he threw on deck handfuls of frozen words, and they looked like pearly pills in different colours. We saw there words of gules, words of sinople, words of azure, gilded words. When they were warmed a little in our hands, they melted like snow, and we actually heard them' (*Quart Livre*, ch. 56).

[2] See my *Style in the French Novel*, p. 202.

[3] Cf. the Section 'Alchimie du verbe', in *Une Saison en enfer*.

[4] 'Avant d'écrire un mot, je le goûte comme un cuisinier goûte le produit qu'il va mettre dans sa sauce; je l'examine aux lumières comme un décorateur examine un vase chinois qu'il veut mettre en valeur; je le pèse comme un chimiste qui verse dans une éprouvette un corps qui peut faire tout sauter; et je n'emploie que des mots dont je sais la saveur intime et la puissance d'évocation et de retentissement' — 'Before writing down a word I taste it as a cook tastes the ingredient which he is going to put in his sauce; I examine it against the light as a decorator examines a Chinese vase which he wants to set against a suitable background; I weigh it as a chemist who pours into a test-tube a substance capable of blowing up everything; and I use only those words whose intimate flavour and whose power of evocation and resonance are known to me' (cf. *Style in the French Novel*, p. 228, n. 3).

Dickens drew a similar picture of a 'large superfluous establishment of words' waiting upon us like liveried servants on a state occasion.[1] The supreme form of personification is reached in Victor Hugo's poem *Réponse à un acte d'accusation. Suite*, where a *crescendo* of almost surrealistic images leads up to a veritable apotheosis of the Word. Among the innumerable guises in which the word appears in this poem there are some disturbing animal metaphors: words swarm in our minds, they open their hands, claws and wings, they move like black polyps in the ocean of thought or crawl about like monstrous snakes, devouring everything, darkening the earth like flies over a field. Other personifications assimilate the word to human beings:

> Le mot veut, ne veut pas, accourt, fée ou bacchante ...
> Tel mot est un sourire, et tel autre un regard ...
> Les mots sont les passants mystérieux de l'âme ...

Some of the images conjure up terrifying visions of the word keeping the earth in bondage and sapping the vitality of men:

> ... présent partout, nain caché sous les langues,
> Le mot tient sous ses pieds le globe et l'asservit ...
> Mets un mot sur un homme, et l'homme frissonnant
> Sèche et meurt, pénétré par la force profonde ...,

while others, in a poetic paraphrase of Genesis, celebrate its cosmic power and creative force:

> A son haleine, l'âme et la lumière aidant,
> L'obscure énormité lentement s'exfolie ...[2]

The poem culminates in a *fortissimo* which has already been quoted (p. 4): six powerful images explode in a single line and are followed by a triumphant proclamation echoing the words of the Gospel:

> Il est vie, esprit, germe, ouragan, vertu, feu;
> Car le mot, c'est le Verbe, et le Verbe, c'est Dieu.

The purpose of this digression was to throw light indirectly on the

---

[1] Ch. 52, p. 707 of the Everyman ed. Cf. Jespersen, *Growth and Structure of the English Language*, 6th ed., Leipzig, 1930, p. 126.
[2] 'The word consents or refuses; it comes running, like a fairy or a bacchante ... One word is a smile, another is a look ... Words are the mysterious passers-by of the mind ... present everywhere, a dwarf hidden beneath our tongues, the word holds the globe under its heel and enslaves it ... Place a word upon a man, and the man, shuddering, withers away and dies, penetrated by its deep force ... At its breath, helped by the soul and by light, the dark immensity slowly unfolds itself.'

ordinary speaker's attitude to words by showing how they appear to the heightened sensitivity of the imaginative writer. There can be no doubt that awareness of words, as distinct from other linguistic units, lies at the very root of man's whole conception of language. On the written and the printed page, he is faced with words neatly set out as discrete elements, and in the dictionary he finds them in a 'pure' state, free from contextual associations, each of them set up as an independent entity with its own meaning or meanings. The vocabulary thus gives the impression of a vast filing system in which all items of our experience are docketed and classified. We are so convinced of the validity of our words that we automatically assume the existence of things behind the labels, and implicitly believe in the reality of abstract ideas. It is this uncritical acceptance of -*isms* and other 'phantoms due to the refractive power of the linguistic medium',[1] that philosophers and other critics of language never tire of denouncing (cf. p. 10).

Not only is the ordinary speaker convinced of the value and effectiveness of his words; he is even apprehensive about their power and their 'tyranny'.[2] As a means of self-protection he has surrounded himself with various verbal taboos ranging from crude superstitions to elaborate prohibitions and rituals such as the avoidance of the name of God in some religions. Such taboos, which are found at all levels of civilization, have left their mark on our vocabulary and have played an important part in semantic changes; they will be considered in detail in a later chapter.

Even people who do not normally think much about words can easily be made aware of them. This is confirmed by some observations made by the late Edward Sapir on American Indian speakers: 'The naïve Indian', he writes, 'quite unaccustomed to the concept of the written word, has nevertheless no serious difficulty in dictating a text to a linguistic student word by word; he tends, of course, to run his words together as in actual speech, but if he is called to a halt and is made to understand what is desired, he can readily isolate the words as such, repeating them as units' (op. cit., pp. 33 f.). This potential awareness of words will naturally be sharpened by literacy; it has actually been suggested that a word could be defined as 'any segment of a sentence bounded by successive points at which pausing is possible'.[3]

The ordinary speaker's awareness of words, as far as it can be

---

[1] Ogden-Richards, op. cit., p. 96.
[2] See esp. S. Chase, *The Tyranny of Words*, London ed., 1938; Id., *The Power of Words*, London ed., 1955; T. T. Segerstedt, *Die Macht des Wortes*, German transl., Zurich, 1947.
[3] Hockett, op. cit., p. 167.

D

ascertained by objective methods, is a psychological fact of considerable importance;[1] it does not, however, provide a safe guide to the actual structure of language. One must therefore look for purely linguistic criteria which will confirm, invalidate or limit this implicit belief in the independence of the word. To this end I shall briefly consider words from three points of view: as phonological elements, as grammatical units, and as carriers of meaning.

1. The Word as a Phonological Unit

In the flow of speech, individual words seldom stand out as phonetic units. Two or more words may combine to form a breath-group, and within these groups, words may lose their stress and may even be mutilated and run together. In French, this process of telescoping and loss of stress may sometimes lead to ambiguity, as in the pun attributed to Louis XVIII on his death-bed: 'Allons, finissons-en, *charlatans*',[2] where the last word may also be interpreted as 'Charles attend'.[3] In an often quoted couplet by Marc Monnier, the two lines are phonetically identical although they are made up of entirely different words:

Gal, amant de la reine, alla, tour magnanime,
Galamment de l'Arène à la Tour Magne, à Nîmes.[4]

Such loss of independence in connected speech may have permanent effects on the form of a word. It may result either in a 'reshaping'[5] of its substance, or in the use of two or more variant forms according to context. There are several examples of reshaping in English. Some words have lost an initial |n| because it was felt to belong to the indefinite article; thus, Old English *nafu-gār* 'nave-borer' has become *an auger*, Old English *nædre* has given *an adder*, and, among foreign words, Old French *naperon* has changed to *an apron*, Old French *nonper* to *an umpire*, and Arabic *nāranj* to English and French *orange*.[6] The opposite process, where an |n| is detached from the indefinite article and joined to the following word, is also attested: *a newt* comes from *an ewt*, and a *nickname*

[1] Cf. A. Mirambel, 'Essai sur la notion de "conscience linguistique" ', *Journal de Psychologie*, lv (1958), pp. 266-301.
[2] 'Come on, let us get it over, charlatans.'
[3] 'Charles is waiting' — a reference to the future Charles X, Louis XVIII's brother and heir to the throne.
[4] 'Gal, the queen's lover, walked — a noble feat — gallantly from the Arena to the Great Tower in Nîmes.'
[5] Hockett, op. cit., pp. 287 f., considers 'reshaping' as a special case of 'reinterpreting' or 'metanalysis'. Cf. Jespersen, *Language: its Nature, Development and Origin*, London, repr. 1934, p. 173.
[6] Cf., however, Spanish *naranja* and Hungarian *narancs* where the n- has been preserved.

from *an eke-name*, literally an 'additional name'. Not all reshapings are due to confusion with the indefinite article: *for the nonce* should really be *for then once*; the verb *to atone* comes from the phrase *at one*; the three *Ridings* of Yorkshire were originally *thridings*, 'third parts', whose initial |th| was confused with the final |t| or |th| of *East*, *West* and *North*. Similarly, French *lierre* 'ivy' goes back to *l'ierre* (Latin *hedera*) where the definite article *l'* was wrongly joined to the word; *dinde* 'turkey' derives from *coq d'Inde, poule d'Inde* 'India cock, India hen', whereas Greek *apothēkē* has lost its initial vowel to the definite article in French *la boutique* 'shop'. A more recent and drastic mutilation is French *chandail* 'sweater' which comes from *marchand d'ail* 'garlic-seller', as this garment was popular among vegetable dealers in the Paris Central Market (Bloch-Wartburg).

The existence of two or more variant forms used in different phonetic contexts is known in linguistics as *sandhi*, a term taken over from ancient Hindu grammar, which literally means 'putting together'. A well-known example is elision and liaison in French: *le garçon — l'homme, les garçons — les_hommes*. These features may play an important role in differentiating between homonyms: *l'être* 'being' — *le hêtre* 'beech', plural *les_êtres — les hêtres*. The reason why there is a so-called 'aspirate *h*', in other words compulsory hiatus, in *le héros* 'hero', but not in the feminine *héroïne* or in the adjective *héroïque*, is the need to avoid confusion in the plural between *les héros* 'the heroes' and *les ʒéros* 'the zeroes'.[1] A few French words have three different forms according to their phonetic environment: the numeral *six* is pronounced |sis| at the end of a breath-group, |siz| before a word beginning with a vowel (*six ans*), and |si| before one beginning with a consonant (*six garçons*). The Celtic languages have an even more intricate system of sandhi rules: in Modern Irish, |'uv| 'egg' acquires a *t-* in |an 'tuv| 'the egg', an *n-* in |na 'nuv| 'of the eggs', and an *h-* in |a 'huv| 'her egg'.[2]

It is clear from the foregoing that single words are not normally treated as *phonetic* units in speech. The question now arises whether they should be regarded as *phonological* units in language. A quarter of a century ago K. Bühler suggested that words have a distinctive 'phonematic stamp',[3] and recent investigations have in fact discovered a number

[1] This was already recognized by the seventeenth-century grammarian Vaugelas; cf. J. Orr, *Words and Sounds in English and French*, Oxford, 1953, p. 138.

[2] Bloomfield, *Language*, p. 188.

[3] Op. cit., pp. 297 f. See on these problems Reichling, Rosetti and Trubetzkoy, op. cit.; Ch. Bally, *Linguistique générale et linguistique française*, 3rd ed., Berne, 1950, pp. 320 ff., and articles by B. Collinder (*Språkvetenskapliga Sällskapets in Uppsala Förhandlingar*, 1937-39, pp. 63-75), P. Delattre (*Le Français Moderne*, viii (1940), pp. 47-56), H. Galton

of features which serve to indicate word-limits[1] or to bring out in a more general way the phonological unity of the word:

(1) *Accent.* — In languages with a fixed accent, the latter will obviously have no distinctive function (see above, pp. 24 f.), but will act merely as a 'delimitative sign' showing where a word begins or where it ends. In Finnish, Hungarian and Czech, every word is stressed on the first syllable, in Polish on the penult, in French — in so far as there is any independent word-stress at all — on the last syllable. Latin rules of accentuation are more complex, but as long as there are any general rules, accent can be regarded as an indication of word-boundaries.

(2) *Compensatory lengthening.* — In some languages, the loss of a sound is compensated by the lengthening of another sound in the same word. To the Finnish *antura* 'keel' there corresponds in Estonian the form *andur* where the loss of the final vowel is offset by the lengthening of the |n|.[2]

(3) *Initial sounds and sound-combinations.* — Each language has its own characteristic forms of word-structure. Certain sounds or sound-combinations, for example, are never or very seldom found at the beginning of words in a particular language. Thus the sound |z|, which is very common in the interior or at the end of English and French words, is extremely rare in initial position: there are less than 200 examples in the *Shorter Oxford English Dictionary*,[3] and about the same number in the *Nouveau Petit Larousse* (1954 ed.), and most of the few words beginning with a |z| are rare, learned and foreign terms. Similarly, some languages do not tolerate certain initial sound-combinations which are common elsewhere and which were once acceptable in the same language; thus the plosive in the initial groups |kn-| and |gn-| has been silent in English since the seventeenth century although we still write *knave, gnaw,* etc., and the sequence |ps-| has been developing in the same way, thus giving P. G. Wodehouse his celebrated pun: 'Psmith — the *p* is silent'. It is common knowledge that words borrowed from a foreign language are often adapted to the phonetic structure of the receiving idiom: both the Finnish and the Hungarian words for 'free' are based on Slavonic forms of the *svobod* type, but the initial |sv-| has been reduced by dropping either the first or the second element: Finnish *vapaa,* Hungarian *szabad.*

(4) *Vowel harmony.* — In some languages the phonological unity of

(*Archivum Linguisticum,* vii (1955), pp. 123-39), A. W. de Groot (*Neophilologus,* xxiv (1939), pp. 221-33), D. Jones (*Le Maître Phonétique,* ix (1931), pp. 60-5), etc. On connexions between word-limits and 'juncture' ('sharp transition' as in *night rate* as opposed to *nitrate*), see Hockett, op. cit., pp. 58 f.

[1] 'Delimitative signs' (Grenzsignale) in Trubetzkoy's terminology. Cf. recently V. M. Zhirmunskij, *Voprosy Jazykoznanija,* 1961, no. 3, pp. 3-21.
[2] Collinder, loc. cit., p. 67.   [3] 3rd ed. revised, repr. 1952.

the word is effectively underlined by vowel harmony, which means that the vowel structure of the stem determines that of the suffixes and inflexions which follow it. Many of the latter have two forms, one with a front and the other with a back vowel (or vowels), and it will depend on the stem which of the two variants will be appended to it.[1] As languages of this type (Finnish, Hungarian, Turkish) are highly agglutinative, given to the use of numerous inflexions and suffixes aligned in a fixed order, one can often find a whole series of such elements all conforming to the same vowel pattern, as in the following Hungarian words:

> *kegy-etlen-ség-ük-ben* 'in their cruelty', literally: 'pity-less-ness-their-in'
>
> *gond-atlan-ság-uk-ban* 'in their carelessness', literally: 'care-less-ness-their-in'

where the inflexions and suffixes are welded into a unified word by the predetermined pattern of vowel harmony, reinforced by a strong stress on the initial syllable.

It will thus be clear that languages have their own means, some quite forcible, others more discreet, for bringing out the unity of the word on the phonological plane, irrespective of what may happen to it on the phonetic plane, in the actual flow of speech.

2. *The Word as a Grammatical Unit*
Full Words and Form-words

The status of the word as a grammatical element raises first of all a rather trivial question: are inflected forms of the same stem to be regarded as one word or as several? In dictionaries and word-counts they are usually treated as one word, even in the extreme case known as 'suppletion' where a paradigm is recruited from two or more separate stems: *good* — *better*, *go* — *went*, French *je vais* 'I go' — *nous allons* 'we go' — *j'irai* 'I shall go', etc. This question leads on to a more interesting one: the contrast between 'concrete' and 'abstract' word-structure.[2] In Latin and other highly inflected languages it often happens that a word does not exist in an abstract state, as a pure designation of the thing it stands for: there is *annus*, nominative singular, *annum*, accusative singular,

---

[1] There may even be three variants, one with a back vowel, one with a rounded front vowel, and the third with an unrounded front vowel: Hungarian *ajtó* 'door' — *ajtóhoz* 'to the door', *tüz* 'fire' — *tuzhöz* 'to the fire', *víz* 'water' — *vízhez* 'to the water'.

[2] See A. Meillet, 'Le Caractère concret du mot', op. cit., II, pp. 9-13, and P. Naert, 'Réflexions sur le caractère concret du mot dans les langues anciennes et dans les langues modernes', *Acta Linguistica*, ii (1940-41), pp. 185-91.

annorum, genitive plural, etc., but no single form denoting the idea of 'year' as such, without specifying its function in the sentence. In this sense, the Latin word is concrete, i.e. grammatically determined, whereas the French *an* or the English *year* are abstract, grammatically neutral until they are embedded in a specific utterance.

A more important distinction connected with the grammatical status of the word is that between '*full words*' and '*form-words*'. This dichotomy goes back to Aristotle[1] and has recurred, in various forms and under different names, in many philosophical and linguistic works; the terms here used were introduced by Henry Sweet in his *New English Grammar*.[2] The distinction is based on a purely semantic criterion. Consider the following two groups of words:

tree	the
sing	it
blue	of
gently	and

It is obvious that the words in the first column have some meaning even if they appear in isolation, as they do on this page, whereas those in the second column have no independent meaning proper: they are grammatical elements which will contribute to the meaning of the phrase or the sentence when used in conjunction with other words.[3] As one modern school of thought would put it, full words are 'autosemantic', meaningful in themselves, whereas articles, prepositions, conjunctions, pronouns, pronominal adverbs and the like are 'synsemantic', meaningful only when they occur in the company of other words.[4]

Leaving aside for the moment the question whether any word may be regarded as meaningful in itself, the contrast between the two types of words seems both self-evident and fundamental. There is, however, one difficulty. Modern linguists are disinclined to recognize any grammatical category on semantic grounds alone; they recognize only such categories as are given formal expression in a particular language. Form-words cannot therefore be set up as a special category unless it can be proved that there exist some phonological or grammatical features distinguishing them from full words.

[1] See Robins, *Ancient and Mediaeval Grammatical Theory*, pp. 19 f.; cf. above, p. 3.
[2] Oxford, 1892, vol. I, pp. 22 ff.
[3] This is why Aristotle called them σύνδεσμοι 'conjunctions', giving this term a much wider meaning than the one in which we use it today.
[4] This distinction was first proposed by A. Marty and was subsequently developed by O. Funke; see most recently the *Proceedings of the Seventh International Congress of Linguists*, pp. 252 ff. Cf. B. Trnka, *Omagiu lui Al. Graur*, Bucharest, 1960, pp. 761-3.

At the phonological level such features are not numerous, but there are some quite clear-cut examples. The most striking case in English is the treatment of initial *th-*. In full words, this sound is always voiceless: *thank, theft, thin, thorn, thread, thump*, etc., whereas form-words regularly have the voiced variety: *than, the, then, there, they, this, those, though, thus*, etc. There is only one exception: *through*, which is the only form-word beginning with *th-* plus consonant; here the presence of the *r* would make it difficult to pronounce a voiced *th-*. A more precise formulation of the rule would be that initial *th-* followed by a vowel is voiced in form-words and voiceless in full words.

In French a number of form-words are made up of one consonant plus the so-called 'mute *e*', and the *e* is usually elided when the next word begins with a vowel, so that the form-word is reduced to a single consonant. This minimal word-structure is found in the article and pronoun *le*, the preposition *de*, the conjunction *que*, the negative particle *ne*, and in a number of pronominal forms: *ce, je, me, se, te*. It is not found in any full word in French.

In the grammatical system, certain form-words not only play the same role as inflexions but are in some cases interchangeable with them. 'My friend's mother' means exactly the same thing as 'the mother *of* my friend'. In Latin, *aptus* 'fit' may be construed either with the dative or with the preposition *ad* plus the accusative. In English, some comparatives and superlatives are formed with the endings *-er, -est*, others with the adverbs *more, most*, and there are cases where both are permissible: *stupidest — most stupid*. The stylistic effect of Alice's 'curiouser and curiouser' is due to this possibility of choice. This affinity between inflexions and form-words distinguishes the latter very sharply from ordinary words.

The difference between the two types of words may also be brought out in word-order. In French, the unstressed personal pronoun may be separated from its verb by one or more form-words but never by a full word: *je crois* 'I believe', *je ne le crois pas* 'I do not believe it', *je n'y crois pas* 'I do not believe in it'. English structure is very different from French in this respect: 'I *rarely* see HIM' — je LE vois *rarement*'.

In the light of such formal criteria one may safely accept the traditional distinction between form-words and full words. But another question will immediately arise: if form-words are thus differentiated from full words and if they are purely grammatical in function, can they be regarded as words at all? This question, like the previous one, will have to be answered in the first place by formal rather than semantic arguments.

The first point to consider is whether form-words are covered by the definition of the word given on p. 28: whether they are 'minimum free forms' capable of acting as a complete utterance. Some form-words, such as pronouns or pronominal adverbs, often appear in isolation, but prepositions, conjunctions and articles will seldom stand by themselves though one can imagine highly elliptical sentences where they do: an impatient person may interrupt somebody else's words with an isolated '*And?*' to speed up the story. In the case of the article, Bloomfield has suggested an ingenious way out of this difficulty: since the use of the article is closely parallel to that of the pronouns *this* and *that*, which are undoubtedly free forms, the article too should be classed as such:

this thing: *that thing*: *the thing*
this   : *that*   : (*the*)[1]

From the phonological point of view, form-words are subject to the same rules of word-structure as full words, in addition to having, as we have seen, some peculiarities of their own. If every word in a language is stressed on the first syllable, every form-word will be stressed that way. If initial |kn| and |gn| are impermissible in English words, no form-word will start with these groups. In languages with vowel harmony, form-words will be governed by the same rules as the rest of the vocabulary: in Hungarian, the postposition *alatt* 'below' gives the possessive form *alatt-am* 'below me', whereas *fölött* 'above' gives *fölött-em* 'above me'. The criterion of 'potential pause' after each word, which was mentioned above (p. 39), is applicable to form-words too: the ordinary speaker, accustomed as he is to writing them and seeing them written as separate words, has no doubts whatever about their independent status.

Can form-words be regarded as independent units from the grammatical point of view? Many scholars would answer in the negative. They would argue that the articles, prepositions and personal pronoun subjects in English and French are exactly parallel to the declensions and verb endings in Latin — the only real difference being that the latter are suffixes whereas the former are prefixed to the words they modify. To take the contrast between Latin and French:

soror-*i* 'to the sister'   *à la* sœur
soror-*is* 'of the sister'   *de la* sœur
dic-*o* 'I say'   *je* dis
dic-*is* 'you (sing.) say'   *tu* dis

[1] *Language*, p. 179.

One linguist has described the Modern French construction as a kind of 'inflexion by prefix' (flexion par l'avant).[1] There is undoubtedly some truth in this argument; yet it would be wrong to equate the form-words of English and French with the inflexional endings of Latin. There are two important differences. Firstly, English and French form-words are separable from the terms they modify whereas Latin inflexions are not.[2] Thus, an adjective may be fitted in between the article and the noun: 'à la sœur — à la *jolie* sœur' 'to the sister — to the *pretty* sister', whereas the Latin dative singular *sorori* is an indivisible unit. Similarly personal pronoun subjects may be separated from their verb in English and in French (see above, p. 45), but nothing can come in Latin between the verb stem and the ending. Secondly, some personal pronoun subjects are inversible in English and in French: '*il* dit — dit-*il*' '*he* says — says *he*', whereas inflexional endings in Latin can never be inverted. It is thus abundantly clear that English and French form-words are not on all fours with Latin inflexions and have a great deal more independence than the latter.

To sum up: it can be proved by purely formal criteria, without any recourse to meaning, that form-words have some features in common with full words but differ from them in other respects. In view of their hybrid character, I have suggested elsewhere that they might be called 'pseudo-words'.[3] It must not be thought, however, that the boundary between the two categories is absolute and immutable; like most boundaries in language, it can be crossed, and some elements may even lie astride it. It has been crossed, for example, when the Latin noun *casa* 'house' became the French preposition *chez* 'at', and the Latin noun *homo* the French indefinite personal pronoun *on* 'one, people', or when the Spanish phrase *vuestra merced* coalesced to give the pronoun of address *usted* 'you'. Other elements, such as *considering* and *notwithstanding* used as prepositions ('*considering* his age' = 'in view of ... ', '*notwithstanding* his resistance' = 'despite ... '), seem to lie astride the demarcation line: as far as their function is concerned they are form-words, yet, thanks to their connexion with the verbs *consider* and *withstand*, they retain some of the semantic autonomy of full words. An interesting case is that of some French past participles such as *compris* 'included', *vu* 'seen', etc.,

---

[1] J. Vendryes in Meillet, op. cit., vol. I, p. 17; cf. Bally, op. cit., p. 301.
[2] This is not, however, a universally valid criterion. In Portuguese, for instance, the Future is formed by adding certain endings to the Infinitive, but the two can be separated by a personal or reflexive pronoun object: *servir-ei* 'I shall serve' — *servir-me-ei* 'I shall help myself.'
[3] *The Principles of Semantics*, p. 59.

which, when used prepositionally, do not agree in number and gender with the noun which follows: '*compris* quelques réponses' 'including some replies' (instead of *comprises*), '*vu* sa charge énorme' 'seeing his enormous burden' (instead of *vue*).[1] This lack of agreement clearly shows that they are to be regarded as form-words, yet once again they retain some of their independent semantic status because of their association with their verbs.

It may even happen that the same term belongs to several word-classes some of which are full words and others form-words. *Down* as an adverb and a preposition is a form-word, but it can also be used as a full word: as an adjective in '*down* train', as a verb in 'to *down* tools', as a noun in 'ups and *downs*' and the colloquial 'have a *down* on somebody'. But although the border-line is not definitive, and may be fluid at certain points, there can be no doubt about its fundamental importance in the structure of language.

Enough has been said about form-words to show that their function is syntactical rather than lexical. Though they possess some measure of autonomy, they are functionally more akin to inflexions than to full words: their role in the economy of language is that of grammatical tools rather than independent terms. It follows that their study will fall within syntax, not lexicology, and that the important and complicated semantic problems connected with them will be dealt with in the semantic division of syntax. As the present book is concerned with lexical meaning only, no further attention will be paid to the semantics of form-words.

3. *The Word as a Unit of Meaning*
The Role of Context

'When *I* use a word', said Humpty Dumpty, 'it means just what I choose it to mean — neither more nor less.' Some linguists, in their eagerness to underline the importance of context and to demolish the belief that there is a 'proper' meaning inherent in each word, go almost as far as Humpty Dumpty in their dogmatic utterances. Statements like 'le mot n'est que par le contexte et n'est rien par lui-même',[2] which are frequently heard nowadays, are neither accurate nor realistic. While it is perfectly true, and even a truism, that words are almost always found embedded in specific contexts, there are cases when a term stands entirely by itself, without any contextual support, and will still make sense. A

[1] Cf. M. Grevisse, *Le bon Usage*, 7th ed., Gembloux — Paris, 1959, pp. 692 ff.
[2] 'The word exists only through the context and is nothing in itself' (Rosetti, op. cit., p. 38). On this whole problem see now T. Slama-Cazacu, *Langage et contexte*, The Hague, 1961, esp. Pt. II, ch. 3. Cf. also L. Antal, 'Sign, Meaning Context', *Lingua*, xi (1961), pp. 211-19.

one-word title such as Tolstoy's *Resurrection*, Ibsen's *Ghosts* or Jane Austen's *Persuasion* can be heavily charged with meaning, and even such elliptical titles as Kipling's *If* and Henry Green's *Nothing* will conjure up some sort of idea. In everyday life one is often asked: 'What does word so-and-so mean?' or 'How would you say word so-and-so in French?', and while in some cases it is difficult or even impossible to answer, in others one can do so without a moment's hesitation; no one knowing French would have any difficulty in giving the equivalent of an adjective like *yellow*, a verb like *write*, a concrete noun like *pencil*, or an abstract noun like *equality*. If words had no meaning outside contexts it would be impossible to compile a dictionary. 'There is no getting away from the fact', writes an eminent semanticist, 'that single words *have* more or less permanent meanings, that they actually do refer to certain referents, and not to others, and that this characteristic is the indispensable basis of all communication.'[1] This is only common sense, and it has recently been confirmed by experimental data. A series of tests designed to study the influence of context has shown that there is usually in each word a hard core of meaning which is relatively stable and can only be modified by the context within certain limits.[2]

At the same time no one would deny the crucial importance of context in the determination of word-meanings. As far as the role of *verbal context* is concerned, this was already recognized as fundamental by some of the pioneers of modern semantics; Darmesteter, for example, spoke of the various elements of a sentence 'conspiring', by their distribution and their collocations, to modify the meaning of individual words.[3] Similarly, the citing of contexts was acknowledged as a guiding principle in lexicography by Dr. Johnson and later on by the editors of the *Oxford English Dictionary*.[4] Modern linguists, however, have not only placed greater emphasis on context but have considerably broadened its scope and have also probed more deeply into its influence on word-meanings.

The range of the term 'context' has been widened in several directions.[5] Even the strictly verbal context is no longer restricted to what immediately precedes and follows, but may cover the whole passage, and sometimes the whole book, in which the word occurs. This tendency is particularly noticeable in stylistic criticism where it has often been found that the

---

[1] Stern, op. cit., p. 85.
[2] T. Cazacu, 'Le principe de l'adaptation au contexte', *Revue de Linguistique*, i (1956), pp. 79-118, esp. pp. 93 f. (Editions de l'Académie de la République Populaire Roumaine.)
[3] Op. cit., Paris, 1946 ed., p. 126; cf. Bréal, op. cit., 6th ed., Paris, 1924, pp. 145 f., and J. Stöcklein, *Bedeutungswandel der Wörter*, Munich, 1898.
[4] Cf. J. R. Firth, *Papers in Linguistics*, London, 1957, p. 7.
[5] Cf. I. A. Richards, *The Philosophy of Rhetoric*, New York, 1936, pp. 32 ff.

complete significance of an important term can be grasped only in the light of the work as a whole. When one begins to read Camus's novel *La Peste*, the word *peste* 'plague' seems at first to refer to a specific disease which devastated the town of Oran in the 1940s. As one reads on one gradually realizes that the term also has several superimposed layers of symbolic significance: it is an allegory of the German occupation of France and, in a wider sense, of evil in all its metaphysical and moral aspects, and these implications continue to be broadened and deepened until the final sentence of the book.[1]

In addition to the verbal context, the linguist must also pay attention to the so-called '*context of situation*', which has already been briefly mentioned (p. 32). This useful concept was introduced into linguistics by the anthropologist Bronislaw Malinowski who derived it from his field-work on the language and culture of the Trobriand Islanders in the South Pacific.[2] It means in the first place the actual situation in which an utterance occurs, but leads on to an even broader view of context embracing the entire cultural background against which a speech-event has to be set. 'The conception of context', writes Malinowski, 'must burst the bonds of mere linguistics and be carried over into the analysis of the general conditions under which a language is spoken ... The study of any language, spoken by a people who live under conditions different from our own and possess a different culture, must be carried out in conjunc-tion with the study of their culture and of their environment' (op. cit., p. 306).

This principle is of vital importance for historical semantics. The full meaning and overtones of certain words can be recaptured only if we replace them in the cultural context of the period. The Latin *rex* is not an exact equivalent of English *king* or French *roi*; since the overthrow of the monarchy in the early days of Roman history it acquired a heinous connotation and became the symbol of tyranny: 'after the expulsion of Tarquinius the Roman people could not bear to hear the word "king"'', writes Cicero in *De Re Publica* (Lewis and Short). The cultural context is even more relevant to a full understanding of so-called 'key-words'[3] which epitomize the ideals of a particular civilization: the καλοκἀγαθός[4] of ancient Greece, the *cortegiano* of the Italian Renaissance, the *honnête*

---

[1] See J. Cruickshank, *Albert Camus and the Literature of Revolt*, London, 1959, ch. 8.

[2] 'The Problem of Meaning in Primitive Languages', Supplement I to Ogden-Richards's *Meaning of Meaning*. Cf. J. R. Firth, op. cit., pp. 181 ff.

[3] On key-words see G. Matoré, *La Méthode en lexicologie. Domaine français*, Paris, 1953, pp. 67 ff.

[4] 'A perfect man, a man as he should be' (literally: 'beautiful and good') (Liddell and Scott).

homme of seventeenth-century France,[1] and above all the English *gentleman*.[2] The latter has outlived his Continental counterparts, but there have been subtle shifts of emphasis and changes in implication and nuance, which one can gauge by comparing the following passages:

> I do not think a braver *gentleman*,
> More active-valiant or more valiant-young,
> More daring or more bold, is now alive
> To grace this latter age with noble deeds.
> *King Henry the Fourth*, Part One, Act V, scene 1.

> He was the mildest manner'd man
> That ever scuttled ship or cut a throat,
> With such true breeding of a *gentleman*,
> You never could divine his real thought.
> *Byron, *Don Juan*, Canto III, st. 41.

> And thus he bore without abuse
> The grand old name of *gentleman*,
> Defamed by every charlatan,
> And soil'd with all ignoble use.
> *Tennyson, *In Memoriam*, CXI.

> Tea, although an Oriental,
> Is a *gentleman* at least;
> Cocoa is a cad and coward,
> Cocoa is a vulgar beast.
> *G. K. Chesterton, *The Song of Right and Wrong*.

This widening of contexts, linguistic and non-linguistic, has opened new horizons for the study of meaning. What we have to aim at is a 'serial contextualization of our facts, context within context, each one being a function, an organ of the bigger context and all contexts finding a place in what may be called the context of culture'.[3]

Modern semantics has also begun to grasp more precisely the impact of context upon word-meanings. This impact, which has a number of aspects, will become clearer in the later chapters of this book, and it will be sufficient at this stage to mention briefly some of its main forms.

[1] On the development of this concept see recently M. Wandruszka, *Der Geist der französischen Sprache*, Hamburg, 1959, pp. 92 ff.

[2] K. Nyrop, 'Qu'est-ce qu'un gentleman?', in *Linguistique et histoire des mœurs*, Paris 1934, ch. 2.

[3] Firth, op. cit., p. 32.

Broadly speaking there are two kinds of contextual influences: those which affect any word, and those which affect some words more than others. Every word, no matter how precise and unambiguous, will derive from the context a certain determinateness which, by the very nature of things, can arise only in specific utterances. Even proper names, the most concrete of all words, have a variety of aspects only one of which will be relevant to a particular situation; only the context will show whether, when speaking of Queen Victoria, we are referring to the young Queen advised by Lord Melbourne, to the aged monarch reigning at the time of the Boer War, or to any other stage in the 82 years of her life. Another factor which depends largely on the context is the emotive side of word-meaning. In principle, practically any term may acquire emotive overtones in a suitable context; conversely, even words with a strong emotional charge may on occasion be employed in a purely objective manner. *Home*, for example, is one of the great emotional words of the language, and is used that way in many contexts ('*Home*, sweet *home*'; *'England, home* and beauty'; *'Home* is the sailor, *home* from the sea', etc.), but it is stripped of all emotion in *Home Office* or *B.B.C. Home Service*.

Apart from this general influence, context may also play a vital part in fixing the meaning of words which are too vague or too ambiguous to make sense by themselves. To take an extreme case, the verb *do* has such a wide variety of uses that it is virtually meaningless in itself. It is interesting to note, however, that in less advanced cases of ambiguity there is some-times a kind of hierarchy between the various meanings, which is largely independent of context. Recent experiments have shown, for example, that when German speakers were asked to make up a sentence containing the word *Nagel*, all the subjects automatically took it in the sense of 'metal nail'; apparently it did not even occur to them that it also means 'finger-nail, toe-nail'.[1]

Another type of ambiguity which only the context will dispel is found in words belonging to more than one word-class. This is particularly common in English where words can pass freely — by a process known as 'conversion' — from one class to another. We have already seen (p. 48) that the word *down* may belong to no less than five parts of speech. Here too there is no doubt a hierarchy of functions: *fire* is primarily a noun, though it can be used as a verb; *have* is first and foremost a verb though it becomes a noun in 'the *haves* and the have-nots'; *savage*, normally adjective or noun, is sometimes employed as a verb: 'he was

[1] H. Wissemann, 'Erlebte und abstrahierte Wortbedeutung', *Sybaris. Festschrift H. Krahe*, Wiesbaden, 1958, pp. 195-202: p. 201.

savaged by his horse'. Conversion can also become a stylistic device as in Shakespeare's 'it *out-herods* Herod', Sir Walter Scott's *'but* me no *buts'* (*NED*), or Gerard Manley Hopkins's *'feel-of-primrose* hands' (*The Habit of Perfection*).

The role of context is even more essential in the case of homonyms. It would obviously be meaningless to ask someone to find the equivalent of the English word *sole* in a foreign language; one would first have to specify which of the three *soles* is meant: the adjective, the fish, or the bottom of the foot — not to mention *soul* which, though spelt differently, is pronounced in the same way. The Shakespearean pun:

> Not on thy *sole*, but on thy *soul*, harsh Jew,
> Thou mak'st thy knife keen.
> *The Merchant of Venice*, Act IV, scene 1,

is based on this ambiguity.

It is thus clear that the influence of context is highly variable: it differs from one word to another and from one language to another. Idioms infested with homonyms, for example, will rely extensively on context to clear up that particular form of ambiguity. The frequency of conversion in English increases the importance of context in that language. A number of factors governing the role of context will gradually emerge as we come to consider the semantic peculiarities of our words. First, however, it will be necessary to look more closely at the hub of all semantic theory: the nature of meaning itself.

CHAPTER 3

MEANING

I. The Concept of Meaning

MEANING is one of the most ambiguous and most controversial terms in the theory of language. In *The Meaning of Meaning*, Ogden and Richards collected no less than sixteen different definitions of it—twenty-three if each subdivision is counted separately.[1] Since then, many new uses, implicit or explicit, have been added to this formidable growth of ambiguity,[2] and in the opinion of some scholars the term has become unusable for scientific purposes. As a recent book on the theory of signs wittily puts it: 'Accounts of meaning usually throw a handful of putty at the target of sign phenomena, while a technical semiotic (= theory of signs) must provide us with words which are sharpened arrows ... ; hence it is desirable for semiotic to dispense with the term and to introduce special terms for the various factors which "meaning" fails to discriminate.'[3] Most scholars, however, are reluctant to abandon such a fundamental term; they prefer to redefine it and to add various qualifications to it.

The ambiguity can be reduced, but by no means resolved, if one narrows one's attention to word-meanings. Many linguistic elements other than words may be said to have 'meaning' of some kind: all morphemes are by definition significant (p. 26), and so are the combinations into which they enter, and all these various meanings play their part in the total meaning of the utterance. As Professor J. R. Firth wrote in a pioneering article a quarter of a century ago:

> I propose to split up meaning or function into a series of component functions. Each function will be defined as the use of some language form or element in relation to some context. Meaning, that is to say, is to be regarded as a complex of contextual relations, and phonetics, grammar, lexicography and semantics each handles its own components of the complex in its appropriate context.[4]

[1] Op. cit., pp. 186 f.
[2] See C. C. Fries, 'Meaning and Linguistic Analysis', *Language*, xxx (1954), pp. 57-68: pp. 62 f.
[3] Morris, op. cit., p. 19.
[4] Op. cit., p. 19 (the original article appeared in 1935 in the *Transactions of the Philological Society*, under the title 'The Technique of Semantics').

Other scholars have found it expedient to distinguish between 'lexical' and 'structural meaning'[1] — rather an unfortunate choice of terms since it seems to imply that the vocabulary has no structure; 'lexical' and 'grammatical' meaning would perhaps be preferable.[2] Be that as it may, the present book is concerned solely with the meaning of words.

A great deal has been written in recent years on the definition of word-meaning, and although we are no nearer to an answer — there can indeed be no single and definitive answer to such a question — we are at least beginning to see more clearly the main lines of contemporary thinking on the problem.[3] There are, broadly speaking, two schools of thought in present-day linguistics: the 'analytical' or 'referential' approach, which seeks to grasp the essence of meaning by resolving it into its main components, and the 'operational' approach, which studies words in action and is less interested in what meaning is than in how it works.

1. *Analytical (Referential) Definitions of Meaning*

The best known analytical model of meaning is the 'basic triangle' of Ogden and Richards (p. 11):

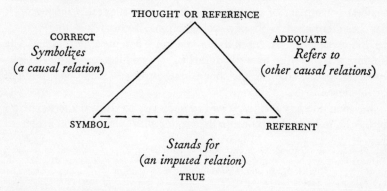

THOUGHT OR REFERENCE

CORRECT
Symbolizes
(a causal relation)

ADEQUATE
Refers to
(other causal relations)

SYMBOL   REFERENT

Stands for
(an imputed relation)
TRUE

The essential feature of this diagram is that it distinguishes between three components of meaning. On this reading, there is no direct relation

[1] Fries, op. cit., pp. 65 ff.

[2] Bloomfield, *Language*, p. 264. Cf. A. Raun, 'Grammatical Meaning', *Verba Docent (Festschrift L. Hakulinen)*, Helsinki, 1959, pp. 346-8; A. V. Isačenko, 'O grammaticheskom znachenij', *Voprosy Jazykoznanija*, 1961, no. 1, pp. 28-43.

[3] The following books and articles will help to orient the reader in the vast literature on the subject: Bloomfield, *Language*, ch. 9, and 'Meaning', *Monatshefte für deutschen Unterricht*, XXXV (1943), pp. 101-6; Firth, op. cit., chs. 3 and 15; Fries, loc. cit.; Gill, loc. cit.; W. Haas, loc. cit.; R. S. Hattori, 'The Analysis of Meaning', *For Roman Jakobson. Essays on the Occasion of his Sixtieth Birthday*, The Hague, 1956, pp. 207-12; W. Henzen, 'Wortbedeutung und Wortnatur', *Sprachgeschichte und Wortbedeutung. Festschrift A. Debrunner*, Berne, 1954,

E

between words and the things they 'stand for': the word 'symbolizes' a 'thought or reference' which in its turn 'refers' to the feature or event we are talking about. There is nothing fundamentally new in this analysis of meaning; the mediaeval schoolmen already knew that 'vox significat mediantibus conceptibus' (the word signifies through the medium of concepts), and Robert Browning expressed the same insight when he wrote in a somewhat different context:

> Art may tell a truth
> Obliquely, do the thing shall breed the thought,
> Nor wrong the thought, missing the mediate word.
> *The Ring and the Book*, XII, ll. 858-60.[1]

For a linguistic study of meaning, the basic triangle offers both too little and too much. Too much because the referent, the non-linguistic[2] feature or event as such, clearly lies outside the linguist's province. An object may remain unchanged and yet the meaning of its name may change for us if there is any alteration in our awareness of it, our knowledge about it, or our feelings towards it. The atom is the same as it was fifty years ago, but since it has been split we know that it is not the smallest constituent of matter, as its etymology suggests;[3] moreover, it has been enriched with new connotations, some fascinating, others terrifying, since the advent of the atomic age — and the atomic bomb. The linguist will therefore be well advised to confine his attention to the left-hand side of the triangle, the connexion between 'symbol' and 'thought or reference'.

Before going any further, it will be necessary to adapt the terminology to the job in hand. Our concern here is not with symbolization in general

pp. 179-94; C. E. Osgood, G. J. Suci, P. H. Tannenbaum, *The Measurement of Meaning*, Urbana, Ill., 1957, pp. 2-10; A. W. Read, 'The Term *Meaning* in Linguistics', *Etc.*, xiii (1956), pp. 37-45; R. H. Robins, 'A Problem in the Statement of Meanings', *Lingua*, iii (1952-53), pp. 119-37; S. Ullmann, 'The Concept of Meaning in Linguistics', *Archivum Linguisticum*, viii (1956), pp. 12-20; R. Wells, 'Meaning and Use', *Word*, x (1954), pp. 235-50. See also the *Proceedings of the Seventh International Congress of Linguists*, pp. 5-17 and 181-233; K. L. Pike, *Language in Relation to a Unified Theory of the Structure of Human Behavior*, Part III, Preliminary ed., Glendale, California, 1960, ch. 16; K. Ammer, *Einführung in die Sprachwissenschaft*, vol. I, Halle a.S., 1958, Part I, ch. 6; H. S. Sørensen, *Word-classes in Modern English, with Special Reference to Proper Names, with an Introductory Theory of Grammar, Meaning and Reference*, Copenhagen, 1958; P. Ziff, *Semantic Analysis*, ch. 5.

[1] Cf. S. W. Holmes, 'Browning: Semantic Stutterer', *Publications of the Modern Language Association of America*, lx (1945), pp. 231-55: p. 236.

[2] The referent may be a linguistic phenomenon in the rare cases when we use language to talk about language; cf. Bloomfield, 'Secondary and Tertiary Responses to Language' *Language*, xx (1944), pp. 45-55.

[3] From Greek *atomos* 'that cannot be cut, indivisible'.

but with the definition of word-meaning. One could choose, or coin, some specialized technical terms such as Saussure's 'signifiant' and 'signifié' (op. cit., pp. 97 ff.), but I personally have found it more expedient, in teaching and research, to use simple, everyday English words, giving them a little more precision than they have in ordinary usage. The three terms I would suggest are: 'name', 'sense', and 'thing'. The '*name*' is the phonetic shape of the word, the sounds which make it up and also other acoustic features such as accent. The '*sense*', put in general terms without committing oneself to any particular psychological doctrine, is 'the information which the name conveys to the hearer', whereas the '*thing*' is Ogden and Richards's 'referent', the non-linguistic feature or event we are talking about. The latter, as we have seen, lies outside the linguist's province, but the relation between name and sense will have to be looked at more closely.

It is at this point that the Ogden-Richards model does not go far enough. It gives an account of how the word acts on the hearer but seems to neglect the speaker's point of view. For the hearer, the sequence of events will be as shown in the basic triangle: hearing the word, say, *door*, he will think of a door and thus understand what the speaker was saying. For the speaker, the sequence will be just the reverse: he will, for some reason or another, think of a door, and this will make him pronounce the word. There is therefore a *reciprocal and reversible relationship between name and sense*: if one hears the word one will think of the thing, and if one thinks of the thing one will say the word. It is this reciprocal and reversible relationship between sound and sense which I propose to call the '*meaning*' of the word. The choice of terms is, of course, of secondary importance as long as the analysis itself is accepted.[1]

The above definition of meaning, and the analysis underlying it, are by no means new: they were explicitly stated by some semanticists more than thirty years ago,[2] and are implicit in Saussure's theory of the linguistic sign and in various developments of his doctrine.[3] It is sympto-

---

[1] 'Experience shows that it is not profitable to begin the study of a subject by trying to define the popular or technical terms that are connected with it. It is much better simply to examine the object of one's curiosity and then, when one comes across some feature which seems to deserve a name, to assign to this feature a familiar term which seems roughly to fit the case. Or else, we may prefer to invent some new word to name the feature we have seen' (Bloomfield, 'Meaning', p. 101).

[2] Z. Gombocz, *Jelentéstan* ('Semantics'), Pécs, 1926, pp. 31 ff., and L. Weisgerber, 'Die Bedeutungslehre — ein Irrweg der Sprachwissenschaft?', *Germanisch-Romanische Monatsschrift*, ix (1927), pp. 161-83.

[3] For example the distinction between 'expression' and 'content' by the Danish school of 'glossematics'; see L. Hjelmslev, *Prolegomena to a Theory of Language* (transl. F. J. Whitfield), Baltimore, 1953.

matic of the popularity of this approach that, at a conference on semantics held at Nice in 1951, a definition of meaning on the lines just mentioned was one of the few fundamental principles on which there was a large measure of agreement.[1] On the other hand, the theory has come under heavy fire from various directions in recent years, and the discussions have revealed a deep-seated cleavage of opinion on the aims and methods of linguistics. The criticisms fall under three main heads:

(a) The fear has been expressed that, by excluding the 'referent', the non-linguistic feature or event referred to, semantics will 'fall prey to an extreme esoteric formalism'.[2] A moment's reflection will show that this is not so. It is true that the referent as such is excluded, but all its linguistically relevant features are included as they form part of the 'sense'. By excluding the referent we merely separate what is linguistically relevant from what is irrelevant. In Bloomfield's words,

> it is clear that we must discriminate between *non-distinctive* features of the situation, such as the size, shape, colour, and so on of any particular apple, and the *distinctive*, or *linguistic meaning* (the *semantic* features) which are common to all the situations that call forth the utterance of the linguistic form, such as the features which are common to all the objects of which English-speaking people use the word *apple* (*Language*, p. 141).

The distinction is inherent in the generic nature of our words, which will be discussed in Chapter 5.

(b) The second objection is far more serious and more difficult to counter. It is intimately connected with one of the great philosophical issues in contemporary linguistics: the controversy between 'mentalists' and 'mechanists'.[3] American structuralists in particular[4] are disinclined to operate with vague and elusive mental entities which are inaccessible to scientific analysis and can be observed only by the notoriously unreliable method of introspection. They are unwilling to assume that, 'prior to the utterance of a linguistic form, there occurs within the speaker a non-physical process, a *thought, concept, image, feeling, act of*

---

[1] G. Devoto, 'La "Conferenza di semantica" di Nizza', *Archivio Glottologico Italiano*, xxxvi (1951), pp. 82-4.

[2] H. Werner, *Language*, xxviii (1952), p. 255.

[3] On this controversy see esp. Bloomfield, *Language*, pp. 32 ff., and his article on secondary and tertiary responses in language (see above, p. 56, n. 2), as well as L. Spitzer's rejoinder in *Language*, xx (1944), pp. 245-51.

[4] For a similar objection by a non-structuralist see A. Gill's article referred to on p. 19, n. 2, above.

will, or the like, and that the hearer, likewise, upon receiving the sound-waves, goes through an equivalent or correlated mental process' (Bloomfield, *Language*, p. 142). In order to avoid recourse to these psychological factors, the antimentalists prefer to eliminate the apex at the top end of the triangle and to posit a direct relation between 'name' and 'thing'. Hence Bloomfield's famous definition of the meaning of a linguistic form as 'the situation in which the speaker utters it and the response which it calls forth in the hearer' (ibid., p. 139). This definition refers primarily to the meaning of a whole utterance, but the meaning of individual words is obtained in the same way; as he explains elsewhere in the form of an amusing parable, a visitor from another planet would soon notice that human utterances are connected with certain situations and accompanied by certain responses, and he would 'learn to recognize recurrent parts of utterances, and to see that words like *shut, door, apple* occurred in speeches that were connected with acts of shutting something and objects of certain definite types' ('Meaning', p. 101).

It is easy to prove that Bloomfield's conception of meaning, which virtually equates the latter with the 'referent', is untenable. To mention only one or two of its weaknesses, it takes no account of the innumerable cases where the thing referred to is not present at the time of speaking — not to mention statements about abstract phenomena. Bloomfield regards such situations as 'displaced uses of speech' which are 'derived in fairly uniform ways from its primary value, and require no special discussion' (*Language*, p. 141); yet it is perfectly clear that a statement about an earthquake thousands of miles away, or about the evils of totalitarianism, can be understood only if the words *earthquake* and *totalitarianism* correspond to something in the hearer's memory. Another difficulty is that the outside world is not merely registered in language, but divided up, analysed and classified in each idiom in a different manner. This fact, which will be discussed in the last chapter, is recognized by Bloomfield (ibid., p. 280), but there is no way of fitting it into his definition of meaning.

An inevitable consequence of Bloomfield's conception of meaning is that the latter is relegated outside linguistics proper. Since meaning is a feature or event in the non-linguistic world, it is natural for Bloomfield to suggest that we should define it, whenever we can, in terms of some other science, saying, for example, that 'the ordinary meaning of the English word *salt* is "sodium chloride" (NaCl)' (ibid., pp. 139 f.). But one may wonder whether this is really the meaning of the word for the average speaker who probably has no idea of the chemical composition of salt. When it comes to defining feelings and other states of mind, the antimentalistic bias which is at the root of Bloomfield's theory leads to methods which can only be called 'Procrustean':[1]

> Terms which relate to social behaviour such as *love, friend, kind, hate* could be defined in terms of ethnology, folklore, and sociology, provided these studies had reached a perfection and accuracy undreamed of today. Terms which relate to states of the speaker's body that are perceptible only to him, such as *queasy, qualmish, sad, gay, glad, happy*, could be defined only if we had a minute knowledge of what goes on inside a living person's body (ibid., p. 280).

Quite apart from the attempt to reduce sadness, happiness and other feelings to 'states of the body',[2] one may again wonder whether a rigorously scientific definition of such words, even if it were feasible, would correspond to what they mean to the ordinary speaker. In view of these unrealistic standards,[3] it is not surprising that Bloomfield should have arrived at a discouraging conclusion: 'The statement of meanings is therefore the weak point in language-study, and will remain so until human knowledge advances very far beyond its present state' (ibid., p. 140). While it is quite wrong to say that Bloomfield paid no attention to meaning,[4] there can be no doubt that his attitude had a negative influence on many of his followers and helped to turn them away from semantic problems.

The failure of the Bloomfield experiment clearly shows that one cannot have a referential definition of meaning without positing a middle term between the name and the referent. This does not mean, however, that we should relapse into a naïve form of mentalism, set up spurious psychological entities, and operate with loose and nebulous concepts such as 'ideas', 'mental images' and the like. The experience of meaning, as far as it can be scientifically ascertained at all, is for the psychologist to elucidate, and although recent studies on conditioned reflexes and similar

[1] Cf. Robins, *Lingua*, iii, p. 131. As Mr. Robins rightly points out, 'feelings and thoughts should be recognized as an irreducible part of many contexts of situation, contexts in turn being defined simply as abstractions analysed out by us from the totality of our experience' (ibid., p. 134).

[2] Cf. M. Schlauch, 'Early Behaviorist Psychology and Contemporary Linguistics', *Word*, ii (1946), pp. 25-36.

[3] 'What he [Bloomfield] seems to want has been shown by recent philosophy of science to be hopeless. What he wants, in principle, is to dispense with all "constructs" and "intervening variables", and to correlate observables directly with observables. Seeing that the hopelessness of this widespread dream was not shown until the mid thirties, and is still not common knowledge ... , we need not blame Bloomfield for ignorance. It is enough to recognize that what was plausible in his day is not now plausible two decades later' (R. Wells, *Word*, x, p. 241).

[4] See on this question Fries, *Language*, xxx, pp. 58 ff.

processes have begun to throw some light on the problem,[1] it would be unwise for the linguist to commit himself to any particular psychological theory. The exact psychological nature of meaning is of no outstanding importance to the linguist: he is more interested in the information which a word actually conveys to the ordinary speaker. Even this is, of course, extremely difficult to establish since the same term may be used in countless situations by millions of people. Patient study of a large and representative sample of contexts, as in the compilation of a major dictionary, can go some way towards solving the problem, and the linguist may also receive some help from modern experimental techniques, as will be seen later on in this chapter.

(c) Another criticism directed against referential theories of meaning is that they are inspired by the old — and allegedly obsolescent — metaphysics of body and soul. 'As, in a human person, a soul or mind is supposed to accompany the body and its overt behaviour, so in a linguistic sign, a meaning is supposed to accompany the form in its various occurrences. The linguistic sign is supposed to emerge from a correspondence, a kind of psycho-physical parallelism, between a form and a meaning.'[2] It should be noted that this criticism is not confined to 'mentalistic' definitions of meaning but applies to all referential theories, including even the attempt to define meaning in terms of distribution.[3]

This objection, if valid, would strike at the very root of all the definitions mentioned so far, since it calls into question the dualism on which they are based. It seems, however, that the criticism springs from a misunderstanding suggested by a much-abused metaphor which was already dismissed as unsatisfactory by Saussure half a century ago (op. cit., p. 145). The dualism of sound and sense, which is implicit in all referential theories, has nothing to do with the metaphysics of body and soul. It is a totally different kind of dualism: that inherent in any sign, linguistic or other. All signs, by definition, point to something else, refer to something beyond themselves (see above, p. 15). This is true of any sign, from the simplest to the most complex, from traffic lights to the most recondite symbols of the poet; and words are no exception to the rule. To deny the dual, 'Janus-like' nature of words would be tantamount

---

[1] Osgood, et al., The Measurement of Meaning, pp. 3 ff.

[2] Haas, Transactions of the Philological Society, 1954, p. 71; cf. Firth, op. cit., pp. 19 and 227; Id., 'A Synopsis of Linguistic Theory, 1930-1955', Studies in Linguistic Analysis. Special Volume of the Philological Society, Oxford, 1957, pp. 1-32; Read, Etc., xiii, p. 38.

[3] Haas, loc. cit., pp. 72 ff. The distributional theory referred to is that put forward by Z. S. Harris, Methods in Structural Linguistics, Chicago, 1951.

to denying that they are signs, and most linguists would be reluctant to take that step.

If any analogy were required to illustrate the relation between sound and sense, one could, with Saussure, compare a word to a sheet of paper whose two sides are two facets of an indissoluble whole, so that you cannot cut out one side without also cutting out the other.[1] But perhaps it is safer to avoid metaphors and similes when defining fundamental concepts. It is sufficient to say that words have a dual structure simply because they are signs; whether one interprets that dual structure in 'mentalistic' or any other terms is a question which does not arise in this context,

None of the above criticisms will, then, compel the linguist to abandon referential definitions of meaning. Such definitions will, however, have to be expanded in two directions before they can be used in actual research. Provision will have to be made, first of all, for multiple meaning. In the ideally simple situations envisaged so far, only one name and one sense were involved — a relationship which may be symbolically represented by a single line connecting two poles:

where n = name, s = sense, and the two arrows show that the relation is reciprocal and reversible. As will be seen in greater detail in Chapters 6 and 7, this scheme may be complicated in two ways: several names may be connected with one sense, as in the synonyms *little* and *small*, and conversely, several senses may be attached to one name, as in *conductor* 'director of orchestra; official on bus or tram; thing that transmits heat or electricity'. Diagrammatically:

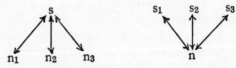

Secondly, the referential definition of meaning must not lead to an

[1] 'La langue est ... comparable à une feuille de papier: la pensée est le recto et le son le verso; on ne peut découper le recto sans découper en même temps le verso; de même dans la langue, on ne saurait isoler ni le son de la pensée, ni la pensée du son' (op. cit., p. 157). While this extract refers to language in general, it is clear from other passages in the book (cf. pp. 99 ff. and 144 f.) that the same principle applies to individual words.

atomistic view of language, in which each word would be regarded as an isolated and self-contained unit. In addition to the very special and *sui generis* relationship which binds the name to the sense, words are also associated with other words with which they have something in common, in sound, in sense, or in both. The noun *light*, for example, will be connected with *darkness, day, sun*, etc., by associations between the senses; with the adjective *light* 'not heavy' because the two words are homonymous;[1] and with the adjective *light* 'not dark', the verb *to light*, the noun *lightning*, etc., on both formal and semantic grounds. This principle plays a significant part in changes of meaning and in the structure of the vocabulary, as will be seen in the last two chapters of this book. It could be diagrammatically represented in this way:

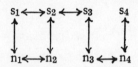

The first two words are connected by both sound and sense, the second and third by sense only, and the third and fourth by sound only. If one bears in mind that all three types of association may radiate in various directions from a single word, and that the pattern may be further complicated by multiple meaning, one will have some idea of the infinite complexity of semantic relations.

Referential definitions of meaning raise an interesting point of linguistic method. Since meaning is a reciprocal and reversible relation between name and sense, it can be investigated by starting from either end: one can start from the name and look for the sense or senses attached to it, as do all alphabetical dictionaries; but one can also start from the sense and look for the name or names connected with it. It has been categorically affirmed that 'in all study of language we must start from forms and not from meanings'.[2] This is not entirely true. In most inquiries there will be obvious advantages in taking forms as our starting-point; there are, however, important and fruitful types of research in which one has to proceed the other way round.[3] Dialectologists and linguistic geographers will often be interested in finding out the words for particular objects or processes in a given area. Conceptual dictionaries

---

[1] For a stylistic exploitation of this homonymy see below, p. 192.
[2] Bloomfield, 'Meaning', p. 103.
[3] See, in the field of syntax, F. Brunot's monumental *La Pensée et la langue*, 3rd ed., Paris, 1936. Cf. also Jespersen, *The Philosophy of Grammar*, pp. 39 ff., and, for stylistics, my *Style in the French Novel*, p. 20.

such as Roget's *Thesaurus* are compiled on the same principle,[1] and the study of certain closely organized nomenclatures ('semantic fields'), which will be discussed in the last chapter, has a similar orientation. That branch of semantics which starts from the sense and seeks to identify the name, or names, attached to it is known as '*onomasiology*'.[2] Attempts have been made in the past to detach onomasiology from semantics and to regard the two as parallel sciences, semantics dealing with meaning and onomasiology with 'designation'.[3] This is quite unnecessary if a referential definition of meaning is adopted: the two approaches will then be seen, not as two distinct disciplines but as parallel methods starting at opposite ends. The two methods are complementary, and in certain types of inquiries they may even be combined with interesting results.[4]

2. *Operational (Contextual) Definitions of Meaning*

In recent years, a new and entirely different conception of meaning has begun to take shape inside and outside linguistics. It received its most pointed and most provocative formulation in L. Wittgenstein's *Philosophical Investigations* which were published posthumously in 1953. A quarter of a century earlier, P. W. Bridgman had emphasized, in *The Logic of Modern Physics*, the purely operational character of scientific concepts like 'length', 'time' or 'energy'. 'We mean by any concept', he argued, 'nothing more than a set of operations; the concept is synonymous with the corresponding set of operations.'[5] This approach, known by the name of 'operationalism', was extended from scientific concepts to words in general, and summed up in the well-known formula: 'The true meaning of a word is to be found by observing what a man does with it, not what he says about it.'[6] Wittgenstein goes one step further: he does not merely say that we can establish the meaning of a word by observing its use; he boldly asserts that the meaning of a word *is* its use: 'For a *large* class of

---

[1] See esp. the introduction to F. Dornseiff, *Der deutsche Wortschatz nach Sachgruppen*, 5th ed., Berlin, 1959.

[2] From the Greek *onoma* 'name'. A useful survey of research in this field will be found in B. Quadri, *Aufgaben und Methoden der onomasiologischen Forschung*, Romanica Helvetica XXXVII, Berne, 1952.   [3] See my *Principles of Semantics*, pp. 161 ff.

[4] K. Jaberg, *Aspects géographiques du langage*, Paris, 1936.

[5] New York, 1927, p. 5. Cf. ibid.: 'If the concept is physical, as of length, the operations are actual physical operations, namely, those by which length is measured; or if the concept is mental, as of mathematical continuity, the operations are mental operations, namely those by which we determine whether a given aggregate of magnitudes is continuous.' Cf. also p. 6: 'the proper definition of a concept is not in terms of its properties but in terms of actual operations'.

[6] Cf. Stuart Chase, *The Tyranny of Words*, p. 7 and ch. 8; Firth, *Proceedings of the Seventh International Congress of Linguists*, p. 8.

cases — though not for all — in which we employ the word "meaning" it can be defined thus: the meaning of a word is its use in the language' (p. 20). This idea reappears in varying forms in the book, though at times it would seem that Wittgenstein had some hesitations about it (pp. 53, 215); it is as if he felt that there was something more in the meaning of a word than its use, but that this something eluded our grasp and nothing could profitably be said about it.

Wittgenstein uses several analogies to show the implications of his formula. 'Language', he writes, 'is an instrument. Its concepts are instruments' (p. 151). Elsewhere he develops the similarity between words and tools: 'Think of the tools in a tool-box: there is a hammer, pliers, a saw, a screw-driver, a rule, a glue-pot, glue, nails and screws. — The functions of words are as diverse as the functions of these objects' (p. 6). Like Saussure,[1] but no doubt independently of him, he compares language to a game of chess: 'The question "What is a word really?" is analogous to "What is a piece in chess?" ' (p. 47); and again: 'Let us say that the meaning of a piece is its role in the game' (p. 150). He also speaks of the 'field of force of a word' (p. 219) and of 'all the extensive ramifications of the tie-up effected by each of the words' (ibid.). All these comparisons show a remarkable affinity between his thinking and contemporary linguistic theory. It is not surprising, therefore, to find him using a procedure which is known in modern linguistics as the 'substitution test'. Discussing the verb *is* in the two sentences 'The rose *is* red' and 'Twice two *is* four', he writes: 'The rule which shows that the word *is* has different meanings in these sentences is the one allowing us to replace the word *is* in the second sentence by the sign of equality, and forbidding this substitution in the first sentence' (p. 149). This is the method used by linguists for the identification of phonemes and other distinctive elements: by substituting phonemes for each other we obtain different words (*pat — bat — pet — pad*), and by substituting words for each other we get different sentences ('A young man came into the garden — An *old* man came into the garden — A young *woman* came into the garden — A young man *ran* into the garden — A young man came into the *house*). As far back as 1935, Professor J. R. Firth had defined the word as a 'lexical substitution-counter',[2] and this conception fits very smoothly into Wittgenstein's philosophy of language.

Wittgenstein's ideas had some immediate repercussions in linguistics,[3]

---

[1] Op. cit., pp. 125 ff.; cf. above, p. 8.
[2] Op. cit., p. 20. Cf. also Haas, loc. cit., p. 80.
[3] See esp. Wells, loc. cit. Cf. also Haas, loc. cit., p. 81, n. 1, and my article, 'The Concept of Meaning in Linguistics', mentioned above.

and have strengthened the case of those linguists who, before him, had defined meaning on similar lines.[1] His formula will appeal to the student of language not only because of its neatness and simplicity and because it is very much in line with current trends in linguistics, but also because it offers several solid advantages. On the negative side, it avoids any recourse to vague, intangible and subjective mental states or processes. On the positive side, it has the merit of defining meaning in contextual, i.e. in purely empirical terms. The crucial question which now arises is this: how does the operational definition compare with the referential (a) as a tool of research, and (b) as a working hypothesis in semantic theory?

(a) What is the value of the operational definition in the study of particular words, for example in lexicography? The answer will depend on how the definition is interpreted. If it is taken to mean that the student must confine himself to collecting and analysing contexts in which the word occurs, then the task would seem to be thankless as well as inconclusive. It has been suggested that 'substitutions for *cat*, in more comprehensive units such as *The — caught the mouse, I bought fish for my —*, etc., display its meaning; its privilege of occurring in those contexts, with a certain distribution of frequencies among the occurrences, *is* the linguistic meaning of *cat*.'[2] Such contexts could of course be multiplied indefinitely, and some of the most frequent among them would be the least informative: *I saw a —; The — is hungry; Our — is black*. What would be the ultimate value of such a roundabout method?

If, on the other hand, the lexicographer tried, as he surely would, to identify some typical uses of the word by extracting the common feature or features from a representative selection of contexts, then he would immediately relapse into the referential theory of meaning. The terminology would be different, but the basic dualism would reappear, with 'use' playing the same role as 'sense', 'reference' or other terms in more overtly referential theories.

(b) Any definition of meaning should be regarded as no more than a working hypothesis. Its value will depend on how it works: on the help it can give in the description, interpretation and classification of semantic phenomena. From this point of view it would be premature to choose

---

[1] 'I propose to split up meaning or function into a series of component functions. Each function will be defined as the use of some language form or element in relation to some context' (Firth, op. cit., p. 19; cf. above, p. 54); 'the meaning of a portion of speech is a function of it ... the function of a portion of speech is its distinctive occurrence in certain environments' (Haas, *Proceedings of the Seventh International Congress of Linguists*, p. 191; cf. loc. cit., pp. 79 f.). Dr. Haas calls his theory 'functional', but in view of the ambiguity of this term in linguistics it might be better to call it 'operational' or 'contextual'.

[2] Haas, *Transactions of the Philological Society*, 1954, p. 80.

between the two types of definition. All major works on semantic theory have so far been based on referential concepts of meaning; the operational doctrine has had as yet no chance to prove its worth,[1] though it must be admitted that it is difficult to see how a comprehensive and orderly survey of the field of semantics could be devised on such a basis. It would seem, for example, that certain important aspects of the subject would have no place in a strictly operational theory. Where would conceptual dictionaries, 'semantic fields', onomasiological studies and atlases fit into such a frame-work?[2] To adopt a doctrine which would exclude such vital parts of the subject would involve limitations which few semanticists would be prepared to accept.

All this does not mean in any way that the operational definition has to be discarded. It should be viewed, not as an alternative to, but as a valuable complement of, the referential theory. It contains the salutary warning, which both semanticists and lexicographers would do well to heed, that the meaning of a word can be ascertained *only* by studying its use. There is no short cut to meaning, through introspection or by any other method. The investigator must start by collecting an adequate sample of contexts and then approach them with an open mind, allowing the meaning or meanings to emerge from the contexts themselves. Once this phase has been completed, he can safely pass on to the 'referential' phase and seek to formulate the meaning or meanings thus identified. The relation between the two methods, or rather between the two phases of the inquiry, is ultimately the same as that between language and speech: the operational theory is concerned with meaning in speech, the referential with meaning in language. There is absolutely no need to set the two approaches against each other: each handles its own side of the problem, and neither is complete without the other.

Since this book deals primarily with meaning in language, not speech, it will adopt the referential definition cited on p. 57, according to which meaning is a 'reciprocal and reversible relationship between the name and the sense',[3] with the correctives mentioned on pp. 62 f. concerning multiple meaning as well as associative relations between words.

---

[1] R. Wells's attempt (loc. cit., pp. 245 ff.) to study the use of some English adjectives in the light of Wittgenstein's theory, though interesting in itself, is too limited in scope to give any idea of the possibilities of this approach.

[2] See above, pp. 63 f.

[3] While this definition differentiates carefully between the 'sense' and the 'meaning' of a word, it would be unnecessary and pedantic to adhere systematically to this distinction throughout the present book. On occasion, 'meaning' can be safely used as a synonym of 'sense'; in definitions or wherever there is any risk of ambiguity, the two terms will of course have to be employed in the technical acceptations given on p. 57.

II. Can Meaning be Measured?

The referential theory of meaning has recently been vindicated by an interesting experiment which could not possibly be fitted into a contextual theory as it dispenses with context altogether. For the past few years, a group of American researchers calling themselves 'psycholinguists' have been working on a method for 'measuring meaning'. A series of papers on the subject was followed by the publication in 1957 of a major book, *The Measurement of Meaning*, by C. E. Osgood, G. J. Suci and P. H. Tannenbaum. Although the procedure includes some elaborate mathematical operations involving the use of an electronic computer, the basic principle is quite simple. The starting-point is a series of tests carried out by means of a device called the 'semantic differential'. This is made up of a number of scales, each with seven divisions, whose poles are formed by opposite adjectives: *rough — smooth, fair — unfair, strong — weak*, etc., and the various subjects are asked to locate a given 'concept' in that division of each scale which seems most appropriate to them. To take an example given by the authors themselves (p. 26):

FATHER

happy____:____: X :____:____:____:____sad

hard____: X :____:____:____:____:____soft

slow____:____:____:____: X :____:____fast, etc.

The meaning of the seven divisions is, taking as an example the first of the above scales, from left to right: extremely happy; quite happy; slightly happy; neither happy nor sad, equally happy and sad; slightly sad; quite sad; extremely sad. In the above test, 'father' is described as 'slightly happy', 'quite hard', and 'slightly fast'. Needless to say, both concepts and adjectival scales were carefully sampled. It should be noted that not all the concepts were common nouns; there were also some proper names (for example names of well-known American politicians), pronouns and pronominal combinations (*myself, my mother*), and 'compound concepts' such as *abstract art, Red China*, and *flexible price supports*. The adjectival scales were subjected to an operation known as 'factor analysis', and this revealed that they fell into three groups, according to the predominance of one of the following factors: evaluation (*good — bad*), potency (*hard — soft*), and activity (*active — passive*). Several other factors were identified but were found to be of subsidiary importance. This had the advantage of yielding a three-dimensional 'semantic space' in which each concept could be assigned its place by subjecting the various answers to statistical analysis.

The new technique, if properly developed and extended to a far larger sample of vocabulary, could be of considerable importance to lexicography. 'One can envisage', the authors claim, 'the gradual construction of a functional dictionary of connotative meanings — a quantized Thesaurus — in which the writer would find nouns, adjectives, verbs and adverbs (all lexical items) listed according to their locations in the semantic space, as determined from the judgments of representative samples of the population' (p. 330). In this way a new science, which the authors call 'experimental semantics', would come into being. Apart from purely lexical problems, the semantic differential has a variety of other applications, some of them only tenuously connected with linguistics: they include such diverse topics as 'attitude measurement', aesthetic judgments, advertising, personality studies, and psychotherapy. One of the most interesting of the experiments recorded in the book was the 'blind' analysis of a famous case of multiple personality.[1] Each of the three personalities was subjected to tests with the semantic differential, and the results, arrived at quite independently, not only confirmed the diagnosis of the two psychiatrists in charge, but gave them some useful hints about further treatment.

On the eve of its publication, *The Measurement of Meaning* was hailed at the Oslo congress of linguists in rather extravagant terms.[2] Since then, various aspects of the method have been criticized: the linguistic theory on which it is based, the way the sampling and the factor analysis were conducted, the inappropriateness of some of the scales, and other points.[3] The most serious criticism concerns the title of the book, or rather the claim which is implicit in the title. Is it really 'meaning' that Osgood and his colleagues have been measuring? This objection was anticipated by the authors when they candidly declared: 'It is certain that we are not providing an index of what signs refer to, and if reference or designation

---

[1] Pp. 258 ff.; see also C. H. Thigpen-H. M. Cleckley, *The Three Faces of Eve*, London ed., 1957.

[2] U. Weinreich, *Proceedings of the Eighth International Congress of Linguists*, p. 790.

[3] See esp. J. B. Carroll, *Language*, xxv (1959), pp. 58-77, and U. Weinreich, 'Travels through Semantic Space', *Word*, xiv (1958), pp. 346-66; cf. also Osgood's rejoinder in *Word*, xv (1959), pp. 192-200. See also R. Wells, 'A Mathematical Approach to Meaning', *Cahiers Ferdinand de Saussure*, xv (1957), pp. 117-36. On a different technique for measuring semantic data, see F. Hiorth, 'Distances of Meaning and Semantical Tests', *Synthese*, xi (1959), pp. 33-62. See also J. Cohen, E. J. Dearnley, C. E. M. Hansel, 'A Quantitative Study of Meaning', *The British Journal of Educational Psychology*, xxviii, 2 (1958), pp. 141-8.

is the *sine qua non* of meaning, as some readers will insist, then they will
conclude that this book is badly mistitled' (p. 325). It must be perfectly
clear to any impartial observer that what the semantic differential
measures is not 'meaning' in any of the accepted senses of the term.[1] But
it is equally clear that what it does measure is an important component of
meaning: it comes very close to what is usually called 'emotive connotation', a factor which will be examined in Chapter 5. It is perhaps a pity
that the authors claimed more than they had actually achieved, but this
must not obscure the fact that it is no mean feat to have reduced a major
component of meaning to quantitative analysis.

The significance of the Osgood experiment, and of the vistas it opens
up for future research, becomes clear if one recalls some of the difficulties
mentioned earlier on in this chapter (pp. 58 f.). The great stumbling-
block in referential theories of meaning has always been that they had to
operate with subjective and intangible mental processes. As one of the
acutest critics of these theories wrote: 'An empirical science cannot be content to rely on a procedure of people looking into their minds, each into
his own.'[2] This was the main reason why various scholars turned away
from the traditional approach and tried to define meaning on entirely
different lines. Now it seems possible at last to envisage a referential theory
resting on sound empirical foundations. In the authors' own words: 'It
may be argued that the data with which we deal in semantic measurement
are essentially subjective — introspections about meanings on the part of
subjects — and that all we have done is to objectify expressions of these
subjective states. This is entirely true, but it is not a criticism of the
method. Objectivity concerns the role of the observer, not the observed.
Our procedures completely eliminate the idiosyncrasies of the investigator
in arriving at the final index of meaning, and this is the essence of
objectivity' (pp. 125 f.). In other words, each person records his own
private, entirely subjective reactions, but by the time the analysis has
been completed the result will represent a kind of 'semantic average'
reached by purely objective statistical methods.[3]

---

[1] 'The meaning of "meaning" for which we wish to establish an index is a psychological
one — that process or state in the behaviour of a sign-using organism which is assumed to be
a necessary consequence of the reception of sign-stimuli and a necessary antecedent for the
production of sign-responses' (*The Measurement of Meaning*, p. 9).

[2] Haas, *Transactions of the Philological Society*, 1954, p. 74.

[3] 'Techniques such as those utilized by Osgood and his collaborators make greater
objectivity possible in that the describer, instead of asking himself, asks a representative
sample of the speech community, and treats the degree of agreement between answers as a
significant and measurable variable. In order to keep answers from varying too wildly and
to make them suitable for quantitative analysis, the technique prescribes that the subjects
make a multiple choice from among a preselected set of possible answers. The resulting

Experiments like Osgood's are also bound to have a beneficial effect on the status of semantics. Ever since scientific rigour became the main aspiration of linguists, the 'unscientific' nature of meaning brought that concept, and with it semantics at large, into disrepute. A leading American structuralist recently admitted that 'for many linguistic students the word *meaning* itself has become almost anathema'.[1] The situation has been ably summed up by Professor W. S. Allen in his inaugural lecture at Cambridge: 'Meaning, as at least one linguist has expressed it, has become a "dirty word"; but if the name tends to be avoided, there is no doubt that every linguist employs the concept, though some would be unwilling to admit to such improper thoughts. And surely, without meaning linguistics cannot exist.'[2] At the London congress of linguistics, this ambivalent attitude was described as 'crypto-semantics'.[3] It is to be hoped that further progress along the trail blazed by Osgood and his team will put an end to this state of affairs.

III. PROPER NAMES

Possession of a name is, and has been from time immemorial, the privilege of every human being. 'No one, whether of low or high degree, goes nameless once he has come into the world', we read in the *Odyssey*; 'everybody is named by his parents the moment he is born.'[4] Herodotus, and Pliny after him, mention as a freak of nature the Atarantes (or Atlantes) of North Africa who are the only human beings known to have no names for one another.[5] Names play such an important part in human relations that they are often endowed with magic potencies and surrounded by elaborate superstitions and taboos. To cite but one example out of many, among the Masai of Africa, the name of a dead person is never mentioned, and if an ordinary word happens to sound like that name, it will have to be replaced: 'if an unimportant person called Ol-onana (he who is soft, or weak, or gentle) were to die, gentleness would not be

---

quasi-semantic description is then condensed further, by means of statistical manipulation. All these are features which an experimental lexicography may in future want to accept' (Weinreich, *Word*, xiv, p. 364).

[1] Fries, loc. cit., p. 58.
[2] *On the Linguistic Study of Languages*, Cambridge, 1957, p. 22.
[3] O. Funke (quoting C. L. Wrenn) in *Proceedings of the Seventh International Congress of Linguists*, p. 197.
[4] VIII, ll. 552-4; quoted in E. Pulgram, 'Theory of Names', *Beiträge zur Namenforschung*, v (1954), pp. 149-96: p. 151.
[5] Ibid., p. 150.

F

called *en-nanai* in that kraal, as it is the name of a corpse, but it would be called by another name, such as *epolpol* (it is smooth)'.[1] Such superstitions are by no means confined to primitive societies: Cicero tells us that in their levies, the Romans took care to enrol first people with such auspicious names as Victor or Felix, and to head the roll of the census with a name of happy augury.[2]

The name is so closely identified with its owner that it soon came to stand for his reputation, good or bad. The synonymy of name and fame is already attested in Homer,[3] and recurs in various Greek and Roman authors. Shakespeare's Juliet may, under the stress of thwarted love, implore Romeo to 'doff thy name, And for thy name, which is no part of thee, Take all myself' (Act II, scene 2); but for a responsible person it is a major decision to change his name. One of Hamlet's last thoughts is about his name: 'Horatio, what a wounded name, Things standing thus unknown, shall live behind me!' (*Act V, scene 2), and Iago embroiders on the same theme in greater detail:

> Good name in man and woman, dear my lord,
> Is the immediate jewel of their souls:
> Who steals my purse steals trash; 'tis something, nothing;
> 'Twas mine, 'tis his, and has been slave to thousands;
> But he that filches from me my good name
> Robs me of that which not enriches him
> And makes me poor.
>
> (*Act III, scene 3)

In a novel by F. Molnár, a member of a boys' gang, accused of unworthy behaviour, experiences the supreme humiliation of seeing his 'poor honest name' written with a small initial.

The concept of proper name is thus deeply rooted in tradition, and in everyday life we have no difficulty in recognizing such names and distinguishing them from common nouns by writing them with a capital letter. Yet it is not always easy to state the grounds on which the distinction is made. A number of criteria have been put forward at various times for the definition of a proper name:

(1) *Uniqueness.* — In the second century B.C., the Greek grammarian Dionysius Thrax summed up the difference between proper name and

---

[1] R. M. Estrich-H. Sperber, *Three Keys to Language*, New York, 1952, p. 6. On name-taboos, see R. F. Mansur Guérios, *Tabus lingüísticos*, Rio de Janeiro, 1956, pp. 41 ff.

[2] Ogden-Richards, op. cit., p. 37.

[3] *Odyssey*, XIII, l. 248; see Liddell and Scott, s.v. ὄνομα.

common noun in the following terms: 'A name[1] is a declinable part of speech signifying a body or an activity, a body like "stone" and an activity like "education", and may be used both commonly and individually; commonly like "man", "horse", and individually like "Socrates" '. Elsewhere the same writer defines a proper name as 'that which signifies individual being, such as "Homer", "Socrates" '.[2] This view, which recurs in some later authors, overlooks the fact that many different and unrelated persons, and even several different places, may have the same name. If, on the other hand, the formula is taken to mean that most proper names are used in actual speech with reference to a specific person or thing, then this criterion coincides with the next which expresses the same idea in more precise terms.

(2) *Identification.* — Many philosophers and linguists are agreed in regarding proper names as identification marks. Unlike common nouns whose function it is to subsume particular specimens under a generic concept — say, various houses, irrespective of material, size, colour or style, under the class-concept 'house' — a proper name merely serves to identify a person or object by singling it out from among similar items. The *locus classicus* of this doctrine is in Book I, chapter 2 of John Stuart Mill's *A System of Logic*. Mill crystallized his meaning in a striking and apposite simile:

> If, like the robber in the Arabian Nights, we make a mark with chalk on a house to enable us to know it again, the mark has a purpose, but it has not properly any meaning ... The object of making the mark is merely distinction ... Morgiana chalked all the other houses in a similar manner, and defeated the scheme: how? simply by obliterating the difference of appearance between that house and the others ... When we impose a proper name, we perform an operation in some degree analogous to what the robber intended in chalking the house. We put a mark, not indeed upon the object itself, but, so to speak, upon the idea of the object. A proper name is but an unmeaning mark which we connect in our minds with the idea of the object, in order that whenever the mark meets our eyes or occurs to our thoughts, we may think of that individual object.[3]

Another comparison which is frequently used to illustrate the same idea is that of a 'label' stuck on a person or a thing in order to identify it

[1] The Greek word ὄνομα may mean either 'name' or 'noun'.
[2] Quoted after Sir Alan Gardiner, *The Theory of Proper Names*, 2nd ed., Oxford, 1954, p. 5. See also Pulgram, loc. cit., pp. 177 f.
[3] *A System of Logic, Ratiocinative and Inductive*, 10th ed., London, 1879, vol. I, pp. 36 f.

by distinguishing it from similar elements. This analogy, in spite of its modern appearance, seems to be very ancient: labels containing proper names are already found on Egyptian inscriptions and papyri.[1]

(3) *Denotation versus connotation.* — Another famous criterion advanced by Mill is the 'denotative' function of proper names as opposed to the 'connotative' value of common nouns. 'Proper names', he says, 'are not connotative: they denote the individuals who are called by them; but they do not indicate or imply any attributes as belonging to those individuals.' Even if they were originally derived from significant elements the meaning is irrelevant: *Dartmouth* no doubt received its name from its situation at the mouth of the Dart, but it would continue to have that name even if the mouth of the river were to be choked up by sand, or its course diverted by an earthquake. And Mill concludes that 'whenever the names given to objects convey any information, that is, whenever they have properly any meaning, the meaning resides not in what they *denote*, but in what they *connote*. The only names of objects which connote nothing are *proper* names; and these have, strictly speaking, no signification'.[2]

It has been argued that while proper names have no meaning in isolation, they will 'connote' a great deal when applied in a specific context to a particular person or place. Jespersen has actually reversed Mill's formula by claiming that 'proper names (as actually used) "connote" the greatest number of attributes'.[3] But surely there is some confusion here between language and speech. It is perfectly true to say that proper names are filled with rich connotations when applied to persons or places well known to both speaker and hearer, but in themselves, torn out of context, they will often mean nothing at all. A common noun used in isolation will, as we have seen (pp. 48 f.), have some meaning, however vague and ambiguous, whereas a proper name like *Thomas* or *Alexander* will convey no information beyond the bare fact that it denotes a person; we do not even know whether to take it as a surname or as a Christian name. This is just another way of saying that the specific function of a proper name is to identify and not to signify, so that this is not really a new criterion but merely a special aspect of the previous one.

(4) *Distinctive sound.* — In his treatise *The Theory of Proper Names*, Sir Alan Gardiner accepts identification as the essential purpose of proper names, but adds to it another criterion, that of distinctive sound. It is, of

[1] B. Migliorini, *Dal Nome proprio al nome comune*, Geneva, 1927, p. 5, n. 1.
[2] Mill, op. cit., pp. 33-6; cf. Gardiner, op. cit., pp. 41 f.
[3] *The Philosophy of Grammar*, p. 66.

course, a characteristic of all words (except in the rather special case of homonyms) to have a distinctive shape of their own which differentiates them from other terms; the whole phonemic principle is based, as already noted (pp. 24 ff.), on this need. Sir Alan feels, however, that in the case of proper names, such distinctiveness is of special importance. He gives two main reasons for this view:

> In the first place, the things called by proper names are mostly members of a set in which the resemblances considerably outweigh the differences, so that special labels, as it were, are required to mark the distinction. And in the second place, the actual name forces itself upon our attention more prominently than do other words. Think of the place in our lives occupied by christenings and introductions of persons by name, inquiries after the name of places, and so forth (p. 38).

The fusion of the two criteria, identification and phonetic distinctiveness, yields the following carefully worded definition, which occurs in its final form in the Retrospect to the second edition of the book:

> A proper name is a word or group of words which is recognized as having identification as its specific purpose, and which achieves, or tends to achieve, that purpose by means of its distinctive sound alone, without regard to any meaning possessed by that sound from the start, or acquired by it through association with the object or objects thereby identified.[1]

(5) *Grammatical criteria.* — The semantic and functional difference between proper names and common nouns is also reflected in certain grammatical peculiarities. These vary from one language to another and sometimes from one period to another in the same language. Some of them are purely conventional, others are dictated by the special function of proper names. In Fijian, for example, place-names and names of persons are preceded by the prefix *ko*, common nouns by the prefix *na*: |na vanua levu| 'the (or a) big land, big island' — |ko vanua levu| 'Big Island', the name of the largest island of the Fiji group.[2] In English, the

---

[1] Op. cit., p. 73. On rather different lines, E. Pulgram defines a proper name as follows: 'a noun used κατ' ἐξοχήν, in a non-universal function, with or without recognizable current lexical value, of which the potential meaning coincides with and never exceeds its actual meaning, and which is attached as a label to one animate being or one inanimate object (or to more than one in the case of collective names) for the purpose of specific distinction from among a number of like or in some respects similar beings or objects that are either in no manner distinguished from one another or, for our interest, not sufficiently distinguished' (loc. cit., p. 196).

[2] Hockett, op. cit., pp. 311 f.

same contrast would be marked by the presence or absence of the article: '*the* (or *a*) long island — Long Island', '*the* (or *a*) white chapel — White-chapel'. The syntax of the article and other 'determiners' is indeed one of the most widespread grammatical criteria distinguishing between proper names and common nouns,[1] but it operates differently in various languages. In English, names of persons take no article except in special circumstances ('*the* Lloyd George we knew'). In French, the article is not normally used with names of persons, but names of famous (or infamous) women are often preceded by it, as in Musset's poem to an actress, 'Stances à *la* Malibran', and so are some well-known names of Italian origin: *Le Tasse* (Tasso), *Le Tintoret* (Tintoretto). In Italian, it is quite normal for a surname to be preceded by the definite article, except when it is accompanied by a Christian name: *il Croce*, but *Benedetto Croce*. In German, the definite article can be used with Christian names: *die Marie* 'our Mary'. The treatment of place-names is equally varied. In English, place-names either take no article at all or are regularly accompanied by the definite article, as in names of rivers, mountain ranges, island groups and some others (*the Thames, the Alps, the Shetlands*, etc.). French differs from English in that names of countries are regularly preceded by the definite article: *la France, l'Angleterre* — France, England. This was not so in Old French where names of countries and provinces had no article. It is thus clear that every language has its own rules which may change in the course of time. Quite apart from these variations, the presence or absence of the article is not a universally valid criterion since many languages, such as Latin, Finnish and most Slavonic idioms, have no article at all.

Another grammatical criterion which has often been adduced is that the great majority of proper names have no plural.[2] As a general tendency this is no doubt true and even inevitable since the identifying function of proper names does not go easily with the idea of plurality. There are, however, numerous exceptions. Certain proper names are used only in the plural: they include some of the collectives just mentioned, such as island groups and mountain ranges, and also constellations (*The Pleiades*), some tribal names (the Latin *Ramnes*, etc.), as well as an occasional place-name such as the city of Athens in Greek and in Latin ('Αθῆναι, *Athenae*). Some categories of proper names can be used both in the singular and in the plural: national names (*a Spaniard* — *two Spaniards*),

[1] See esp. Bloomfield, *Language*, p. 205; Gardiner, op. cit., pp. 21 f.; Pulgram, loc. cit., pp. 190 ff.
[2] For a thorough examination of this problem see E. Coseriu, 'El Plural en los nombres propios', *Revista Brasileira de Filologia*, i (1955), pp. 1-15. Cf. also Gardiner, op. cit., pp. 15 ff.

families and dynasties, etc. As regards families, there is an interesting difference between English and French: where English uses the plural form, as in 'I had dinner with the *Martins*', French has the singular, as in the title of Roger Martin du Gard's family chronicle, *Les Thibault*. A final group of exceptions includes the use of the plural in special contexts: 'there are two *Pauls* in this form'. These cases must be distinguished from the plural of proper names used as common nouns: 'I saw several *Turners* (= paintings by Turner) in the gallery.'

It would seem, then, that of the five criteria just discussed, the second is the most useful. The essential difference between common nouns and proper names lies in their function: the former are meaningful units, the latter mere identification marks. This criterion can be supplemented by the important but not very precise factor of phonetic distinctiveness. The other criteria are either limited in scope or are already implicit in the identifying function of names.

While it is fairly easy to distinguish between proper names and common nouns, the border-line between the two categories is by no means final. Many proper names derived from common nouns still show clear traces of their origin: place-names like *Blackpool* and *Newcastle*, surnames like *Smith* and *Carpenter*, Christian names like *Pearl* and *Heather*. Others, though less transparent, have at least some analysable element, like the various place-names ending in *-caster*, *-cester* and *-chester*, all derived, as everybody knows, from the Latin *castra* 'camp'. Many other names have become entirely opaque though the etymologist may reconstruct or at least conjecture their derivation; thus the name *Bordeaux*, Latin *Burdigala*, has been resolved into two pre-Indo-European elements: the Iberian **burdo* 'mule' (cf. Spanish *burro* 'ass' and French *bourrique* 'she-ass') and the Ligurian **cala*, **gala* 'rock' (cf. Latin *calculus* and French *caillou* 'pebble').[1] The study of proper names, which may throw light on many aspects of political, economic and social history, has recently established itself as a quasi-independent branch of linguistics, and has its own specialized congresses and journals. This science, known as *onomastics*, has two main divisions: *toponymy*,[2] the study of place-names, and *anthroponymy*,[3] the study of personal names.

No less frequent is the converse process where a proper name is turned into a common noun. These changes are too well known to require detailed discussion. They fall, broadly speaking, into two groups.

---

[1] G. Alessio, *Le Origini del francese*, Florence, 1946, pp. 36 ff.
[2] From Greek *topos* 'place' + *onoma* 'name'.
[3] From Greek *anthrōpos* 'man' + *onoma*.

Some are 'metaphorical', based on some kind of similarity or common feature. This is the operative factor when a person or place gives its name to a whole class of similar persons or places: Cicero to all the garrulous guides known as *cicerone*-s, or the Belgian town of *Spa*, renowned for the curative influence of its mineral springs, to all watering-places of the same kind. The second group is 'metonymic', founded on some relation other than similarity: that between inventor and invention, between product and place of origin, etc. Examples of all these processes will spring readily to everybody's mind. The transparency of the common noun will mainly depend on how widely known the proper name is: one cannot even suspect that *chauvinism* originated in a name until one is told of the existence of one Nicolas Chauvin of Rochefort, a soldier in Napoleon's army, whose naïvely demonstrative patriotism was ridiculed in drawings and on the stage (Bloch-Wartburg and *NED*). The derivation of a common noun from a proper name may also be obscured by phonetic differences. *Sherry* comes from the Spanish town *Xeres* (now Jerez de la Frontera), but the English word has lost its final -*s* which was wrongly interpreted as the sign of the plural: a 'good *sherris-sack* hath a twofold operation in it', says Falstaff in *King Henry the Fourth*, Part II.[1] Opacity may also result from the lack of an ostensible link between a proper name and a homonymous common noun. What possible connexion could there be between the French word for a 'cab', *fiacre*, and the Irish saint of the same name who lived in the seventh century? Yet there is a connexion, though a purely fortuitous one: an eye-witness, the seventeenth-century lexicographer Ménage, has recorded that these carriages were so called because they used to be stationed in front of a house in the rue Saint-Antoine in Paris, on which was hung a picture of the saint (Bloch-Wartburg).

It should be noted that when a proper name becomes an ordinary word it is not always turned into a common noun; it may, for example, be used as a verb. In 1818, a Dr. T. Bowdler published an expurgated edition of Shakespeare, and the verb to *bowdlerize* arose from his name twenty years later (*NED*). An even more interesting case is that of Burke who was executed in Edinburgh in 1829 for strangling people and then selling their bodies for dissection. According to a newspaper report published at the time, the spectators shouted during the execution: '*Burke* him, *Burke* him — give him no rope!' The verb is found in the physical sense in the *Ingoldsby Legends*: 'The rest of the rascals jump'd on him and *Burk'd* him'; yet barely ten years after the event, it had already acquired the

[1] Act IV, scene 3; cf. E. Weekley, *The Romance of Words*, 3rd ed., London, 1917, p. 116.

figurative meaning in which it is still used (*NED* and Weekley, op. cit., p. 41).

Semantically, the change of a proper name into an ordinary word involves a considerable extension in range. To cite one more example, a certain Poubelle, prefect of the Seine department in the latter half of the last century, made the use of dust-bins compulsory, and since then all these objects have been called *poubelle* after him. When a common noun is made into a proper name, the change may be accompanied by a restriction in range, but this is not necessarily the case.[1] There certainly is a restriction when a common noun becomes a place-name: there are many *black forests* and *new markets*, but as a proper name *The Black Forest* and *Newmarket* will denote only one place or possibly a small number of homonymous places. But there is no restriction in some of the surnames and Christian names which derive from common nouns; it would be idle to speculate whether there are more *smiths* or *Smiths* in the world, more people called *George* or more 'husbandmen', this being the meaning of the word γεωργός in Greek. In all these processes, the extension or restriction that may have occurred is of secondary importance; the main point is that an identification mark has become a meaningful symbol, or vice versa.

Having thus surveyed some of the fundamental principles of semantic theory, we can now turn to more empirical questions. The next four chapters will deal with certain aspects of descriptive semantics: the transparency or opacity of our words; the logical and emotive factors which enter into their meaning; the problems raised by synonymy and ambiguity. In these chapters, historical data will be freely used, but only in order to throw light on the state of the language at a given moment. In Chapter 8, the approach will change from descriptive to historical, whereas in Chapter 9 the emphasis will shift from individual words to the structure of the vocabulary as a whole.

---

[1] Cf. Pulgram, loc. cit., p. 171.

CHAPTER 4

TRANSPARENT AND OPAQUE WORDS

What's in a name? That which we call a rose
By any other name would smell as sweet.
Romeo and Juliet, Act II, scene 2.

'Tis not enough no harshness gives offence,
The sound must be an echo to the sense.
Pope, *Essay on Criticism*, ll. 364-5.

THESE two passages sum up in a poetic form the two rival theses which have time and again confronted each other in the philosophy of language. The Greeks, it will be remembered,[1] were already divided into two camps: the naturalists, who believed that words possess their meanings 'by nature' (φύσει), by virtue of an intrinsic correspondence between sound and sense, and the conventionalists, who maintained that meaning is a matter of tradition and convention, of a kind of linguistic 'contrat social' (θέσει). It is interesting to find Rabelais, a past-master at exploiting the onomatopoeic resources of language, siding with the conventionalists: 'C'est abus dire que ayons langage naturel: les langages sont par institutions arbitraires et convenances des peuples; les voix, comme disent les dialecticians, ne signifient naturellement, mais à plaisir.'[2] In subsequent centuries, the naturalist theory gained ground in discussions about the origin of language. Leibniz, and many others after him, saw in onomatopoeia the primeval form of human speech.[3] These views were echoed by the Romantics, notably by Charles Nodier who published in 1808 a *Dictionnaire raisonné des onomatopées françoises*. This interest in onomatopoeia led to fanciful and dilettantish speculations which brought the whole subject into discredit and tended to obscure the important issues involved.

Among modern linguists, Saussure was most emphatic on what he called 'l'arbitraire du signe', the conventional character of our words, in which he saw one of the basic principles of language (op. cit., pp. 100 ff.). He realized that there were some exceptions to this principle, but dismissed

[1] See above, p. 1.
[2] 'It is wrong to say that we have a natural language: languages are based on arbitrary institutions and on the conventions of peoples; words, as the dialecticians say, signify not by nature, but arbitrarily' (Book III, ch. 19; cf. J. Vendryes, 'Sur la dénomination', *Bulletin de la Société de Linguistique de Paris*, xlviii (1952), pp. 1-13: p. 9).
[3] G. Révész, *The Origin and Prehistory of Language*, English transl., London, 1956, pp. 37 ff.

them as unimportant. Linguists of a different temperament, such as Schuchardt and Jespersen, tended to attach rather more importance to these 'exceptions'. Some twenty years ago, the old debate flared up again in the opening volumes of the journal *Acta Linguistica*. These discussions have helped to clarify the whole problem and to put it in its proper perspective.[1] We now know that it is pointless to ask whether language is conventional or 'motivated': every idiom contains words which are arbitrary and opaque, without any connexion between sound and sense, and others which are at least to some degree motivated and transparent. There are three main aspects of motivation which we can now see more clearly: how it works in a particular language; how it can change in the course of time; finally, how its scope varies from one language to another.

I. THREE TYPES OF MOTIVATION

That many words are entirely opaque and unanalysable is a fact so self-evident that it hardly requires any proof.[2] Nevertheless, it might be useful to mention briefly some of the objective arguments which confirm this subjective impression. These arguments are of three kinds: descriptive, historical and comparative. I shall try to illustrate them on a single example: the English word *meat*.

(1) If there were a necessary connexion between name and sense, one would expect the same sounds to mean always the same thing, and conversely, the same thing to be always denoted by the same sounds. Yet English *meat* has several homonyms with totally different meanings: the verb *to meet*, the archaic adjective *meet* 'fit, suitable', the noun *mete* 'boundary', and the verb *to mete (out)* 'allot'. On the other hand, *meat* has a quasi-synonym in the word *flesh*: the two terms are very close in meaning and yet have not a single sound in common.

(2) If the link between name and sense were a necessary one, we would expect both elements to remain unchanged. Yet they have both changed, independently of each other, since Anglo-Saxon times. The form of the word in Old English was |mẹte|, and it originally meant food in general, as it still does in *sweetmeats* and in the phrase *meat and drink*.[3]

---

[1] For the vast literature on the subject, see my *Principles of Semantics*, pp. 83 f.; cf. also E. Buyssens, 'Le Structuralisme et l'arbitraire du signe', *Omagiu lui Al. Graur*, pp. 403-16; J. Engels, 'Het Probleem der motivering', *Levende Talen*, clxxxii (1955), pp. 521-39; Guiraud, *La Sémantique*, pp. 17 ff.; Vendryes, loc. cit. It may be recalled that as far back as 1868, the American linguist W. D. Whitney had declared: 'Inner and essential connexion between idea and word ... there is none, in any language upon earth' (Jespersen, *Language*, p. 397, n. 1).

[2] See above, pp. 13 and 17.   [3] Cf. Bloomfield, *Language*, pp. 430 ff.

(3) Various languages have entirely different words for the same object. To English *meat* there corresponds *viande* in French, *carne* in Italian, *kött* in Swedish, *hús* in Hungarian, etc. Conversely, the same — or approximately the same — sounds stand for different things in other languages: German *miet-* 'hire', French *mite* 'cheese-mite, moth' and *mythe* 'myth', etc.

While a great many words are thus entirely conventional, others are motivated in various ways. The motivation may lie either in the sounds themselves, or in the morphological structure of the word, or in its semantic background. Each of these possibilities raises different problems and has therefore to be considered separately.

1. *Phonetic Motivation (Onomatopoeia)*[1]

In a passage from which some lines have already been quoted, Pope has clearly defined the principle of motivation by sound, and has illustrated it by some apposite examples:

'Tis not enough no harshness gives offence,
The sound must be an echo to the sense.
Soft is the strain when zephyr gently blows,
And the smooth stream in smoother numbers flows;
But when loud surges lash the sounding shore,
The hoarse, rough verse should like the torrent roar:
When Ajax strives some rock's vast weight to throw,
The line too labours, and the words move slow;
Not so when swift Camilla scours the plain,
Flies o'er the unbending corn, and skims along the main.
Essay on Criticism, ll. 364-73.[2]

The applications of this principle in poetry are innumerable. They range from the evocation of comic and grotesque scenes such as the rats' progress in Browning's *Pied Piper*:

And the muttering grew to a grumbling;
And the grumbling grew to a mighty rumbling;
And out of the houses the rats came tumbling ...

to the sinister portrayal of hallucinations heralding the onset of madness, as in Racine's famous line:

[1] From Greek *onomatopoiía* 'word-making': *onoma*, *-atos* 'name'+*poieō* 'make'. Various other terms have been suggested, such as 'echoism' (Jespersen) and 'phonaesthetic function' (Firth).
[2] Cf. Orr, *Words and Sounds in English and French*, p. 17.

> Pour qui *s*ont *c*es *s*erpents qui *s*ifflent *s*ur vos têtes?
>
> *Andromaque*, Act V, scene 5,[1]

which, in its orchestration, is reminiscent of some passages in *Paradise Lost*:

> The *S*erpent *s*ubtle*s*t bea*s*t of all the field.
>
> *Book IX, l. 86.
>
> he hear*s*,
> On all *s*ides, from innumerable tongue*s*
> A di*s*mal univer*s*al hi*ss*, the *s*ound
> Of public *s*corn.
>
> Book X, ll. 506-9.

The device is as old as poetry itself. In the first book of the *Odyssey* (lines 56-7) there is a striking example of the evocative effect of liquids and kindred sounds:

> αἰεὶ δὲ μαλακοῖσι καὶ αἱμυλίοισι λόγοισι δέλγει.[2]

The pattern is thus set for one of the great onomatopoeic themes of Western poetry:

> *L*es souff*l*es de *l*a nuit f*l*ottaient sur Ga*lg*a*l*a.
>
> Victor Hugo, *Booz endormi*.[3]

> Wi*l*d thyme and va*ll*ey-*l*i*l*ies whiter sti*ll*
> Than *L*eda's *l*ove, and cresses from the ri*ll*.
>
> Keats, *Endymion*, Book I.

More discreetly, such effects can also arise in artistic prose. Take for instance the impression of liquidness produced by the following sentence in Gide's novel *L'Immoraliste*: 'L'air lui-même semble un fluide lumineux où tout baigne, où tout plonge, où tout nage.'[4] Such examples, which are a great challenge to the translator, could be multiplied indefinitely.

In the use of onomatopoeia as a stylistic device, the effect is based not so much on individual words as on a judicious combination and modulation of sound values, which may be reinforced by such factors as alliteration, rhythm, assonance and rhyme. The semanticist is more immediately interested in the onomatopoeic quality of particular words, although the

---

[1] 'For whom are these snakes that hiss on your heads?'
[2] 'And ever with soft and wheedling words she beguiles him.'
[3] 'The breezes of the night floated over Galgala.'
[4] 'The air itself is like a luminous fluid where all things bathe, where all things plunge, where all things swim.'

two problems are often inseparable, as will be seen presently. From the semantic point of view, a distinction has to be made between primary and secondary onomatopoeia. Its primary form is the imitation of sound by sound. Here the sound is truly an 'echo to the sense': the referent itself is an acoustic experience which is more or less closely imitated by the phonetic structure of the word. Terms like *buzz*, *crack*, *growl*, *hum*, *plop*, *roar*, *squeak*, *squeal*, *whizz* and a great many others fall into this category. In secondary onomatopoeia, the sounds evoke, not an acoustic experience but a movement (*dither*, *dodder*, *quiver*, *slink*, *slither*, *slouch*, *squirm*, *wriggle*), or some physical or moral quality, usually unfavourable (*gloom*, *grumpy*, *mawkish*, *slatternly*, *slick*, *slimy*, *sloppy*, *sloth*, *slovenly*, *sluggish*, *wry*.)

It will have been noticed that some of these onomatopoeic terms have certain elements in common; in Bloomfield's words, there is a 'system of initial and final root-forming morphemes, of vague signification', with which the 'intense, symbolic connotation' of such terms is associated. To mention one initial group which has not yet been exemplified, the sounds |sn| may express, according to Bloomfield, three types of experiences: 'breath-noises' (*sniff*, *snuff*, *snore*, *snort*), 'quick separation or movement' (*snip*, *snap*, *snatch*), and 'creeping' (*snake*, *snail*, *sneak*, *snoop*). Final groups have similar functions: are, for instance, suggests 'big light or noise' as in *blare*, *flare*, *glare*, *stare*.[1]

Another interesting feature of onomatopoeic patterns is that they often work by vowel alternation. By substituting one vowel for another one can express different noises: *snip* — *snap*, *sniff* — *snuff*, *flip* — *flap* — *flop*. This may even occur in secondary onomatopoeia, as in the pair *gleam* — *lo cm* whose contrast is neatly brought out in this passage by Zangwill: The *gloom* of night, relieved only by the *gleam* from the street-lamp.'[2] Similar examples are found in other languages: French *craquer* 'crack, crackle' — *croquer* 'scrunch', *siffler* 'whistle' — *souffler* 'blow'; Hungarian *dong* 'buzz' — *döng* 'resound'. It is interesting to learn that the same feature has also been noticed in some African idioms.[3] Akin to this tendency are reduplicated words and phrases like *riff-raff*, *wishy-washy*, *tit for tat*; French *cahin-caha* 'so-so', *clopin-clopant* 'limping along', *et patati et patata* 'and so forth and so on'. 'Vowel antiphony', as it has been

[1] Bloomfield, *Language*, p. 245. On onomatopoeic patterns see, e.g., Firth, op. cit., chs. 4 and 15; H. Marchand, 'Motivation by Linguistic Form', *Studia Neophilologica*, xxix (1957), pp. 54-66; Orr, op. cit., ch. 3; Richards, op. cit., ch. 3; G. V. Smithers, 'Some English Ideophones', *Archivum Linguisticum*, vi (1954), pp. 73-111.

[2] Jespersen, *Language*, p. 401.

[3] Smithers, loc. cit., pp. 83 f.

called,[1] plays an important part in purely imitative and interjectional forms which are on the fringes of organized language: *tick-tock, click-clack, pit-a-pat, ding-dong,* French *pif, paf*! 'bang, bang!' Such vowel alternations are strangely reminiscent of the so-called 'ablaut' forms in verbs (*sing — sang — sung*), and of pronominal or adverbial pairs expressing proximity versus remoteness: *these — those*; French *comme ci comme ça* 'so-so'; Hungarian *ez* 'this' — *az* 'that', *itt* 'here' — *ott* 'there', *így* 'this way' — *úgy* 'that way'. It should be noted that many onomatopoeic forms are based on alternations not of vowels but of initial consonants: *higgledy-piggledy, helter-skelter, namby-pamby, roly-poly*, etc.

Hardly any aspect of semantics has aroused as much interest as onomatopoeia. The voluminous literature on the subject ranges from whimsical fantasies on the colour of speech-sounds to experiments carried out under laboratory conditions.[2] The stylistic[3] as well as the purely linguistic implications of the phenomenon have received equal attention,[4] and the values attaching to particular sounds — especially the vowel |i| — have been fully explored.[5] It would be impossible here to survey this vast problem in all its ramifications, but it may be useful to mention a few points of semantic interest:

(1) Since onomatopoeia involves an intrinsic resemblance between

---

[1] Orr, op. cit., pp. 19 ff., where many excellent examples will be found.

[2] H. Wissemann, *Untersuchungen zur Onomatopoiie I: Die sprachpsychologischen Versuche*, Heidelberg, 1954.

[3] See esp. M. Cressot, *Le Style et ses techniques*, Paris, 1947, Part I, ch. 1; J. Marouzeau, *Précis de stylistique française*, 3rd ed., Paris, 1950, ch. 1; Trubetzkoy, op. cit., pp. 16-29. Cf. also D. I. Masson, 'Some Problems in Literary Phonaesthetics', *Literature and Science*, Oxford, 1955, pp. 61-4, and I. Fónagy, *A költői nyelv hangtanából* ('From the Phonetics of the Language of Poetry'), Budapest, 1959.

[4] A good bibliographical survey of the whole field will be found in M. Chastaing, 'Le Symbolisme des voyelles. Significations des *i*', *Journal de Psychologie*, lv (1958), pp. 403-23, 461-81. In addition to the works already mentioned, the following may be noted: M. Grammont, *Traité de phonétique*, 3rd ed., Paris, 1946, Part III; J. M. Kořínek, 'Laut und Wortbedeutung', *Travaux du Cercle Linguistique de Prague*, viii (1939), pp. 58-65; R. Lehmann, *Le Sémantisme des mots expressifs en Suisse romande*, Romanica Helvetica XXXIV, Berne, 1949; W. Schneider, 'Über die Lautbedeutsamkeit,' *Zeitschrift für deutsche Philologie*, lxiii (1938), pp. 138-79; A. Sieberer, 'Primäre oder sekundäre Lautbedeutsamkeit?', *Österreichische Akademie der Wissenschaften, Philosophisch-Historische Klasse, Anzeiger*, lxxxiv (1947), pp. 35-52; M. Wandruszka, 'Ausdruckswerte der Sprachlaute', *Germanisch-Romanische Monatsschrift*, xxxv (1954), pp. 231-40. Cf. also Jespersen, *Language*, ch. 20; Kronasser, op. cit., ch. 19; K. Knauer, 'Grenzen der Wissenschaft vom Wort', *Akademie der Wissenschaften und der Literatur, Abhandlungen der Geistes- und Sozialwissenschaften*, Klasse 13, Mainz, 1950.

[5] Chastaing, loc. cit.; O. Jespersen, 'Symbolic Value of the Vowel *i*', *Linguistica*, Copenhagen — London, 1933, pp. 283-303; M. Wandruszka, 'Der Streit um die Deutung der Sprachlaute', *Festgabe E. Gamillscheg*, Tübingen, 1952, pp. 214-27. Cf. on a different sound W. Havers, 'Zur Entstehung eines sogenannten sakralen *u*-Elementes in den indogermanischen Sprachen.' *Österreichische Akademie der Wissenschaften, Philosophisch-Historische Klasse, Anzeiger*, lxxxiv (1947), pp. 139-65.

name and sense one would expect such formations to be similar in different languages. This is actually so in many cases, best known among them the names of the *cuckoo* which are closely parallel in a large number of idioms: French *coucou*, Spanish *cuclillo*, Italian *cuculo*, Rumanian *cucu*, Latin *cuculus*, Greek κόκκυξ, German *Kuckuck*, Russian *kukushka*, Hungarian *kakuk*, Finnish *käki*, etc. The parallelism is striking and cannot be accounted for by common origin or mutual influence; it is a case of what has been called 'elementary affinity', of a fundamental similarity in the way different people hear and render the same noise. Comparative philologists must be careful to eliminate such correspondences when trying to adduce evidence for historical kinship or influence. At the same time it would be unwise to make too much of such elementary affinities. Even where there is a genuine similarity of perception there are also marked differences, due to the fact that the imitation is only partial and that each language has conventionalized it in its own way. Moreover it often happens that patently onomatopoeic formations in different idioms bear little or no resemblance to each other. The Englishman transcribes the crow of the cock as *cock-a-doodle-do*, the Frenchman as *cocorico*, the German as *kikeriki*. The dog's bark is reproduced as *bow-wow* in English and as *ouâ-ouâ* in French. The sound of a shot is rendered as *bang* or *crack* in English and as *pum* or *paf* in Spanish.[1] While it is an exaggeration to say, as one linguist has done: 'Even onomatopoeia is conventional. The imitations serve, not because they are good, but because they are conventional',[2] there can be no doubt that a strong element of conventionality enters into most onomatopoeic formations, including even interjections. Bloomfield was nearer the truth when he wrote: 'Languages that have symbolic forms show some agreement, but probably more disagreement as to the types of sounds and meanings which are associated' (*Language*, p. 156).

(2) It is a *sine qua non* of phonetic motivation that there should be some similarity or harmony between the name and the sense. Sounds are not expressive in themselves; it is only when they happen to fit the meaning that their onomatopoeic potentialities come into their own. As a recent student of these problems very aptly put it: 'Onomatopoeia will ignite only when the expressive possibilities latent in a given sound are, as it were, brought to life by contact with a congenial meaning.'[3] This

---

[1] Entwistle, op. cit., p. 15, n. 1.
[2] Ibid., p. 15; cf. Smithers, loc. cit., pp. 110 f.
[3] 'Lautbedeutsamkeit entzündet sich erst, wenn die in einer bestimmten Lautung schlummernden Ausdrucksmöglichkeiten durch die Berührung mit einer kongenialen Bedeutung gleichsam zum Leben erweckt werden' (Sieberer, loc. cit., p. 40).

can best be seen by contrasting certain pairs of homonyms one of which is onomatopoeic while the other is not: the *pealing* of a bell with the *peeling* of potatoes, the *tolling* of a bell with the *toll* paid at a gate, a *grating* laugh with the adjective *great*, a *ring* at the door with a wedding-*ring*. A particularly interesting example is the French word for 'poppy', *coquelicot*. This term, whose earlier form was *coquelicoq*, was originally an onomatopoeic imitation of the cock's crow; it denoted first the cock itself and then, by metaphor, the flower whose red colour reminded people of a cockscomb. In this secondary meaning, which is the only one to have survived, the word is no longer onomatopoeic since the sounds bear no relation to the sense (Bloch-Wartburg).

The principle of harmony between sound and sense explains some apparent anomalies which have often perplexed students of onomatopoeia. It is, for instance, generally agreed that the vowel |i| is admirably adapted to convey an idea of smallness and is frequently found in adjectives and nouns of that meaning: *little*, *wee*, French *petit*, Hungarian *kicsi*; *bit*, *tit*, *whit*, *jiffy* and many more. Yet this tendency seems to be contradicted by the adjectives *big* and *small*, and also by such examples as German *Riese* 'giant' and Hungarian *apró* 'tiny'. The explanation is quite simple: where a sound happens to occur with a meaning to which it is naturally attuned, it will become onomatopoeic and will add its own expressive force to the sense by a kind of 'resonance' effect.[1] Where there is no intrinsic harmony the sound will remain neutral, there will be no resonance, the word will be opaque and inexpressive.

It has often been suggested that the vitality of words may be affected, among other things, by phonetic motivation. The Latin word for 'small', *parvus*, for example, was ill fitted by its form to convey that meaning and was therefore replaced by more expressive rivals such as French *petit*, Italian *piccolo*, Rumanian *mic*, etc. This sounds plausible enough, but the undiminished vitality of English *small*, which must have suffered from the same handicap and has yet withstood the pressure of its more expressive synonym *little*, is a warning that too much importance should not be attached to such factors.

(3) Even where the sound seems naturally adapted to express the meaning, onomatopoeia will come into play only if the context is favourable to it. 'Context' should be taken here in the wider sense defined in Chapter 2: it includes both verbal setting and context of situation. The former can influence onomatopoeia in two main ways. No matter what expressive force may be latent in a word, it will come to life only if it

---

[1] Sieberer, loc. cit., p. 50.

G

fits into the general effect of the utterance. The verb *ring* in the acoustic sense is, as already noted, onomatopoeic in itself, but this is merely a potential quality waiting for a favourable opportunity to manifest itself. The verb will have no expressive value in an ordinary sentence like 'Please *ring* the back-door bell', but it is fraught with onomatopoeic overtones in Ariel's song: 'Sea-nymphs hourly *ring* his knell' (*The Tempest*, Act I, scene 2).

The context can also reinforce the expressive quality of a word by fitting it into a suitable sound-pattern. Thus, the onomatopoeic value of the word *silver*, which remains dormant in many neutral contexts, is strikingly brought out by the phonetic structure of the following passage:

> And the enchanted moonlight seemed transformed
> Into the *silvery* tinkling of an old
> And gentle music-box ...
>
> Edith Sitwell, *Colonel Fantock*.

Onomatopoeic effects will also depend on the situation in which a word or sentence is spoken. Nothing could be simpler and more banal than the French question; 'Qui te l'a dit?' 'Who told you so?' And yet these words are filled with tragic significance, powerfully assisted by onomatopoeia, in Racine's *Andromaque* where Hermione, blinded by jealousy, orders Orestes to assassinate Pyrrhus and, when he comes to tell her that he has done so, turns on him like a fury, shrieking hysterically: 'Qu*i* te l'a d*i*t?' (Act V, scene 3).

In a more general way, certain situations and environments are hospitable to onomatopoeia while others are practically impervious to it. It will flourish in emotional and rhetorical speech whose general effect it helps to reinforce. It will also be at home in spontaneous, unsophisticated and expressive forms of language such as nursery talk, colloquial and popular speech, dialect and slang. The poet and the writer of artistic prose will naturally exploit these resources to the full. On the other hand, the more restrained, neutral and matter-of fact varieties of style used by scientists, diplomats, civil servants, businessmen, etc., will have little or no room for onomatopoeia; in these unemotional forms of speech expressiveness would be out of place and will very seldom come to the fore.[1]

(4) More than half a century ago, Maurice Grammont enunciated an important principle concerning onomatopoeia: 'Un mot n'est une onomatopée qu'à condition d'être senti comme tel.'[2] This introduces a

---

[1] See esp. Kořínek, loc. cit.
[2] 'A word is onomatopoeic only if it is felt as such' ('Onomatopées et mots expressifs', *Revue des Langues Romanes*, xliv (1901), pp. 97-158: p. 125).

subjective element into the study of phonetic motivation. While there would be a fair measure of agreement on the more obvious types of onomatopoeia, such as imitative interjections, the more subtle and more interesting cases will often be a matter of personal opinion; their evaluation will depend on the speaker's sensitivity, his imagination, his cultural background, and other imponderables. It might be possible to devise some statistical method, on the lines of the experiments discussed in the last chapter, to establish a kind of average reaction to specific words, but there would still be the influence of context to reckon with, and one may wonder whether the statistical net would be fine enough to catch these delicate and elusive phenomena. Meanwhile, there are many examples of creative writers detecting onomatopoeic overtones where the ordinary speaker would find little or no motivation. In the *Ode to a Nightingale*, Keats speculates on the suggestiveness of the word *forlorn*:

> Charm's magic casements, opening on the foam
> Of perilous seas, in faery lands forlorn.
> *Forlorn!* the very word is like a bell
> To toll me back from thee to my sole self.

The French Romantics' interest in onomatopoeia (see above, p. 80) produced some queer notions on the subject. Balzac discovered a 'fantastic rectitude' and a 'chaste nakedness' in the adjective *vrai* 'true' (*Louis Lambert*, p. 4), while Nodier, the chief authority on onomatopoeia, was struck by the expressiveness of the word *catacombe*: 'Il est impossible de trouver une suite de sons plus pittoresques, pour rendre le retentissement du cercueil, roulant de degrés en degrés sur les angles aigus des pierres, et s'arrêtant tout à coup au milieu des tombes.'[1] Foreign words are particularly apt to give rise to onomatopoeic fantasies which may strike the native as rather strange. The English word *Angels*, used as a place-name, reminds Verlaine of the calmness and freshness of a swan,[2] while Vigny waxes enthusiastic over the phrase *for ever* which seems to him even more melancholy than the French *pour toujours*, with sounds as vague as the voice of spirits in the clouds.[3]

Needless to say, proper names have their fair share in these speculations. As we have seen, the sound element in names tends to force itself on one's attention with particular intensity (see above, p. 75), and this

---

[1] 'It is impossible to find a sequence of more picturesque sounds in order to render the noise of the coffin rolling from step to step on the sharp corners of the stones, and suddenly coming to a halt in the midst of the tombs' (quoted by Nyrop, *Sémantique*, p. 7).
[2] '*Angels!* ô nom "revu", calme et frais comme un cygne' (*There*).
[3] *Correspondance*, ed. by Sakellaridès, p. 139.

is bound to enhance their onomatopoeic possibilities: unhampered by any meaning, the writer's fancy will have free scope. Some of the associations seem perfectly arbitrary, though they may well have a personal background, as when the German poet Christian Morgenstern cryptically remarks that all sea-gulls look as if their name was *Emma*.[1] Elsewhere, a chance assonance seems to have started the process of reading hidden meanings into a name. Jules Romains, for example, discussing the noises of the *rue Réaumur* ('la rumeur de la rue Réaumur'), says that the name itself sounds like a song of wheels and walls, like the vibration of buildings and the tremor of concrete under the pavement, and like the rumbling of underground trains.[2] It is a safe guess that the author's imagination was set in motion by the phonetic similarity between the words *rumeur* and *Réaumur* which occurred side by side at the beginning of the passage.

In other cases, the onomatopoeic values attributed to a proper name are dictated by external associations. Alphonse Daudet, for example, felt that *Bethlehem* was a 'legendary and sweet name, warm like the straw in the miraculous manger'.[3] Proust developed a veritable *mystique* around the latent potencies of proper names. By a kind of auto-suggestion he discovered in the sound and shape of a name some of the things he knew about its bearer; *Coutances*, for instance, appeared to him as a 'Norman cathedral which its fat and yellowing final diphthong [*sic*] crowns with a tower of butter' — an obvious reference to the butter trade for which the town is renowned.[4]

The expressiveness of certain sound-combinations may influence a writer in choosing names for his characters. Boileau already warned poets:

> D'un seul nom quelquefois le son dur ou bizarre
> Rend un poëme entier ou burlesque ou barbare.
> *L'Art poétique*, Canto III.[5]

---

[1] On this often-quoted passage, see recently the comments of P. Trost in *Omagiu lui Iorgu Iordan*, Bucharest, 1958, p. 869, n. 1.

[2] 'La rumeur de la rue Réaumur. Son nom même qui ressemble à un chant de roues et de murailles, à une trépidation d'immeubles, à la vibration du béton sous l'asphalte, au bourdonnement des convois souterrains ...' (*Les Amours enfantines*, Paris, Flammarion, p. 302).

[3] 'Légendaire et doux, chaud comme la paille de l'étable miraculeuse' (*Le Nabab*, quoted after Nyrop, *Sémantique*, p. 5).

[4] 'Coutances, cathédrale normande, que sa diphtongue finale, grasse et jaunissante, couronne par une tour de beurre' (*Du Côté de chez Swann*, Paris, 1954 ed., vol. II, p. 222). On Proust's theory of names, see J. Vendryes, 'Marcel Proust et les noms propres', *Choix d'études linguistiques et celtiques*, Paris, 1953, pp. 80-8. Cf. also my *Style in the French Novel*, ch. 5.

[5] 'The harsh or bizarre sound of a single name will sometimes make a whole poem burlesque or barbarous.'

Many comic or grotesque effects have been obtained from the queer shape of fictitious names such as Professor *Teufelsdröckh* in *Sartor Resartus*, Baron *Thunder-ten-tronckh* in Voltaire's *Candide*, and the quaint names which occur in *Gulliver's Travels*.

This quest for motivation has even been extended to the written word. Some writers profess to feel an analogy between the meaning of certain words and their visual shape. The poet Leconte de Lisle once said that if the French word for 'peacock', *paon* (pronounced *pã*), were to be written without an *o* he would no longer see the bird spreading out its tail.[1] Going even further, Paul Claudel detects in the two *t*-s of the French noun *toit* 'roof' the two gables of a house, and discovers a funnel and wheels in the word *locomotive*.[2] These vagaries seem to hark back to an earlier form of writing when visual symbols were directly representative of the things they stood for and had not yet become ancillary to the spoken word (see above, p. 17).

2. *Morphological and Semantic Motivation*

Another large category of words are motivated by their *morphological* structure. A word like *preacher* is transparent because it can be analysed into component morphemes which have themselves some meaning: the verb *preach* and the suffix *-er* which forms agent nouns from verbs (*speak-er, read-er, sing-er, think-er*, etc.). A foreigner hearing the word *preacher* for the first time will understand it if he is familiar with the verb and the suffix. Occasionally he may be misled by false analogy: a *poser* is not a person who poses, nor is a *supper* a person who sups. In most cases, however, the system will work.

Compound words are motivated in the same way. Anyone who knows their components will understand formations like *penholder* or *penknife*; with a little imagination he will also be able to guess the meaning of *pen-friend, penman*, or *pen-name*. In many cases the connexion between the two elements may be remote or obscure, as for instance in *butterfly, kingfisher* or *lady-bird*, but it is none the less obvious that such words are morphologically motivated.

A third and last type of motivation is based on *semantic* factors. When we speak of the *bonnet* or the *hood* of a car, of a *coat* of paint, or of potatoes cooked in their *jackets*, these expressions are motivated by the similarity between the garments and the objects referred to. In the same way, when we say *the cloth* for the clergy, *silk* for a Q.C., or 'town and *gown*' for

---

[1] Orr, op. cit., p. 27.
[2] Bally, *Linguistique générale et linguistique française*, p. 133, n. 1.

town and University', there is semantic motivation due to the fact that the garments in question are closely associated with the persons they designate. Both types of expression are figurative: the former are meta-phorical, based on some similarity between the two elements, the latter are metonymic, founded on some external connexion.

The three types of motivation account between them for a very considerable proportion of the vocabulary: they include all onomatopoeic terms, derivatives, compounds and figurative expressions in the language. Only those words which are not motivated in either of these ways can be put down as conventional.

Although there are some important differences between morphological and semantic motivation, they have certain features in common which distinguish them from onomatopoeia:

(1) In many cases, a word is motivated both morphologically and semantically. The plant name *blue-bell*, for example, has such mixed motivation: it is a transparent compound and at the same time a metaphor based on the bell-like shape of the flower. Likewise, the bird name *redbreast* is motivated by its morphological structure and also by the metonymy which underlies it: the robin is called after its red breast, the part gives its name to the whole.[1]

(2) These two types of motivation have also this in common that they are both 'relative': they enable us to analyse words into their elements but cannot explain these elements themselves. To take some of the examples just quoted: *preacher* is motivated, but *preach* and the suffix *-er* are not; *penknife* is transparent but *pen* and *knife* are opaque; the *bonnet* of a car is so called because it looks like the head-dress, but the name of the head-dress itself is conventional. There always comes a point where morphological and semantic analysis has to stop: beyond that, there is either onomatopoeia or pure conventionality. In this sense, onomatopoeia is the only form of motivation which can be described as 'absolute'. The principle of relative motivation was first formulated by Saussure,[2] but he limited it to compounds and derivatives whereas figurative language obviously works in the same way.

Sometimes there are several layers of motivation which can be identified by a process of 'semantic reduction'. The word *coxcomb* may serve as an

---

[1] This is the figure known in rhetoric as 'synecdoche' or 'part for the whole'. The relation between these various figures will be discussed in Chapter 8.

[2] Op. cit., pp. 180 ff.; cf. Bally, *Linguistique générale et linguistique française*, pp. 127 ff.; Engels, loc. cit.; L. Zawadowski, 'The So-called Relative Motivation in Language', *Omagiu lui Iorgu Iordan*, pp. 927-37; Id., *Constructions grammaticales et formes périphrastiques*, Cracow, etc., 1959, ch. 6, section 1.

illustration of this process.[1] When applied to human beings, this word originally meant a 'simpleton', then a 'foolish, conceited, showy person, a fop'. The following two extracts show the difference between the two meanings:

> O murderous *coxcomb*! What should such a fool
> Do with so good a wife?
> > *Othello*, Act V, scene 2.

> Some are bewildered in the maze of schools,
> And some made *coxcombs* nature meant but fools.
> > Pope, *Essay on Criticism*, ll. 26-7.

Both these uses are semantically motivated: they are metaphors derived from the word *cockscomb* in the literal sense. Between the proper and the figurative meanings there was once an intermediate link which has since disappeared: the use of the term *coxcomb* to denote, by a picturesque metaphor, the red cap of a jester:

> Katherina: What is your crest — a *coxcomb*?
> Petruchio: A *combless cock*, so Kate will be my hen.
> > *The Taming of the Shrew*, Act II, scene 1.

Nor does motivation stop at this stage: the use of the word *comb* to describe the cock's crest is itself a metaphor based on the similarity of the two objects. It is only at this point that the analysis reaches its limits: we are left with two simple, unanalysable elements, *cock* and *comb*, which must be either conventional or onomatopoeic. Of the two, *comb* is entirely opaque whereas *cock* could probably be regarded as vaguely imitative.[2]

(3) Like onomatopoeia, but to a much lesser extent, morphological and semantic motivation involves a subjective element. For a word to be so motivated, it must be *felt* to be a compound, a derivative, or a figurative expression. Once again it might be possible to devise a statistical method in order to determine, in marginal cases, how far people are aware, or can be made aware, of the motivation of such words. The main factors which may influence such awareness will become clearer when we have considered the ways in which motivation may change.

II. Changes in Motivation

Two opposite tendencies are at work all the time in the development of language: many words lose their motivation while others which

---

[1] For the examples that follow, see the *NED* and the *Shorter OED*.
[2] Cf. Bloch-Wartburg, *s.v. coq*, and Lewis and Short, *s.v. coco*.

were, or had grown, opaque become transparent in the course of their history.

1. Loss of Motivation

(1) *Loss of phonetic motivation.*[1] — The main factor which tends to obscure the phonetic motivation of words is sound-change. Although 'sound-laws' do not operate with 'blind necessity', as the Neo-Grammarian school of linguists believed at the end of the last century, they do affect words with a fair measure of uniformity, regardless of the harm they may do to their motivation. Moreover, words are exposed to all kinds of phonetic accidents — assimilation, dissimilation and the like — which may also cancel out their onomatopoeic effects. Without going into details, it will be sufficient to cite a few words which have lost their motivation in this way:

> Latin *mūgire* > French *mugir* 'to low, to bellow'. Owing to the change from Latin |ū| to French |y|, the French word, which is itself a late formation modelled on Latin, is less expressive than its Latin counterpart.
>
> Vulgar Latin *pīpio, pīpionem* > French *pigeon* (whence English *pigeon*). The Vulgar Latin term, formed from the onomatopoeic verb *pīpīre* 'peep, pip, chirp', was an imitation of the cheeping of the young bird, and the word originally meant 'young dove' both in French and in English (see Bloch-Wartburg and the *Shorter OED*). Subsequently, every trace of motivation was eliminated by sound-change, and this no doubt made it easier for the word to acquire its present meaning; the Vulgar Latin form with its high-pitched vowels would not have fitted in very well with the cooing of pigeons.
>
> Latin *cicada* > French *cigale* 'cicada'.
> Latin *ciconia* > French *cigogne* 'stork'.
> Latin *cycnus* > French *cygne* 'swan'.

These three words had some onomatopoeic force in Latin, due to the reduplication of the |k| sound (Marouzeau, loc. cit., p. 291); in their passage from Latin to French, however, they lost all their imitative value.[2]

How far a word can drift in form and meaning from its onomatopoeic origins is seen in the modern descendants of Greek βάρβαρος, Latin

---

[1] See especially J. Marouzeau, 'L'Usure des onomatopées', *Le Français Moderne*, iii (1935), pp. 289-92; most of the examples that follow are taken from this article. Cf. also Orr, op. cit., pp. 17 ff.

[2] *Cigale* and *cigogne* are not directly descended from Latin but were borrowed from Provençal (Bloch-Wartburg).

barbarus. This began as an imitation of the bizarre noises made in an incomprehensible foreign language, but nothing of the original meaning and motivation is left in English *brave*, French *brave*, German *brav*, etc., which derive in all probability from the Latin word.[1] On the other hand, the learned forms borrowed directly from Latin, such as English *barbarous* and *barbaric*[2] or French *barbare*, have retained some of the expressive force of their ancestry; the effect is not far removed from the original one in Milton's '*barbarous* dissonance' (**Paradise Lost*, Book VII, l. 32) or in Walt Whitman's line: 'I sound my *barbaric* yawp over the roofs of the world' (**Song of Myself*).

The destruction of onomatopoeia by sound-change is not always passively accepted. There are three ways in particular in which the damage can be prevented or repaired:

(*a*) Sounds which would normally have changed or dropped out are sometimes retained or modified to safeguard expressive values. The French *charivari* 'din, row, racket', which comes from a Greek word meaning 'headache', would, if it had developed regularly, have lost its first *i*, but this would have weakened the onomatopoeic effect of the word, so the vowel has been preserved (Bloch-Wartburg). The Latin verb *tinnitare* would have given **tenter* in French; instead, we have the modified form *tinter* 'to ring, to tinkle', which is far better suited to the meaning of the word (ibid.).

(*b*) A form whose motivation has been weakened by sound-change may be replaced by a more expressive new formation. Thus the Latin *cucūlus* 'cuckoo' had given, by a somewhat irregular development, *cocu* in Old French. This was felt to be inexpressive and was ousted by the purely imitative *coucou*; it has survived, however, in French *cocu* and English *cuckold* as a crudely jocular metaphor based on the notorious habits of the bird (ibid. and Marouzeau).

(*c*) It may even happen that a phonetic change modifies the onomatopoeic effect of a word without cancelling it out altogether, and that the meaning is altered to conform to the new sound-pattern. When the Latin *murmur*, which was admirably expressive of roaring, rumbling and similar noises, was borrowed into French, the $|u|$-s were changed into $|y|$-s and the word came to denote softer and lighter sounds. The English *murmur*, which comes from French, has again a different vowel scheme

---

[1] Marouzeau, *Le Français Moderne*, iii, p. 291; Wandruszka, *Germanisch-Romanische Monatsschrift*, xxxv, p. 239; Id., *Der Geist der französischen Sprache*, pp. 51 f.
[2] Via Old French *barbarique* (*NED*).

and onomatopoeic value. One example from poetry in each language will help to bring out the contrast:

> magno misceri *murmure* caelum.
> *Aeneid*, Book IV, l. 160.[1]

> Ou l'onde qui *murmure* en caressant ces rives.
> Lamartine, *Chant d'amour*.[2]

> The surgy *murmurs* of the lonely sea.
> Keats, *Endymion*, Book I.

An interesting case is that of the Vulgar Latin **retinnitire* which belongs to the same family as the verb *tinnitare*, French *tinter*. As we have just seen, the latter retained its motivation by modifying the crucial vowel sound. In **retinnitire*, the sound-laws were allowed to take their course, giving Modern French *retentir*, but the meaning has been slightly altered to fit the form: from the idea of 'ringing' or 'tinkling' it has shifted towards that of 'resounding' (Marouzeau).

(2) *Loss of morphological and semantic motivation.* — Loss of *morphological* transparency may come about in three main ways:

(a) Phonetic changes may once again play a decisive role in destroying motivation. The parts of which a compound is made up may coalesce to such a degree that it becomes an opaque, unanalysable unit. The English word *lord*, for example, comes from the Old English *hlāford*, earlier *hlāfweard*, a perfectly transparent compound of *hlāf* 'loaf' and *weard* 'ward' (*NED*). Since the two elements have merged the word has become an indivisible morpheme. Some compounds have not travelled so far on the road towards coalescence. Though the etymology of *breakfast*, *blackguard*, *boatswain* and a number of similar words has been obscured by phonetic and other factors (cf. above, p. 29), the traditional spelling still preserves a modicum of transparency. The process can even be reversed before it has gone too far: *grindstone* was formerly pronounced |grinstən| but has been restored to its etymological pronunciation.[3]

Sound-change may also sever the link between a derivative and its root-word, thus robbing the former of its motivation. From the Latin *directus*, a transparent verb **directiare* was formed in Vulgar Latin. Subsequently, *directus* became *droit* 'straight, right' in French whereas **directiare* developed into *dresser* 'to set up, to train, etc.'. For the modern

---

[1] 'A confused rumbling sound started in the sky' (W. F. Jackson Knight's translation).
[2] 'Or the wave which whispers when stroking these shores.'
[3] O. Jespersen, *A Modern English Grammar on Historical Principles*, Part I, 4th ed., Heidelberg, 1928, p. 118.

speaker there is no longer any connexion between the two terms, nor do they bear any resemblance to the learned form *direct*, borrowed from Latin in the Middle Ages (Bloch-Wartburg). This is reflected in English too, where no one but an etymologist would connect *dress* with *direct*.

(*b*) Compounds and derivatives may also lose their motivation if any of their elements falls into disuse. The days of the week are a case in point. Only *Sunday* and, perhaps, *Monday* are fully analysable in English; the rest have become opaque since the disappearance of the names of pagan deities on which they were based. The English words are at least partially motivated by the presence of the element -*day*, but the French names do not even have that support: the -*di*, from Latin *dies* 'day', has not survived as an independent word, only as an obscure suffix in *lundi*, *mardi*, etc., and in *midi*, and as a prefix in *dimanche*; the ordinary word for 'day', *jour*, comes from the Latin *diurnum*.[1]

The same factor may also cancel out the motivation of derivatives. *Visage* was motivated in Old French by the existence of its root-word, the noun *vis* 'face'; since the disappearance of the latter, *visage* has ceased to be analysable.

(*c*) Even where the elements are alive and phonetically intact, compounds and derivatives will lose their motivation if there is too wide a gulf in meaning between them and their components. French *débonnaire*, which has also passed into English, arose from the phrase *de bonne aire*, which originally meant 'of good stock', but only the etymologist will be aware of its connexion with *aire* 'eyrie': for the ordinary speaker, *débonnaire* is entirely opaque (cf. Bloch-Wartburg, *s.v. aire*). Derivatives are exposed to the same process: who would connect *contemplate* with *temple*, *consider* with *sideral*, or French *regarder* with *garder*? In English, the latter pair are even spelt differently: *regard* — *guard*, which is usually a sign that no connexion is perceived between two words.

Loss of *semantic motivation* may result from the same factors. Sound-change is not of great importance here, though it can make itself felt in special circumstances. Thus French *pavillon* initially meant a 'tent' and came from Latin *papilio*, *papilionem* 'butterfly'; it was, to begin with, a graphic metaphor suggested by the similarity between a tent and the spread-out wings of the insect. But no trace of this connexion remains in Modern French where the butterfly is called *papillon*, an irregular form which does not show the normal French change from |p| to |v| between vowels (Bloch-Wartburg). It may also happen that the literal and transferred meanings of a word are differentiated by being attached to variant

[1] Cf. W. v. Wartburg, *Von Sprache und Mensch*, Berne, 1956, ch. 3.

forms: German *Rabe* 'raven' — *Rappe* 'black horse'; English *person* — *parson*, etc.[1]

If the literal sense of a word falls into disuse, its figurative meaning will lose its motivation.[2] Perhaps the most famous example of this process is the French word for 'head', *tête*, whose Latin ancestor, *testa*, meant 'pot, jug, shell' and was applied to the head by metaphor in Vulgar Latin.[3] When the earlier meaning disappeared, *tête* 'head' became opaque and is now surrounded by more expressive and jocular synonyms such as *poire* 'pear' and *citrouille* 'pumpkin'. A less known example is the history of the word *scruple*. In Latin, *scrupulus* meant literally a 'small sharp or pointed stone', and figuratively 'uneasiness, scruple, anxiety'.[4] Since the literal meaning has disappeared and only the figurative has survived, the word has become unmotivated.[5]

When the gap between original and transferred meaning becomes too wide, motivation is lost and the two senses will be felt to belong to two separate words. There are many examples of this tendency: *pupil* 'ward, scholar' and 'apple of the eye'; *collation* 'comparison' and 'light repast', etc. To re-establish the link between the two senses of the last word, one requires some special information about its history; it is then found that passages from Cassian's *Collationes Patrum* used to be read before compline in Benedictine monasteries, and these readings were followed by a light meal which was called *collation* because of its chance connexion with the book (*NED*). In some cases, loss of motivation may be accompanied by differences in spelling, but this is not an infallible criterion.

---

[1] See already H. Paul, *Prinzipien der Sprachgeschichte*, ch. 14. On the semantic development of the word *person*, see H. Rheinfelder, *Das Wort 'Persona'*, Beihefte zur Zeitschrift für Romanische Philologie, LXXVII (1928).

[2] The same applies to figurative phrases and locutions which become opaque when their literal meaning can no longer be understood. There is an interesting analysis of the process in a recent English novel describing the state of the world after a nuclear war: 'As little did she know of what the future held for her as she had known before; she only knew that instead of dreading it she looked forward to it, that instead of a frost numbing her faculties, it was a soft spring morning, pregnant with promise. So indeed she thought of it, in metaphors drawn from long ago. Mental habit dies hard; the survivors of the Third World War helped out their thoughts with pre-war images. In the New World there was no frost, no soft spring mornings — the war had swept them away, along with all the other changes of climate, temperature and season; they had this uniform, perpetual March, with an east wind that did indeed grow keener towards evening and a grey sky which the sun never quite pierced. But the language hadn't adapted itself to the new meteorological conditions; it was still, as ours is now, a storehouse of dead metaphors, still retained phrases like "at daggers drawn", though no one in the New State had a dagger' (L. P. Hartley, *Facial Justice*, London, 1960, pp. 115 f.).

[3] On the exact meaning of this metaphor, see recently Benveniste, *Word*, x, pp. 255 f.

[4] See Lewis and Short.

[5] The existence of another word *scruple*, meaning 'a unit of weight or time, a small amount or portion' (*NED*, *s.v. scruple*, sb.[1]), does not furnish any motivation for *scruple* in the abstract sense.

English *metal* and *mettle*, which were originally one word, are spelt differently and yet it may be doubted that the connexion has been completely forgotten; in *Julius Caesar*, Act I, scene 1, we find the spelling *metal* in the figurative sense: 'See whe'r their basest *metal* be not mov'd', and there is some evidence that the two words are still connected with each other by certain modern speakers.[1]

As has already been noted (p. 93), morphological and semantic motivation is to some extent a subjective matter. A writer interested in words, sensitive to their nuances and implications, and familiar with their history will be more aware of their derivation than an unsophisticated speaker. He might even attempt, when opportunity offers, to *revitalize* them by bringing them back to their etymological origins. This can be done either by explicit comment or implicitly, by placing the word in a context which will suddenly reveal its hidden background. Chaucer uses the first method when he unveils the etymology of the word *daisy*:

> That men by resoun wel it callè may
> The *dayésie*, or elles the *ye of day*,
> The emperice, and flourè of flourès alle.
> *The Legend of Good Women*, Prologue, ll. 183-5.

T. S. Eliot chooses the more subtle technique of contrast effect when trying to restore to the word *revision* its full etymological value:

> And time yet for a hundred indecisions,
> And for a hundred *visions* and *revisions*,
> Before the taking of a toast and tea.
> *The Love Song of J. Alfred Prufrock*.[2]

Rabelais proceeds in the same way when he 're-motivates' the verb *avaler*. This verb, derived from the old substantive *val* 'valley', originally meant 'to lower', and still does so in some technical uses; its main meaning, however, is 'to swallow'. Rabelais boldly revives the connexion by using the verb in its ordinary meaning and yet contrasting it with *monter* 'to mount, to climb': 'Si je *montasse* aussi bien comme je *avalle*, je feusse désjà au dessus la sphere de la lune.'[3]

[1] See Weekley, op. cit., pp. 144 f., where a newspaper article is quoted as saying that an increasing number of persons do not discriminate between *metal* and *mettle* and would write for example: 'Margaret was on her *metal*.'

[2] Cf. M. Schlauch, *The Gift of Tongues*, London ed., 1943, pp. 247 f. (subsequently renamed *The Gift of Language*, New York, 1955).

[3] 'If I could *climb* as well as I can *swallow*, I would be already above the sphere of the moon' (quoted by W. v. Wartburg, *Evolution et structure de la langue française*, 5th ed., Berne, 1958, p. 161). Other examples of revitalized metaphors in French will be found in V. Väänänen, 'Métaphores rajeunies et métaphores ressuscitées', in the Proceedings of the Eighth International Congress of Romance Linguistics, pp. 471-6.

This revival of etymologies is usually a form of wit or humour, but it can acquire serious and even sinister implications. In his short novel *Thésée*, Gide sums up the symbolic significance of Oedipus's self-mutilation by playing on the *double entendre* of the phrase *crever les yeux* 'to put out someone's eyes — to be obvious, to stare one in the face': 'J'ai *crevé mes yeux* pour les punir de n'avoir pas su voir une évidence qui, comme on dit, aurait dû me *crever les yeux*.'[1] In Camus's play *L'État de siège*, the Plague, symbol of the Nazi occupation, enlarges cynically on the appropriateness of the everyday expression *s'exécuter* 'to submit, to comply, to oblige', by connecting it with the idea of an *execution*: 'Magnifique! On y trouve tout! L'image de l'*exécution* d'abord qui est une image attendrissante et puis l'idée que l'*exécuté* collabore lui-même à son *exécution*, ce qui est le but et la consolidation de tout bon gouvernement.'[2]

This technique of 'etymological reduction', as it has been called, can become a veritable obsession with some writers and thinkers.[3] Valéry, who, like other French Symbolists, was an assiduous student of etymologies, revived the motivation of some of the words discussed on the preceding pages. The old connexion between a pebble and a scruple comes to life in the phrase 'le ruisseau *scrupuleux*' 'the "scrupulous" brook'; the link between *temple* and *contemplate* and that between *sideral* and *consider* is reforged in the pregnant formula: 'En insistant un peu sur les étymologies, on pourrait dire, avec une sorte de précision, que le croyant *contemple* le ciel, tandis que le savant le *considère*.'[4] Some philosophers go even further and believe that they can grasp the essential significance of words by uncovering their derivation. The German language, where motivation is, as we shall see, particularly strong, lends itself admirably to this kind of etymologizing. This method plays a prominent part in the philosophy of Martin Heidegger who argues, for instance, that the German word *Entschlossenheit* 'resoluteness' really means 'openness, opening up' since it is formed by joining the privative particle *ent-* to the verb *schliessen* 'to close'. Such analyses seem to revert

---

[1] 'I have torn out my eyes to punish them for not having been able to see a fact so obvious that it should, as the saying goes, have stared me in the face' (59th ed., Paris, 1946, p. 117).

[2] 'Splendid! You find everything in it! First of all the image of an *execution* which is a touching image, and then the idea that the *executed* person co-operates himself in his own *execution*, which is the purpose and consolidation of any good government' (Paris, 1948, pp. 117 f.).

[3] See on this matter M. Wandruszka's interesting article, 'Etymologie und Philosophie', *Etymologica*, pp. 857-71. The examples which follow are taken from this essay.

[4] 'By dwelling a little on etymologies, one might say, with a kind of precision, that the believer *contemplates* the sky whereas the scientist *considers* it' (quoted by Wandruszka, loc. cit., p. 865, from *Variété II*, p. 52).

to the pre-scientific stage of etymology when it was firmly believed that the derivation of words can give a clue to their 'real' and 'proper' meaning; the term *etymology* itself comes from the Greek τὸ ἔτυμον 'truth'. Heidegger's reconstructions are not as naïve as those of the seventh-century etymologist Isidore of Seville, who connected Latin *mors* 'death' with *amarus* 'bitter' and with the god *Mars*, but they are just as unrealistic: thus, he draws all kinds of conclusions from the relation between German *hell* 'clear' and *hallen* 'to resound', but forgets that the connexion is purely historical and has no relevance to the present state of the language.

2. *Acquisition of Motivation*

(1) *Acquisition of phonetic motivation.* — The caprice of sound-change, which cancels out the expressiveness of many words, may endow others with new onomatopoeic effects. From the inexpressive Latin *fagus* 'beech-tree', French has derived the diminutive form *fouet* 'whip' and the verb *fouetter*, which have a certain imitative quality (cf. Saussure, p. 102). The French verbs *gémir* 'to groan, to moan, to wail' and *geindre* 'to whine, to whimper' have more onomatopoeic force than the Latin *gemere* from which they have developed through a series of phonetic and morphological changes. The proper name *Cicero* has become more expressive in Italian *cicerone* where the |k|-s have changed to |tʃ|-s, and this may in its turn have influenced the meaning since the new sound was admirably adapted to imitate the garrulousness of a guide.[1]

(2) *Acquisition of morphological and semantic motivation.* — Morphological motivation can be acquired by the process commonly known as '*popular etymology*'.[2] This term has often been criticized, and 'popular' is indeed hardly a fitting description since some of these errors were committed not by the 'people' but by the learned or the semi-learned: mediaeval scribes, Renaissance humanists and the like. 'Associative etymology', suggested by Professor Orr,[3] would be a more appropriate term, but it is probably too late to change linguistic usage on this point. The

---

[1] Migliorini, op. cit., p. 141; cf. above, p. 78.

[2] For the rich literature on the subject, see the works listed in my *Principles of Semantics*, p. 91, n. 2, to which the following recent contributions may be added: G. Gougenheim, 'La fausse étymologie savante', *Romance Philology*, i (1948), pp. 277-86; J. Orr, 'L'Étymologie populaire', *Revue de Linguistique Romane*, xviii (1954), pp. 129-42; V. Pisani, 'Über Volksetymologie', *Omagiu lui Al. Graur*, pp. 633-43; A. W. Read, 'English Words with Constituent Elements having Independent Semantic Value', *Philologica: The Malone Anniversary Studies*, Baltimore, 1949, pp. 306-12; J. Vendryes, 'Pour une étymologie statique', *Bulletin de la Société de Linguistique de Paris*, xlix (1953), pp. 1-19.

[3] *Words and Sounds in English and French*, p. 96.

driving force behind popular etymology is the desire to motivate what is, or has become, opaque in language. As a French linguist recently put it, 'l'étymologie populaire est une réaction contre l'arbitraire du signe. On veut à tout prix expliquer ce dont la langue est bien incapable de fournir l'explication'.[1] The motivation which words receive in this way is psychological rather than historical; it is based on associations of sound and sense, and has nothing to do with the facts of scientific etymology.

Popular etymology is one of the best known aspects of semantics; it will therefore be sufficient to mention briefly its most characteristic forms and illustrate them by one or two examples:

(1) In some cases, the new motivation will affect the meaning of a word but will leave its form intact. The French adjective *ouvrable* is derived from the old verb *ouvrer* (Latin *operari*) 'to work', which was replaced by *travailler* in the seventeenth century and has survived only in technical usage. Since the virtual eclipse of *ouvrer*, *ouvrable* has been drawn into the orbit of the verb *ouvrir* 'to open', so that *jour ouvrable* 'working day' is commonly interpreted as a day when shops, offices, etc., are open.

(2) Conversely, there are cases where the new motivation will alter the form of a word while the meaning remains unchanged. A well-known example is English *bridegroom* which comes from Old English *brydguma*, a compound of *bryd* 'bride' and *guma* 'man'. When the latter term disappeared, the second element of the compound became opaque and was subsequently identified with the word *groom* 'lad'; hence the modern form which goes back to the sixteenth century (*NED*).

(3) In many cases, popular etymology will impinge both on the form and on the meaning of words. The German name of the biblical Flood, *Sündflut*, was originally *sint-vluot* 'universal flood', which was altered under the influence of the word *Sünde* 'sin'. This historically erroneous interpretation has not only affected the form but has also introduced the idea of sin, and of punishment for sins, into the meaning of the word. An interesting example is the archaic and dialectal term *sand-blind* 'half-blind, dim-sighted, purblind'. This is usually considered to be a deformation of Old English **samblind* whose first syllable, the prefix **sam* 'half', became opaque and was wrongly identified with *sand*. This association is not only responsible for the modern form but seems also to reverberate in its meaning; in Dr. Johnson's dictionary, we find the

---

[1] 'Popular etymology is a reaction against the conventionality of signs. People want to explain at any cost what remains unexplained in language' (Vendryes, *Bulletin de la Société de Linguistique de Paris*, xlviii, p. 6).

definition; 'having a defect in the eyes, by which small particles appear to fly before them'.[1] In *The Merchant of Venice*, Act II, scene 2, the spurious connexion with *sand* is forcefully brought out when Launcelot Gobbo says: 'This is my true-begotten father, who, being more than *sand-blind*, high-gravel blind, knows me not.'

(4) In languages with a non-phonetic system of spelling, popular etymology may be confined to the written word without affecting its pronunciation. Thus, English *island* owes its *s* to the influence of the historically unconnected *isle*, and the *g* in *sovereign* (from French *souverain*, Mediaeval Latin *superānus*) is due to confusion with *reign*.[2] There is always a possibility that such silent letters may come to life by what is known as a 'spelling pronunciation'. The French *legs* 'legacy, bequest' was originally spelt *lais* and was derived from the verb *laisser* 'to leave'; it was then remodelled in writing under the influence of Latin *legatum* 'bequest', and attached to the verb *léguer* 'to bequeath'. Eventually, the spelling began to react on the sound, and today many people pronounce the word with a $|g|$.[3]

Foreign words are particularly vulnerable to popular etymology: they are unmotivated and without roots in the receiving idiom, so that sound and sense associations will have free scope. There are many well-known examples: French *choucroute* from Alsatian *sûrkrût* (German *Sauerkraut*), as if it were a compound of the French words *chou* 'cabbage' and *croûte* 'crust'; English *crayfish* or *crawfish* from Old French *crevice* (Modern French *écrevisse*); French *contredanse* from *country dance*, and *âne salé* (literally 'salt donkey') from *Aunt Sally*, and many more.

The contrast between scientific and popular etymology is another reminder of the necessity to distinguish between historical and descriptive viewpoints in linguistics. The ordinary speaker's ideas about the derivation of words are a linguistic fact worthy of the philologist's attention even if they contradict his own knowledge of etymologies. This was already clear to some of the Sanskrit grammarians and has been strongly emphasized by Gilliéron and other linguistic geographers. It is perhaps a sign of the times that in the first edition of Saussure's book, popular etymology was dismissed as a 'pathological phenomenon', but that this description disappeared from subsequent editions.[4] The scope of popular etymology might well be much wider than has been realized so far. It

---

[1] *NED* and Stern, op. cit., p. 234.   [2] *Shorter OED*; cf. Bloch-Wartburg.
[3] See Bloch-Wartburg, and P. Fouché, *Traité de prononciation française*, Paris, 1956, p. 421.
[4] Op. cit., p. 241; cf. I. Iordan-J. Orr, *An Introduction to Romance Linguistics*, London, 1937, p. 173, n. 1.

H

would be interesting to conduct a statistical inquiry to find out how many
people actually connect *noise* with *noisome*, *scare* with *scarify*, *nigger* with
niggard,[1] and similar pairs of historically unrelated words. Meanwhile,
Professor Orr has summed up very neatly the fundamental affinity between
learned and popular etymology:

> L'étymologie populaire ... ne diffère pas essentiellement de sa soeur
> savante, l'étymologie des philologues. Plus vivante, plus 'opérative'
> que cette dernière, elle fait instinctivement, intuitivement et du premier
> jet ce que fait l'autre intentionnellement, à grand renfort de bouquins
> et de fiches.[2]

Popular etymology can also furnish *semantic motivation* for an opaque
term. When two words are identical in sound and not too dissimilar in
meaning, there will be a tendency to regard them as one word with a
literal and a transferred sense. An interesting example in English is *ear*,
name of the organ, and its homonym *ear* which means a 'spike or head
of corn'. The two come from entirely different roots, the former being
related to German *Ohr* and Latin *auris*, the latter to German *Ähre* and
Latin *acus*, *aceris*. Their homonymy in English has led to the invention
of a semantic link totally unjustified by history: most people would
probably regard '*ear* of corn' as a metaphor based on the similarity
between the spike and the organ (Bloomfield, *Language*, p. 436). Once
again it would be useful to have some objective statistical data to show
how many people are, or can be made, aware of these spurious connexions.

Popular etymology may even come into play when two words are not
identical but merely similar in sound. In such cases the form of one of the
words will be altered to make it homonymous with the other. Thus
French *souci* 'marigold' comes from Late Latin *solsequia* and had originally
nothing to do with *souci* 'care, worry', derived from Latin *sollicitare*. In
the sixteenth century, however, the flower came to be regarded as the
symbol of care,[3] and its name was adjusted accordingly: from an earlier
soucie and other variants, it changed to its modern form and thus became

---

[1] Cf. the following quotations in Read, loc. cit.: 'Skiing down a vast open side of a valley,
with clear expanses of snow on all sides (a less *noisome* place would be difficult to find)';
'truly a *scarifying* experience'; 'Such conduct I should call, sir — with no disrespect to the
coloured population — *niggardly*.'

[2] 'Popular etymology does not essentially differ from its learned sister, the etymology of
philologists. More vital, more "operative" than the latter, it does instinctively, intuitively
and at the first attempt what the other does deliberately, with a great array of books and
index cards' (*Revue de Linguistique Romane*, xviii, p. 142).

[3] Cf. a similar symbolism in the flower-name *pensée* 'pansy', regarded as the symbol of
pensée 'thought, remembrance'. In the sixteenth century, the flower was also known as
herbe de la pensée 'plant of remembrance' (Bloch-Wartburg, *s.v. penser*).

identical with the other *souci* (Bloch-Wartburg). A similar example is French *flamme*, 'fleam, lancet', which has no historical connexion with *flamme* 'flame': it comes from Graeco-Latin *phlebotomus* and had the form *flieme* in Old French, which passed into English as *fleam*. Subsequently, it became associated with the other *flamme*, and its form was changed to make the identification complete (ibid.). In Modern French, both *souci* 'marigold' and *flamme* 'fleam' are motivated; they are regarded as transferred meanings of the words for 'care' and 'flame'.

III. CONVENTIONALITY AND MOTIVATION IN LANGUAGE

It was one of Saussure's most important discoveries that the proportion of transparent and opaque words varies characteristically from one language to another and sometimes from one period to another in the same idiom. He even foresaw the possibility that languages might one day be classified on this ground, and outlined a rudimentary 'typology' based on morphological motivation: he distinguished between 'lexicological' languages, which have a preference for the conventional word, and 'grammatical' languages, which favour the transparent type. English, in his view, is less motivated than German; Chinese represents the extreme form of opaqueness, whereas Primitive Indo-European and Sanskrit are at the opposite end of the scale. In the history of the same language, there may be a movement from motivation to conventionality or vice versa, and the balance of the two elements may be considerably altered in the course of time. Thus French as compared to Latin shows an enormous increase in the proportion of opaque terms: the Latin *fabrica* 'workshop', based on *faber* 'forger, smith, etc.', has been reduced by sound-change to the unanalysable *forge*; *magister*, supported by *magis* 'more', has become purely conventional in *maître*, and many other words have evolved on similar lines.[1]

Although the terms 'lexicological' and 'grammatical' are not very happily chosen, Saussure had the merit of formulating the problem in all its main aspects. His ideas were followed up by Bally and others, and the conclusions which have emerged from these studies have not only thrown fresh light on word-structure but have also had repercussions outside linguistics.[2]

[1] Op. cit., pp. 183 f.
[2] See Bally, *Linguistique générale et linguistique française*, pp. 341 ff.; V. Grove, *The Language Bar*, London, 1949; E. Leisi, *Das heutige Englisch*, 1st ed., ch. 12; Wartburg,

It will have been noticed that Saussure's remarks apply only to morphological motivation. In order to obtain a complete picture of the interplay of transparent and opaque words, all three types of motivation would have to be examined separately. This, however, is at present beyond our power: though one may have some quite definite impressions about the frequency of onomatopoeia or metaphor in a given language, it would be difficult to formulate them with any degree of precision. With morphological motivation one is on firmer ground: it is the most clear-cut and least subjective of the three types, and certain broad tendencies stand out very clearly even though they may not be statistically formulable.[1] I shall therefore confine myself to this type of motivation, and shall illustrate the problem on a concrete example: the structure of Modern French as compared to English and German as well as to earlier periods in the history of French itself.

1. *English, French and German*

(1) *Compounds.* — Even a perfunctory glance at a German dictionary will reveal that compounds are far more numerous, and far more easily formed, in that language than in French or in English. Consider the following examples where a transparent compound in German is matched by a simple, unanalysable term or by a learned Graeco-Latin formation in the other two languages:

Schlittschuh ('sledge-shoe')	*skate*	*patin*
Schnittlauch ('cut-leek')	*chive*	*cive*
Fingerhut ('finger-hat')	*thimble*	*dé*

Evolution et structure, pp. 263 f.; Id., *Problèmes et méthodes de la linguistique*, pp. 171 ff.; Id., *La Posizione della lingua italiana*, Florence, 1940, pp. 89-97; cf. also my *Précis de sémantique française*, pp. 125 ff.

[1] In his interesting review of my *Précis de sémantique française* in *Language*, xxxi (1955), pp. 537-43, Professor Weinreich refuses to admit the relative paucity of morphological motivation in French until it has been demonstrated by statistical data. It is, however, difficult to imagine a statistical test for a feature embracing the entire vocabulary of a language; moreover, one of the essential points is the ease with which *new* compounds and derivatives are formed in German as opposed to French, and no statistical inquiry could cover these fluid and elusive processes. In any case the tendency is so obvious that no numerical demonstration is needed; hence the general consensus of opinion on this point. When Professor Weinreich suggests that a contrary example can be found for every one of the instances I have quoted, this may be true of the limited number of illustrations given in the text, but it would be difficult to do so for the scores of similar cases which can easily be collected from any dictionary. In fact, Professor Weinreich gives only two such examples, one of which, French *parce que* — German *weil* 'because', is not relevant as it concerns form-words, while the other, French *petit-fils* — German *Enkel* 'grandson', is a very special case which arose in the sixteenth century, partly under the influence of *grand-père* 'grandfather' and allied terms, partly because of the ambiguity of the word *neveu* (Latin *nepos*) which could mean either 'grandson' or 'nephew' (Bloch-Wartburg). On the need for statistics see also G. Mounin, *Bulletin de la Société de Linguistique de Paris*, lv (1960), p. 50.

Handschuh ('hand-shoe')	*glove*	*gant*
Erdteil ('earth-part')	*continent*	*continent*
Wasserleitung ('water-conduit')	*aqueduct*	*aqueduc*
Kehlkopf ('throat-head')	*larynx*	*larynx*
Nilpferd ('Nile-horse')	*hippopotamus*	*hippopotame*

The same pattern of a German compound facing a Graeco-Latin word in English and French recurs in the terminology of many sciences.[1] Take for instance linguistics and its main divisions:

Sprachwissenschaft ('language-science')	*linguistics*	*linguistique*
Lautlehre ('sound-lore')	*phonetics*	*phonétique*
Formenlehre ('form-lore')	*morphology*	*morphologie*
Bedeutungslehre ('meaning-lore')	*semantics*	*sémantique*

Or take some of the traditional names of chemical elements in German:

Wasserstoff ('watery substance')	*hydrogen*	*hydrogène*
Sauerstoff ('acid substance')	*oxygen*	*oxygène*
Stickstoff ('choky substance')	*nitrogen*	*azote*

There are also many German compounds which are rendered in English and French not by one word but by a phrase: *Kammerzofe* 'lady's maid', *Bedeutungswandel* 'change of meaning', *Schuldbewusstsein* 'sense of guilt' (literally: 'being conscious of guilt'), *Kadavergehorsam* 'blind obedience' (literally: 'obedience of a corpse'), *Minderwertigkeitskomplex* 'inferiority complex', etc. The ease with which examples can be multiplied shows, without any need for statistics, how fundamental this feature is in all three languages. As all readers of German academic prose will readily agree, some of these compounds are extremely difficult to translate into English and French, especially when derivatives are formed from them; one then has to resort to clumsy paraphrases, rendering *geistes-wissenschaftlich* by 'pertaining to the humane sciences', *geistesgeschichtlich* by 'connected with the history of ideas', etc.[2]

(2) *Derivatives.* — A comparison of derivatives in English, French and German tells a very similar story. The extraordinary richness of German in such forms is well known; in his book *The Language Bar*, Dr. Victor Grove has collected over seventy words derived by means of prefixes and suffixes from the one verb *nehmen* 'to take' (op. cit., pp. 41 ff.). In

---

[1] It should be noted that in many of these cases the learned term exists also in German.
[2] Cf. R. Priebsch-W. E. Collinson, *The German Language*, 3rd ed., London, 1952, p. 439.

many cases, such German derivatives correspond to simple, opaque terms in the other two languages:

Vergangenheit ('bygone-ness')	*past*	*passé*
Scheidung ('part-ing')	*divorce*	*divorce*
Ehelosigkeit ('marriage-less-ness')	*celibacy*	*célibat*
Ursache ('original matter')	*cause*	*cause*
anfangen ('put one's hand to')	*begin*	*commencer*

Occasionally, English is closer to German than to French: it will use a verb followed by a preposition where German has a prefix and French a simple term: *eintreten — come in — entrer*; *hinausgehen — go out — sortir*; *überfahren — run over — écraser*, etc.[1] In most cases, however, English will show the same pattern as French.

Here again, as with compounds, it often happens that a German derivative has to be translated by a phrase in English and in French. Diminutives are a case in point. In German, the diminutive suffixes *-chen* and *-lein* can be freely appended to nouns with a suitable meaning: *Schwester* 'sister' — *Schwesterchen*, *Frau* 'woman' — *Fräulein*. In English and French, this can be done only on a very limited scale (*lamb — lambkin*, *pig — piglet*; *roi — roitelet* 'king — kinglet', etc.); normally, German diminutives will have to be rendered by an adjectival phrase: *Schwesterchen* — '*little* sister' — '*petite* sœur'. Other German derivatives may also have to be translated by a phrase: *Urtext* 'original text', *verdeutschen* 'translate into German', *Ausnahmslosigkeit* 'working without exceptions', and many more.

Where it is necessary to have a derivative, French and English are often unable, or unwilling, to form one from their existing resources, and use a Graeco-Latin term instead. This pattern is found in a number of hybrid pairs — nouns and adjectives or other combinations — where an ordinary word is flanked by a learned derivative:

Gesetz — gesetzlich	*law — legal*	*loi — légal*
Kirche — kirchlich	*church — ecclesiastical*	*église — ecclésiastique*
Bischof — bischöflich	*bishop — episcopal*	*évêque — épiscopal*
Stadt — städtisch	*town — urban*	*ville — urbain*
Mund — mündlich	*mouth — oral*	*bouche — oral*
Sprache — sprachlich	*language — linguistic*	*langue — linguistique*[2]

[1] See J. Orr, 'English and French — a Comparison', *Words and Sounds in English and French*, ch. 8, p. 59.

[2] Some of these words also have regular derivatives like *churchy*, *mouthy*, French *loyal* and *vilain* 'nasty, ugly', but these have specialized meanings and overtones whereas the learned terms are purely descriptive and closely parallel to the noun.

From a historical point of view, some of these pairs go back to the same root (*language* and *linguistic* to Latin *lingua*, *bishop* and *episcopal* to Christian Latin *episcopus*, of Greek origin, etc.), whereas others come from totally different sources: thus, the native English *mouth* is paired off with the Latin *oral*; the Old Norse word *law* with the Latin *legal*; *church*, a term of Greek origin, with *ecclesiastical* which is derived from another Greek word, etc. For the descriptive linguist, these etymologies are of course irrelevant: whether the two terms go back to the same root or not, the ordinary speaker is unaware of any connexion between them.

French goes a good deal further than English in the avoidance of derivation.[1] To many of the commonest French words it is quite impossible to attach any suffix. Thus, where we have transparent derivatives like *water — watery*, *fire — fiery* in English, the corresponding French nouns are unproductive, and learned adjectives have to be introduced to fill the gap: *eau — aqueux*, *feu — fougueux*. The same disparity recurs in many other cases:

soot — sooty	suie — fuligineux
month — monthly	mois — mensuel
week — weekly	semaine — hebdomadaire
heaven — heavenly	ciel — céleste
blind — blindness	aveugle — cécité[2]

In words like *eau*, *feu* or *suie*, it would be phonetically difficult to join certain suffixes to the stem since this would create an awkward hiatus (*eau-eux*), but in many other cases there would be no such difficulty, and the reluctance to form derivatives springs from a deeper reason: the time-honoured custom of filling gaps in vocabulary by drawing on the two classical languages.

Enough examples have been cited to show that French inclines very markedly towards opaqueness in word-structure whereas German prefers just as clearly the motivated type. English, true to its mixed origins, oscillates between the two solutions but is on the whole closer to the French pattern. All this does not mean of course that there are not a great many transparent compounds and derivatives in English and in French; certain derivational processes are in fact more productive than ever, though they are mainly confined to the more learned parts of the vocabulary (*automation*, *electronic*, *supersonic*, *deration*, *decontrol*,

[1] See especially A. Dauzat, 'L'Appauvrissement de la dérivation en français', *Le Français Moderne*, v (1937), pp. 289-300, and J. Marouzeau, 'Les Déficiences de la dérivation française', ibid., xix (1951), pp. 1-8.
[2] The word *aveuglement* exists in French, but refers to 'moral blindness'.

decongest, disinflate, disincentive, meritocracy, etc.). On the whole, however, it is clear that English, and especially French, are more sparing than German in the use of transparent forms made up of native elements. A glance at the history of French will show the main factors which have brought about the present situation.

2. *From Motivation towards Conventionality*

As Saussure rightly saw (see above, p. 105), sound-change has played an important part in making French into a relatively opaque idiom. The phonetic substance of Latin words has been drastically reduced; sounds have developed differently according to their environment, their place in the word, and the influence of accent, and all these factors have severed many etymological connexions and have increased the conventional element in the language.[1] One example out of many will be sufficient to show how phonetic change has obscured the transparency of words. Take the following Latin terms and their French descendants:

pes, pedem	*pied* 'foot'
pedō, pedōnem	*pion* 'junior master; pawn'
*pedaticum	*péage* 'toll, charge'
pedica	*piège* 'trap'
impedicare	*empêcher* 'to prevent, to hinder'
pedestris	*piètre* 'wretched, paltry'

The net result of all these changes is that five words which were transparent derivatives of *pes, pedem* in Classical or Vulgar Latin have since passed into the category of opaque terms. This has of course happened in other languages as well: the connexion between English *thumb* and *thimble,* or between the verb *to sew* and the nouns *seam* and *seamstress* (or *sempstress*), has been disrupted in much the same way. But while sound-changes usually work against transparency, there are few languages where they have played havoc with it on the same scale as in French.

The main reason for the opaqueness of French lies, however, in the history of the vocabulary. During the Renaissance, Latin and Greek words were introduced into French in very considerable numbers, and this process has never been reversed. As a result, native resources have remained largely untapped, and many of the transparent words coined in Old French were discarded as redundant or replaced by classical forms.

---

[1] Cf. above, pp. 96 f.; see also, in addition to the works already cited in this section, A. Meillet, 'La Notion de radical en français', op. cit., vol. II, pp. 123-7.

Before the vogue of learned terms set in, the language was rich in derivatives; sometimes there was indeed a plethora of them. From the substantive *fin* 'end' and the verb *finir*, the following abstract nouns could be formed in Old French: *finage, finail, finaille, finance, fine, finée, finement, finie, finiment, finison, finissement, finité, finitive*.[1] Out of these thirteen derivatives, only *finance* has survived, and even that with a specialized meaning which has isolated it from its root. In many other cases, a transparent formation has been replaced by a classical term: *murison* 'ripeness', from the adjective *mûr* (Latin *maturus*) 'ripe', has been supplanted by the learned *maturité; feintise* 'pretence', from the verb *feindre* (Latin *fingere*) 'to feign', by *fiction*, etc.[2] Even where the native and the Latin term come from the same root this will provide no motivation as the French word has usually changed beyond recognition since Roman times; cf. such pairs as *éteindre* 'extinguish' — *extinction*, as opposed to Italian *estinguere* — *estinzione; chien* 'dog' — *canin* as against Italian *cane* — *canino*, and many others.

Learned influence has also been the main factor making for opaqueness in English. Old English was a plastic medium in which compounds and derivatives could be formed very freely. Dr. Grove has collected nearly fifty terms derived from the word *heofon* 'heaven'; they include such picturesque compounds as *heofon-candel* 'sun, moon, stars', and *heofon-weard* 'Heaven's Keeper, God' (op. cit., pp. 45 f.). The language relied extensively, though by no means solely, on native formations for the rendering of the new religious and scientific concepts introduced by Christianity: *priness* for 'trinity'; *tungol-wītegan* (literally: 'star+wise men') for the three Magi; *sunfolgend* ('sun+follower') for 'heliotrope'; *foresetness* for 'preposition', etc.[3] With the subsequent influx of French and classical words, these resources were allowed to atrophy. Attempts were made time and again to turn back the tide: in the sixteenth century, Sir John Cheke tried to replace *lunatic* by *mooned, publican* by *toller, prophet* by *foresayer*, etc.,[4] and three centuries later, the Dorset poet William Barnes suggested *sky-sill* for *horizon, folkwain* for *omnibus, hearsomeness* for *obedience*, and other 'Saxonisms' of the same type.[5] In some cases, the purists' efforts were successful: thus, *foreword* and *folklore*, formed in the middle of the last century, have taken root,

---

[1] Quoted after Godefroy, *Lexique de l'ancien français*, Paris, 1901, p. 232.
[2] Wartburg, *Evolution et structure*, p. 263.
[3] See Jespersen, *Growth and Structure of the English Language*, pp. 41 ff.
[4] A. C. Baugh, *A History of the English Language*, 2nd ed., New York — London, 1959, p. 277.
[5] Grove, op. cit., p. 103; Leisi, op. cit., p. 71.

and a little earlier, the word *handbook*, which had existed in Old English but was subsequently ousted by *manual*, was reintroduced on the model of German *Handbuch*. These isolated successes did not, however, affect the main pattern of English word-formation. Commenting on the reception of *handbook*, which had to establish itself in the face of fierce opposition — Archbishop Trench denounced it as a 'very ugly and very unnecessary' term — Jespersen declared: 'I cannot help thinking that state of language a very unnatural one where such a very simple, intelligible, and expressive word has to fight its way instead of being at once admitted to the very best society' (*Growth and Structure*, p. 46). Whether 'unnatural' or not, such reactions are highly symptomatic of the English attitude to this form of motivation.

Far-reaching conclusions have sometimes been drawn from the predominance of transparent or opaque terms. It has been suggested, for example, that the preference of the French language for purely conventional words containing no clue whatever to their meaning, has encouraged the French fondness for contrast and antithesis, the coining of terse and memorable formulas, and also the formation of clichés.[1] There may be a grain of truth in these ideas, but it would be very difficult to support them with tangible evidence. Meanwhile, there are other important effects of motivation which can be demonstrated far more precisely. Since these effects transcend semantics proper they can only be mentioned very briefly.

(1) The preponderance of the transparent or the opaque type in a given language will have a direct bearing on the treatment of foreign words. In a flexible idiom, rich in compounds and derivatives, purism and linguistic chauvinism will find a more fertile soil than in a language where such resources are sparingly used. In the case of German, this was already recognized in the seventeenth century by a certain Justus Georg Schottel who praised his mother tongue for being firmly attached to its native roots. In his famous *Speeches to the German Nation*, written at a time when Berlin was occupied by French troops, Fichte extolled the same quality of the German vocabulary; in his patriotic fervour, he went so far as to equate word-formation with vitality in language, whereas an idiom like French had, in his view, only a 'semblance of life' and was really dead at the roots.[2] The German habit of replacing international terms by native compounds — so-called 'loan-translations'[3] — is well known and still very much in evidence, as seen from the rendering of

1 Bally, *Linguistique générale et linguistique française*, pp. 344 f. and *passim*.
2 See Wandruszka, *Etymologica*, pp. 865 ff.
3 For the literature on this subject, see my *Principles of Semantics*, p. 40, n. 1, and L. Deroy, *L'Emprunt linguistique*, Paris, 1956.

television by *Fernsehen* 'far-seeing', on the model of earlier words where Greek *tēle* 'far' was translated by German *fern*: *telescope — Fernrohr* 'far-tube', *telephone — Fernsprecher* 'far-speaker'. It is worth noting that some of these native forms live side by side with the international term, and it may even happen that the latter has wider currency while its German rival remains confined to official usage; thus *Telephon*, not *Fernsprecher*, is the everyday word, and there is only one verb: *telephonieren*.

When a wave of nationalism swept over Europe in the nineteenth century, many of the new or resurgent countries began to purify their vocabulary. Some went even further than Germany. In Hungarian, which is a highly motivated language, the international term *theatre* disappeared before its native rival *színház*, literally 'stage-house'. Similar replacements occurred in Czech and in Serbo-Croat; indeed, nationalism developed into parochialism when the Serbs and the Croats chose different terms for the same object, so that a theatre is called *kazalište* in Zagreb and *pozorište* in Belgrade.[1]

(2) Motivation is of direct relevance to the learning and teaching of foreign languages. One could not say in general that transparent idioms are easier to acquire than opaque ones, for the advantages and disadvantages are very neatly balanced; but the methods of study ought to be adapted to the basic design of the language. The learning of ordinary everyday terms in German will in many cases involve less memorizing than in French; thus the French words *gare* 'railway station', *camion* 'lorry' and *avion* 'aeroplane' have to be learnt by heart, whereas the corresponding German terms are self-explanatory compounds made up of well-known elements: *Bahnhof* 'railway-yard', *Lastauto* 'load-automobile', *Flugzeug* 'flying-thing'. The pattern of derivation is certainly simpler in German than in French: *Russ, russig* is easier to remember than *suie, fuligineux*, and *Woche, wöchentlich* more coherent than *semaine, hebdomadaire*. On the debit side there are all the international words, especially scientific terms, which must be relearnt in German: it is not likely to help a doctor to find that *pleurisy* is called *Rippenfellentzündung* 'inflammation of the rib membrane', and the *duodenum Zwölffingerdarm* 'twelve finger-gut', nor will the chemist readily recognize his familiar *oxygen* in *Sauerstoff*, quite apart from the fact that it may not be very accurate to describe that element as 'acid substance'.

(3) The contrast between transparent and opaque languages may also have important social and cultural consequences. In English, the presence

---

[1] A. Meillet, 'Les Interférences entre vocabulaires', op. cit., vol. II, pp. 36-43: p. 38.

of countless Greek and Latin words — 'inkhorn terms', as they were called in the sixteenth century — has helped to build a 'language bar' between those with and without a classical education. For the more privileged, many of these words will be motivated and will easily fit into a pattern; to their less fortunate fellow-citizens they will appear as opaque, 'highbrow', forbidding and confusing. The problem, which was cogently diagnosed in Dr. Grove's book, is not a new one, though the growing importance of science in everyday life makes it more acute than ever. Educational facilities and human attitudes have changed out of recognition since Goldsmith's portrait of the village schoolmaster:

> While words of learned length and thund'ring sound
> Amazed the gazing rustics rang'd around,
> And still they gaz'd, and still the wonder grew,
> That one small head could carry all he knew.
>
> *The Deserted Village*, ll. 213-6;[1]

yet the problem is still with us and is bound up with the fundamental structure of the language.

The worst feature of the language bar is that it perpetuates and aggravates class differences and fills people on the wrong side of the bar with a sense of insecurity and inferiority. There are frequent hesitations about the pronunciation, meaning and use of Graeco-Latin terms. Alice in Wonderland could safely risk using *latitude* and *longitude* although she 'had not the slightest idea what Latitude was, or Longitude either, but she thought they were nice grand words to say'. She was less confident about *Antipodes*: ' "The Antipathies, I think" — she was rather glad there *was* no one listening, this time, as it didn't sound at all the right word.' Indeed, malapropism is endemic in English and must have been so long before Sheridan's Mrs. Ma'aprop; it is already a common device in Shakespeare:

> 'She is given too much to allicholy and musing.'
> (Mrs. Quickly in *The Merry Wives of Windsor*, Act I, scene 4)

> 'O villain! thou wilt be condemn'd into everlasting redemption for this.'
> (Dogberry in *Much Ado about Nothing*, Act IV, scene 2)

> Quince: 'He is a very paramour for a sweet voice.'
> Flute: 'You must say "paragon". A paramour is — God bless us! — a thing of naught.'
> (*A Midsummer Night's Dream*, Act IV, scene 2)[2]

[1] Cf. Grove, op. cit., p. 84.   [2] Cf. Leisi, op. cit., pp. 64 and 68.

Jespersen once remarked that 'no literature in the world abounds as English does in characters made ridiculous to the reader by the manner in which they misapply or distort "big" words' (*Growth and Structure*, p. 133). It would be wrong to reduce the whole problem of malapropism and of the language bar to a question of transparency and opaqueness; the issues are far more delicate and complex. Yet it cannot be denied that lack of motivation is one of the chief factors responsible for this state of affairs: learned Greek and Latin terms are felt to be 'hard words' precisely because they are unmotivated, without roots in the language, and without any of 'those invisible threads that knit words together in the human mind'.[1]

---

[1] Jespersen, ibid.

CHAPTER 5

LOGICAL AND EMOTIVE FACTORS IN MEANING

I. Words with Blurred Edges

THROUGHOUT the centuries, writers and thinkers have been critical of the shortcomings of language. Some of their complaints were kept in general terms; others singled out the word as the chief offender. In his *Seventh Epistle*, Plato made some extravagant statements on the subject: 'No intelligent man will ever be so bold as to put in language those things which his reason has contemplated; ... if he should be betrayed into so doing, then surely not the gods but mortals have utterly blasted his wits.'[1] In one of his epigrams, Schiller expressed the problem in the form of a paradox: 'Why cannot the living spirit appear to the spirit! When the mind *speaks*, alas, it is no longer the *mind* that is speaking.'[2] Some modern writers are equally sceptical about words. Valéry has compared them to light planks thrown over an abyss: you may cross over, but you must not stop.[3] Camus has even envisaged the possibility of a meaningless language expressing the fundamental isolation of man: 'Il s'agit de savoir si même nos mots les plus justes et nos cris les plus réussis ne sont pas privés de sens, si le langage n'exprime pas, pour finir, la solitude définitive de l'homme dans un monde muet.'[4]

More specific criticisms of the word centre mostly on its lack of precision. Goethe's Faust sums up the position in a terse and forceful image when he explains why he has no name for God: 'Names are sound and smoke, befogging a heavenly glow.'[5] Voltaire is more explicit about the vagueness of words: 'Il n'est aucune langue complète, aucune qui puisse exprimer toutes nos idées et toutes nos sensations; leurs nuances

[1] Quoted by W. M. Urban, *Language and Reality*, London, 1939, p. 53.

[2] 'Warum kann der lebendige Geist dem Geist nicht erscheinen! *Spricht* die Seele, so spricht ach! schon die *Seele* nicht mehr' (*Votivtafeln*, 84: 'Die Sprache').

[3] 'J'en suis venu, hélas, à comparer ces paroles par lesquelles on traverse si lestement l'espace d'une pensée, à des planches légères jetées sur un abîme, qu souffrent le passage et point la station' (*Monsieur Teste*, 32nd ed., Paris, p. 74).

[4] 'The question is whether even our most exact words and our most successful cries are not devoid of meaning, whether, in the last analysis, language does not express the final loneliness of man in a silent world' ('Sur une philosophie de l'expression', *Poésie* 44, no. 17, pp. 15-23, quoted by J. Cruickshank, *French Studies*, x, 1956, p. 245).

[5] 'Name ist Schall und Rauch, umnebelnd Himmelsglut.'

sont trop imperceptibles et trop nombreuses ... On est obligé, par exemple, de désigner sous le nom général d'*amour* et de *haine*, mille amours et mille haines toutes différentes; il en est de même de nos douleurs et de nos plaisirs.'[1] Byron too complains about the ineffectiveness of our words:

> Oh that my words were colours! but their tints
> May serve perhaps as outlines or slight hints.
>
> *Don Juan*, Canto VI, stanza cix.

In our own day, Wittgenstein has spoken of concepts with 'blurred edges' and has compared them to indistinct photographs, adding: 'Is it even always an advantage to replace an indistinct picture by a sharp one? Isn't the indistinct one often exactly what we need?' (op. cit., p. 34). Some modern schools of poetry would wholeheartedly agree with Wittgenstein, and would value the suggestive and evocative power of words far higher than any logical precision. This was a basic principle of the Symbolist movement and was developed in Verlaine's famous poem, *Art poétique*:

> Il faut aussi que tu n'ailles point
> Choisir tes mots sans quelque méprise:
> Rien de plus cher que la chanson grise
> Où l'Indécis au Précis se joint.[2]

Mallarmé put the same point more briefly and ironically in his poem *Toute l'âme résumée*:

> Le sens trop précis rature
> Ta vague littérature.[3]

Gide notes in his autobiography[4] that in his early days, when he was under the influence of Symbolism, he was fond of words like *incertain*, *infini* and *indicible*, which give free scope to the imagination. Such words abound in German, and they endowed it, in the eyes of the young writer,

---

[1] 'There is no complete language, none which could express all our ideas and all our sensations; their shades are too imperceptible and too numerous ... One is forced, for example, to denote by the general terms *love* and *hatred* a thousand entirely different loves and hatreds; and the same happens with our pains and our pleasures' (quoted by Nyrop, *Sémantique*, p. 444).

[2] 'It is also necessary that you should not always choose the right word: there is nothing more precious than the grey song where Vagueness and Precision meet.'

[3] 'Too precise a meaning will erase your vague literature.'

[4] *Si le grain ne meurt*, 37th ed., Paris, 1928, p. 246.

with an aura of poetry. It was not till much later that he understood that his own language is dominated by a need for precision.

It would seem, then, that the vagueness of our words is a handicap in some situations and an advantage in others. If one looks more closely at this vagueness one soon discovers that the term is itself rather vague and ambiguous: the condition it refers to is not a uniform feature but has many aspects and may result from a variety of causes. Some of these are inherent in the very nature of language, whereas others come into play only in special circumstances.[1]

(1) One of the principal sources of vagueness is the *generic* character of our words. Except for proper names and a small number of common nouns referring to unique objects, words denote, not single items but classes of things or events bound together by some common element. As Bloomfield very clearly put it in a passage already quoted (p. 58), we must discriminate between 'non-distinctive features', such as the size, shape or colour of any particular apple, and the 'distinctive features' which are common to all the objects of which we use the word *apple*. In the case of more complex terms, the process of generalization works somewhat differently. Wittgenstein has examined, for example, the nature of the concept of *game*. By comparing various types of games — board-games, card-games, ball-games, Olympic games, etc. — he found a 'complicated network of similarities overlapping and criss-crossing', with common features appearing and disappearing as we consider more and more games: some are amusing, others are not; some are competitive, others solitary; some involve skill, others mere chance, and so on. Wittgenstein concludes that these similarities are rather like 'family resemblances': 'the various resemblances between members of a family: build, features, colour of eyes, gait, temperament, etc., etc., overlap and criss-cross in the same way.' In this sense one could say that the various phenomena known as *games* form a family (op. cit., pp. 31 f.).

Except in the case of rigorously defined scientific or technical terms,[2] this process of generalization will inevitably involve an element of vagueness. This has led some philosophers to describe the word as crude

---

[1] See on these matters H. Delacroix, *Le Langage et la pensée*, Paris, 1924, pp. 361 ff.; K. O. Erdmann, *Die Bedeutung des Wortes*, 4th ed., Leipzig, 1925; K. Jaberg, 'Sprache als Äusserung und Sprache als Mitteilung', *Sprachwissenschaftliche Forschungen und Erlebnisse*, Paris — Zurich — Leipzig, 1937, pp. 137-85; F. Paulhan, 'Qu'est-ce que le sens des mots?', *Journal de Psychologie*, xxv (1928), pp. 289-329; C. Spearman, *The Nature of 'Intelligence' and the Principles of Cognition*, London, 1923, ch. 11. Cf. also I. Coteanu, 'Contributions à l'établissement d'un système en sémantique' (in Rumanian, with French summary), in *Probleme de Lingvistică Generală*, vol. I, Bucharest, 1959, pp. 11-33.

[2] On the various methods of definition, see R. Robinson, *Definition*, Oxford, 1950.

and banal, robbing our experiences of their personal content and finer nuances, and interposing a screen between us and the non-linguistic world. Bergson speaks of 'le mot brutal, qui emmagasine ce qu'il y a de stable, de commun et par conséquent d'impersonnel dans les impressions de l'humanité, écrase ou tout au moins recouvre les impressions délicates et fugitives de notre conscience intellectuelle'.[1] Elsewhere the same philosopher writes: 'Le mot, qui ne note de la chose que sa fonction la plus commune et son aspect banal, s'insinue entre elle et nous ... Nous ne saisissons de nos sentiments que leur aspect impersonnel, celui que le langage a pu noter une fois pour toutes parce qu'il est à peu près le même, dans les mêmes conditions, pour tous les hommes.'[2] This is perfectly true and in some ways regrettable, but it is the price we have to pay for having a means of social communication flexible enough to cope with the infinite variety of our experiences.

The generic nature of our words has often been described as an element of 'abstractness' in language. There is some danger of ambiguity here since the usual opposition between abstract and concrete does not correspond to that between generic and particular. A word may be extremely general in meaning and yet remain on the concrete plane; thus, the terms *animal* and *plant* are the widest in range in the whole system of zoological and botanical classification, and yet they are concrete in the sense that specific animals and plants are tangible, material things as opposed to pure abstractions such as *liberty* or *immortality*. In a wider sense, however, generic terms can be regarded as 'abstract', i.e. more schematic, poorer in distinguishing marks than particular terms; as the logician would say, they have greater extension and lesser intension: they apply to a wider range of items but tell us less about them. The word *tree*, for example, is more general and therefore more 'abstract' than *beech*; in the same way, *plant* is more abstract than *tree* — in fact, it is such a wide and general concept that it did not exist in Classical Latin and only emerged in the course of the Middle Ages: the Latin word *planta* meant 'sprout, slip, cutting', not 'plant'.[3]

---

[1] 'The crude word, which stores up that which is stable, common and therefore impersonal in the experiences of mankind, and crushes or at least overlays the delicate and fleeting impressions of our intellectual consciousness' (quoted from *La Conscience* in Nyrop, *Sémantique*, p. 448).

[2] 'The word, which notes only the commonest function and the banal aspect of the object, interposes itself between the object and ourselves ... We can grasp only the impersonal aspect of our feelings, that which language has noted once and for all because it is approximately the same for all men under the same conditions' (*Le Rire*, 15th ed., Paris, 1916, pp. 156 f.; cf. Nyrop, *Sémantique*, p. 447).

[3] Quoted, from an article by Wartburg, in Baldinger, *Cahiers de l'Association Internationale des Etudes Françaises* xi, p. 259.

I

Practically all our words are generic to a greater or lesser extent, yet there is a great deal of variation between different languages: some seem to favour particular terms while others lean towards the abstract and general type. For a long time it was customary for linguists, psychologists and anthropologists to regard the languages of primitive races as rich in specific terms and poor in generic ones. This was commonly interpreted as a sign of 'pre-logical mentality', of undeveloped powers of generalization. These races, it was thought, literally could not see the wood for the trees: they were immersed in particular experiences and unable to rise above them, to analyse and classify them. The Zulus, for instance, were reported to have no word for 'cow', only specific expressions for 'red cow', 'white cow', etc.; the Tasmanian aborigines had no single term for 'tree' but possessed names for each variety of gum-tree and wattle-tree; in the Bakaïri language of Central Brazil each parrot has its special name but there is no word for 'parrot' in general.[1] There are so many reports of this kind, and they sound so plausible, that there may well be some truth in the theory. Unfortunately, however, the evidence is suspect; it is sometimes based on faulty observations by early missionaries, which were uncritically accepted by successive generations of linguists quoting one another. In this way, the myth that there is no term for 'washing' in the language of the Cherokee Indians was perpetuated until it was exploded a few years ago by an American specialist.[2] American linguists, who have done much valuable field-work on Indian tongues, are, as a matter of principle, opposed to the notion of 'primitive languages'; as a philosopher pointed out during a recent symposium on language and culture, everyone was 'quite willing to talk about the primitiveness of a culture', but most people were 'quite unwilling to talk about the primitiveness of language'.[3] Until all the evidence has been carefully sifted by modern scientific methods it is better to withhold judgment on this issue.[4]

It should also be noted that richness in particular terms is not necessarily a symptom of inability to generalize; it may be due to the influence of environment and living conditions. Thus it is not altogether surprising to learn that the Eskimos and the Lapps have a multiplicity of terms for different kinds of snow, whereas the Aztecs use the same word stem for

---

[1] Jespersen, *Language*, p. 429; cf. also Kronasser, op. cit., ch. 11.

[2] A. A. Hill, 'A Note on Primitive Languages', *International Journal of American Linguistics*, xviii (1952), pp. 172-7.

[3] H. Hoijer (ed.), *Language in Culture. Conference on the Interrelations of Language and other Aspects of Culture*, Chicago, 1954, p. 219.

[4] On the evidence of child language on this point, cf. W. Kaper, *Kindersprache mit Hilfe des Kindes*, Groningen, 1959, p. 11.

'cold', 'snow' and ice'.[1] Each environment creates its own particular needs and problems; for the inhabitants of the arctic region snow is a factor of such overriding importance that every state and aspect of it has to be carefully specified. Similarly the Paiute Indians, who live in a desert area, 'speak a language which permits the most detailed description of topographical features, a necessity in a country where complex directions may be required for the location of water holes'.[2] Language is, in the words of Sapir, 'a complex inventory of all the ideas, interests, and occupations that take up the attention of the community'.[3] This problem will come up again in the last chapter as it has a direct bearing on the structure of the vocabulary.

Even between languages based on the same civilization there can be marked differences in the use of general and specific terms. French is usually regarded as a pre-eminently 'abstract' language,[4] whereas German and even English are 'concrete' in comparison. There are various symptoms of this abstract streak in French. In some cases, a single generic term in French — supplemented, if need be, by the context — will correspond to three or four particular expressions in German. The latter language will specify, for example, the various forms of locomotion which are all lumped together in French in the generic term *aller* 'to go': *gehen* 'to go, to walk', *reiten* 'to ride on horseback', *fahren* 'to drive, to travel by train or car, etc.'. It is of course possible to indicate the means of locomotion in French by adding a supplementary phrase to the verb (*aller à pied* 'on foot', *à cheval* 'on horseback', etc.), but this will be done only when necessary, whereas the more differentiated German terms will automatically convey this extra information. Consider also the following groups of words in English, German and French:

to sit	sitzen	⎫
to stand (intransitive)	stehen	⎬ *être, se trouver* 'to be'
to lie	liegen	⎭

Here again French will add supplementary details whenever necessary: *être assis* 'to sit', *debout* 'to stand', *couché* 'to lie'; but it will not dot the i's

[1] See Segerstedt, op. cit., pp. 56 ff., and Henle, op. cit., p. 5.
[2] Ibid.
[3] Ibid. (quoted from *Selected Writings by Edward Sapir*, ed. D. Mandelbaum, Berkeley, 1949, pp. 90 f.).
[4] See esp. V. Brøndal, *Le Français, langue abstraite*, Copenhagen, 1936; Bally, *Linguistique générale et linguistique française*, pp. 346 ff.; W. J. Entwistle, 'French, Audible, Visible and "Real" ', *Studies ... Presented to John Orr*, pp. 82-9; A. Ewert, *Of the Precellence of the French Tongue* (Zaharoff Lecture), Oxford, 1958; E. Lerch, *Französische Sprache und Wesensart*, Frankfurt, 1933, pp. 178 ff.; J. Orr, 'English and French — a Comparison', *Words and Sounds in English and French*, ch. 8. Cf. also Weinreich, *Language*, xxxi (1955), p. 539.

and cross the t's where there is no need to do so. The corresponding transitive verbs show the same pattern:

> to set   setzen   ⎫
> to stand (transitive)   stellen   ⎬ mettre 'to put'
> to lay   legen   ⎭

In many other cases, the 'abstractness' of French is connected with its preference for simple, unmotivated words. We have already seen (p. 108) that German likes to join prefixes to the verb in order to specify its various aspects and nuances. These shades of meaning, which can be expressed in English by adding a preposition to the verb, are, more often than not, left unformulated in French:

> to set   setzen   ⎫ mettre
> to put on   ansetzen   ⎭
> to write   schreiben   ⎫ écrire
> to write down   niederschreiben ⎭
> to grow   wachsen   ⎫ grandir
> to grow up   heranwachsen   ⎭

The German fondness for precision can also be seen in certain compound adverbs. 'High German', write Professors Priebsch and Collinson, 'is unique in distinguishing between a relation directed towards the speaker (*herein, heraus, herunter,* etc.) and one directed away from the speaker (*hinein, hinaus, hinunter,* etc.).'[1] These details are usually neglected in French as they are in English. German will also introduce all kinds of adverbs and prepositions to specify every aspect of an action, to 'trace the whole trajectory of a movement' (Bally, op. cit., p. 350). The following sentence is typical of this superabundance of details: 'Wir segelten *vom* Ufer *her über* den Fluss *hin nach* der Insel *zu*' 'We sailed from the bank (here) over the river (there) (on) towards the island' (ibid.). French, like English, would confine itself to one preposition in each case.

Two further symptoms of 'abstractness' in French may be mentioned here. One is the frequent use of a derivative where English and German have a more explicit compound:

ashtray	Aschenbecher ('ash-cup')	cendrier ('ash' +suffix)
teapot	Teekanne (id.)	théière ('tea' +suffix)
apple-tree	Apfelbaum (id.)	pommier ('apple' +suffix)
chimney-sweep	Schornsteinfeger (id.)	ramoneur ('to sweep' +suffix)

[1] Op. cit., p. 441. For further details see M. Staub, *Richtungsbegriff, Richtungsausdruck; Versuch zu einem Vergleich von deutscher und französischer Ausdrucksweise,* Berne, 1949.

Another factor making for 'abstractness' in French is the popularity of 'nominal syntax':[1] the use of an abstract noun where English, for instance, would prefer a verb. Professor Orr has collected some amusing examples from posters and placards (*Words and Sounds*, pp. 59 ff.):

Stick no bills	*Défense d'afficher* (literally: 'Prohibition to stick (bills)')
No smoking allowed	*Défense de fumer* (literally: 'Prohibition to smoke')
Please do not touch	*Prière de ne pas toucher* (literally: 'Request not to touch')

The vogue of the so-called 'style substantif' in modern French prose is symptomatic of the same tendency. Thus the sentence: 'Ils cédèrent parce qu'on leur promit formellement qu'ils ne seraient pas punis' ('They gave in because they were formally promised that they would not be punished') is considered less elegant than the more concise and abstract 'Ils cédèrent à une *promesse* formelle d'*impunité*' ('They yielded to a formal *promise* of *impunity*'). In recent years, some misgivings have been expressed about the spread of these nominal constructions, but the tendency itself is deeply rooted in the structure of the language.

All these features, to which others could be added,[2] make Modern French into a highly abstract, intellectual, discreet and allusive instrument. They also mean that the individual French word is in many cases more schematic, less rich in expressive details than its German counterpart. English is in this respect much closer to German than to French, though it does not go so far as the former in the accumulation of details. The abstract and generic character of the French vocabulary increases the importance of context in that language: a vague, undifferentiated word like *aller*, *mettre* or *être* obviously has less autonomy and is more dependent on the context than a more particularized term (see above, p. 52). The same lack of autonomy is, as we have seen, characteristic of the French word as a phonetic unit (pp. 40 f.). Professor Orr has neatly summed up this fundamental trait of French when he wrote:

> In French, the word is more submerged in the sentence and its component sounds are functionally less apparent than in English. The detail is subservient to the ensemble as in a classical building. This supremacy of the general over the particular, this more complete dominance of the physical by the intellectual is just as evident in word-formation and phraseology (op. cit., p. 59).

[1] See esp. A Lombard, *Les Constructions nominales dans le français moderne*, Stockholm — Uppsala, 1930; cf. also my *Style in the French Novel*, ch. 3.
[2] Cf. ch. 5 of my *Précis de sémantique française*.

(2) Our words are never completely homogeneous: even the simplest and the most monolithic have a number of different facets depending on the context and situation in which they are used, and also on the personality of the speaker using them. This *multiplicity of aspects* is another important source of vagueness. As we have already seen (p. 52), even proper names, the most concrete of all words, are subject to such 'shifts in application': only the context will specify which aspect of a person, which phase in his development, which side of his activities we have in mind. If we take an ordinary common noun with a concrete meaning, such as *book*, its significance will vary according to its users: it will mean rather different things to an author, a publisher, a printer, a bookseller, a book-collector, a librarian, a specialist reader, a non-specialist reader, a bibliographer and others. With abstract words, such differences in application are even more marked. Take, for instance, the following three examples of the adjective *mortal* in *Paradise Lost*:

> chase
> Anguish and doubt and fear and sorrow and pain
> From *mortal* and immortal minds.
>
> > Book I, ll. 557-9.
>
> the fruit
> Of that forbidden tree whose *mortal* taste
> Brought death into the World.
>
> > Book I, ll. 1-3.
>
> to redeem
> Man's *mortal* crime.
>
> > Book III, ll. 214-15.

Clearly, the adjective has three different shades of meaning in the three passages: in the first one it means 'subject to death, destined to die', in the second 'causing death', and in the third 'deadly', as opposed to 'venial', sin. In fact, Milton obtains a very striking effect by playing on the diversity of these overlapping meanings. A fuller version of the last extract reads:

> Which of ye will be *mortal*, to redeem
> Man's *mortal* crime, and just, the unjust to save?

In some words, the process of diversification can go to remarkable lengths without destroying the fundamental unity of their meaning. The term *style* is an example in point. It comes from the Latin *stilus*, the name of the writing-rod, and was originally applicable to writing alone, but in the course of the centuries it has vastly extended its range. In the words of Sir Walter Raleigh:

> ... the fact that we use the word *style* in speaking of architecture and sculpture, painting and music, dancing, play-acting, and cricket, that we can apply it to the careful achievements of the housebreaker and the poisoner and to the spontaneous animal movements of the limbs of man or beast, is the noblest of unconscious tributes to the faculty of letters.[1]

As can be seen from these examples, such shifts in application can easily lead to multiple meaning; we shall encounter them again in the chapter on ambiguity.

(3) A further factor making for vagueness is the *lack of clear-cut boundaries* in the non-linguistic world. Here again it is necessary to distinguish between concrete and abstract experiences. Even in our physical environment we are often faced with phenomena which merge into one another and which we have to divide up, as best we can, into discrete units. The spectrum of colours is, for example, a continuous band; it is we who introduce into it a certain number of more or less arbitrary distinctions which may vary from one language to another, and sometimes even from one period to another within the same idiom. The consequences of this situation will be considered in the last chapter of this book. Another concrete sphere where sharp lines of demarcation are often lacking is the human body. This explains certain shifts in meaning where the name of one part of the body has come to denote a neighbouring region.[2] Thus, the Latin word for 'hip', *coxa*, has given *cuisse* in French, which means 'thigh', not 'hip'. As will be seen later, this was part of a whole series of changes, of a kind of semantic chain-reaction; nevertheless it could not have occurred if there were a definite boundary between the two areas in our anatomy. There have been similar shifts of meaning between various parts of the facial region. Most of the Romance words for 'mouth' which have replaced the Latin *os, oris*: French *bouche*, Italian *bocca*, Spanish *boca*, derive from Latin *bucca* 'puffed up cheek'; the Rumanian *bucă* still means 'cheek' (Bloch-Wartburg). A more intricate interchange can be seen in the history of English *chin* and cognate terms. The German *Kinn* and the Dutch *kin* have the same meaning as the English word, but Swedish *kind* means 'cheek' and

---

[1] *Style*, 2nd ed., 1897, pp. 1-2.
[2] See already A. Zauner, 'Die romanischen Namen der Körperteile', *Romanische Forschungen*, xiv (1895), pp. 339-530.

so does the Latin *gena* from the same family, whereas another related form, Sanskrit *hanuh*, signifies 'jaw', and the Greek γένυς can mean either 'jaw' or 'cheek'.[1]

When we turn to abstract phenomena, this lack of boundaries is even more conspicuous since the distinctions are largely man-made: they have no real existence without the linguistic forms in which they are clothed. Delimiting such concepts is often a difficult and delicate operation. The classic example is of course the frontier between *talent* and *genius*. Owen Meredith once wrote: *'Genius does what it must, and Talent does what it can', but whether one accepts this formula or any other, there will always be border-line cases lying astride the boundary wherever one may trace it.[2]

For the specialist it is of the utmost importance to define his terms clearly and to distinguish them sharply from one another. Hence the endless and often acrimonious discussions in philosophical works, in the law courts and at diplomatic conferences, on the precise definition and delimitation of abstract words. A lawyer will carefully avoid any confusion between *felony* and *misdemeanour*, a theologian between *venial* and *deadly* (*mortal*) sins, a psychiatrist between *neurosis* and *psychosis*, a linguist between *phonemes* and *allophones*. The abstract terms of ordinary language are, however, far less precise, and it is left to the dictionary to introduce some semblance of order into their overlapping uses. It occasionally happens that a particularly language-conscious period makes a systematic effort to redefine its abstract vocabulary. This was done in France on a large scale during the seventeenth century. The distinctions then made will often strike the modern reader as strained, over-subtle, or outright pedantic; they are, however, of outstanding interest when they refer to key-terms of the period, to the words which sum up its ideals and aspirations, its hatreds and its fears. Here, for example, is Vaugelas's definition — one might almost say 'chemical analysis' — of the crucial term *galant*: 'un composé où il entroit du je ne sçay quoy ou de la bonne grâce, de l'air de la Cour, de l'esprit, du jugement, de la civilité, de la courtoisie et de la gayeté, le tout sans contrainte, sans affectation, et sans vice'.[3] Half a century later La Bruyère tried, in rather a different mood,

---

[1] Cf. Bloomfield, *Language*, pp. 425 ff.

[2] See on this problem L. P. Smith, 'Four Words: Romantic, Original, Creative, Genius', *Society for Pure English Tracts*, xvii (1924), reprinted in his book *Words and Idioms*; cf. also P. Zumthor in *Zeitschrift für Romanische Philologie*, lxvi (1950), pp. 170-201, and G. Matoré-A.-J. Greimas in *Le Français Moderne*, xxv (1957), pp. 256-72.

[3] 'A compound into which entered an indefinable quality or gracefulness, a courtly air, wit, judgment, civility, courtesy and gaiety, all this without constraint, affectation or vice' (quoted after F. Brunot, *Histoire de la langue française*, vol. iii, pt. 1, pp. 238 f.).

to distinguish between three other key-terms of the period: an able man ('habile homme'), a gentleman ('honnête homme'), and a good man ('homme de bien'). His analysis is expressed in quasi-mathematical terms. The gentleman, he says, stands somewhere between the other two types, but is nearer to the able man than to the good man; indeed, he adds with a touch of cynicism, the distance between a gentleman and an able man is shrinking every day and is about to vanish altogether. He then goes on to examine, in tersely ironical terms, the distinctive features of the three human types, and points out that while every good man is by definition a gentleman, the reverse is obviously not true.[1] These exercises in definition and analysis have played a significant part in the tradition of linguistic discipline which is still one of the pillars of the French educational system.

(4) Yet another source of vagueness in words is *lack of familiarity* with the things they stand for. This is of course a highly variable factor, dependent on the general knowledge and the special interests of each individual. Many townspeople will have extremely hazy notions about the meaning of animal and plant names or agricultural terms which will be perfectly clear to any gardener or farmer. How many readers, for example, will be able to visualize some of the plants mentioned by Ophelia: 'There's *fennel* for you, and *columbines*. There's *rue* for you; and here's some for me' (Act IV, scene 5)? On quite a different plane, how many people would be able to give a reasonably clear account of what is meant by *existentialism, logical positivism, surrealism, relativity, enzyme, electron,* or *cybernetics*? Yet these words, and many others like them, are key-terms in twentieth-century civilization, and some at least are apt to be used, in non-technical writings and even in the press or over the wireless, without any explanation.

Quite apart from these specialized terms, there are countless others which English has taken over from foreign languages, living or dead, and whose meaning is obscure for many speakers. The language bar, which was discussed in the preceding chapter, is a potent factor making for vagueness in English. The malapropisms quoted above (p. 114) are but extreme symptoms of this deep-seated linguistic insecurity. Jespersen tells the amusing but revealing story of a ploughman who, when asked by a parson what the word *felicity* meant for him, replied: 'Summut in the inside of a pig, but I can't say altogether what' (*Growth and Structure*, p. 91). This happened nearly a century ago, and since then

[1] 'Des Jugements', in *Caractères*, Nelson ed., p. 420. On these and allied concepts see recently M. Wandruszka, *Der Geist der französischen Sprache*, pp. 94 f.

the situation has improved beyond recognition; nevertheless, this form of vagueness continues to represent a serious social and educational problem.

II. EMOTIVE OVERTONES

It has been realized for a long time, and has been strongly re-emphasized in recent years, that language is not merely a vehicle of communication: it is also a means of expressing emotions and arousing them in others. Indeed it could be argued that both elements, the communicative as well as the emotive, must be present in any utterance even though one of them may completely overshadow the other. As a French psychologist put it, 'all language has some emotive value: if what I say were indifferent to me I would not say it. At the same time, all language aims at communicating something. If one had absolutely nothing to say one would say nothing'.[1]

These considerations have led some scholars to distinguish between two uses of language, one symbolic or referential, the other emotive. This doctrine, which has been called the theory of the Great Divide, has been stated in simple terms by Ogden and Richards: 'The symbolic use of words is *statement*; the recording, the support, the organization and the communication of references. The emotive use of words is a more simple matter, it is the use of words to express or excite feelings and attitudes.'[2] It will be noted that the duality is more apparent than real since emotive language combines a number of diverse functions: to express feelings is not the same thing as to excite them, and there is also a vast difference between feelings and attitudes. Hence Dr. Richards's finer mesh of distinctions, in *Practical Criticism* and elsewhere, between four aspects of meaning: sense, tone, feeling and intention.

---

[1] H. Delacroix, op. cit., pp. 41 f.

[2] Op. cit., p. 149; cf. also I. A. Richards, *Principles of Literary Criticism*, London, 1938 ed., ch. 34. Among the numerous works dealing with emotive language and allied problems, the following may be mentioned: M. Black, E. L. Stevenson, I. A. Richards, 'Symposium on Emotive Meaning', *The Philosophical Review*, lvii (1948), pp. 111-57; B. Bourdon, *L'Expression des émotions et des tendances dans le langage*, Paris, 1892; W. Empson, *The Structure of Complex Words*, London, 1951; E. Gamillscheg, 'Zur Einwirkung des Affekts auf den Sprachbau', *Zeitschrift für französische Sprache und Literatur*, Suppl., 1937; L. Havas, 'Words with Emotive Connotations in Bilingual Dictionaries', *Acta Linguistica Academiae Scientiarum Hungaricae*, vi (1957), pp. 449-68; C. S. Lewis, *Studies in Words*, Cambridge, 1960, ch. 9; F. Paulhan, 'La double fonction du langage', *Revue Philosophique*, civ (1927), pp. 22-73; M. Piron, 'Caractérisation affective et création lexicale. Le cas du wallon *ramponô*', *Romanica Gandensia*, i (1953), pp. 119-70; A. Sieberer, 'Vom Gefühlswert der Wörter', *Österreichische Akademie der Wissenschaften*, *Phil.-Hist. Kl.*, *Anzeiger*, lxxxiv (1947), pp. 35-52. A useful survey of current ideas on the subject will be found in chs. 5-6 of Henle, op. cit. (by W. K. Frankena). Emotive meaning is one of the central problems of stylistics, and many aspects of it are discussed in the works of Ch. Bally, M. Cressot and J. Marouzeau on that subject.

Other scholars have tried to refine the original scheme in various ways. An early semanticist, K. O. Erdmann, recognized three factors: 'essential or central meaning', 'applied or contextual meaning', and 'feeling-tone'.[1] In recent years, a number of more complex schemes have been put forward; one of the latest would distinguish between no less than nine different components of meaning.[2] Rather than going into the intricacies of these theories, some of which transcend the limits of semantics proper, I shall consider three specific problems, in the light of concrete examples: the sources of emotive overtones, the linguistic devices which help to reinforce them, and the various ways in which they may be weakened or lost.

1. Sources of Emotive Overtones

(1) *Phonetic factors.* — The phonetic structure of a word may give rise to emotive effects in two different ways. The first of these is onomatopoeia. Where there is an intrinsic harmony between sound and sense, this may, in suitable contexts, come to the fore and contribute to the expressiveness and the suggestive power of the word. This process has been examined in the last chapter.

Sounds may also produce purely aesthetic effects, pleasant or unpleasant, irrespective of the meaning they express. This is often an entirely subjective factor; it is also rather rare since the meaning and associations of the word will almost inevitably colour the impression made by the sounds. It can best be seen in some marginal elements of language — place-names, foreign words, neologisms and the like — where there is less interference by semantic factors. Some French poets have extolled the sheer phonetic beauty of certain place-names:[3]

> S'il est un nom bien doux, fait pour la poésie,
> Oh, dites, n'est-ce pas le nom de la *Voulzie*?
>
> (Hégésippe Moreau)[4]

> *Créqui, Fronsac*, beaux noms chatoyants de satin.
>
> (Albert Samain)[5]

Even here, external associations may creep in; when, for example,

---

[1] Op cit. The English terms are those suggested by Professor Firth, in 'The Technique of Semantics', loc. cit.
[2] W. K. Frankena, loc. cit.
[3] See J. Marouzeau, *Précis de stylistique française*, 3rd ed., Paris, 1950, pp. 126 ff., from where the next three examples are taken.
[4] 'If there ever was a soft name, made for poetry, tell me, is it not the name of the *Voulzie*?'
[5] '*Créqui, Fronsac*, beautiful names chatoyant like satin.'

Théophile Gautier ridiculed the name of a village in the rugged Basque country:

> *Urrugne,*
> Nom rauque dont le son à la rime répugne,[1]

his reactions were probably influenced by the situation of the place. Similar judgments are sometimes passed on neologisms and foreign terms. Vaugelas, for example, described the new word *exactitude* as a monster against which everybody protested at first, though in the end they became used to it.[2] English words adopted into French have been subjected to a great deal of adverse criticism because of their alleged harshness: *keepsake,* for instance, which was very fashionable in the early nineteenth century, was denounced in a magazine article as a 'hard word whose perilous pronunciation will prevent it from becoming popular'.[3] The Italian poet Alfieri went even further: he wrote an epigram on the sonorous quality of the Italian word *capitano,* which was deformed and 'nasalized' in French *capitaine,* and reduced to a mere *captain* in harsh English throats.[4]

Occasionally, even ordinary terms are judged by purely aesthetic criteria, though once again considerations of meaning will tend to influence the result. In *De Vulgari Eloquentia,* Dante worked out an elaborate classification of words, based on euphony and other factors. Professor Ewert has explained in a recent article some of the obscure textile metaphors in which his categories are expressed.[5] Words like *amore* or *donna* appear to him as *pexa,* like 'fine velvet with its full but evenly and smoothly combed out pile', whereas *terra* is *hirsutum,* having 'the more abundant and less smoothly finished nap of a high-grade wool', and *corpo* is *reburrum,* 'suggesting the somewhat excessive shagginess of fustian'.

(2) *Context.* — As has already been mentioned (p. 52), any word, even the most ordinary and prosaic, may, in certain contexts, be surrounded by an emotive aura. A concrete noun like *wall,* for example, will be used in countless situations in a perfectly neutral and matter-of-fact way; yet it is capable of acquiring powerful overtones. A wall can even be apostrophized:

---

[1] *'Urrugne,* a harsh name whose sound is unfit for rhyme.'
[2] See F. Brunot, *Histoire de la langue française,* vol. iii, pt. 1, p. 211.
[3] See A. Weil, *Le Français Moderne,* xiii (1945), p. 133.
[4] Quoted by A. Graf, *L'Anglomania e l'influsso inglese nel secolo XVIII,* Turin, 1911, p. 229.
[5] A. Ewert, 'Dante's Theory of Diction', *MHRA, Annual Bulletin of the Modern Humanities Research Association,* no. 31 (1959), pp. 15-30: pp. 24 f.

PYRAMUS: Thou *wall*, O *wall*, O sweet and lovely *wall*,
Show me thy chink, to blink through with mine eyne.
Thanks, courteous *wall*. Jove shield thee well for this ...
O wicked *wall*, through whom I see no bliss;
Curs'd be thy stones for thus deceiving me!
THESEUS: The *wall*, methinks, being sensible, should curse again.
A Midsummer Night's Dream, Act V, scene 1.

For the prisoner or the invalid hemmed in by walls, these will be filled with intense emotional significance:

I saw the dungeon *walls* and floor
Close slowly round me as before ...
These heavy *walls* to me had grown
A hermitage — and all my own.
Byron, *The Prisoner of Chillon*, X and XIV.

Similarly, in Camus's novel *La Peste*, people dying in Oran are tersely described as 'trapped behind hundreds of *walls* crackling with heat'.[1] In this way, walls may become a symbol of imprisonment and claustrophobia, physical as well as moral. It is significant that one of Sartre's short stories, and indeed the whole volume in which it appears, should be entitled *Le Mur*.

Even prison walls will have a different meaning for the captive confined within them and for the law-abiding citizen, let alone the custodian of the law. In one of Anatole France's novels there is an interesting passage on what a wall means to the mind of a judge: 'Son âme de juge jubilait à la vue d'un *mur*, de la chose sourde, muette et sombre qui rappelait à sa pensée ravie les idées de prison, de cachot, de peines subies, de vindicte sociale, de code, de loi, de justice, de morale, un *mur*.'[2]

(3) *Slogans*. — It often happens that political and other slogans become so heavily charged with emotion that the latter will completely supersede their objective sense. Professor C. S. Lewis has recently coined the expression 'verbicide' to describe these and similar perversions of meaning.[3] The history of words like *democracy* is a warning against the

---

[1] 'Qu'on pense alors à celui qui va mourir, pris au piège derrière des centaines de *murs* crépitants de chaleur' (Paris, 1958 ed., p. 15). On the symbolism of walls see my book, *The Image in the Modern French Novel*, Cambridge, 1960, pp. 18 f., 54 f., 264 ff.

[2] 'His mind, the mind of a judge, was jubilant at the sight of a *wall*, that deaf, dumb and dark thing which called up to his delighted imagination ideas of a prison, of a cell, of punishment, social retribution, a penal code, law, justice, morality — a *wall*' (from *L'Anneau d'améthyste*, quoted by Nyrop, *Sémantique*, p. 24).

[3] Op. cit., pp. 7 f., 131 f., 221 ff.

lengths to which the process can go.[1] A French critic has given a penetrating analysis of this tendency:

At certain moments, in the life of a nation or of mankind at large, there are words in which is concentrated a force of feeling and of will-power which makes them singularly beneficial or particularly formidable. A mere mention of them will unleash the anger or enthusiasm of crowds, of parties, of immense groups of people. *Liberty, equality, order, fatherland, justice* have shown in turn their temporary power ... In a word, in a phrase, in certain associations of sounds are vested possibilities of suggestion, means of acting almost automatically on the minds of individuals who form a more or less extensive group.[2]

(4) *Emotive derivation.* — There are certain suffixes — diminutive, augmentative, pejorative and others — which add an emotive note or a value-judgment to the meaning of the stem. In English and French, where derivatives are not formed as freely as, say, in German or in Italian (see ch. 4), the emotive use of suffixes is not very common, but examples are not lacking: *poet — poetaster; prince — princelet, princeling, princekin;* French *roi* 'king' — *roitelet* 'kinglet, petty king'; *papier* 'paper' — *paperasse* 'red tape'; *traîner* 'drag' — *traînasser* 'draw out, spin out'. Other languages are richer in such resources; in Italian, for example, a whole series of emotive derivatives can be formed from the word *donna* 'woman': diminutives (*donnina, donnetta, donnettina*), pejoratives (*donnaccia, donnuccia, donnicciuola*), and others. The overtones conveyed by these suffixes would have to be expressed in English by one or more separate words: a *donnetta* is a '*little* woman', a *donnettina* a '*graceful little* woman', a *donnuccia* a '*sickly little* woman', etc.[3]

(5) Some words contain an element of *evaluation* superimposed on the main meaning. A *hovel* is a '*rude* or *miserable* dwelling-place'; *to scrawl* is defined by the dictionary as 'to write or draw in a *sprawling, untidy* manner'; *scribble* combines the idea of writing with that of haste and carelessness. The translator will be careful to preserve such nuances even where there is no exact equivalent in English; thus the French *grabat*, well known to readers of Balzac's *Le Père Goriot*, will have to be rendered by '*mean* bed' or some similar phrase.

---

[1] See esp. T. D. Weldon, *The Vocabulary of Politics*, Penguin Books, London, 1955, ch. 4.
[2] Paulhan, *Revue Philosophique*, civ, p. 44.
[3] Cf. Wartburg, *La Posizione della lingua italiana*, pp. 89 f.; see also above, p. 108.

(6) There are words whose main function is to express evaluation or emotive comment. Such are, for instance, adjectives like *good, brave, funny, stupid, horrible* and their opposites. In such words, the emotive element is more than an overtone: it is an integral part of their central meaning.

(7) *'Evocative values'*. — Many of our words owe their expressiveness and their emotive effect to the associations which they call forth. Terms peculiar to a given milieu or level of style will evoke their usual environment even when they occur in totally different contexts. Archaisms, foreign words, technical and dialect terms, vulgarisms and slang, will transport the reader into the stylistic climate to which they normally belong. As Proust once said, 'chaque mot a sur notre imagination une puissance d'évocation aussi grande que sa puissance de stricte signification'.[1] These values, which are known since Bally as 'evocative effects',[2] embrace the whole range of the language system; they involve pronunciation and grammar as well as vocabulary.

A glance at one of these resources, the stylistic use of *foreign words*, will give some idea of how the mechanism works. It is essential to distinguish between primary and secondary evocative effects. The primary stylistic function of foreign terms is to produce local colour:[3] to portray an alien speaker or environment by using words peculiar to them. This is a simple device, but it has to be handled with discretion. Few modern playwrights would dare to use a foreign language on such a lavish scale as Shakespeare did with French in *King Henry the Fifth*, except possibly for comic purposes, as for instance in Tristan Bernard's vaudeville, *L'anglais tel qu'on le parle*, where the main source of comedy is the broken English of Frenchmen and the broken French of Englishmen. In most cases, foreign words and tags will be used more sparingly, which does not, however, lessen their evocative force; take for example this caricature of an Englishman in the stage directions of Vigny's play *Chatterton*: 'John Bell, gonflé d'*ale*, de *porter* et de *roast beef.*'[4]

Poetry is of course less hospitable than prose to foreign words, but even here there are occasionally some light and suggestive touches of local colour:

[1] 'Every word has on our imagination an evocatory power as great as its power of meaning in the strict sense' (quoted by Marouzeau, *Précis de stylistique française*, p. 100).

[2] Ch. Bally, *Traité de stylistique française*, 2 vols., 3rd ed., Geneva — Paris, 1951: vol. I, pp. 203-49. A survey of these effects will be found in my *Précis de sémantique française*, pp. 157-72.

[3] On local colour see ch. 1 of my *Style in the French Novel*; on English words in French, F. Mackenzie, *Les Relations de l'Angleterre et de la France d'après le vocabulaire*, vol. I, Paris, 1939-46; cf. also my articles in *Publications of the Modern Language Association of America*, 1947, *Mélanges Albert Dauzat*, Paris, 1951, and *Vie et Langage*, 1957.

[4] 'Puffed up with *ale, porter* and *roast beef.*'

Même alors que l'aurore allume
Les *cottages* jaunes et noirs.
Verlaine, *Aquarelles: Streets.*[1]

A foreign word may even be used because of its general aura of exotic-
ism, without any precise local colour. The English *steamer* — perhaps
because it rhymes with French *mer* — fits admirably into the mood of
Mallarmé's poem *Brise marine*:

Je partirai! *Steamer* balançant ta mâture,
Lève l'ancre pour une exotique nature![2]

When a foreign word is employed, not because there is any real need
for it, but because of its snob value, the air of distinction it confers on the
speaker, we have what may be called 'secondary evocative effects'. The
affectations of Gallomaniacs in England and Anglomaniacs in France
have been ridiculed by many writers. The technique is applied with
some gusto in Sir George Etherege's *The Man of Mode* (1676):

Sir Fopling Flutter: 'In Paris, the *mode* is to flatter the *prude*,
laugh at the *faux-prude*, make serious love to the *demi-prude*, and only
rally with the *coquette*.'[3]

In France, where Anglomania did not start till much later, the speech
of Anglicized 'dandies' was strikingly parodied by Musset, both in verse
and in prose. 'Il te sied bien de faire le *fashionable* (Que le diable soit
des mots anglais!)', says an uncle to his nephew in one of Musset's
plays.[4] Such satire is even more effective in poetry where the English
words fit strangely into the French alexandrine and will sometimes result
in a halting metre:

Dans le *bol* où le *punch* rit sur son trépied d'or,
Le *grog* est *fashionable*.
Les secrètes pensées de Rafael.[5]

And how do you do, mon bon père, aujourd'hui?
Mardoche.[6]

---

[1] 'Even when dawn lights up the yellow and black *cottages*.'
[2] 'I shall leave! *Steamer* trimming your masts, weigh anchor for an exotic land.' Cf. Y. Le
Hir, *Commentaires stylistiques de textes français modernes*, Paris, 1959, p. 91.
[3] Act IV, scene 1, quoted by F. Mossé, *Esquisse d'une histoire de la langue anglaise*, Lyons,
1947, p. 174, n. 1.
[4] 'It becomes you to act the *fashionable* (To hell with English words!)' (*Il ne faut jurer
de rien*, scene 1).
[5] 'In the *bowl* where *punch* is smiling on its golden tripod, *grog* is *fashionable*.'
[6] '*And how do you do*, good father, today?'

Even a single English word may produce an explosive effect if it suddenly appears in an unexpected context. In a modern play, a husband comments ironically on the fashionable parties given by his wife: 'Ce devait être charmant! J'aurais bien voulu arriver un peu plus tôt. Enfin, c'est manqué! Ah! Mais non! *Miousic!* Venez donc, cher ami!'[1]

If the speaker had used the French word *musique* instead of its mock English counterpart, the ironical effect would have been almost completely lost.

The emotive overtones of foreign words are not always favourable; in many cases they are distorted by xenophobia or chauvinistic bias, and this may result in a permanent depreciation of meaning. Thus, the ordinary Spanish verb for 'to speak', *hablar*, has been taken over into French as *hâbler* 'to boast, to brag, to talk big', whereas the Spaniards have adopted the French *parler* 'to speak' in the form of *parlar* and given it the meaning 'to chatter' (Bloch-Wartburg).

2. *Emotive Devices*

In addition to the factors just discussed, there exist in every language specific devices which help to reinforce the emotive significance of words. Some of these devices are universal; others are peculiar to a given language. All sectors of the linguistic system may be involved in the process, so that the devices fall into three groups: phonetic, lexical and syntactical.

(1) *Phonetic devices.* — Under the stress of emotion, the shape of our words may be altered in different ways. In the exclamation: 'Well, I never!', the adverb *never* is pronounced with heavy emphasis and its initial consonant tends to be lengthened. In some languages, these 'phonostylistic' devices, as they have been called,[2] are systematically organized. As has already been mentioned (p. 25), French possesses a special emotive accent which falls on the first syllable of words beginning with a consonant and on the second syllable of those beginning with a vowel: *'misérable! — é'pouvantable!* This accent may be accompanied by other phonetic features: *é'pouvantable!* will be pronounced with a long |p| and preceded by a glottal stop. Apart from this emotive stress, French also has a so-called emphatic accent (accent d'insistance) which always falls on the first syllable of words and helps to throw them into relief or to contrast them with one another: 'Ce n'est pas *'subjectif*, c'est *'objectif.'*

---

[1] 'It must have been charming. I should really have liked to arrive a little earlier. Well, it is too late. Oh, no! *Miousic!* Come on, my dear fellow!' (from a play by Nozière and Savoir, quoted by M. Kuttner, 'Anglomanie im heutigen Französischen', *Zeitschrift für französische Sprache und Literatur*, lxviii (1926), pp. 446-65).

[2] See N. S. Trubetzkoy, op. cit., pp. 16-29.

K

Of the two, the second type is the more discreet; it also differs in quality
from the other since it is a purely musical pitch-accent whereas emotive
stress takes the form of a strong expiratory beat.[1]

(2) *Lexical devices.* — The most potent lexical device available for
emotive and expressive purposes is figurative language. This can work
either explicitly, by *comparison*, or implicitly, by *metaphor*. Instead of
merely stating that a person is very keen or that a meeting is very dull,
we can put our meaning more incisively by saying: 'he is as keen as
mustard', 'it is as dull as ditch-water'. Although these clichés have lost
much of their pristine force, they are still far more energetic than a simple
statement. Metaphor works in the same way but is expressed in a more
condensed form: rather than saying that someone is as silly as a goose, as
stupid as an ass, as timid as a mouse, or as clumsy as a bull in a china
shop, we can suppress the comparison and identify him or her with these
animals: 'she is a little goose', 'he is a perfect ass', etc. On an infinitely
higher and more original level, the creative writer will proceed in a
similar way. He may prefer the explicit type and may even delight in the
leisurely unfolding of an epic simile; or he may aim at surprise effects
and shock tactics by the bald juxtaposition of totally different experiences.
Mallarmé once declared: 'J'ai rayé le mot *comme* du dictionnaire',[2] and
many modern writers would agree with him. Yet Shakespeare could
achieve powerful effects by explicit comparisons:

> whose phrase of sorrow
> Conjures the wand'ring stars, and makes them stand
> *Like* wonder-wounded hearers.
>
> > *Hamlet,* Act V, scene 1.

> The quality of mercy is not strain'd;
> It droppeth *as* the gentle rain from heaven
> Upon the place beneath.
>
> > *The Merchant of Venice,* Act IV, scene 1.

The nature of imagery and its role in style will be considered in
chapter 8; here it is sufficient to note that simile and metaphor are among
the most effective devices available for the expression of emotive meaning.

A kindred figure of speech, whose chief function is to give vent to
strong feelings, is exaggeration or '*hyperbole*'. Echoing Virgil's phrase

---

[1] See J. Marouzeau, *Le Français Moderne,* ii (1934), pp. 123 ff., and xvi (1948), pp. 8 ff.
Cf. also Wartburg, *Évolution et structure,* pp. 251 ff.

[2] 'I have struck out the word *like* from the dictionary' (quoted by G. Davies, *French
Studies,* ix, p. 326).

about piling Ossa on Pelion, Hamlet vies with Laertes in finding extravagant expressions for his grief over Ophelia's death:

> let them throw
> Millions of acres on us, till our ground,
> Singeing his pate against the burning zone,
> Make Ossa like a wart!

Act V, scene 1.

In a less extreme form, the same tendency to overstatement is responsible for countless hyperbolical expressions in everyday life: *awful, dreadful, frightful, terrific, tremendous, abysmal, bottomless, deadly*, and many more. The meaning of some of these words has been completely cancelled out by their emotional tone: to speak of a '*terrific* success', a '*tremendous* welcome', or of something '*awfully* funny', is really a contradiction in terms.

(3) *Syntactical devices.* — One of the most valuable emotive devices in syntax is *word-order*. Stendhal once said that there is a certain 'physiognomy' in the position of words, which no translation can render.[1] This is particularly true of synthetic, highly inflected languages such as Latin, where words can be freely moved about for purposes of emphasis and emotive effect. But even analytical languages like English and French have retained some mobility which the experienced writer can put to good use.[2] A well-known example is the place of the adjective in French.[3] Many French adjectives may either precede or follow the noun, according to whether they are used emotively or objectively. 'Une découverte *importante*' merely states that the discovery was of some importance; 'une *importante* découverte' also implies some degree of emotional participation by the speaker. In this way some adjectives have acquired two distinct values according to their position. 'Un quartier *misérable*' means a 'poverty-stricken' quarter, whereas 'un *misérable* franc' is a 'paltry' franc. Similarly *pauvre* in 'un homme *pauvre*' 'a poor man', as opposed to 'le *pauvre* homme!' 'poor fellow!' — a phrase made famous by Molière's *Tartuffe*. By placing before the noun a factual or classifying adjective which would normally come after it, a skilful writer can achieve subtly ironical effects: 'ils abdiqueront peut-être jusqu'à leur *républicaine* prétention à la souveraineté'.[4] The emotive value of the adjective in

---

[1] *La Chartreuse de Parme*, Pléiade ed., p. 293.
[2] See ch. 4 of my *Style in the French Novel*.
[3] See recently K. Wydler, *Zur Stellung des attributiven Adjektivs vom Latein bis zum Neufranzösischen*, Berne, 1956.
[4] 'They will perhaps renounce even their very republican claim to sovereignty' (Roger Martin du Gard, *Les Thibault*, pt. VIII, p. 195).

anteposition can be reinforced by repeating it:

> Le ciel faisait sans bruit avec la neige épaisse
> Pour cette *immense* armée un *immense* linceul.
>
> Victor Hugo, *L'Expiation*,[1]

or by using the same adjective in two opposite places within the same sentence — a form of inversion known as *chiasmus*, from the Greek letter *khi* which has the form of an X: 'Non, pas un *admirable* ambassadeur, mais un ambassadeur *admirable*.'[2] In English, where the adjective has a fixed position, these delicate shifts of emphasis will have to be conveyed by other means.

3. *Loss of Emotive Meaning*

Some emotive overtones are ephemeral, contextual or purely subjective; others are fairly constant in a given period but may weaken, or disappear altogether, in the course of time. Among the factors which may reduce or destroy them, the following four seem to be particularly significant:

(1) Slogans and key-words which held the stage at one time in politics, art, philosophy and other spheres may, with changed circumstances, lose their relevance and cease to arouse strong feelings. *Home Rule, suffragette, prohibitionism, dreyfusard*, all of them burning issues not so very long ago, have become mere historical terms; even *New Deal, appeasement, quisling* and *collaborator* have little emotional impact on the young generation.

(2) Loss of motivation — a process discussed in the previous chapter — may also deprive words of their emotive colouring. A term which is no longer felt to be onomatopoeic will lose the expressiveness it had derived from the harmony between sound and sense. Diminutives will no longer carry any special connotations once they become unanalysable: Vulgar Latin **avicellus* 'little bird' was a transparent derivative of *avis* 'bird', but no diminutive nuance is left in its Romance descendants, French *oiseau* and Italian *uccello*, which are the ordinary words for 'bird' in those languages. Loss of semantic motivation has similar consequences. French *lézarde* 'split, crack' owes its name to a picturesque metaphor based on the similarity between a crack and a lizard, *lézard*; subsequently, the connexion was forgotten and *lézarde* has become inexpressive (Bloch-Wartburg).

(3) A third factor which may cancel out emotive meaning is what one

---

[1] 'The sky made noiselessly, with the thick snow, a vast shroud for this vast army.'
[2] 'No, not an admirable ambassador but an ambassador worthy of admiration' (quoted by F. Boillot, *Psychologie de la construction dans la phrase française moderne*, Paris, 1930, pp. 76 f.).

might call the 'law of diminishing returns'. The more often we repeat an expressive term or phrase, the less effective it will be. This is particularly noticeable in the case of figurative language. Constant repetition has taken the edge off many comparisons and metaphors. 'He is as sharp as a needle' must once have been a highly expressive image; now it is a mere cliché. When, a few years ago, the term *bulge* began to be used to denote an increase in the birth rate, it had the effect of an illuminating metaphor; now we are so accustomed to it that we no longer visualize the image. Hyperbolical terms are even more affected by the law of diminishing returns. We all know how quickly such expressions become fashionable and how quickly they go out of fashion. In our own time, modern forms of publicity and propaganda consume such words at an unprecedented rate and are constantly on the look-out for fresh alternatives: even such recent technical terms as *supersonic* have been drawn into their orbit.

(4) Finally, words may lose their evocative power as they pass from a restricted milieu into common usage. When the English term *sport* was introduced into French in 1828, the writer who first used it was at pains to explain that the word had no equivalent in his own language. For several decades, *sport* remained an Anglicism of limited currency in French; as late as 1855, the purist Viennet protested against it in a poem about English words, which he read to the Institut:

> Faut-il, pour cimenter un merveilleux accord,
> Changer l'arène en *turf*, et le plaisir en *sport*?[1]

Since then, the word has become part of everyday French and has lost all evocative force. The same has happened to many successful neologisms. The adjective *international*, for example, was formed in 1780 by Jeremy Bentham who apologized for his temerity in coining a new term: 'The word *international*, it must be acknowledged, is a new one, though, it is hoped, sufficiently analogous and intelligible.'[2] Subsequently the word became an indispensable element of our political vocabulary and lost any air of neologism it may have had in Bentham's day.[3]

---

[1] 'Must we, to cement a wonderful agreement, change arena to *turf*, and pleasure to *sport*?' (*Epître à Boileau*, quoted by Nyrop, *Grammaire historique*, vol. I, 4th ed., p. 104). On the history of the word in French, see Bloch-Wartburg and Mackenzie, op. cit. The English word itself is ultimately of French origin.

[2] See B. Migliorini, *The Contribution of the Individual to Language* (Taylorian Lecture), Oxford, 1952, p. 9.

[3] See on this process G. Matoré, 'Le Néologisme: naissance et diffusion', *Le Français Moderne*, xx (1952), pp. 87-92, and M. Riffaterre, 'La Durée de la valeur stylistique du néologisme', *Romanic Review*, xliv (1953), pp. 282-9.

Rather more subtle are the movements of words up and down the social scale. One is quite surprised to learn that some ordinary English words such as *joke* or *banter* began their careers as slang terms, and that many others — *cajole, clever, fun, job, width,* etc. — were stigmatized as 'low' by Dr. Johnson.[1] Similarly, the French *blaguer* 'to joke, to banter' is today a harmless colloquialism; yet a little more than a century ago it must have had powerful social overtones. In one of Balzac's novels, a reformed courtesan deliberately uses it to show that she is relapsing into her former way of life, and the word has such an explosive effect that even her chambermaid is staggered; it is, says Balzac, as though she had heard an angel utter a blasphemy.[2] In this instance, a highly language-conscious writer has recorded for posterity the precise social status of the word. In most cases we have no such information, and even the most sensitive critic will often be unable to recapture the evanescent overtones of words in older texts.[3]

[1] See an interesting list in G. E. Van Dongen, *Amelioratives in English I*, Rotterdam, 1933, pp. 15 ff.
[2] Cf. my *Style in the French Novel*, pp. 88 f.
[3] Cf. my article, 'Un Problème de reconstruction stylistique', in the Proceedings of the Eighth International Congress of Romance Linguistics, pp. 465-9.

CHAPTER 6

SYNONYMY

I. DIFFERENCES BETWEEN SYNONYMS

'WORDS', Dr. Johnson once remarked, 'are seldom exactly synonymous.'
Macaulay has expressed the same idea in terms which will commend
themselves to the modern linguist: 'Change the structure of the sentence;
substitute one synonym for another; and the whole effect is destroyed.'[1]
In contemporary linguistics it has become almost axiomatic that complete
synonymy does not exist. In the words of Bloomfield, 'each linguistic
form has a constant and specific meaning. If the forms are phonemically
different, we suppose that their meanings are also different ... We
suppose, in short, that there are no actual synonyms'.[2] Long before
Bloomfield, Bréal had spoken of a 'law of distribution' in language,
according to which 'words which should be synonymous, and which
were so in the past, have acquired different meanings and are no longer
interchangeable' (*Essai de sémantique*, p. 26).

While there is of course a great deal of truth in these statements, it would
be wrong to deny the possibility of complete synonymy. Paradoxically
enough, one encounters it where one would least expect it: in technical
nomenclatures. The fact that scientific terms are precisely delimited and
emotionally neutral enables us to find out quite definitely whether any
two of them are completely interchangeable, and absolute synonymy is by
no means infrequent. Recent studies on the formation of industrial
terminologies[3] have shown that several synonyms will sometimes
arise around a new invention, until they are eventually sorted out.
Such synonymy may even persist for an indefinite period. In medicine

---

[1] Both quotations are from the *NED*.

[2] *Language*, p. 145; cf. also Hockett, op. cit., pp. 130 f. For a somewhat different view
see Pike, op. cit., pt. III, p. 91 and pp. 95 f. On synonymy in general, the following works
may be consulted: Bally, *Traité de stylistique*, vol. I, *passim*, esp. pp. 140-54; W. E. Collinson,
'Comparative Synonymics: Some Principles and Illustrations', *Transactions of the Philological Society*, 1939, pp. 54-77; A. Dauzat, 'L'Etude des synonymes', *Etudes de linguistique
française*, 2nd ed., Paris, 1946, pp. 3-24; Jespersen, *Growth and Structure*, pp. 91 ff. and 123 ff.;
Y. D. Apresyan, 'Problema sinonima', *Voprosy Jazykoznanija*, 1957, no. 6, pp. 84-8; G. Poale-
lungi, 'Sinonimia gramaticală,' *Omagiu lui Al. Graur*, pp. 645-56.

[3] P. J. Wexler, *La Formation du vocabulaire des chemins de fer en France* (1778-1842),
Geneva – Lille, 1955; S. Stubelius, *Airship, Aeroplane, Aircraft. Studies in the History of
Terms for Aircraft in English*, Gothenburg, 1958; Id., *Balloon, Flying-machine, Helicopter.
Further Studies in the History of Terms for Aircraft in English*, Gothenburg, 1960.

there are two names for the inflammation of the blind gut: *caecitis* and *typhlitis*; the former comes from the Latin word for 'blind', the latter from the Greek word.[1] In phonetics, consonants like *s* and *ʒ* are known both as *spirants* and as *fricatives*, and the same writer may employ both terms synonymously.[2] The word *semantics* itself has a somewhat cumbrous synonym in *semasiology*, which is now hardly used in English and French but is firmly established in some other languages. A different form of synonymy results from the co-existence of native and Graeco-Latin terms in certain technical nomenclatures. The German linguist, for instance, can choose between *Lautlehre* and *Phonetik*, *Formenlehre* and *Morphologie*, *Bedeutungslehre* and *Semantik* (or *Semasiologie*), and as these synonyms are used in the same contexts, and sometimes even in the title of the same book,[3] one can hardly speak even of stylistic differences between them. In ordinary language, one can rarely be so positive about identity of meaning, since the matter is complicated by vagueness, ambiguity, emotive overtones and evocative effects; but even there one can occasionally find words which are for all intents and purposes interchangeable; it has been suggested, for example, that *almost* and *nearly* are such 'integral' synonyms.[4]

Nevertheless, it is perfectly true that absolute synonymy runs counter to our whole way of looking at language. When we see different words we instinctively assume that there must also be some difference in meaning, and in the vast majority of cases there is in fact a distinction even though it may be difficult to formulate. Very few words are completely synonymous in the sense of being interchangeable in any context without the slightest alteration in objective meaning, feeling-tone or evocative value.

Professor W. E. Collinson has made an interesting attempt at tabulating the most typical differences between synonyms.[5] He distinguishes between nine possibilities:

(1) One term is more general than another: *refuse — reject*.
(2) One term is more intense than another: *repudiate — refuse*.

---

[1] On these words see recently C. Schick, *Il Linguaggio*, Turin, 1960, p. 188.

[2] 'Examples of such "spirants" or "fricatives", as they are called, are *s* and *ʒ* and *y*' (Sapir, *Language*, p. 51).

[3] As e.g. in Kronasser's *Handbuch der Semasiologie*, which has the subtitle: *Kurze Einführung in die Geschichte, Problematik und Terminologie der Bedeutungslehre*, or in E. Struck's *Bedeutungslehre. Grundzüge einer lateinischen und griechischen Semasiologie*.

[4] Collinson, loc. cit., p. 58.

[5] Ibid., pp. 61 f. As Professor Collinson points out, his system is based on G. Devoto's article 'Sinonimia' in the *Enciclopedia Italiana*, xxxi, p. 857. It will be noted that a single word may be synonymous with a phrase: *refuse — turn down*.

(3) One term is more emotive than another: *reject — decline.*

(4) One term may imply moral approbation or censure where another is neutral: *thrifty — economical.*

(5) One term is more professional than another: *decease — death.*

(6) One term is more literary than another: *passing — death.*

(7) One term is more colloquial than another: *turn down — refuse.*

(8) One term is more local or dialectal than another: Scots *flesher — butcher.*

(9) One of the synonyms belongs to child-talk: *daddy — father.*

Some of the above categories include several subdivisions. Under (6), literary terms may be divided into poetic, archaic and others; under (7), colloquial language comprises several varieties such as familiar, slangy and vulgar speech.

If one looks more closely at this series one notices that the nine categories fall into several distinct groups. Numbers (8) and (9) stand apart from the rest since dialect and child-talk are really outside, or at best on the fringes of, Standard English. Number (1) refers to objective differences between synonyms, number (2) combines objective and emotive factors, (3) and (4) are emotive, whereas (5), (6) and (7) involve evocative effects which, as we already know, are a special type of emotive meaning.

The best method for the *delimitation of synonyms* is the substitution test recommended by Macaulay. This, it will be remembered, is one of the fundamental procedures of modern linguistics, and in the case of synonyms it reveals at once whether, and how far, they are interchangeable. If the difference is predominantly objective, one will often find a certain overlap in meaning: the terms involved may be interchanged in some contexts but not in others. Thus, *broad* and *wide* are synonymous in some of their uses: the '*broadest* sense' of a word is the same thing as its '*widest* sense', etc. In other contexts, only one of the two terms can be used: we say 'five foot *wide*', not *broad*; a '*broad* accent', not a *wide* one, etc. If, on the other hand, the difference between synonyms is mainly emotive or stylistic, there may be no overlap at all: however close in objective meaning, they belong to totally different registers or levels of style and cannot normally be interchanged. It is difficult to imagine any context — except a deliberately comical or ironical one — where *mingy* could replace *avaricious* or where *pop off* could be substituted for *pass away.*

One can also distinguish between synonyms by finding their opposites (antonyms). Thus, the verb *decline* is more or less synonymous with *reject* when it means the opposite of *accept*, but not when it is opposed to *rise*. *Deep* will overlap with *profound* in 'deep sympathy', where its opposite would be *superficial*, but not in 'deep water', where its antonym is *shallow*.

Yet another way of differentiating between synonyms is to arrange them into a series where their distinctive meanings and overtones will stand out by contrast, as for instance the various adjectives denoting swiftness: *quick, swift, fast, nimble, fleet, rapid, speedy*.[1]

There is an amusing demonstration of differences between synonyms in *As You Like It*, Act V, scene 1, where Touchstone, the court jester, exercises his professional wit at the expense of an uneducated young peasant:

> Therefore, you clown, abandon — which is in the vulgar leave — the society — which in the boorish is company — of this female — which in the common is woman — which together is: abandon the society of this female; or, clown, thou perishest; or, to thy better understanding, diest; or, to wit, I kill thee, make thee away, translate thy life into death.[2]

Distinctions between synonyms are a great challenge to the ingenuity of the lexicographer. For many languages there exist special dictionaries of synonyms;[3] in France, in particular, there is a long tradition of these, which culminated a century ago in B. Lafaye's famous *Dictionnaire des synonymes de la langue française*.[4] Inevitably, there is a great deal of arbitrariness in some of these verbal subtleties. In the seventeenth century, an attempt was made to distinguish between the two French words for 'gratefulness', *reconnaissance* and *gratitude*, by ruling that the former should be used when one is requiting a good turn and the latter when one is unable to do so.[5] An eighteenth-century synonymist tried to sort out four synonyms meaning 'lazy' or 'casual' by suggesting that *indolent*

---

[1] Cf. on this group of synonyms G. Stern, 'Swift, Swiftly' and their Synonyms. A Contribution to Semantic Analysis and Theory, Göteborgs Högskolas Årsskrift, XXVII, 1921, and E. Oksaar, Semantische Studien im Sinnbereich der Schnelligkeit. 'Plötzlich, schnell' und ihre Synonymik ... , Uppsala, 1958.

[2] Cf. Jespersen, Growth and Structure, p. 91.

[3] See esp. C. D. Buck, A Dictionary of Selected Synonyms in the Principal Indo-European Languages, Chicago, 1949; Collinson, loc. cit., pp. 56 f.; F. Dornseiff, 'Buchende Synonymik', Neue Jahrbücher für das klassische Altertum, xlvii (1921), pp. 422-33, and his book, Der deutsche Wortschatz nach Sachgruppen, which has already been mentioned.

[4] See L. C. Harmer, The French Language Today. Its Characteristics and Tendencies, London, 1954, pp. 93 ff.

[5] Brunot, Histoire de la langue française, IV, 1, p. 522.

implies lack of sensitivity, *nonchalant* lack of eagerness, *paresseux* lack of action, and *négligent* carelessness proper.[1] More recently, the long-standing synonymy of the two words for river, *fleuve* and *rivière*, has been resolved by reserving *fleuve* for a river which falls into the sea whereas a *rivière* flows into another river.[2] Needless to say, ordinary speakers will not always abide by these sophisticated rules; many will not even be aware of them, and in any case there is nothing like uniformity in the dictionaries. Nevertheless, these exercises in logical analysis have certainly sharpened the Frenchman's sense for the finer nuances of his language; in fact, as Professor Harmer has recently pointed out, many of the celebrated moralists of the eighteenth century applied, in a wittier and more literary form, the same method as the synonymists.[3]

II. Synonymic Patterns

The synonymic resources of a language tend to form certain characteristic and fairly consistent patterns. In English, for instance, synonyms are organized according to two basic principles, one of them involving a double, the other a triple scale.

The *double scale* — 'Saxon' versus 'Latin', as it is usually called — is too well known to require detailed comment.[4] There are in English countless pairs of synonyms where a native term is opposed to one borrowed from French, Latin or Greek. In most cases the native word is more spontaneous, more informal and unpretentious, whereas the foreign one often has a learned, abstract or even abstruse air. There may also be emotive differences: the 'Saxon' term is apt to be warmer and homelier than its foreign counterpart. Phonetically too, the latter will sometimes have an alien, unassimilated appearance; it will also tend to be longer than the native word which has been subjected to the erosive effect of sound-change. There are many exceptions to this pattern;[5] yet it recurs so persistently that it is obviously fundamental to the structure of the language. It may be noted that the term 'native' need not be taken in a narrowly etymological sense: it may include words of foreign origin which have become thoroughly Anglicized in form as well as in meaning, such as for instance the adjective *popish* as opposed to the learned *papal*.

[1] Harmer, op. cit., p. 99.
[2] L. Foulet, '*Fleuve et rivière*', *Romance Philology*, ii (1949), pp. 285-97.
[3] Op. cit., pp. 106 f.; cf. above, pp. 126 f.
[4] See, e.g., Jespersen's masterly discussion in *Growth and Structure*, chs. 5 and 6.
[5] Cf. A. C. Baugh, op. cit., pp. 225 f.

It will be sufficient to quote a few examples of this synonymic pattern. All major parts of speech are involved in the process: adjectives:

bodily	*corporeal*
brotherly	*fraternal*
heavenly	*celestial*
idle	*otiose*
inner	*internal* (*interior*)
learned	*erudite*
lying	*mendacious*
sharp	*acute*
sooty	*fuliginous*
starry	*sidereal*

verbs:

answer	*reply*
buy	*purchase*
read	*peruse*
tire (*weary*)	*fatigue*

nouns:

fiddle	*violin*
friendship	*amity*
help	*aid*
player	*actor*
wire	*telegram*
wireless	*radio*
world	*universe*

The ease with which examples can be multiplied shows how all-pervasive this pattern is in English. In his Taylorian lecture on 'The Impact of French upon English', Professor Orr has outlined the psychological and social climate in which the pattern first took shape after the Norman Conquest:

> For two hundred years and more, things intellectual, things pertaining to the spirit, were symbolized by words that had a flavour of remoteness, of higher courtliness, words redolent of the school rather than of the home, words that often had by their side humbler synonyms, humbler, yet used to express the things that are closer to our hearts as human beings, as children and parents, lovers and workers.[1]

[1] *Words and Sounds in English and French*, p. 42.

In subsequent centuries, the influx of Graeco-Latin terms during and since the Renaissance introduced new overtones into the pattern without altering its basic structure. It is symptomatic of our instinctive reactions that, when in danger, we call for *help*, not *aid*, and that we speak of *self-help* but *mutual aid*.

In a few cases, these synonymic values are reversed and the native term is rarer or more literary than the foreign:

dale	*valley*
deed	*action*
foe	*enemy*
meed	*reward*
to heed	*to take notice of*

The explanation of the anomaly will no doubt lie in the history of the two words involved. In the case of the first pair, for example, '*valley* [from French *vallée*] is the everyday word, and *dale* [from Old English *dæl*, cognate with German *Tal*] has only lately been introduced into the standard language from the dialects of the hilly northern counties'.[1]

An interesting aspect of this pattern is that it enables one to avoid native (or quasi-native) terms which, for some reason or another, have become tainted and might call up undesirable associations:

bloody	*sanguinary*
blooming	*flourishing*
devilish	*diabolical*
hell	*inferno*
popish	*papal*

Side by side with this main pattern there exists in English a subsidiary one based on a *triple scale* of synonyms: native, French, and Latin or Greek:[2]

begin (start)	*commence*	*initiate*
end	*finish*	*conclude*
food	*nourishment*	*nutrition*
kingly	*royal*	*regal*
rise	*mount*	*ascend*
time	*age*	*epoch*

In most of these combinations, the native synonym is the simplest and

[1] Jespersen, *Growth and Structure*, p. 93.
[2] Cf. Baugh, loc. cit., and Mossé op. cit., p. 206.

most ordinary of the three terms, the Latin or Greek one is learned, abstract, with an air of cold and impersonal precision, whereas the French one stands between the two extremes. The notorious slogan: 'Peace in our *time*' would have had less popular appeal if Mr. Chamberlain had said 'Peace in our *age*', let alone 'Peace in our *epoch*.' It should be noted, however, that here too there is an occasional reversal of values: in the series *kingly — royal — regal*, for example, the ordinary term is the French one, *royal*, whereas the native *kingly* is comparatively rare and most at home in literary contexts like Mark Antony's 'I thrice presented him a *kingly* crown.'

The French synonymic pattern is similar to the main English one, though there are important differences. It is a system with two scales, one native (including some old-established loan-words), the other borrowed from Latin or Greek. The latter, usually known as 'learned terms' (mots savants), have a cold, abstract, quasi-scientific air and belong to a completely different stylistic register than their native synonyms:

frêle 'frail'	*fragile* 'fragile'
froid 'cold'	*frigide* 'frigid'
nourriture 'food, nourishment'	*nutrition* 'nutrition'
pourriture 'rot, decay'	*putréfaction* 'putrefaction'
raide 'stiff'	*rigide* 'rigid'
sûreté 'safety'	*sécurité* 'security'

It will have been noticed that each of the above pairs comes from the same Latin root: in the first column we have the ordinary French descendants of these words, showing the effects of normal sound-change, whereas the second column consists of learned borrowings from Latin. There are, however, many pairs of French synonyms where the two words come from different sources: *aveuglement* 'moral blindness' — *cécité* 'physical blindness' (cf. above, p. 109); *haïr* (an old borrowing from Germanic related to English *hate*) — *détester*, etc.

In recent centuries, French has also borrowed many words from living languages: Italian during and since the Renaissance, English since the eighteenth century, and others. Some of these borrowings have been fitted into the same pattern of two synonymic scales:

chanteuse 'female singer'	Italian *cantatrice* 'female professional singer, cantatrice'
chevalier 'knight'	Italian *cavalier* 'rider, horseman; gentleman, gallant'[1]

[1] See on this pair G. Gougenheim, *Mélanges E. Hoepffner*, Paris, 1949, pp. 117-26.

| *entrevue* 'interview' | English *interview* (in the journalistic sense) |
| *humeur*[1] 'mood, temper' | English *humour* 'humour' |

The last two words were borrowed from French into English at an early date, and were subsequently reintroduced into French with a different shade of meaning.

It is clear from these examples that the main factor responsible for the pattern of English and French synonymy is the presence of large numbers of foreign words: French and classical in English, mainly classical in French. Similar tendencies have been at work in many other languages, but the nature and scope of the synonymic pattern will depend in each case on the historical background; in German, for example, purism, combined with the innate flexibility of the language, has produced many native synonyms for international words of classical origin; *dichterisch — poetisch*, *Sauerstoff — Oxygen*, *Fernsehen — Television*, etc.[2]

A very different pattern unfolds itself when one considers the *distribution of synonyms* in a given language. It is then found that there are in each idiom and each period certain significant clusters of synonyms, or 'centres of attraction', as they have been called.[3] Subjects in which a community is interested will attract synonyms from all directions; many of these will be metaphorical in character. If there is some lessening of interest in these themes, then the synonyms relating to them will be thinned out. Victor Hugo has described the process in a memorable simile:

Toute époque a ses idées propres, il faut aussi qu'elle ait les mots propres à ces idées. Les langues sont comme la mer, elles oscillent sans cesse. A certains temps, elles quittent un rivage du monde de la pensée et en envahissent un autre. Tout ce que leur flot déserte ainsi, sèche et s'efface du sol. C'est de cette façon que des idées s'éteignent, que des mots s'en vont.[4]

Some interesting statistics are available for these centres of synonymic

[1] Borrowed from Latin in the Old French period.
[2] See above, pp. 107 ff. and 142; cf. Priebsch-Collinson, op. cit., pp. 276 ff. For other languages, cf. e.g. H. Regnéll, *Semantik*, Stockholm, 1958, p. 77, and Weinreich, *Language*, xxxi (1955), p. 540, n. 1.
[3] H. Sperber, *Einführung in die Bedeutungslehre*, 2nd ed., Bonn — Leipzig, 1930, ch. 8. Cf. recently O. Ducháček, 'Au Problème de la migration des mots d'un champ conceptuel à l'autre', *Lingua*, x (1961), pp. 57-78.
[4] 'Each period has its own ideas; it must also have the words appropriate to these ideas. Languages are like the sea: they oscillate continuously. At certain times they leave one shore of the world of ideas and invade another. Whatever is thus deserted by their waves withers and fades away from the soil. This is how ideas die out and how words depart' (*Préface de Cromwell*). Cf. Ch. Bruneau in F. Brunot, *Histoire de la langue française*, vol. XII, p. 211.

attraction. It has been found, for example, that in the Old English epic *Beowulf* there are thirty-seven words for 'hero' or 'prince', at least a dozen for 'battle' or 'fight', seventeen for 'sea', and eleven for 'ship' or 'boat'. Nor does this exhaust the reservoir of synonyms for these concepts in Old English: in other poems thirteen further words have been found for 'sea' and at least sixteen for 'boat' or 'ship'.[1] A somewhat similar picture, less the seafaring element, emerges from the vocabulary of the twelfth-century French epic poet Benoît de Sainte-Maure who has eighteen verbs for 'attack', thirteen verbs for 'vanquish', and thirty-seven nouns for 'fight' or 'battle'.[2] In French dialects, there is a plethora of words for 'rich' and 'poor', and especially for 'miserly'; Professor Wartburg has counted nearly two hundred expressions denoting this vice, and has found in one case nine different synonyms for it within a single dialect.[3] In slang, there are heavy concentrations of synonyms around certain characteristic themes: stealing, cheating, drunkenness and the like. A perennial centre of synonymic attraction is of course the idea of death; the cluster of synonyms and periphrases surrounding it includes legal expressions like *decease*, euphemisms like *depart this life* or *pass away*, and a rich assortment of jocular and picturesque slang phrases: *go west*, *kick the bucket*, *peg out*, *snuff out*, and many more.[4]

A third type of synonymic pattern arises when two or more synonyms develop on *parallel* lines. Since words with similar meanings are closely associated with each other, a change in one of them may set off an analogous change in another or in several others. When, in early Modern English, the verb *overlook* acquired the meaning of 'deceive', its synonym, *oversee*, soon began to be used in the same transferred sense. Similarly, when *cram* came to mean 'deceive', its synonym, *stuff*, underwent the same change of meaning.[5] In French dialects, the synonyms *maison* and *hôtel* are both employed in the sense of 'kitchen'.[6] Elsewhere, such parallel developments have affected a whole series of words, by a process which has been described as 'synonymic radiation'.[7] This is particularly noticeable in slang where a racy and picturesque metaphor will often be extended

---

[1] Jespersen, *Growth and Structure*, p. 48

[2] See Wartburg, *Problèmes et méthodes de la linguistique*, pp. 175 f.

[3] Ibid., p. 135.

[4] Further examples in Jespersen, *Mankind, Nation and Individual from a Linguistic Point of View*, pp. 166 f.

[5] S. Kroesch, 'Analogy as a Factor in Semantic Change', *Language*, ii (1926), pp. 35-45; cf. by the same author: 'Change of Meaning by Analogy', *Studies in Honor of H. Collitz*, Baltimore, 1930, pp. 176-89.

[6] J. Gilliéron, *Pathologie et thérapeutique verbales*, Paris, 1921, pp. 124 ff.

[7] B. Migliorini, 'Calco e irradiazione sinonimica', *Boletín del Instituto Caro y Cuervo*, iv (1948), pp. 3-17, reprinted in *Saggi linguistici*, Florence, 1957.

to a wide range of synonyms. As Chesterton once said, *'all slang is metaphor, and all metaphor is poetry'. In French argot, for example, the verb
chiquer 'beat', used in the sense of 'steal', started off a similar change in a
number of its synonyms (*torcher*, *taper*, *estamper*, *toquer*, etc.); in the
same way, the use of *polir* in the meaning of 'steal' set the pattern for a
parallel development in other verbs for 'cleaning' and 'polishing', such as
nettoyer and *fourbir*.[1] The amusing euphemism *être noir* 'to be black' in
the sense of 'to be drunk', established a firm associative link between
blackness and drunkenness in argot: witness such expressions as *être
chocolat*, *réglisse*, *coaltar* 'to be (as black as) chocolate, liquorice, tar', *se
poisser* 'to be pitchy', and others, all referring jocularly to the effect of
drink.[2]

III. Synonymy and Style

In his *Rhetoric* Aristotle made an interesting remark on the difference
between synonymy and ambiguity. Synonyms, according to him, are
'useful to the poet', whereas 'words of ambiguous meaning are chiefly
useful to enable the sophist to mislead his hearers'.[3] Synonymy is indeed
an invaluable stylistic resource not only to the poet but to any writer,
and it lends itself to a variety of uses. These fall into two broad categories
according to whether the speaker has to choose between synonyms or
prefers to combine them for some specific purpose.

(1) *Choice between synonyms.* — The possibility of choosing between
two or more alternatives is fundamental to our modern conception of
style,[4] and synonymy affords one of the most clear-cut examples of such
choice. If more than one word is available for the expression of the same
idea, the writer will select the one which is best suited to the context:
the one which will carry the right amount of emotion and emphasis,
which will fit most harmoniously into the phonetic structure of the sentence, and which will be best attuned to the general tone of the utterance.
The study of manuscripts and variants is most revealing in this respect.
It shows how often a writer will cross out a word and replace it by another
which may not have exactly the same meaning but offers definite stylistic
advantages. For Victor Hugo, for example, the adjectives *âpre* 'harsh'

[1] See M. Schwob-G. Guieysse, 'Etudes sur l'argot français', *Mémoires de la Société de
Linguistique de Paris*, vii (1892), pp. 33-56.
[2] See G. Esnault, 'La Sémantique', in *Où en sont les études de français*, ed. by A. Dauzat,
2nd ed., Paris, 1949, pp. 123 ff.
[3] Quoted by Collinson, loc. cit., p. 57.
[4] Cf. my paper 'Choix et expressivité', to be published in the proceedings of the Ninth
International Congress of Romance Linguistics, held in Lisbon in 1959.

L

and *austère* 'austere', *morne* 'dejected, gloomy' and *triste* 'sad', *funèbre* 'funereal, dismal' and *sinistre* 'sinister', seem to have been virtually interchangeable, in spite of the semantic differences between them; as Professor Charles Bruneau has put it, for this poet *âpre* and *austère* had the same emotive value whereas their meaning proper was of little importance.[1]

(2) More interesting and varied are the stylistic uses of *combinations of synonyms*. Here again there are two possibilities: the synonyms involved may occur at intervals or they may be in close contact with each other. The former may be described as 'variation', the latter as 'collocation' of synonyms.

(a) *Variation.* — We all make use of synonyms to avoid repeating the same word for the same idea. There are, however, two dangers one should carefully guard against. Firstly, the use of another term may easily suggest that the meaning too is slightly different, and this may lead to ambiguity and misunderstanding. Whenever there is such a risk the good stylist will weigh carefully the pros and cons of employing the same word, and, if there is no suitable alternative, he will not shrink from repeating it rather than distorting his thought. As Pascal said, 'quand dans un discours se trouvent des mots répétés et qu'en essayant de les corriger, on les trouve si propres qu'on gâterait le discours, il les faut laisser'.[2]

Another risk inherent in this use of synonyms is what H. W. Fowler has called 'elegant variation'. If it becomes obvious to the reader that the writer has studiously tried to avoid repetition and to vary the expression of the same thought, then the device will defeat its own ends and the style will have a false elegance, a slightly artificial air. This at least will be the reaction of a modern reader, for earlier periods were by no means averse to this form of symmetry. In the following passage, which is a comparison between punch and conversation, Dr. Johnson uses four different expressions for the same idea:

'The spirit, volatile and fiery, is the *proper emblem* of vivacity and wit; the acidity of the lemon will very *aptly figure* pungency of raillery and acrimony of censure; sugar is the *natural representative* of luscious adulation and gentle complaisance; and water is the *proper hieroglyphic* of easy prattle, innocent and tasteless.'[3]

---

[1] In F. Brunot, *Histoire de la langue française*, vol. XII, p. 217.

[2] 'If, in a text, some words are repeated and, on trying to correct them, one finds that they are so exact that one would only spoil the text, one should let them stand.' Cf. Marouzeau, *Précis de stylistique française*, p. 173.

[3] Quoted by Jespersen, *Growth and Structure*, p. 126.

(b) Collocation. — This may have a number of different uses. It may, for example, provide an outlet for strong emotions. Hamlet's very first soliloquy starts with such an impassioned accumulation of synonyms:

> O, that this too too solid flesh would melt,
> Thaw, and resolve itself into a dew!
>
> Act I, scene 2.

In a comic vein, Molière's miser, on finding that he has been robbed, vents his horror and despair in the same kind of extravagant language:

'Au voleur! au voleur! à l'assassin! au meurtrier! Justice, juste ciel! je suis perdu, je suis assassiné! on m'a coupé la gorge: on m'a dérobé mon argent! Qui peut-ce être? Qu'est-il devenu? Où est-il? Où se cache-t-il?'[1]

An important function of such collocations of synonyms is to make one's meaning clearer and more emphatic. In the Middle Ages it was customary to explain a French word by adding to it a native synonym.[2] 'Cherité þet is luve', 'ignoraunce þet is unwisdom and unwitnesse', we read in the thirteenth-century *Ancren Riwle*. In the course of time this developed into a literary mannerism which is found in Chaucer, Shakespeare and other writers. The phrase 'liberty and freedom', which has become so popular in modern times, occurs already in Caxton who seems to have been particularly fond of this construction: '*Fredome* and *lyberte* is better than ony gold or syluer' (*NED*). Some of our tautological compounds and phrases: *courtyard, mansion-house, lord and master, pray and beseech*, and others, go back to the same tradition. But the device was by no means confined to England; it was common in French literature during the Renaissance:

> Des arbres et des murs, lesquels tour dessus tour,
> Plis dessus plis il *serre, embrasse* et *environne*.
>
> Ronsard, *Sonnets pour Hélène*, II, 29.[3]

'Dieu ... ne peult s'*augmenter* et *accroistre* au dedans; mais son nom se peult *augmenter* et *accroistre* par la benediction et louange que nous donnons à ses ouvrages exterieurs.'

Montaigne, 'De la gloire' (*Essays*, Book II, ch. 26).[4]

---

[1] 'Stop thief! stop thief! assassin! murderer! Justice, just heavens! I am lost, I am murdered! they have cut my throat: they have stolen my money! Who can it be? What has become of him? Where is he? Where is he hiding?' (*L'Avare*, Act IV, scene 7).

[2] Cf. Mossé, op. cit., pp. 94 f.

[3] 'Trees and walls which, turn by turn, fold by fold, it *clasps, embraces* and *surrounds*.'

[4] 'God ... cannot *augment* and *increase* himself from within; but his name can be *augmented* and *increased* by the blessing and praise we give to his external works.'

These repetitive constructions were later on proscribed by the purists of the seventeenth century.

One form of language where synonymy is endemic is legal style. As everyone knows, the law abounds in expressions like 'goods and chattels', 'last will and testament', 'good repair, order and condition', which, to the layman at any rate, seem tautological. Occasionally, some laymen have demurred against this jargon. Wesley protested fiercely against 'that villanous tautology of lawyers, which is the scandal of our nation'.[1] In the style of Mr. Micawber, who 'had a relish in this formal piling up of words' and appeared 'majestically refreshed' by their sound, Dickens has parodied the legal manner with great gusto. Professor R. Quirk has recently suggested that 'it is a regular symptom of Micawber's retreat from reality that he should find a sufficient reality in words'.[2] This is no doubt true, but Dickens was at pains to emphasize that this habit was more than a personal idiosyncrasy. 'I have observed it,' he wrote, 'in the course of my life, in numbers of men. It seems to me to be a general rule. In the taking of legal oaths, for instance, deponents seem to enjoy themselves mightily when they come to several good words in succession, for the expression of one idea; as, that they utterly detest, abominate, and abjure, or so forth; and the old anathemas were made relishing on the same principle. We talk about the tyranny of words, but we like to tyrannize over them too.'[3]

When one encounters this kind of gratuitous tautology in poetry one has the impression of mere padding designed to fill out the line. Thus in the following passage from *Childe Harold's Pilgrimage*:

> Away! — there need no *words* nor *terms* precise,
> The paltry jargon of the marble mart ...
>
> Canto IV, 50,

one feels, rightly or wrongly, that the collocation of the synonyms *words* and *terms* was dictated, not by any desire for clarity or emphasis, but by the exigencies of the metre.

Occasionally, a collocation of synonyms will help to produce a contrast effect. The contrast may be either serious or humorous. It is serious when Soames Forsyte indignantly declares on withdrawing from a board of directors: 'I do not tender my resignation to the meeting; I

---

[1] See the *NED*, s.v. *tautology*.

[2] *Charles Dickens and Appropriate Language*, Inaugural Lecture, University of Durham, 1959, p. 21.

[3] *David Copperfield*, ch. 52 (p. 707 of the Everyman ed.). Cf. Jespersen, *Growth and Structure*, p. 126.

resign.'[1] It is humorous when Mr. Micawber explains, in his inimitable style: 'It is not an avocation of a remunerative description — in other words, it does *not* pay.'[2]

It may also happen that a writer, or one of his characters, will add a synonym in order to correct himself, to change a word which, on second thoughts, he wishes to replace by a more appropriate one. 'Perhaps, after all, America never has been *discovered* ... I myself would say that it had merely been *detected*', says Wilde in *Dorian Gray*.[3] When the alternative is not more appropriate but merely has a more learned or more refined air, it may throw an ironical sidelight on the speaker's personality. In George Eliot's *Middlemarch* there is a character for whom 'things never *began* ... they always *commenced* both in private life and on his handbills ... He was an amateur of superior phrases, and never used poor language without immediately correcting himself'; thus he would say: 'Anybody may *ask*. Anybody may *interrogate*. Any one may give their remarks an *interrogative turn*.'[4]

Elsewhere, an author will leave in the final text all the various synonyms which came to his mind as he was trying to formulate his thoughts. Such collocations are a real mannerism in the style of Charles Péguy. In the following passage, half a dozen different nouns are used to describe the posture of an author bending over his desk:

'Je sens déjà l'*incurvation*, l'*incurvaison* générale ... Il faut dire aussi que c'est le *courbement*, la *courbure*, la *courbature*, l'*inclinaison* de l'écrivain sur sa table de travail.'[5]

This heavy battery of synonyms, nearly all from the same root (Latin *curvare*, French *courber*), is brought into play to convey the sheer physical effort involved in the process of literary creation.

As will be seen from this small selection of examples, Aristotle's claim that 'synonyms are useful to the poet' was, if anything, an understatement. Among the effects just discussed, collocation, though quite common in some of its forms, is on the whole a stylistic device, but choice and variation, if discreetly handled, are not merely useful: they are indispensable to any style worthy of that name.

---

[1] J. Galsworthy, *A Modern Comedy*, London, 1952 impr., p. 316.
[2] Quoted by Jespersen, *Growth and Structure*, p. 127, n. 1.
[3] Quoted by Apresyan, loc. cit., p. 88.
[4] London, Dent, 1959 impr., Vol. I, Book III, ch. 23, pp. 273 ff.; cf. Mossé, op. cit., p. 207.
[5] 'I am already feeling the *incurvation*, the general *incurving* ... One should also say that it is the *bowing*, the *curving*, the *backache*, the *bending* of the writer over his desk' (*Cahiers de la Quinzaine*, October 23rd, 1910).

CHAPTER 7

AMBIGUITY

AMBIGUITY is a linguistic condition which can arise in a variety of ways. Professor Empson has distinguished between seven different types of it in literature.[1] From a purely linguistic point of view there are three main forms of ambiguity; phonetic, grammatical and lexical.

(1) As we have already seen (pp. 40 f.), ambiguity may result, in spoken language, from the *phonetic structure of the sentence*. Since the acoustic unit of connected speech is the breath-group, not the individual word, it may happen that two breath-groups made up of different words become homonymous and thus potentially ambiguous. If this occurs often enough, it may leave a permanent mark on the language. In English, for example, there was once a noun *near* meaning 'kidney' (related to German *Niere*), but it fell subsequently into disuse because *a near* could be confused with *an ear*.[2] The 'aspirate' *h-* in French *héros* is due, as already mentioned (p. 41), to the desire to distinguish in the plural between *les héros* 'the heroes' and *les ʒéros* 'the zeroes'.

(2) Another large group of ambiguities are caused by *grammatical* factors. There are two possibilities here: the equivoque may result from the ambiguousness of grammatical forms or from the structure of the sentence.

(a) Many *grammatical forms*, free as well as bound (see above, p. 28), are ambiguous. Some prefixes and suffixes have more than one meaning, and this may, on occasion, create misunderstandings. The suffix *-able* does not mean the same thing in *desirable* or *readable* as it does in *eatable, knowable, debatable*; this ambiguity led J. S. Mill to an erroneous analysis of the adjective *desirable* as though it were on all fours with *knowable* and similar formations.[3] There are also homonymous prefixes and suffixes. The prefix *in-*, meaning 'into, within, towards, upon' (e.g. *indent, inborn, inbreeding, inflame*), has a homonym in the prefix *in-* expressing negation or privation (e.g. *inappropriate, inexperienced, inconclusive*). Though the two enter into different combinations, they can occasionally give rise to confusion and uncertainty. The following two passages from Shakespeare

---

[1] W. Empson, *Seven Types of Ambiguity*, 2nd ed., London, 1949.
[2] See E. R. Williams, *The Conflict of Homonyms in English*, Yale Studies in English 100 (1944), pp. 47 ff.
[3] Cf. Ogden-Richards, op. cit., p. 133.

show that the adjective *inhabitable* could sometimes have the same sense as its logical opposite, *uninhabitable*:[1]

> Even to the frozen ridges of the Alps,
> Or any other ground *inhabitable*
> Where ever Englishman durst set his foot.
> *King Richard the Second*, Act I, scene 1.

Though this island seem to be desert, ... *uninhabitable*, and almost inaccessible ...
> *The Tempest*, Act II, scene 1.

Inflexional endings may also be ambiguous; in Latin the nominative and accusative forms of all neuters are identical, and so are all dative and ablative plurals. In actual speech, such homonymy will seldom lead to confusion, but there are cases where it has done so. When, in Vulgar Latin, a -*b*- between two vowels came to be pronounced in the same way as a -*v*-, a future like *amabit* 'he will love' became indistinguishable from the perfect of the same verb: *amavit* 'he has loved'. This confusion was no doubt one of the main reasons for the disappearance of the old future tense in the Romance languages most of which have replaced it by the combination: infinitive + 'to have': *amare habet* > French *aimera*.

Even languages which have reduced or obliterated case endings tend to have distinct forms for singular and plural. Yet there are many examples where the two forms are identical: Latin *dies* 'day — days', French *temps* 'time — times', German *Dichter* 'poet — poets', etc. Usually no ambiguity will arise since agreement with the verb and other grammatical features will make the meaning perfectly clear. A curious case where this homonymy was felt to be embarrassing is that of the Spanish word for 'God'. In mediaeval Spanish, the singular of this word was *Dios*, from the Latin nominative singular *deus*, and its plural was also *dios*, from the Latin accusative plural *deos*. This enabled the Jews of Spain to taunt the Christians with polytheism since they could not speak of one God, only of gods. Eventually, the problem was solved by forming a new analogical plural: *dioses*.[2]

Form-words too may have several meanings which may make for confusion in some contexts. When a married man is invited to a semi-official function in these terms: 'Will *you* join us for dinner tomorrow?',

---

[1] Cf. Jespersen, *Growth and Structure*, p. 130. On grammatical homonymy, see recently S. Stati, *Probleme de linguistică generală*, vol. II, Bucharest, 1960, pp. 125-42.
[2] R. Menéndez Pidal, *Manual de Gramática Histórica Española*, 5th ed., Madrid, 1934, p. 177.

he often has to ask the awkward question: 'Do you mean *you* in the singular or in the plural?'

(*b*) Another fertile source of grammatical ambiguity is *equivocal phrasing* ('amphibology').[1] Here the individual words are unambiguous but their combination can be interpreted in two or more different ways. To take a trivial example, in the sentence: 'I met a number of old friends and acquaintances', the adjective *old* may be taken to refer either to both *friends* and *acquaintances* or only to the former. As Professor Hockett recently put it, we have here two 'alternative hierarchical organizations'.[2] The following simple sentence, found in Romain Rolland: 'Sophie quitte Anna rassurée', can mean two different things according to whether the adjective *rassurée* is attached to *Sophie* or to *Anna*: 'Sophie, reassured, leaves Anna' or 'Sophie leaves Anna who now feels reassured'.[3] Defenders of the split infinitive argue that it sometimes helps to avoid such ambiguities. Thus the sentence: 'A vicious back-hander, which I failed *to entirely avoid*' makes it clear that I did not altogether succeed in avoiding it, whereas the alternative construction: 'I failed entirely to avoid' could also mean complete failure.[4]

Most ambiguities of this kind will be clarified by the context and, in the spoken language, by intonation. Take for instance Hamlet's reply to his mother when she and Claudius try to persuade him not to go to Wittenberg: 'I shall in all my best obey you, madam' (Act I, scene 2). By placing heavy emphasis on *you*, an actor could give the sentence an aggressive edge; the implication then would be: 'obey *you*, not your husband'. A glance at the context will show that this interpretation, though grammatically correct, is psychologically wrong for it does not fit in with the King's answer: 'Why, 'tis a loving and a fair reply. Be as ourself in Denmark.'

(3) By far the most important type of ambiguity, and the only one with which the present chapter is concerned, is that due to *lexical* factors. In countless cases more than one sense will be connected with the same name; according to the diagram given on p. 62:

$$S_1 \quad\searrow \quad S_2 \quad\downarrow\swarrow \quad S_3 \searrow \\ n$$

---

[1] From Greek *amphi* 'on both sides' and *ballein* 'to throw'. The form *amphiboly* is also used.
[2] Op. cit., p. 152.
[3] Cf. Bally, *Linguistique générale et linguistique française*, p. 26.
[4] See Jespersen, *Essentials of English Grammar*, London, 1933, p. 346.

This '*polyvalency*' of our words, as it is sometimes called, may take two different forms:

(*a*) The same word may have two or more different meanings. This situation has been known since Bréal as '*polysemy*'.[1] The noun *board*, for example, may mean a thin plank, a tablet, a table, food served at the table, persons sitting at the council-table, and various other things. Normally, only one of these will fit into a given context, but occasionally there may be some confusion in people's minds, as when Oliver Twist, told by Bumble that he should bow to the *board*, 'seeing no *board* but the table, fortunately bowed to that'.[2]

(*b*) Two or more different words may be identical in sound ('*homonymy*'): *mean* 'middle' and *mean* 'inferior'; *seal*, name of an animal, and *seal* 'piece of wax fixed on a letter'. Needless to say, words which sound alike but are spelt differently (*root — route, site — sight — cite*) must also be regarded as homonyms.

It should be noted that both polysemy and homonymy may be accompanied by syntactical differences. When a word belongs to several parts of speech — as for instance *double* which can be an adjective, an adverb, a verb and a noun — these uses will differ not only in meaning but in grammatical function. Homonyms too may come from different word-classes: *grave* (adjective) — *grave* (noun), *bear* (noun) — *bear* (verb); French *sang* 'blood' — *sans* 'without' — *cent* 'hundred' — (*il*) *sent* '(he) feels'.

Although, as will be seen, the border-line between polysemy and homonymy is sometimes fluid, the two types are so distinct that they will have to be considered separately. We shall have to examine two main questions: the way in which the two phenomena arise, and the effect they have on ordinary language. In a concluding section the stylistic uses of both forms of ambiguity will be briefly discussed.

I. POLYSEMY

1. *Sources*

Polysemy is a fundamental feature of human speech, which can arise in a multiplicity of ways. I shall confine myself to the examination of five sources, four of them native, the fifth involving the influence of a foreign language.

(1) *Shifts in application.* — As we saw when discussing the various

---

[1] Op. cit., p. 144; from Greek *polys* 'many'+*sēmeion* 'sign'.
[2] Chapman and Hall ed., ch. 2, p. 12; cf. the *NED*.

forms of vagueness in meaning (pp. 124 f.), our words have a number of different aspects according to the contexts in which they are used. Some of these aspects are purely ephemeral; others may develop into permanent shades of meaning and, as the gap between them widens, we may eventually come to regard them as different senses of the same term. In the dictionaries, these various stages are systematically distinguished, but in actual fact they merge imperceptibly into one another.

Shifts in application are particularly noticeable in the use of adjectives since these are apt to change their meaning according to the noun they qualify. The semantic ramifications of some common English adjectives have been investigated by a Swedish scholar, Arne Rudskoger, in a valuable monograph published a few years ago.[1] To take one of his simpler examples, the adjective *handsome* has been used, in the course of its history, in the following senses, grouped according to the noun to which they refer:

Persons:
1. Apt, skilled, clever.
2. Proper, fitting, decent.
3. Beautiful with dignity.

Concretes:
1. Easy to handle.
2. Of fair size.
3. Beautiful with dignity.
4. Proper, fitting (of dress).

Actions, speech:
1. Appropriate, apt, clever.

Conduct:
1. Fitting, seemly.
2. Gallant, brave.
3. Generous, magnanimous.

Sizes, sums:
1. Fair, moderately large.
2. Ample, liberal, munificent.

Most of these senses arose through shifts in application, though another factor, figurative usage, may also have been at work. Naturally, not all

---

[1] *'Fair, Foul, Nice, Proper.' A Contribution to the Study of Polysemy*, Gothenburg Studies in English, I; Stockholm, 1952.

these meanings have survived. Dr. Rudskoger's conclusions concerning the present position are worth quoting: '*Handsome* has become a comparatively strong and positive word. The three chief senses of today are "beautiful", "generous", and "considerable, ample", and this general character of positive strength may, as I see it, have brought about the fall of older, neutral or less positive senses' (p. 371).

It must not be thought, however, that other word-classes are not exposed to such shifts. To take an example at random, the *Shorter Oxford Dictionary* lists the following senses for the verb *rush* used intransitively:

1. *Of persons or animals*:
   (*a*) To run, dash, or charge with violence or impetuous rapidity.
   (*b*) Figuratively: To make an attack or descent on a person.
   (*c*) Figuratively: Denoting rash or precipitate action.
   (*d*) To pass or travel rapidly.
2. *Of things*:
   (*a*) To move, flow, fall, etc., with great speed or impetuosity.
   (*b*) To come suddenly into view.

Once again, shifts in application were the main agency behind this wealth of meanings, with figurative usage as an important contributory factor. To have a complete picture of the semantic range of the verb *rush*, one would also have to take into account its transitive uses, listed by the same dictionary under five main headings, one of them with as many as five subdivisions.

(2) *Specialization in a social milieu.* — Michel Bréal drew attention to the fact that polysemy often arises through a kind of verbal shorthand. 'In every situation, in every trade or profession', he wrote, 'there is a certain idea which is so much present to one's mind, so clearly implied, that it seems unnecessary to state it when speaking' (*Essai de sémantique*, p. 154). For a lawyer, *action* will naturally mean 'legal action'; for the soldier it will mean a military operation, without any need for a qualifying epithet. In this way the same word may acquire a number of specialized senses only one of which will be applicable in a given milieu. We have already seen an example of this process in the polysemy of the word *style* (pp. 124 f.). Similarly, *paper* can refer not only to the material in general but to a variety of other things: legal or official documents; a newspaper; a set of examination questions; a communication read or sent to a learned society; in the plural it can also denote identity documents; certificates accompanying the resignation of an officer; documents showing the

ownership, nationality and destination of a ship, etc. In the past there were also some other specialized uses; the word could mean, for example, a note fastened on the back of a criminal, specifying his offence:

> Methinks I should not thus be led along,
> Mail'd up in shame, with *papers* on my back.
> *King Henry the Sixth, Part Two*, Act II, scene 4.[1]

One could indefinitely multiply examples of words which have a general meaning in ordinary language and specialized senses in more restricted spheres: *company, interest, security, share* in commerce; *overture, key, score* in music; *signature* in music and printing; *stage, pit, curtain* in the theatre; *screen* in the cinema; *broadcasting* in radio; *viewing* in television; *score, goal, back, centre, bat, century* in various sports, to mention only a few.

The extreme form of specialization is reached when a common noun virtually becomes a proper name denoting a single object in a particular environment. This has happened in the case of some famous London districts and landmarks: the *City*, the *House*, the *Abbey*, the *Tower*, the *Yard*. The name *Provence* is the regular French continuation of the Latin *provincia*, as if that region were the province *par excellence*; the ordinary French word, *province*, which has been taken over into English, is a learned borrowing from Latin.

(3) *Figurative language.* — We have already encountered metaphor and other figures as an important factor in motivation and in emotive overtones; now we have to consider yet another facet of the same device. A word can be given one or more figurative senses without losing its original meaning: old and new will live on side by side as long as there is no possibility of confusion between them. In this way a number of metaphors may, as a pioneer of modern semantics put it, 'radiate' from the central sense.[2] The word *eye*, for example, may be applied to a wide range of objects reminiscent of the organ. The *Shorter Oxford Dictionary* lists the following metaphorical uses of this term:

1. An object resembling the eye in appearance, shape, or position: the centre of a flower, the leaf-bud of a potato, a spot on a peacock's tail, etc.
2. The opening through which the water of a fountain wells up.
3. A central mass; the brightest spot (of light).
4. The centre of revolution.

---

[1] Cf. the *NED*.
[2] Darmesteter, op. cit., pp. 73 f.

5. A hole or aperture in a needle or tool, etc.
6. A loop of metal, thread, cord, or rope.
7. In architecture: the centre of any part, as in 'the *eye* of a dome'.
8. In typography: the enclosed space in letters like *d*, *e* and *o*.

To these may be added other uses cited by the dictionary, where the word is applied to abstract phenomena, as when we speak of the *eye* of the law, or when Hamlet says: 'Methinks I see my father ... in my mind's *eye*' (Act I, scene 2).

There is the same kind of polysemy based on metaphor when we talk of the *bed* of a river, the *boot* of a car, the *cock* of a gun, a *saddle* in the mountains, a *sheet* of paper, iron or water, or when, in the abstract sphere, we *tackle* a problem, come to *grips* with it, *wrestle* with it, get down to *brass tacks*, or find ourselves on the *horns* of a dilemma. This possibility of metaphorical transposition is fundamental to the working of language. In the words of a philosopher, W. M. Urban:

> The fact that a sign can intend one thing without ceasing to intend another, that, indeed, the very condition of its being an *expressive* sign for the second is that it is also a sign for the first, is precisely what makes language an instrument of knowing. This 'accumulated intension' of words is the fruitful source of ambiguity, but it is also the source of that analogous predication, through which alone the symbolic power of language comes into being.[1]

At a far higher level, the images and symbols of the poet spring from the same 'double vision'. When Lady Macbeth apostrophizes the night:

> Come, thick night,
> And pall thee in the dunnest smoke of hell,
> That my keen knife see not the wound it makes,
> Nor heaven peep through the *blanket* of the dark
> To cry 'Hold, hold!'
>
> *Act I, scene 5,

the effect of the powerful imagery will depend in no small measure on the ordinary meaning of *blanket* being present to the reader's mind.

Metaphor is not the only figure which can give rise to polysemy. Metonymy, which is based not on similarity but on some other relation between two terms, may work in the same way. We have already seen (p. 159) how *board* can mean, among other things, a table as well as the

---

[1] *Language and Reality*, pp. 112 f.

persons sitting around the council-table. *Surgery* can refer to the art of a surgeon, and also to the room where patients are seen and medicine is dispensed. *Youth* originally meant 'youngness, the fact, state or time of being young'. Already in Old English it received the additional meaning: 'young persons collectively'. In Middle English it was given yet a third sense: 'young man between boyhood and maturity'. In Modern English these three meanings, connected not by similarity but by other associations, coexist without interfering with each other.[1]

(4) *Homonyms reinterpreted.* — Polysemy can also arise through a special form of popular etymology, which has already been discussed (pp. 104 f.). When two words are identical in sound and the difference in meaning is not very great, we are apt to regard them as one word with two senses. Historically these are cases of homonymy since the two terms come from different sources; but the modern speaker, unaware of etymologies, will establish a link between them on purely psychological grounds.

This type of polysemy is very rare and most of the examples are somewhat doubtful since, as Bloomfield rightly points out, 'the degree of nearness of the meanings is not subject to precise measurement' (*Language*, p. 436). Only a statistical inquiry could show whether most speakers do actually feel some kind of connexion between the two senses. To the examples already cited (*ear*, name of the organ and of a spike of corn, French *souci* 'care' and 'marigold', French *flamme* 'flame' and 'fleam, lancet'), one or two more may be added. Bloomfield suggests that in the following pairs of homonyms the second term is regarded as a marginal or transferred meaning of the first:

corn 'grain' > Old English *corn*	*corn* on the foot < Old French *corn* (Modern French *cor*) < Latin *cornu*
allure 'attract, fascinate, charm' < Old French *alurer* 'to lure'	*allure* 'gait, mien, air' < French *allure*
weed 'wild plant' < Old English *wēod*	widow's *weeds* 'deep mourning worn by a widow' < Old English *wǣd* 'garment'

The gap in meaning between 'wild plant' and 'garment' seems rather wide; yet there are in Shakespeare several puns which suggest that this gap can be bridged:[2]

[1] See on this last word S. Potter, *Modern Linguistics*, London, 1957, pp. 152 f.
[2] See H. Kökeritz, *Shakespeare's Pronunciation*, New Haven, 1953, p. 153, and M. M. Mahood, *Shakespeare's Wordplay*, London, 1957, pp. 17 f., 25, 94.

When forty winters shall besiege thy brow,
And dig deep trenches in thy beauty's *field*,
Thy youth's proud *livery*, so gaz'd on now,
Will be a tatter'd *weed* of small worth held.

Sonnets, 2.

(5) *Foreign influence.* — One of the many ways in which a language can influence another is by changing the meaning of an existing word.[1] Sometimes the borrowed sense will simply supersede the old one; thus French *parlement*, which originally meant 'speaking' (from the verb *parler* 'to speak') and then came to denote a 'judicial court', acquired at a later date, under the influence of English *parliament*, its modern sense of 'legislative assembly', the only meaning in which it is at present used (Bloch-Wartburg). In many cases, however, the old sense will survive alongside of the new, thus giving rise to a state of polysemy.

'*Semantic borrowing*', as it is usually called, will be particularly frequent where there is intimate contact between two languages one of which serves as a model to the other. This happened, for instance, in the early Christian Church where Hebrew exercised a powerful influence on Greek, and the latter on Latin. It is also happening at present in the speech of immigrants to the United States or, to take a more limited field, in the language of sports, which, in many countries, is saturated with Anglicisms. A few examples from each of these three very different linguistic situations will show how the process works.

Many important concepts of the Christian faith owe their name to semantic borrowings from Hebrew or Greek.[2] In the Bible, the Hebrew word *ml'k* 'messenger' was often used in the sense of 'angel'. Since there was no word for 'angel' in Greek, the translators of the Bible copied the polysemy of the Hebrew term by using the Greek ἄγγελος 'messenger' in the meaning of 'angel'. From Greek the word passed into Latin and eventually became an international term: English *angel*, French *ange*, German *Engel*, Russian *ángel*, Hungarian *angyal*, etc. As Meillet rightly says, the word looks Greek but we really owe it to Hebrew.

A different kind of Hebrew influence is responsible for the polysemy

[1] On this problem see recently L. Deroy, *L'Emprunt linguistique*, pp. 93-102, where full bibliographical references will be found. A useful discussion of the various forms of semantic influence will be found in T. E. Hope, 'The Analysis of Semantic Borrowing', in *Essays Presented to C. M. Girdlestone*, Newcastle, 1960, pp. 125-41.

[2] See esp. Meillet, 'Les Interférences entre vocabulaires', op. cit., vol. II, pp. 36-43, and L. R. Palmer, *The Latin Language*, London, 1954, p. 187. On the wider question of Hebrew, Greek and Latin influences on some important modern concepts (*mother tongue*, *race*, *milieu*, etc.), see L. Spitzer, *Essays in Historical Semantics*, New York, 1948. Cf. also W. D. Elcock, *The Romance Languages*, London, 1960, pp. 199 ff.

of Greek κύριος, Latin *Dominus*, English *Lord*, French *Seigneur*, German *Herr*, etc., all of which mean both 'master' and 'God'. Since the Jews were forbidden to utter the name of God, they used the word for 'master' instead. When the Bible was translated into Greek, this usage was imitated by giving κύριος 'master' the additional meaning of 'God', and the same polysemy was then transmitted, through ecclesiastical Latin, to the modern European languages.

A case of polysemy in Greek adopted and handed down by the Latin of the early Church is that of the verb οἰκοδομεῖν 'to build', which, in ecclesiastical Greek, acquired the metaphorical sense 'to edify'. Under Greek influence, the Latin *aedificare* 'to build' was given the same moral meaning which still lives on in English *edify* and its equivalents in other languages.

In totally different circumstances, we find the same linguistic tendency at work in the speech of European immigrants to the United States.[1] In Colorado Spanish, for instance, *ministro* 'cabinet official' has acquired the additional sense of 'Protestant clergymen' under the influence of English *minister*. Various Romance verbs which originally meant 'to bring in' — Louisiana and Canadian French *introduire*, Italian *introdurre*, Portuguese *introduzir* — have also come to mean 'to acquaint, to present formally', thus copying the polysemy of English *introduce*. Semantic borrowing is an equally conspicuous feature of the Anglicized language of sport in France,[2] where the polysemy of English terms like *form*, *open*, *run* and many others has recently spread to their French equivalents:

'to be in great, in fine *form*'	'être en grande, en belle *forme*'
'an *open* race'	'une course très *ouverte*'
'to *run* the race of his life'	'*courir* la course de sa vie'

To those imbued with the French tradition of purity in language, these 'invisible exports', as Professor Orr has called them, are no less disturbing than the more blatant forms of Anglicism, but it is difficult to see how they could be avoided under the changed circumstances of modern life.

As some of these examples have shown, this type of polysemy is not always confined to contact between two particular languages. Many semantic borrowings have wide international currency, with different

[1] See U. Weinreich, *Languages in Contact. Findings and Problems*, New York, 1953, pp. 48 f. Cf. also E. Haugen, 'The Analysis of Linguistic Borrowing', *Language*, xxvi (1950), pp. 210-31: pp. 219 f.

[2] See J. Orr, 'Les Anglicismes du vocabulaire sportif', *Words and Sounds in English and French*, ch. 11.

idioms copying each other or imitating a common model. The grammatical term *case* is a good example of this tendency. When the idea of grammatical case emerged in Greek philosophy, the term πτῶσις 'fall, falling' was used to denote the new concept. The Roman grammarian' Varro copied this usage by giving *casus*, the Latin word for 'fall, falling, event', the additional sense of 'grammatical case'. This double meaning still persists in modern descendants of *casus*: the English *case*, the French *cas* and others; elsewhere the local word for 'fall' or 'event' is used in the meaning of 'grammatical case' (German *Fall*, Hungarian *eset*).[1]

Some forms of polysemy are so widespread and seem so natural that it is difficult to establish their origin. The word *taste*, for example, has two main meanings: 'perceiving the flavour of a thing' and 'discernment and appreciation of beauty' (cf. the *NED*). The same polysemy is found in many languages: French *goût*, Italian *gusto*, German *Geschmack*, etc. It has been suggested[2] that the Spanish *gusto* set the pattern for the whole series; but, since a similar ambiguity existed already in Latin,[3] this may have had some influence on the development of these terms.

Among the five sources of polysemy examined in this section, the first three — shifts in application, specialization of meaning, and figurative use — are by far the most important; reinterpretation of homonyms is very rare, whereas semantic borrowing, though quite common in certain situations, is not a normal process in everyday language.

2. *Safeguards and Conflicts*

Aristotle, as we have seen (p. 151), was highly critical of polysemy. 'Words of ambiguous meaning', he claimed, 'are chiefly useful to enable the sophist to mislead his hearers.' Since then, philosophers have vied with each other in denouncing polysemy as a defect of language and as a major obstacle to communication and even to clear thinking. Occasionally there were some dissentient voices. According to Bréal, Frederick the Great, who was an ardent admirer of French, saw in multiple meaning a sign of the superiority of that language. Bréal himself was inclined to agree with the king. 'The more meanings a word has accumulated', he wrote, 'the more diverse aspects of intellectual and social activity it is likely to represent' (op. cit., p. 144).

A moment's reflection will show that, far from being a defect of

---

[1] See Deroy, op. cit., pp. 95f.
[2] Migliorini, 'Calco e irradiazione sinonimica', loc. cit., p. 7.
[3] See Lewis and Short, *s.v. gustus*.

M

language, polysemy is an essential condition of its efficiency. If it were not possible to attach several senses to one word, this would mean a crushing burden on our memory: we would have to possess separate terms for every conceivable subject we might wish to talk about. Polysemy is an invaluable factor of economy and flexibility in language; what is astonishing is not that the machine occasionally breaks down, but that it breaks down so rarely.

How does this delicate mechanism work in practice? The main guarantee of its smooth working is the influence of *context*. No matter how many meanings a word may have in the dictionary, there will be no confusion if only one of them can make sense in any given situation. To quote again Bréal, 'we do not even have to exclude the other meanings of the word: these meanings do not arise for us, they do not cross the threshold of our consciousness' (ibid., p. 145). This can be seen most strikingly when the same word has two contradictory meanings which live on side by side without any risk of misunderstanding.[1] The Latin *altus*, for example, can mean 'high' or 'deep' according to the speaker's point of view: whether he is looking at an object from below upwards or from above downwards (Lewis and Short). *Sacer* means 'sacred' and also 'accursed', as in Virgil's famous phrase: 'auri *sacra* fames' 'cursed lust of gold'. French *défendre* signifies 'defend' in some contexts and 'forbid' in others. *Chasser* (which has given *chase* in English) is also ambivalent; as Nyrop wittily puts it, 'on *chasse le gibier* pour s'en emparer; on *chasse un domestique* pour s'en débarrasser' 'one "chases" game in order to catch it; one "chases" a servant to get rid of him' (*Sémantique*, p. 47).

Linguistic geographers often talk of 'semantic overload', 'hypertrophy' or 'plethora' of meaning as causes of ambiguity and confusion in language.[2] These terms would seem to suggest that the more senses a word has the more ambiguous it becomes. Actually, the number of meanings attached to a word is of little importance; what matters is their quality and their relation to each other. It is a well-known fact that some of our commonest words are those which have the widest range of meanings. In Littré's dictionary, the verb *aller* has nearly forty different senses, *mettre* nearly fifty, *prendre* and *faire* as many as eighty each (Nyrop, ibid., p. 26). These high figures are partly due to the 'abstract' and generic nature of French words, which was discussed in a previous

---

[1] On ambivalent words cf. recently H. Galton, *Die Sprache*, vi (1960), p. 239.
[2] Iordan-Orr, op. cit., pp. 166 ff.; cf. L. Spitzer's comments in *Archivum Romanicum*, viii (1924), p. 350.

chapter (pp. 121 f.); but the same tendency is noticeable in other languages, as a glance at the verbs *put* and *go* in the Oxford Dictionary will show.

An attempt was made a few years ago by the late G. K. Zipf to study the relation between polysemy and word-frequency by statistical methods. Having discovered that there is a 'direct relationship between the number of different meanings of a word and its relative frequency of occurrences', Zipf proceeded to find a mathematical formula for this correlation. He came to the conclusion that 'different meanings of a word will tend to be equal to the square root of its relative frequency (with the possible exception of the few dozen most frequent words) .[1] This was accepted by Professor J. Whatmough who summed up the result in the following formula where *m* stands for the number of meanings and *F* for relative frequency:[2]

$$m = F^{\frac{1}{2}}$$

Since Zipf's calculations were based on dictionary material, his formula should be taken with a grain of salt; as we have already seen (p. 160), the lexicographer has to distinguish more or less arbitrarily between different shades of the same meaning and different meanings of the same word, and his data are not very suitable for precise statistical analysis. There is, however, no reason to doubt the principle itself, namely, that the more frequent a word is the more senses it is likely to have. It is clear at any rate that diversity of meaning does not in itself weaken in any way the vitality of a word.

In addition to context there are a number of *special safeguards* which help to mitigate the consequences of polysemy. The scope of these devices is limited, but they are highly effective whenever they come into play:

(1) In languages with grammatical *gender*, this can be used to differentiate between meanings of the same word: French *le pendule* 'pendulum' — *la pendule* 'clock', *le manche* 'handle' — *la manche* 'sleeve'; German *der Band* 'volume' — *das Band* 'ribbon', *der See* 'lake' — *die See* 'sea'.

(2) Distinctions in meaning may be marked by differences in *inflexion*. English *brother* has two plurals with different senses: *brothers* and *brethren*; similarly French *aïeul*: *aïeux* 'forbears' — *aïeuls* 'grandfathers'; Italian *muro*: *i muri* 'walls' — *le mura* 'walls of a town'. In German there is a whole group of words differentiated in this way: *Licht*: *Lichte* 'lights'

[1] See his two articles in *The Journal of General Psychology*, vols. xxxii and xxxiii (1945), and his book, *Human Behavior and the Principle of Least Effort*, Cambridge, Mass., 1949.
[2] J. Whatmough, *Language. A Modern Synthesis*, p. 73.

— *Lichter* 'candles'; *Tuch*: *Tuche* 'sorts of cloth' — *Tücher* 'pieces of cloth'; *Wort*: *Worte* 'connected speech' — *Wörter* 'words'.[1] One noun has even three plurals: *Band*: *Bande* 'bonds' — *Bänder* 'ribbons' — *Bände* 'volumes'. Verbal paradigms can diverge in the same way: *hang*: *hung* — *hanged*; French *ressortir*: *il ressort* 'it comes out again; it is evident, it follows' — *il ressortit* 'it is under the jurisdiction of, belongs to (a country, a court, etc.)'.

(3) *Word-order* may also help to discriminate between different senses of the same term. The mobility of the adjective in French (cf. pp. 137 f.) is extensively utilized to this end: 'linge *propre*' '*clean* linen' — 'ses *propres* paroles' 'his *very* (own) words', 'pois *verts*' '*green* peas' — 'une *verte* semonce' 'a *good* dressing-down', 'une assertion *vraie*' 'a *true* statement' — 'un *vrai* diamant' 'a *real* (genuine) diamond'. French can obtain delicate contrast effects by using the same adjective in two different positions within the same sentence:[2] 'On annonce quelques *nouveaux* journaux, mais aucun journal *nouveau*';[3] 'passant difficilement du rang de *jeune* femme au rang de femme *jeune*'.[4] In English, where the adjective normally has a fixed place, this device is confined to a few set phrases: an 'ambassador *extraordinary*' is not the same thing as an '*extraordinary* ambassador', nor is a 'fee-*simple*' the same thing as a '*simple* fee'.[5]

(4) Sometimes the meaning of a word is clarified by *adding* another term to it; thus the adjective *fair*, which has a number of different and potentially conflicting senses, will be unambiguous in the compounds *fair-sized*, *fair-minded* and *fair-haired*.[6]

(5) A more drastic solution, which may weaken or destroy the unity of the word, is to distinguish between meanings by slight *modifications in form*. The modifications may be phonetic, graphic, or both.[7] There is phonetic differentiation in English *gallant* which, according to its meaning, can be stressed on the first or the second syllable, and graphic distinction in cases like English *discreet* — *discrete*, *draft* — *draught*, *metal* — *mettle*,[8] or French *dessein* 'design, plan, scheme' — *dessin* 'drawing, design, pattern'. Phonetic and graphic differences combine to distinguish between *antic* and *antique*, *divers* and *diverse*, *human* and *humane*, *urban* and *urbane*, and a few similar pairs.

---

[1] See Priebsch-Collinson, op. cit., p. 197.
[2] A construction known as *chiasmus*; cf. above, p. 138.
[3] 'Some *new* journals are announced, but none which is *really new* (quoted by Boillot, op. cit., p. 77, n. 1).
[4] Passing with difficulty from the status of a *young* woman to that of a woman *young in spirit*' (Françoise Sagan, *Aimez-vous Brahms?*, Paris, 1959, p. 11).
[5] See Rudskoger, op. cit., p. 477.
[6] Ibid., p. 476.   [7] Ibid., pp. 473-6.   [8] See above, p. 99.

It is only when all these safeguards have broken down that polysemy may lead to genuine *ambiguity*. Such ambiguity may arise in three different situations: in contacts between two languages, in technical usage, and in ordinary speech.

(1) *Semantic borrowing* from a foreign language may, as every translator knows, give rise to confusion and misunderstanding.[1] Some of these are ephemeral, like the case of the legendary Englishwoman who, misled by the double meaning of the word *engaged*, asked a French taxi-driver: 'Êtes-vous *fiancé?*',[2] or the foreign tourist who thought that the hall porter in a French hotel was Swiss because the French *suisse* can mean both 'Swiss' and 'hall porter'. Occasionally, such a misunderstanding may have more lasting effects. A notorious example is the history of the grammatical term *accusative*. This is a Latin translation of the Greek αἰτιατικὴ πτῶσις, derived from the noun αἰτία which could mean either 'cause' or 'charge, accusation'. The translator, misled by this polysemy, took the Greek adjective to mean 'accusative' whereas it really meant 'causative'.[3]

A recent example of confusion due to semantic borrowing is the French verb *réaliser*.[4] The traditional meaning of this verb is 'to carry into effect, to carry out'. Its use in the sense of 'to understand' is an Anglicism which goes back to Paul Bourget and, beyond him, to Baudelaire;[5] in the 1920s, this usage provoked a public discussion in which Gide and other well-known figures took part. The tendency, still frowned upon by the purists, to use the verb in the English sense can lead to comic situations, as in this sentence from a newspaper where the irony is surely unintentional: 'L'État-Major français a pleinement *réalisé* les intentions ennemies', which means in correct French: 'The French General Staff has fully *carried out* the enemy's intentions.'[6]

(2) Ambiguities are most in evidence where one would least expect them: in *scientific and technical usage*. Even where the terms and concepts of a science are precisely defined, every scholar has the right to redefine them as he thinks fit. In this way, even such recent technical terms as *psychoanalysis*, *existentialism*, *stylistics*, *structuralism* or *phoneme*, have developed a number of overlapping senses. *Semantics* itself, which ought

---

[1] See Deroy, op. cit., ch. 11.
[2] Migliorini, 'Calco e irradiazione sinonimica', loc. cit., p. 8.
[3] Ibid., p. 9.
[4] On the history of this verb, see E. Peruzzi, 'Francese *réaliser*', *Zeitschrift für Romanische Philologie*, lxix (1953), pp. 203-35.
[5] See A. Goosse, *Revue Belge de Philologie et d'Histoire*, xxxiii (1955), p. 931.
[6] Quoted in K. Nyrop, 'Réaliser', *Mélanges de philologie et d'histoire offerts à M. A. Thomas*, Paris, 1927, pp. 319-22.

to set an example in verbal consistency, is by no means free from this blemish (see above, p. 10). Scholars often have to waste considerable time, energy, and even money, before they can be satisfied that a book or an article with an ambiguous title lies outside their field. It has been suggested that such scientific terms should be indexed so that one could know at once in what sense they are being used;[1] thus the formula:

existentialism
Sartre

would make it clear that one is dealing with the agnostic form of existentialism professed by Sartre and his school, and not, for example, with the Christian branch of existentialism associated with Gabriel Marcel.

Confusion and misunderstanding are even more likely to arise when a word which is ambiguous in ordinary language is used in a technical, legal, scientific or other context where the utmost precision is required. A great deal of time is spent at diplomatic conferences, in legal proceedings and in academic discussions on defining words (cf. p. 126) and sorting out their various senses. We have seen (p. 54) how the ambiguity of the term *meaning* has hampered progress in semantics, so that some scholars have actually preferred to avoid the word altogether. Nor is *meaning* the worst offender in linguistics: a monograph on the history of the term *sentence* has listed no less than 200 different definitions of that concept.[2] In view of this terminological jungle, the compilation of standardized nomenclatures is of great benefit to scholarship,[3] and it would be in the interest of all concerned to check the growth of this form of polysemy.

In some cases, the ambiguity of certain key-words has had a serious effect on philosophical thought. In the *Critique of Practical Reason*, Kant drew attention to the double meaning of the all-important ethical terms *bonum* and *malum* in Latin. *Bonum* could mean 'anything good' as well as 'prosperity', whereas *malum* could stand for 'anything bad or evil' and also for 'hurt, harm'. 'The German language', Kant added, 'has the good fortune to possess expressions which do not allow this difference to be overlooked. It possesses two very distinct concepts, and especially different expressions, for that which the Latins express by a single word'.[4] It has

[1] A. H. Maslow, *Psychological Review*, lii (1945), pp. 239 f.
[2] J. Ries, *Was ist ein Satz?*, Prague, 1931.
[3] See J. Marouzeau, *Lexique de la terminologie linguistique*, 3rd ed., Paris, 1951; E. P. Hamp, *A Glossary of American Technical Linguistic Usage, 1925-1950*, Utrecht—Antwerp, 1957.
[4] See A. Flew, 'Philosophy and Language', in *Essays in Conceptual Analysis*, ed. A. Flew, London, 1955, p. 5.

also been suggested that 'the persuasiveness of Hegel's central theme, the Dialectic, is derived from a simple ambiguity of the German word *aufheben*. This word has three main uses: (1) to lift up; (2) to preserve; (3) to cancel ... No similarly ambiguous word exists in English, and therefore Hegel's expositors are driven to coin neologisms like *sublate* in order to translate his most important word.'[1]

The most famous ambiguity of this kind is the case of the Greek λόγος. According to Liddell and Scott's dictionary, this word has two chief meanings, one corresponding to Latin *oratio*, 'the word or that by which the inward thought is expressed', the other to Latin *ratio*, 'the inward thought' itself. Since λόγος occurs in the opening verse of St. John's Gospel, the ambiguity of the term has a direct bearing on the interpretation of that crucial passage. When translating that Gospel, Goethe's Faust rejects the traditional version: 'In the beginning was the *Word*'; he experiments with *sense* (Sinn) and *force* (Kraft), and finally decides for 'In the beginning was the *act* (Tat)'.[2]

(3) In *ordinary language* it often happens that a word develops two or more senses capable of arising in the same contexts. In many cases this has led to the disappearance of one or more of the conflicting meanings. This process has been fully investigated by Dr. Rudskoger in his book on the polysemy of English adjectives, and one or two interesting examples collected by him may be mentioned here:[3]

Admirable. — When this adjective first appeared in English in the late sixteenth century, it had the neutral sense 'to be wondered at', which could be favourable or unfavourable according to context. As the positive meaning gained the upper hand the original sense fell into disuse; a sentence like the following: 'It may justly seem *admirable* how that senseless religion should gain so much ground on Christianity', which Dr. Rudskoger quotes from 1639, would be impossible today.

Careful. — Until the end of the sixteenth century this adjective could also mean 'full of care and grief': 'her maydens are *careful*, and she herself is in great heavynesse' (Coverdale). Eventually, this sense was eclipsed by the other meanings of the word.

Peevish. — This term had at one time half a dozen contemporaneous senses: 'silly', 'mad', 'spiteful', 'horrible', 'headstrong', and 'morose,

---

[1] T. D. Weldon, op. cit., p. 107; cf. Flew, loc. cit.

[2] *Faust*, Part I, ll. 1224 ff.; cf. above, pp. 36 and 38.

[3] Op. cit., pp. 463-73. See also R. J. Menner, 'Multiple Meaning and Change of Meaning in English', *Language*, xxi (1945), pp. 59-76; Gamillscheg, *Französische Bedeutungslehre*, pp. 170 ff.; K. Jaberg, *Aspects géographiques du langage*, Paris, 1936, ch. 2; Iordan-Orr, op. cit., pp. 165 ff.

ill-tempered, fretful'. Since several of these could fit into the same type of context, all but the last were discarded.

Vivacious. — In addition to its present-day meaning, *vivacious* could once also mean 'long-lived' and 'difficult to kill'. The latter senses subsequently dropped out because of the risk of ambiguity; the following sentence, which the *NED* quotes from the seventeenth century: 'Hitherto the English Bishops had been *vivacious* almost to wonder', has now a distinctly comic ring.

An extreme example of ambiguity leading to the disappearance of one of the conflicting senses is the adjective *wan* which originally meant 'lacking light or lustre, dark'. The *NED* quotes from Skelton: 'With vysage *wan*, As swarte as tan.' Since this meaning was incompatible with that of 'pallid', which the word had acquired in Middle English, it disappeared in the late sixteenth century (Menner, loc. cit.).

All these examples were taken from adjectives because this word-class has been most thoroughly investigated from this point of view. But other parts of speech can be involved in the same kind of conflict. Thus the French *se passer de* could once mean either 'do without' or 'be content with'; Molière still has: 'un homme qui *s'est passé* durant sa vie d'une assez simple demeure'.[1] Of the two opposite meanings only the first has survived.

Polysemy can also lead to a different type of conflict. If a word develops an unpleasant sense with strong emotive overtones, it may become so tainted that it will be virtually unusable in its older meanings.[2] An interesting example is the adjective *cunning* which originally had a positive value, that of 'learned, intelligent, skilful'. Shakespeare still wrote: 'I thought he had been valiant, and so *cunning* in fence' (*Twelfth Night*, Act III, scene 4). Towards the end of the sixteenth century, however, the adjective began to be used in a distinctly pejorative meaning, that of 'crafty, artful, sly'. Subsequently, this usage cast a shadow on the more positive meanings of the word, and emerged from the contest as the only sense which is really alive. Similarly, *obsequious* still had the favourable meaning of 'obedient, dutiful' when Shakespeare made Falstaff say: 'I see you are *obsequious* in your love, and I profess requital to a hair's breadth' (*Merry Wives*, Act IV, scene 3); but when it came to be used in the pejorative sense of 'fawning, cringing, sycophantic' it gradually disappeared from positive contexts. To take an example from a different

---

[1] 'A man who, throughout his life, was content with a fairly simple dwelling' (*Don Juan*, Act III, scene 6, quoted by Nyrop, *Sémantique*, p. 47).

[2] See Rudskoger, op. cit., pp. 480-4, from where the next two examples are taken; on *cunning*, see also ibid., pp. 354-7 as well as the *NED*.

sphere, when *undertaker* began to be employed in its present sense it was no longer felt to be suitable in the more general meaning of 'contractor' or 'one who embarks on some business enterprise'; the following sentence, quoted from Swift by the *NED*: 'The *undertaker* himself will publish his proposals with all convenient speed', would today provoke a wry smile.

Conflicts between incompatible meanings of the same word are going on all the time in language, though it is impossible to tell beforehand how they will be resolved. In present-day English there is some uneasiness and hesitancy in the use of adjectives like *common, strange*, and especially *funny*, as shown by the current witticism: 'Do you mean *funny* "ha-ha" or *funny* "peculiar"?', or by passages like the following, which Dr. Rudskoger quotes from a recent novel: 'I never dreamed for a moment then that there had been any *funny* business. *Funny? Did I say funny?* God, what a word to use!'[1] Avoidance of adjectives like *blooming* and *bloody* in their respectable senses is another pointer in the same direction (cf. p. 147).

Awkward ambiguity may even affect the vitality of a word. This was forcefully argued by Gilliéron in whose view 'homonymic clashes and hypertrophy of meaning have been a perpetual menace in language, a perennial cause of the disappearance of words'.[2] In his linguistic atlas of France he found several well-authenticated cases of terms which have fallen into disuse because of their 'pathological' polysemy. In certain parts of Northern France, for example, the noun *vaisseau* 'vessel, ship' could also mean 'beehive' and 'swarm of bees'. 'Being super-saturated with meanings it was doomed to disappear',[3] though attempts were made to save it by modifying its form in some of its uses. Gilliéron's reconstructions are brilliant as well as convincing; yet it would appear that, whatever may happen in dialects, words in ordinary language are seldom abandoned for this reason; in most cases it is sufficient to eliminate some of the conflicting senses. It is certainly significant that out of 120 English adjectives, many of them highly ambiguous, which Dr. Rudskoger has investigated, only three — 2½ per cent — have disappeared altogether (p. 439). Although polysemy is omnipresent in language, it is not, apparently, a major factor in the obsolescence of words.

---

[1] Op. cit., p. 479; cf. also Menner, loc. cit.
[2] *Généalogie des mots qui désignent l'abeille*, Paris, 1918, p. 157.
[3] Jordan-Orr, op. cit., p. 167.

II. Homonymy

1. *Sources*

Homonymy is far less common and far less complex than polysemy, though its effects can be just as serious and even more dramatic. There are only three ways in which it can arise, and the third of these is of very subsidiary importance.

(1) *Phonetic convergence.* — The commonest cause of homonymy is converging sound-development. Under the influence of ordinary phonetic changes, two or more words which once had different forms coincide in the spoken language and sometimes in writing as well. The process is so simple that a few examples will suffice to illustrate it:[1]

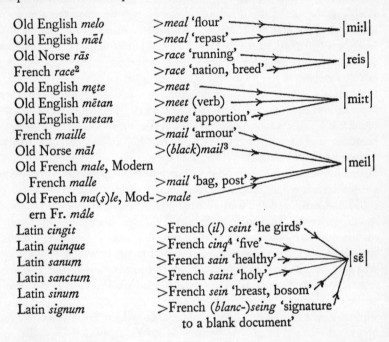

Old English *melo*   >*meal* 'flour'
Old English *mæl*   >*meal* 'repast' |miːl|
Old Norse *rās*   >*race* 'running'
French *race*[2]   >*race* 'nation, breed' |reis|
Old English *męte*   >*meat*
Old English *mētan*   >*meet* (verb) |miːt|
Old English *metan*   >*mete* 'apportion'
French *maille*   >*mail* 'armour'
Old Norse *māl*   >*(black)mail*[3]
Old French *male*, Modern
  French *malle*   >*mail* 'bag, post' |meil|
Old French *ma(s)le*, Mod- >*male*
  ern Fr. *mâle*
Latin *cingit*   >French *(il) ceint* 'he girds'
Latin *quinque*   >French *cinq*[4] 'five'
Latin *sanum*   >French *sain* 'healthy' |sɛ̃|
Latin *sanctum*   >French *saint* 'holy'
Latin *sinum*   >French *sein* 'breast, bosom'
Latin *signum*   >French *(blanc-)seing* 'signature
                             to a blank document'

This form of homonymy is commonest in languages with many monosyllabic terms; it is therefore particularly frequent in English and

---

[1] The English etymologies which follow are all taken from the 1952 impr. of the *Shorter Oxford English Dictionary*.

[2] On the origin of this word see Spitzer, *Essays in Historical Semantics*, ch. 4.

[3] *Mail* is still used in Scotland in the sense of 'payment, tax, tribute, rent'; cf. also the phrase *mails and duties*: 'the rents of an estate, whether in money or grain' (*NED*).

[4] The final consonant is often pronounced; see Fouché, op. cit., p. 479.

in French, and less widespread in, say, German or Italian where the phonetic substance of words has been better preserved.[1] Another factor which favours homonymy is the loss of final consonants. English, for example, has, in spite of its richness in monosyllables, relatively fewer homonyms than French since the retention of final consonants helps to keep words, even the shortest, distinct from each other. In French, both monosyllabism and loss of final consonants combine to produce homonyms on a considerable scale. A number of French words consist of a single vowel: e.g. *au* 'to the' (masculine singular) — *aux* 'to the' (masculine-feminine plural) — *eau* 'water' — *haut* 'high' — *os*[2] 'bones', and *aulx*, the old plural of *ail* 'garlic', all of which are pronounced |o|. Another very common type of word-structure in French is the sequence: consonant + vowel: *tan* 'tan' — *tant* 'so much' — *taon* 'horse-fly' — *temps* 'time' — *(je) tends, (tu) tends, (il) tend, tends!* '(I, you) tend, (he) tends, tend!'. Words of this type would never have coincided in English.

In this branch of semantics, statistical data can be very revealing not only about the frequency of homonyms in a given language, but also about connexions between homonymy, word-length and word-structure.[3] But, while it is perfectly clear that some languages are more infested with homonyms than others, it is not difficult to find examples of chance homonymy in any idiom, even those which have suffered least from the wear and tear of sound-change;[4] cf. such pairs as German *Bauer* 'peasant' — *Bauer* 'cage'; Latin *comparare* 'match, compare' — *comparare* 'prepare, arrange, procure'; Hungarian *ár* 'price' — *ár* 'flood' — *ár* 'awl'.

(2) *Semantic divergence.* — Homonymy can also be brought about through diverging sense-development. When two or more meanings of the same word drift apart to such an extent that there will be no obvious connexion between them, polysemy will give place to homonymy and the unity of the word will be destroyed. We have seen some examples of this process in the section on loss of motivation (p. 98): *pupil* 'ward, scholar' and 'apple of the eye'; *collation* 'comparison' and 'light repast'. Ordinary language is full of 'secondary' homonyms of this type: only an

---

[1] See Jespersen, 'Monosyllabism in English', *Linguistica*, pp. 384-408, and Harmer, op. cit., ch. 4.

[2] Cf. Fouché, op. cit., p. 395.

[3] See B. Trnka, *A Phonological Analysis of Present-day Standard English*, Prague, 1935, pp. 56 ff. Cf. also A. Schönhage, *Zur Struktur des französischen Wortschatzes. Der französische Einsilber*, Bonn, 1948 (unpubl. thesis reviewed by G. Gougenheim, *Le Français Moderne*, xx (1952), pp. 66-8), and P. Miron, 'Recherches sur la typologie des langues romanes', in the Proceedings of the Eighth International Congress of Romance Linguistics, pp. 693-7.

[4] See, e.g., A. Meillet, 'Sur les effets de l'homonymie dans les anciennes langues indo-européennes', *Cinquantenaire de l'Ecole Pratique des Hautes Etudes*, Paris, 1921, pp. 169-80, and E. Öhmann, *Über Homonymie und Homonyme im Deutschen*, Helsinki, 1934.

etymologist would connect the verb *to long* with the adjective *long*; *rake* 'man of loose habits' with the verb *to rake*; *sole*, name of a fish, with the *sole* of a shoe; *still* 'motionless' with the adverb *still* 'yet'; or the French *voler* 'to steal' with *voler* 'to fly'.

This form of homonymy is the exact counterpart of a process discussed in the previous section: the reinterpretation of homonyms as though they were one word with two senses (pp. 164 f.), as in the two *ear*-s or the two *corn*-s. If the two tendencies are represented diagrammatically it becomes clear that they work in opposite directions:

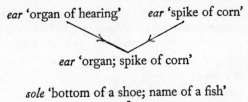

In the first case, two words have merged into one; in the second, one word has split into two. It should be added that the second process seems to be far more common than the first.

The passage from polysemy to homonymy raises the same problem as the converse process. Since we are unable to measure the 'degree of nearness of the meanings', as Bloomfield put it, it is difficult to say in particular cases where polysemy ends and where homonymy begins. The question has a direct bearing on the work of the lexicographer since he has to decide in each case whether to record such doubtful homonyms as one word or two.[1] The decision is bound to be subjective and to some extent arbitrary. Should a purely descriptive dictionary enter the following under one or several headings: *drill* 'instrument for drilling or boring' and *drill* 'military exercise or training'; *fast* 'firmly' and *fast* 'rapid'; *hunch* 'hump' and the Americanism *hunch* 'presentiment'; *suit* 'legal action', *suit* 'garment', and *suit* 'set of cards'? Some speakers would no doubt regard these as single words, though they would find it difficult to guess the connexion between their meanings.

[1] See on this problem R. Godel, 'Homonymie et identité', *Cahiers Ferdinand de Saussure*, vii (1948), pp. 5-15; P. Diaconescu, *Probleme de Lingvistică Generală*, vol. I, pp. 133-53; F. Asan, ibid., vol. II, pp. 113-24; M. M. Falkovich, *Voprosy Jazykoznanija*, 1960, no. 5, pp. 85-8.

In a few cases there are reasonably sound criteria for deciding in favour of homonymy. Difference in spelling may not be necessarily conclusive, as we saw in the discussion of pairs like *draft — draught*, *discreet — discrete*, and *metal — mettle* (pp. 170 f.); nevertheless it is, in conjunction with other factors, an indication that the word is no longer perceived as a unit. This is clearly seen in pairs like *flower — flour*, *gate* 'road, street' (cf. *Gallowgate*) — *gait*, French *penser* 'to think' — *panser* 'to groom a horse, to dress a wound', all of which were originally single words, but are now regarded as homonyms.

If two words identical in form can be used in the same sentence without any sense of repetition, this suggests that the speaker is unaware of any connexion between them. Thus, should there be any doubt about the relationship between French *pas* 'step' and *pas*, negative particle, both of which come from the Latin *passus* 'step', an idiom like 'Cela ne se trouve *pas* dans le *pas* d'un cheval' ('That is not found every day') would suffice to show that they are regarded as two separate words. One must, however, be careful not to use puns as evidence. Thus Pascal's famous paradox: 'Le cœur a ses *raisons* que la *raison* ne connaît point' ('The heart has its *reasons* which *reason* does not know'), is based on the double meaning of the word *raison* and does not prove in any way, as has been suggested,[1] that this is a case of homonymy, not polysemy.

Yet another criterion which may sometimes decide the issue is rhyme. It is quite clear, for instance, that no self-respecting poet would rhyme French *point* 'point' and *point*, negative particle (both from Latin *punctum*) if he felt them to be one word, not two; yet we find in Corneille:

> Et sa mâle vigueur, toujours en même *point*,
> Succombe sous la force, et ne lui cède *point*.
> > *Horace*, Act IV, scene 1.[2]

These and similar criteria might be helpful in some cases but will leave many others unsolved. The suggestion was made recently that 'social science has workable techniques for studying subjective opinions which could be applied to homonymy problems (if it is granted that they are a matter of speakers' opinions) as well as to political issues'.[3] If a statistical

---

[1] Bally, *Traité de stylistique*, vol. I, p. 48.
[2] 'And his virile vigour, standing its ground, succumbs to force but does not yield to it'. This is not an isolated rhyme in Corneille; another example is quoted by Bréal, op. cit., p. 146, n. 2.
[3] Weinreich, *Language*, xxxi, pp. 541 f.

inquiry, a kind of linguistic Gallup Poll, could be devised on these lines, this important and unsatisfactory aspect of lexicography could at last be placed on a solid basis.

(3) *Foreign influence.* — Many words introduced from abroad have swelled the ranks of homonyms in English and other languages, as can be seen from some of the examples already quoted (*race, mail — male*).[1] In some cases, such homonymy has led to serious conflicts, as in the pairs: *gate* 'entrance' (from Old English *geat*) — *gate* 'road, street' (from Old Norse *gata*), and *straight* (from Middle English *stregt*) — *strait* (from Old French *estreit*, Latin *strictus*).[2] When a loan-word becomes firmly established in its new surroundings it will be adapted to the local phonetic system and will thenceforth take part in the normal sound-changes; it may thus come to coincide with other words in the receiving language. This type of foreign influence, then, is not a separate source of homonymy but merely a special form of converging sound-development.

The influence of a foreign language can also lead to homonymy by a different route: through *semantic borrowing*.[3] This is a very rare process, but one or two examples may be quoted here. Upon the model of the German homonyms *Schloss* 'castle' and *Schloss* 'lock', the Czech and Polish words for a 'lock', *zamek*, are also used in the sense of 'castle'. The same 'loan-homonymy' exists also in Russian, though there the mobility of accent makes it possible to distinguish between the two meanings: *za'mok* 'lock' — *'zamok* 'castle' (cf. p. 24).[4] It has also been suggested that the ambiguity of Rumanian *lume* and Hungarian *világ*, both of which mean 'light' as well as 'world', is due to Slavonic influence; the same homonymy (or advanced polysemy?) is found for instance in the Russian noun *svet*.[5]

2. *Homonymic Clashes*

Homonymy differs from polysemy in two vital respects. Unlike the latter it has no positive advantages except for the punster and the rhymester. For reasons which have already been explained (pp. 167 f.), it is

[1] See R. J. Menner, 'The Conflict of Homonyms in English', *Language*, xii (1936), pp. 229-44: pp. 234 ff.

[2] Same word as the French *étroit* 'narrow' and the English *strict*. On the conflict between the two *gate*-s, see E. R. Williams, op. cit., pp. 57-69; on that between *straight* and *strait*, see ibid., pp. 103-11.

[3] See esp. T. E. Hope, loc. cit.

[4] Deroy, op. cit., p. 97.

[5] Ibid.; cf., however, G. Bárczi, *Magyar Szófejtő Szótár* ('Hungarian Etymological Dictionary'), Budapest, 1941, s.v. *világ*.

impossible to imagine a language without polysemy, whereas a language without homonyms is not only conceivable: it would in fact be a more efficient medium. The second difference is that polysemy is incomparably more widespread than homonymy. This does not mean, however, that the latter is not frequent; in some languages, such as English and French, it exists on a scale which some observers find truly alarming. In his entertaining essay 'On English Homophones', published over forty years ago, the late Poet Laureate, Robert Bridges, calculated that there must be between 1600 and 2000 homonyms in English. 'Now it is variously estimated', he went on, 'that 3000 to 5000 words is about the limit of an average educated man's talking vocabulary, and since the 1600 are, the most of them, words which such a speaker will use ... it follows that he has a foolishly imperfect and clumsy instrument.'[1] Bridges's estimate of the average speaker's verbal resources is undoubtedly too low, but even if one multiplies it by ten[2] the proportion of homonyms will still remain substantial.

Since the work done on 'homonymics' by Gilliéron, J. Orr and other linguistic geographers,[3] it is no longer possible to dismiss this form of ambiguity as a mere episode in the life of language. Nevertheless it is true to say that, in the vast majority of cases, homonyms cause no embarrassment in ordinary speech. There are a number of *safeguards* against any possibility of confusion. Most of these are similar to those mentioned in the section on polysemy (pp. 168 ff.), but there are also some characteristic differences.

By far the most important of these safeguards is the influence of *context*. In Professor Palmer's formula, 'homonymity causes linguistic disturbances only when it exists between words that in given contexts would cause misunderstandings'.[4] This is recognized even by linguistic geographers who have given great prominence to the destructive power of homonymy. In the often-quoted words of Gilliéron and Mario Roques: 'L'homonymie n'est pas une force qui va, fatale, inéluctable, détruisant sans merci tout ce que lui livre une phonétique aveugle: pour qu'elle ait à agir, encore faut-il qu'il y ait rencontre, et la rencontre ne se

---

[1] *Society for Pure English Tracts*, II (1919), p. 6.
[2] Cf. Jespersen, *Growth and Structure*, p. 196.
[3] For a general survey see Iordan-Orr, op. cit., ch. 3; see also J. Orr, 'On Homonymics', *Words and Sounds in English and French*, ch. 12, and other chapters of the same book; Wartburg, *Problèmes et méthodes*, ch. 3. In the English field the most important contribution is E. R. Williams, op. cit.; see also R. J. Menner, 'The Conflict of Homonyms in English', loc. cit., and Rudskoger, op. cit., pp. 427-41. There are several articles on homonymy in *Voprosy Jazykoznanija*, 1960, no. 5.
[4] *An Introduction to Modern Linguistics*, London, 1936, p. 113. Cf. also Williams, op. cit., pp. 4 f.

produit que pour des mots engagés dans les mêmes chemins de la pensée.'[1]

Contexts, however, are of infinite diversity, and it may happen that two homonyms with totally different meanings will both make sense in the same utterance. Thus the homonymy between *son* and *sun* seems harmless enough; yet Jespersen reports the case of a small girl who was asked by her mother whether her new doll was her *son* and replied, pointing to the sky: 'No, that's my *sun*.'[2] But the same scholar is on less sure ground when he suggests that the replacement of *son* by *boy* or *lad* in dialects is due to a homonymic clash between *son* and *sun*.[3] Such occasional ambiguities, brought about by freak contexts, are of little importance; it is only when misunderstandings occur time and again that something is done to remove them. To quote again Gilliéron, 'le rôle destructeur de l'homonymie n'apparaît que lorsque le parler a pleinement conscience du caractère intolérable des conflits, on n'essaye d'y remédier qu'après expérience d'une gêne intolérable'.[4]

In addition to context there are, as in the case of polysemy, several *special safeguards* against homonymy. Some of these are very common; others are more limited in range. The cumulative effect of these safeguards goes a long way to reduce the danger of homonymic conflicts.

(1) Many homonyms exist only in theory; in practice there is no risk of any confusion since they belong to different *word-classes*. Thus it was unrealistic to suggest, as Robert Bridges did (loc. cit., p. 22), that the verb *to know* is 'doomed' because of the threefold homonymy in which it is involved: *know — no, knows — nose*, and *knew — new*. Quite apart from differences in meaning it is difficult to imagine any sentence where a verb could occupy the same place as a negative particle, a noun or an adjective. This consideration alone would reduce very drastically the number of 'effective' homonyms in a language. At the same time, difference in class does not automatically rule out any possibility of confusion. There is evidence, for example, of a homonymic entanglement between the French noun *part* (from Latin *pars, partem*), and the preposition *par* (from Latin

---

[1] 'Homonymy is not a force working inevitably, inescapably, destroying mercilessly everything that a blind phonetics delivers to it: it will come into play only if there is an encounter, and such an encounter will arise only in the case of words belonging to the same paths of thought' (Gilliéron-Roques, *Etudes de géographie linguistique*, Paris, 1912, pp. 149 f.). On the authorship of this passage see Iordan-Orr, op. cit., p. 162, n. 1, and M. Roques, *Romania*, lxxiv (1953), p. 140.

[2] *Language: its Nature, Development and Origin*, pp. 120 f.

[3] Ibid., p. 286.

[4] 'The destructive role of homonymy appears only when language is fully aware of the intolerable nature of the conflicts, we try to remedy it only after experiencing an intolerable embarrassment' (*Généalogie des mots qui désignent l'abeille*, p. 58).

per): in phrases like '*de par* le Roi' 'by order, in the name of the King', the original form was *de part*, with the noun, whereas in the phrase *à part moi* 'in my own heart', the noun seems to have been substituted for the preposition.[1]

(2) In languages which possess grammatical *gender*, this can help to distinguish between homonymous nouns: French *le poêle* 'stove' — *la poêle* 'frying-pan', *le vase* 'vase, vessel' — *la vase* 'mud'; German *der Kiefer* 'jaw' — *die Kiefer* 'fir'. Once again this safeguard is not absolute for there are constructions where differences in gender cannot be indicated. Thus the distinction between French *le foie* 'liver' and *la foi* 'faith' will lapse in the combination 'crise de *foie* (*foi*)', and authors who would normally write 'crise *de* (not *de la*) conscience' will put in the article in 'crise de *la* foi' to avoid any confusion between a crisis of faith and a crisis of the liver.[2]

(3) Homonyms belonging to the same word-class are sometimes differentiated by *inflexion*. The plural of French *travail* 'work' is *travaux*, but that of the homonymous *travail*, 'sling or frame where a horse is shod; stocks', is *travails*.[3] Similarly German *die Kiefer* 'jaws' — *die Kiefern* 'firs'. The past tense of *to ring* 'make a circle or ring' is *ringed*, that of *to ring* 'sound loudly' is *rang*.

(4) Occasionally, *compounds* or special *phrases* are formed to show which of two or more homonyms is meant. This device plays an important role in Chinese where all words are monosyllabic and homonymy is therefore particularly common. In English, phrases like '*left*-hand corner' and 'without *let* or hindrance' are employed to remedy the ambiguity of the italicized words.[4] In French, the months May and August are often called 'moi de *mai*', 'moi d'*août*', instead of simply *mai* and *août*, to avoid homonymic complications. An amusing case of ambiguity in the culinary sphere is that of French *pomme* 'apple' and *pomme* 'potato', the latter short for *pomme de terre*. The problem is sometimes solved by referring to the fruit as *pomme de l'air*, *pomme-fruit*, or even *pomme-pomme*.[5]

(5) In languages with non-phonetic writing, *spelling* will often help to differentiate between words identical in sound. This is of course no more than a palliative; it reduces the number of homonyms on the written and the printed page but leaves spoken language unaffected, except in so

[1] See Bloch-Wartburg, *s.v. par* and *part*.
[2] Iordan-Orr, op. cit., p. 163, n. 1.
[3] Originally the same word as the other *travail*. On the history of these terms see esp. C. H. Livingston, *Skein-winding Reels. Studies in Word History and Etymology*, Ann Arbor, 1957.
[4] See Jespersen, *Linguistica*, p. 399.
[5] Gilliéron, *Généalogie des mots qui désignent l'abeille*, p. 58.

N

far as it provides a quick and easy way of dispelling confusion: if there
is any doubt whether we mean *night* or *knight* it is much simpler to spell
them out than to define their meanings. In a language like French, where
both lexical and grammatical homonymy is common, spelling is certainly
of some help in distinguishing between long series of homonyms: *vain*
'vain' (plural: *vains*) — *(je) vaincs* 'I vanquish', *(il) vainc* 'he vanquishes'
— *vin* 'wine' (plural: *vins*) — *vingt* 'twenty' — *(je) vins* 'I came', *(il) vint* 'he
came', all of which are pronounced |vɛ̃|.

The value of spelling as a safeguard against homonymy has been
doubted by some scholars. Bloomfield, for instance, was quite categorical
on this point: 'It is wrong to suppose that writing would be unintelligible
if homonyms (e.g. *pear*, *pair*, *pare* or *piece*, *peace*) were spelled alike;
writing which reproduces the phonemes of speech is as intelligible as
speech.'[1] But surely the point is that in this respect writing is *more*
intelligible than speech, and that homonymy in the language as a whole,
spoken as well as written, is reduced as a result. It is true on the other
hand that non-phonetic spelling produces homonyms of its own: words
like *lead* and *to lead*, a *tear* and *to tear*, a *sow* and *to sow*, which are pronounced differently but written in the same way. But such cases are rather
less common than those where writing helps to discriminate between the
homonyms of speech. It is certainly significant that languages like English,
French and especially Chinese, where homonyms abound, should
have preserved a non-phonetic form of writing while others, less vulnerable to homonymy, are written more or less as they are spoken and have
been repeatedly adjusted to bring spelling closer to pronunciation. It may,
however, be doubted whether the value of writing as a remedy against
homonymy is important enough to provide a serious argument against
spelling reform.

(6) In some cases a homonymic conflict has been averted by slightly
modifying the form of the words involved. The clash between *gate*
'entrance' and *gate* 'road, street', which has already been mentioned (p.
180), has led, in Standard English and in many dialects, to the disappearance of the second word. Other dialects have preserved both terms,
but they are no longer homonymous since the word for 'entrance' has
forms like *yate*, *yett*, etc., which go back to a different Old English
prototype than Standard English *gate*.[2] The same desire to distinguish
between homonyms explains why certain final consonants which would
normally be silent are, or may be, pronounced in French, as in *but* 'aim',

---

[1] *Language*, p. 502; cf. Jespersen, *Linguistica* ,p. 398.
[2] See Williams, op. cit., pp. 57 ff.

joug 'yoke', *sens* 'sense', and others. For the same reason, the final |st| is pronounced in *le Christ* to distinguish it from *le cri* 'cry, shout', whereas in the combination *Jésus-Christ*, where there is no danger of confusion, the last two consonants are silent.

A particularly interesting case of differentiation is the history of the Latin verbs *necare* 'to kill' (in Vulgar Latin 'to drown') and *negare* 'to deny' in French. These verbs became homonymous in Old French both in those forms which were stressed in Latin on the first syllable and those where the stress fell on the second:

$$\left.\begin{array}{l} \text{'}necat \\ \text{'}negat \end{array}\right\} \text{Old Fr. } nie \qquad \left.\begin{array}{l} ne\text{'}care \\ ne\text{'}gare \end{array}\right\} \text{Old Fr. } noyer$$

This ambiguity was removed, and the conjugation of both verbs was regularized, by remodelling each on a different basis: *nier, je nie, nous nions*, etc., became the word for 'denying', whereas *noyer, je noie, nous noyons* was reserved for the meaning 'to drown'.

If, in spite of all these safeguards, a full-scale *homonymic clash* takes place the outcome is usually more serious than in the conflicts due to polysemy. There, as we have seen (p. 176), it is seldom necessary to sacrifice a whole word; normally it will be sufficient to discard one or more of the incompatible senses. In homonymic clashes, one word collides with another, and unless they can be separated by phonetic or grammatical means, one or the other — sometimes even both — will have to be removed from the scene. These processes can best be studied in linguistic atlases where the complex chain of causes and effects can be reconstructed with great precision. The classic example is Gilliéron's analysis of the conflict between the cock and the cat in South-West France.[1] In part of that territory final |-ll| has changed to |-t|; as a result, the Latin word for 'cock', *gallus*, became *gat* and thus fell together with the name of the cat, *gat* from Vulgar Latin *cattus*. As it would have been highly inconvenient to have homonymous names for the two animals, *gat* 'cock' disappeared and was replaced by local forms of French *faisan* 'pheasant' and *vicaire* 'curate'.[2] Outside the area of the change from |-ll| to |-t| there was no confusion between *gal* 'cock' and *gat* 'cat', and both terms have survived. As Bloomfield rightly points out, it is a 'remarkable fact that the isogloss[3] which separates the queer words | azaⁿ | and | begej |

---

[1] See Gilliéron-Roques, op. cit., ch. 12.
[2] Or possibly *viguier* 'provost', which is historically the same word.
[3] 'Boundary of a linguistic feature', from Greek *isos* 'equal'+*glōssa* 'language'.

from the ordinary |gal|, coincides exactly with the isogloss between |-t| and |-ll|; this is highly significant, because isoglosses — even isoglosses representing closely related features — very rarely coincide for any considerable distance' (*Language*, p. 398).

Gilliéron was on the whole more interested in the conflicts themselves than in the *substitutes* which have to be found for discarded homonyms. The problem of replacement has been examined by Professor Wartburg in a series of studies[1] which have thrown valuable light on the close connexion between descriptive and historical linguistics. By exploring further the choice of possible substitutes one finds that the gap caused by the disappearance of a homonym can be filled in a variety of ways:

(1) An ambiguous form may be sacrificed and replaced by a *derivative*. As Gilliéron showed in a special monograph on the subject,[2] the Latin *clavis* 'key' and *clavus* 'nail', which have given *clef* and *clou* in French, both became *claus* in the South of France. To remove this ambiguity, the word for 'nail' was replaced by *clavel*, from *clavellus*, a diminutive of *clavus*. In Latin American Spanish, a voiceless |th| (written as *c* before *e* and *i*, and as *z* elsewhere) has become |s|, and this has created a number of homonyms: *cocer* 'cook' has coincided with *coser* 'sew', *caza* 'hunt' with *casa* 'house', etc. One solution of the problem is to replace one of the homonyms by a derivative: *cocer* by *cocinar*, *caza* by *cacería*.[3]

(2) The place vacated by a homonym may be occupied by one or more ordinary *synonyms*. This happened in the conflict between *let* 'leave, allow' (from Old English *lǣtan*) and *let* 'hinder' (from Old English *lettan*). The latter has been replaced by *hinder* and other synonyms, though it has survived in two special combinations: 'without *let* or hindrance' and a '*let* ball'.

(3) The substitute may be what Professor Wartburg has called a 'satellite' of the disappearing term: a *jocular synonym* which was available at the time when the clash occurred. This is how Wartburg would interpret the use of the word for 'curate' in the sense of 'cock': to compare the bird to the village priest is, in his view, typical of the broad popular humour for which the Gascons are renowned. In much the same way the conflict between *an ear* and *a near* 'kidney' (cf. p. 156) was solved in some areas by dropping the first word and using *lug* instead.[4]

(4) Sometimes a homonym will be replaced by a term denoting some

---

[1] See esp. *Problèmes et méthodes*, pp. 122 ff., where several of the examples that follow (*gat, claus, moudre, nouer*) are discussed in some detail.
[2] *L'Aire Clavellus d'après l'Atlas linguistique de la France*, Neuveville, 1912.
[3] W. J. Entwistle, *The Spanish Language*, London, 1936, p. 265.
[4] See Williams, op. cit, pp. 47 ff.

special aspect of the same object or event. Thus the clash between French *moudre* 'to grind' (from Latin *molere*) and *moudre* 'to milk' (from Latin *mulgere*) led to the replacement of the latter by *traire*, from Latin *trahere* 'to draw'.

(5) Another possibility is to fill the gap with a term belonging to the *same sphere of thought*. When French *nouer* 'to tie' (from Latin *nodare*) became identical with *nouer* 'to swim' (from Latin *natare*), the latter gradually fell into disuse. Its place was taken by *nager* (from Latin *navigare*) which until then had meant 'to sail'. *Nager* itself was replaced in its old sense by the learned Latinism *naviguer*. This example shows that some homonymic clashes have repercussions far beyond their original limits.

(6) In some cases a word has been introduced from a *foreign language* to provide a substitute for a displaced homonym. An example in point is the conflict between *aimer* 'to love' (from Latin *amare*) and *esmer* 'to esteem' (from Latin *aestimare*).[1] The two verbs became homonymous in Old French and *esmer* eventually disappeared, but not without bequeathing some of its functions to its more successful rival. A replacement for *esmer* was found by reintroducing the same word from Latin in the learned form *estimer*.

(7) When one of the conflicting homonyms has an unpleasant meaning it may be dropped and the same idea may be expressed by a *euphemism*. The phonetic similarity between Old English *adela* 'dirt' (Modern English *addle*) and *ādl* 'disease' was no doubt one of the reasons for the disappearance of the latter term. Its replacement, *disease*, was originally a euphemism meaning 'lack of ease, uneasiness', though it has long since lost any euphemistic value.[2]

As this last example shows, homonymic clashes are not always due to genuine ambiguity. An unpleasant or indecent word can cast a shadow on its homonym even if there is no actual risk of confusion between them. We have seen the same factor at work in the case of polysemy (pp. 174 f.). According to Bloomfield, *cock* and *ass* are being replaced by *rooster* and *donkey* in American English in order to avoid homonymy with a 'tabooform' (*Language*, p. 396). In the same way, Professor Orr would explain the obsolescence of the verb *to flee* by a homonymic clash with the *flea*.[3] These associative influences are so potent that they can even affect a word which vaguely resembles a tabooed term. To the hypersensitive ears of the French Précieuses in the seventeenth century, the verbs *inculquer*

[1] See especially Orr, *Words and Sounds in English and French*, ch. 14.
[2] L. R. Palmer, *An Introduction to Modern Linguistics*, p. 111.
[3] Orr, *Words and Sounds in English and French*, ch. 1.

and *confesser* seemed offensive because of the assonance of their middle syllable with an indecent word. In our own time, a group of six players in an American orchestra was called a *quintet* since *sextet* was felt to be too suggestive.[1]

A homonymic clash may even lead to the disappearance of both words; this is what happened when *épi* 'ear of corn' (from Latin *spicum*) and *épine* 'thorn' (from Latin *spina*) fell together in South-West France. This, however, is rarely necessary; in most cases only one of the two conflicting words will be removed. Gilliéron once suggested, in rather general terms, that in a clash between two homonyms, that one will drop out for which a substitute is more readily available, or in whose case replacement is more strongly called for.[2] In practice this is often a matter of chance, and a homonym which disappears in one area may in another prove stronger than its rival, as we saw in the clash between *an ear* and *a near*.

III. Ambiguity as a Device of Style

A great deal of attention has been paid in recent years to the uses of ambiguity in literary style.[3] I shall confine myself to some brief remarks on the stylistic aspects of polysemy and homonymy. Both of them are prolific sources of puns, some feeble or excruciatingly bad, others clever and witty, others again fraught with strong emotion and sometimes bordering on the sublime.

Puns based on *polysemy* are on the whole more interesting than the homonymic type since there is more subtlety in playing on meanings than on chance similarities of sound. From a strictly linguistic point of view, such puns fall into two broad categories: the implicit and the explicit variety. The ambiguity is *implicit* when a word is mentioned only once but carries two or more meanings which the reader has to decipher for himself. This is a higher form of wit than the explicit pun since only an attentive and sensitive reader will notice it. It is particularly effective when it is embodied in the title of a book, where it has no immediate context to support it. In Gide's *Symphonie pastorale*, three meanings are compressed into the adjective. At the literal level it refers to Beethoven's Pastoral Symphony which the parson and his blind protégée go

---

[1] See A. W. Read, 'The Lexicographer and General Semantics', *Papers from the Second American Congress on General Semantics*, Chicago, 1943, pp. 33-42: pp. 41 f.

[2] Cf. Iordan-Orr, op. cit., p. 165, and Bloomfield, *Language*, p. 398.

[3] See especially Professor Empson's two books already referred to: *Seven Types of Ambiguity* and *The Structure of Complex Words*. On other languages, cf. e.g. W. B. Stanford, *Ambiguity in Greek Literature*, Oxford, 1939, and L. Renou, 'L'Ambiguïté dans le vocabulaire du Rg Veda', *Journal Asiatique*, ccxxxi (1939), pp. 161-235.

to hear at Neuchâtel. On a higher and more ironical plane, it signifies a 'pastoral' in the literary sense: set in bucolic surroundings, the parson's friendship with Gertrude appears to him as an innocent idyll until he is forced to realize that it is something more serious and dangerous. A third and equally ironical meaning derives from the circumstance that this 'pastoral symphony' is the story of a Protestant *pastor*, French *pasteur*.

A *double entendre* embedded in a suitable context can be equally rich in suggestive force. When, in Racine's *Andromaque*, Pyrrhus tells his Trojan captive that he is 'brûlé de plus de *feux* que je n'en allumai' (Act I, scene 4),[1] the word *feux* has a physical as well as a moral meaning: it refers to the fires he had kindled in Troy and also to the flames of his love for Andromaque. The image is a little precious and not entirely original, but the sudden shift from a concrete to an abstract plane, and the violent contrast which is expressed in a single line with the utmost economy, have a striking effect in this particular context.

Explicit word-play based on polysemy may seem crude in comparison, yet it can sometimes acquire valuable stylistic overtones. A pun can be made explicit in two ways: by repeating the same word in a different meaning, and by commenting on the ambiguity. Some repetitive puns are trivial, as the Duke's feeble joke in *Twelfth Night*: 'Give me now *leave* to *leave* thee' (Act II, scene 4). Others can throw an interesting side-light on a situation or a character. In one of Jules Romains's novels a veteran trade unionist vents his grievances in a bitter pun: 'La civilisation ne peut pas *se passer* de nous. Mais elle *se passe* au-dessus de nous.'[2] Elsewhere the same technique can produce strong contrast effects and give an impression of epigrammatic wit and brevity, as in Pascal's paradox which has already been mentioned: 'Le cœur a ses *raisons* que la *raison* ne connaît point.' A common form of repetitive word-play is the humorous *quid pro quo*. This too may be trivial, but it can also be symptomatic of deeper undercurrents and tensions:

POLONIUS: What do you read, my lord?
HAMLET: Words, words, words.
POLONIUS: What is the *matter*, my lord?
HAMLET: Between who?
POLONIUS: I mean, the *matter* that you read, my lord.
                                        Act II, scene 2.

---

[1] 'Consumed with more *fires* than I had kindled.' See on this image Professor R. C. Knight's article in *Studies in French Language ... Presented to R. L. Graeme Ritchie*, Cambridge, 1949.

[2] 'Civilization *cannot do without* us. But it *takes place* over our heads' (*Le 6 octobre*, Paris, Flammarion, p. 291).

Sometimes the ambiguity is clarified by explicit comment. At the end of a lecture in the Palais de Justice at Brussels, Verlaine addressed the Belgian police with scathing irony: 'Eh! Messieurs les gens de police, laissez donc les poètes! Ils ne vous *regardent* pas, — dans les deux sens du mot.'[1] In Proust there is a highly significant comment on the polysemy of the adjective *grand* and its effect on the mind of an uneducated speaker. Since *grand* can mean both 'large, big in size' and 'morally great', the maid Françoise believes that the 'grandeur' of the aristocratic Guermantes family is based both on the large number and on the illustriousness of its members. Proust comments on this ambiguity in a graphic image:

'Car n'ayant que ce seul mot de *grand* pour les deux choses, il lui semblait qu'elles n'en formaient qu'une seule, son vocabulaire, comme certaines pierres, présentant ainsi par endroit un défaut et qui projetait de l'obscurité jusque dans la pensée de Françoise.'[2]

Homonymic word-play works in much the same way as that based on polysemy. Here too there are implicit and explicit puns. Numerous examples of both types can be found in Shakespeare who, like his contemporaries, was addicted to punning and derived some extraordinarily powerful effects from this device.[3] His *implicit* puns, in particular, are sometimes heavily laden with sinister significance. In *Macbeth* there is a grim play upon the homonymy of *dear* and *deer*, which strikes the modern reader as somewhat odd in the context but no doubt sounded natural to an Elizabethan audience:

> Your castle is surpris'd; your wife and babes
> Savagely slaughter'd. To relate the manner,
> Were, on the quarry of these murder'd *deer*,
> To add the death of you.
>
> Act IV, scene 3.

But even a modern reader will appreciate the macabre joke which Mercutio makes after being mortally wounded: 'Ask for me to-morrow, and you shall find me a *grave* man' (*Romeo and Juliet*, Act III, scene 1). In a different situation, the same pun would have been clever if somewhat strained; under the circumstances it is sublime. In Professor Mahood's words, 'like many of Shakespeare's characters, Mercutio dies with a

---

[1] 'Officers, leave the poets alone! They do not concern you (do not bother about you) — in both senses of the term' (quoted by Nyrop, *Sémantique*, p. 30).

[2] 'For, having but this one word *grand* for both things, it seemed to her that they were one thing only; her vocabulary, like certain stones, thus showed in some places a flaw which cast darkness into her very thoughts' (*Le Côté de Guermantes*, Paris, 1949 ed., vol. I, p. 26).

[3] See especiallly Mahood, op. cit., and Kökeritz, op. cit., Part II, from where some of the following examples are taken.

quibble that asserts his vitality in the teeth of death. He jests as long as he has breath; only if we ask for him *tomorrow* shall we find him a grave man' (op. cit., p. 69).

Homonymic puns made *explicit* by repetition are again less subtle than the implicit type. They may be no more than a form of purely verbal wit:

> I am too *sore* enpierced with his [Cupid's] shaft
> To *soar* with his light feathers.
>
> *Romeo and Juliet*, Act I, scene 4.

If, however, there is a strong semantic contrast between the two homonyms, the repetitive pun can be very effective:

> Have for the *gilt* of France — O *guilt* indeed! —
> Confirm'd conspiracy with fearful France.
>
> *King Henry the Fifth*, Act II, Prologue.

> And truly not the *morning* sun of heaven
> Better becomes the grey cheeks of the east ...
> As those two *mourning* eyes become thy face.
>
> Sonnet 132.

Once again comical or ironical effects can be obtained from homonymy leading to a *quid pro quo*:

> BÉLISE: Veux-tu toute ta vie offenser la *grammaire?*
> MARTINE: Qui parle d'offenser *grand-mère* ni grand-père?
>
> Molière, *Les Femmes savantes*, Act II, scene 6.[1]

This pun has lost much of its original force since *grammaire* and *grand-mère*, which sounded alike in the seventeenth century, have ceased to be homonymous.

A homonymic pun may also be elucidated by explicit comment. This will often be no more than a brief aside, a kind of semi-apologetic gesture. In Gide's *Faux-Monnayeurs*, a neurotic adolescent, the son and grandson of clergymen, coins an irreverent image based on the homonymy of *foi* 'faith' and *foie* 'liver' (cf. p. 183):

' ... mes parents prétendaient faire de moi un pasteur. On m'a chauffé pour ça, gavé de préceptes pieux en vue d'obtenir une dilatation de la *foi*, si j'ose dire.'[2]

---

[1] BÉLISE: Do you want to offend against *grammar* throughout your life?
MARTINE: Who says I am offending *grandmother* or grandfather?

[2] ' ... my parents intended to make me into a parson. They warmed me for that, they stuffed me with pious precepts so as to produce, if I may say so, a dilation of *faith*' (Paris, 1929 ed., pp. 472 f.).

Most puns are no more than sudden and isolated flashes of wit or humour. But there are, in Shakespeare and elsewhere, examples of intricate patterns of sustained word-play, like the following passage from *Love's Labour's Lost*, which centres on the homonymy of the two adjectives *light*, around which develop a number of subsidiary motifs:

KATHARINE: ... for a *light* heart lives long.
ROSALINE: What's your dark meaning, mouse, of this *light* word?
KATHARINE: A *light* condition in a beauty dark.
ROSALINE: We need more *light* to find your meaning out.
KATHARINE: You'll mar the *light* by taking it in snuff;
Therefore I'll darkly end the argument.
ROSALINE: Look what you do, you do it still i' th' dark.
KATHARINE: So do not you; for you are a *light* wench.
ROSALINE: Indeed, I weigh not you; and therefore *light*.

Act V, scene 2.

This display of verbal acrobatics is not entirely gratuitous, for, as Professor Mahood reminds us, 'a repeated quibble upon *light* points to the play's central theme that words, for all their witty sparkle, are without weight or substance' (op. cit., p. 175).

Punning, like other devices of style, is largely a matter of fashion. After the Elizabethan cult of word-play there came a sharp reaction; Dr. Johnson went so far as to claim that a quibble was for Shakespeare 'the fatal Cleopatra for which he lost the world and was content to lose it.'[1] More recently there has been another swing of the pendulum; to quote again Professor Mahood: 'A generation that relishes *Finnegans Wake* is more in danger of reading non-existent quibbles into Shakespeare's work than of missing his subtlest play of meaning. Shakespearean criticism today recognizes word-play as a major poetic device, comparable in its effectiveness with the use of recurrent or clustered images' (ibid., p. 11). This may be going to the other extreme; one should never forget, amid the hunt for ambiguities that is so fashionable today, that punning is in many cases a low form of wit. Yet it is perfectly clear that word-play brings an element of ease and suppleness into the handling of language and that, if used with discretion, it can provide a valuable vehicle for humour and irony, emphasis and contrast, allusion and innuendo, and a variety of other stylistic effects.

[1] Quoted by Mahood, op. cit., p. 9.

CHAPTER 8

CHANGE OF MEANING

OVER forty years ago, Edward Sapir introduced a valuable new concept into linguistics. 'Language', he wrote, 'moves down time in a current of its own making. It has a *drift* ... Nothing is perfectly static. Every word, every grammatical element, every locution, every sound and accent is a slowly changing configuration, moulded by the invisible and impersonal *drift* that is the life of language.'[1] This Heraclitean conception of a perpetual and all-pervasive drift in language is of particular interest to the student of semantics. Of all linguistic elements caught up in this drift, meaning is probably the least resistant to change. This is due to the interplay of several forces some of which were identified by Antoine Meillet at the turn of the century,[2] whereas others have been noticed only in recent years. Among the factors which facilitate semantic changes, the following seem to be of decisive importance:

(1) Language is handed down, as Meillet put it, in a '*discontinuous*' way from one generation to another: every child has to learn it afresh. It is common knowledge that children will often misunderstand the meaning of words. In most cases, such misconceptions will be corrected before they can go very far; but if, for some reason or another, this does not happen, a semantic change will take place in the usage of the new generation. Most linguists would probably agree that this is a factor of some importance; yet, by the very nature of things, it is difficult to prove that any particular change could have arisen only in child language.[3] Meillet gives a plausible, but not entirely convincing example: the history of the French adjective *saoul* or *soûl*. This comes from the popular Latin *satullus* 'filled with food, satiated', and preserved this meaning until the seventeenth century; the original sense still survives in locutions like *manger tout son soûl* 'to eat one's fill'. Since the sixteenth century, however,

---

[1] Op. cit., pp. 150 and 171 (my italics). On linguistic change in general, see recently E. Coseriu, *Sincronía, diacronía e historia. El problema del cambio lingüístico*, Montevideo, 1958. A useful summary and critique of Coseriu's ideas will be found in N. C. W. Spence, 'Towards a New Synthesis in Linguistics: the Work of Eugenio Coseriu', *Archivum Linguisticum*, xii (1960), pp. 1-34. See also H. M. Hoenigswald, *Language Change and Linguistic Reconstruction*, Chicago, 1960.

[2] In his important article, 'Comment les mots changent de sens', *Linguistique historique et linguistique générale*, vol. I, pp. 230-71, esp. pp. 235 ff.

[3] Cf. G. Stern's critical remarks in *Meaning and Change of Meaning*, pp. 178 ff.

the adjective acquired the new meaning of 'drunk, tipsy', which is its main sense today (Bloch-Wartburg). Meillet argues that this shift is due to a misunderstanding which must have originated in the minds of children: adults would ironically refer to a drunk person as being 'replete', and the child, missing these delicate undertones, would apply the word to the crude fact itself. This may well have been the case, but it is obviously impossible to prove it. The same may be said of other changes which have been attributed to this agency, such as the passage of the word *bead* from the sense of 'prayer' to that of 'small perforated ball':

> The phrase *to count your beads* originally meant 'to count your prayers', but because the prayers were reckoned by little balls, the word *beads* came to be transferred to these objects, and lost its original sense. It seems clear that this misapprehension could not take place in the brains of those who had already associated the word with the original signification, while it was quite natural on the part of children who heard and understood the phrase as a whole, but unconsciously analysed it differently from the previous generation (Jespersen, *Language*, p. 175).

(2) *Vagueness* in meaning is another source of semantic changes. The various forms of vagueness discussed in Chapter 5 — the generic nature of our words, the multiplicity of their aspects, lack of familiarity, absence of clear-cut boundaries — all conspire to facilitate shifts in usage. In this respect, there is a fundamental difference between the meaning of words and their phonetic shape, morphological structure or syntactical use, which are far more strictly defined and delimited and therefore less liable to change.

(3) A further factor which may lead to changes in meaning is *loss of motivation*. As long as a word remains firmly attached to its root and to other members of the same family, this will keep its meaning within certain limits. Once these links are severed, for one of the reasons examined in Chapter 4, the sense may develop untrammelled and may move far away from its origins. In Old English, the words *lord* and *lady* were transparent compounds based on the noun *hlāf* 'loaf': *lord* had the form *hlāford* or *hlāfweard*, 'loaf-ward', and *lady* the form *hlǣfdīge*, from *hlāf* + the root *dīg-* 'to knead', connected with *dough* (*NED*). When the connexion with *loaf* was obscured by phonetic development (cf. p. 96), the two words could evolve unhampered by etymological associations.

To these general factors identified by Meillet, at least another three may be added which are all conducive to mobility of meaning:

(4) The existence of *polysemy* introduces, as we have seen, an element of flexibility into language. There is nothing final about a semantic change: a word may acquire a new sense, or scores of new senses, without losing its original meaning. Some of these innovations are accidental and short-lived, confined to a single author or perhaps even to a single context; others will pass from speech into language and harden into permanent changes, giving rise to one of the forms of polysemy discussed in the previous chapter: shifts in application, specialization in a social milieu, figurative expressions, etc.

(5) Many semantic changes arise in the first instance in *ambiguous contexts* where a particular word may be taken in two different senses while the meaning of the utterance as a whole remains unaffected.[1] The phrase to *count one's beads*, which has just been mentioned, is an example in point. Whether *beads* is taken here to refer to prayers, or to the rosary balls used for counting one's prayers, will make no real difference to the total meaning of the phrase. Similarly, the word *boon* originally meant 'prayer, petition, request';[2] at quite an early date, however, it came to denote the thing prayed or asked for. Here again the change must have been facilitated by ambiguous contexts such as 'he gave her freely all her *boon*' (1300), where the word may be taken either in the first or in the second sense and yet the meaning of the sentence will be practically the same.[3] Ambiguous constructions of this type are fairly common, and the lexicographer will often find it difficult to establish the precise date at which a new meaning emerged.

(6) Perhaps the most important of the general factors governing semantic change is the *structure of the vocabulary*. The phonological and grammatical system of a language is made up of a limited number of closely organized elements. The vocabulary, on the other hand, is a loose aggregate of an infinitely larger number of units; it is therefore far more fluid and mobile, and new elements, words as well as meanings, can be added more freely while existing ones will drop just as easily out of use. More will be said on this question in the last chapter; meanwhile it is sufficient to note that the vocabulary of a language is an unstable structure in which individual words can acquire and lose meanings with the utmost ease.[4]

[1] This process is fully discussed in Stern, op. cit., ch. 13, from where the next two examples are taken.
[2] Cf. for instance: 'But you will take exceptions to my *boon*', *King Henry the Sixth*, Part III, Act III, scene 2 (*Shorter OED*).
[3] Stern, op. cit., p. 351.
[4] For some interesting data on the rate of influx of new meanings into English, see E. L. Thorndike, 'Semantic Change', *American Journal of Psychology*, lx (1947), pp. 588-97.

Change of meaning virtually monopolized the attention of all early semanticists. It will be remembered that the founder of modern semantics, Bréal, and his precursor, Reisig, had set the new science the task of exploring the laws which govern the development of meanings.[1] Until the early 1930s, work in this field centred almost exclusively on two problems: the classification of changes of meaning, and the discovery of semantic laws. The quest for 'laws' met with very limited success, and the classificatory zeal resulted in a number of ambitious schemes built on slender empirical data — it was, as one linguist acidly remarked, as if someone tried to devise a comprehensive classification of plants while his own knowledge was confined to the poplar, the daisy and the toadstool.[2] It must, however, be conceded that these early classifications often showed remarkable ingenuity, and that they made a substantial contribution to our better understanding of semantic processes. The two most outstanding schemes were those put forward by Professors Carnoy and Stern, the former distinguished by the extraordinary richness of its subdivisions, the latter by its clarity, its solid documentation, and the healthy empiricism which informed it.[3]

During the last thirty years, there has been a significant shift of emphasis in research: the interest of most semanticists has turned to descriptive and structural problems, and change of meaning has been relegated to the background. This does not mean, of course, that work in this field has come to a standstill. Monographs on specific problems continue to be published; there have been some valuable theoretical contributions,[4] and changes of meaning occupy a prominent place in most of the latest manuals.[5] Some of the structuralist experiments which will be discussed in the last chapter are likely to rejuvenate the study of semantic change rather than superseding the solid achievements of the past, which

[1] See above, pp. 5 f.

[2] H. Sperber, op. cit., pp. 93 f.; cf. H. Hatzfeld, *Leitfaden der vergleichenden Bedeutungslehre*, Munich, 1924, p. xii.

[3] A detailed survey of these and other schemes will be found in ch. 4 of my *Principles of Semantics*. Cf. also P. Guiraud, *La Sémantique*, Paris, 1955, chs. 3-4; J. Cremona, 'Historical Semantics and the Classification of Semantic Changes', *Hispanic Studies in Honour of I. González Llubera*, Oxford, 1959, pp. 1-6; K. Svoboda, 'Sur la classification des changements sémantiques', *Le Français Moderne*, XXVIII (1960), pp. 249-58.

[4] See, e.g., A. Bachmann, *Zur psychologischen Theorie des sprachlichen Bedeutungswandels*, Munich, 1935; O. Funke, 'Zum Problem des Bedeutungswandels', *Anglo-Americana: Wiener Beiträge zur englischen Philologie*, lxii (1955), pp. 53-61; A. Sauvageot, 'A propos des changements sémantiques', *Journal de Psychologie*, xlvi (1953), pp. 465-72; J. Schröpfer, 'Wozu ein vergleichendes Wörterbuch des Sinnwandels?', *Proceedings of the Seventh International Congress of Linguists*, pp. 366-71; Thorndike, loc. cit.; H. Werner, 'Change of Meaning: a Study of Semantic Processes through Experimental Data', *The Journal of General Psychology*, 1 (1954), pp. 181-208.

[5] See in particular those of Gamillscheg, Guiraud, Kronasser and Zvegintsev.

are sometimes contemptuously dismissed as 'atomistic' or 'anecdotal' semantics.

To survey all the overlapping schemes of classification, based on a variety of different criteria, would be a Herculean as well as a thankless task. I shall therefore confine myself to a few selected problems grouped around three themes: the causes of semantic change, its nature and conditions, and its effects.

I. THE CAUSES OF SEMANTIC CHANGE

Changes of meaning can be brought about by an infinite multiplicity of causes. One early semanticist distinguished no less than thirty-one possibilities,[1] but no matter how fine a mesh of distinctions one may devise, there will always be some cases which will slip through it. Many changes, including some which look deceptively simple, are due to unique causes which can be established only by reconstructing the whole historical background. A classic example of such an unique change is the origin of Latin *monēta* which has given the English words *mint* and *money*, the latter via French *monnaie*. *Monēta* comes from the verb *moneo* 'to admonish, to warn', but at first sight it is difficult to imagine any connexion between the two ideas. The connexion, in fact, was purely fortuitous: *Monēta* was a surname of the goddess Juno in whose temple in Rome money was coined.[2] To take a rather different example, it seems obvious that the French milk-roll known as *croissant* owes its name to the fact that it is crescent-shaped. This is of course true, but it is not the whole story. The French word is a translation of German *Hörnchen*, and the first rolls of this shape were made in Vienna in the late seventeenth century to commemorate a decisive victory over the Turks whose national emblem is the Crescent (Bloch-Wartburg). Such cases contain a salutary warning to the etymologist and lend fresh force to the old slogan: 'words and things' (*Wörter und Sachen*); without close liaison between linguistics and the history of civilization, the origin of *money* would have remained an unsolved mystery and that of *croissant* would have been grossly oversimplified.

Yet, in spite of the complexity of these processes, it is possible to discern several major causes which account between them for a large

---

[1] R. de la Grasserie, *Essai d'une sémantique intégrale*, Paris, 1908, vol. I, pp. 89-139.
[2] See already W. Wundt, *Völkerpsychologie I: Die Sprache*, Leipzig, 1900, vol. I, pp. 426 ff.

proportion of semantic changes. Three of these were clearly identified in Antoine Meillet's fundamental article on the subject:[1]

(1) *Linguistic causes.* — Some semantic changes are due to the associations which words contract in speech. Habitual collocations may permanently affect the meaning of the terms involved; by a process known since Bréal as 'contagion',[2] the sense of one word may be transferred to another simply because they occur together in many contexts. Perhaps the most remarkable example of this tendency is the history of negation in French. A number of words which originally had a positive sense have acquired a negative value because they were often used in conjunction with the negative particle *ne*:

Latin *passus* 'step'	*ne ... pas* 'not'
„ *punctum* 'point'	*ne ... point* 'not, not at all'
„ *persona* 'person'	*ne ... personne* 'nobody'
„ *rem*, accusative of *res* 'thing'	*ne ... rien* 'nothing'
„ *jam* 'now, already' +*magis* 'more'	*ne ... jamais* 'never'

The contagion has been so effective that these terms now have a negative sense even when they stand by themselves, unsupported by *ne*. This has led to the paradoxical situation that the word *personne* has two diametrically opposite uses: as a noun it still means 'person'; used as a particle, as for instance in reply to a question, it means 'nobody':

J'ai vu une *personne*. 'I saw one person.'
Qui a dit cela? — *Personne*. 'Who said that? — Nobody.'

(2) *Historical causes.* — It often happens that language is more conservative than civilization, material as well as moral. Objects, institutions, ideas, scientific concepts change in the course of time; yet in many cases the name is retained and thus helps to ensure a sense of tradition and continuity.[3] The process is too well known to require detailed discussion; one example for each of the main categories will be sufficient to show how it works:

(*a*) *Objects.* — The English word *car* ultimately goes back to Latin

---

[1] See above, p. 193, n. 2. Another important treatise on the causes of semantic change is E. Wellander's *Studien zum Bedeutungswandel im Deutschen*, 3 parts, Uppsala, 1917, 1923, 1928. A summary of his scheme will be found in my *Principles of Semantics*, pp. 206 ff.
[2] *Essai de sémantique*, ch. 21.
[3] Some linguists refuse to regard these processes as changes of meaning; cf. e.g. J. Schwietering, 'Schriften zur Bedeutungslehre', *Anzeiger für deutsches Altertum*, xliv (1925), pp. 153-63. In *The Principles of Semantics*, p. 211, I have suggested to treat such cases as 'semantic changes due to linguistic conservatism', as distinct from those which are due to linguistic innovation.

carrus, a word of Celtic origin which meant a 'four-wheeled wagon' and was repeatedly mentioned in Caesar's commentaries on the Gallic war. Our modern cars bear little resemblance to the Celtic wagons of the first century B.C.; yet the technological development was so continuous that there was no need for the label to be replaced at any point, and the word has remained phonetically almost unaltered since Roman times (cf. also French *char*, Italian, Spanish and Portuguese *carro*, Rumanian *car*).[1]

(*b*) *Institutions.* — The meaning of the word *parliament*, borrowed from Old French *parlement*,[2] has changed beyond recognition since the councils of the early Plantagenet Kings, but the development was gradual, the continuity of tradition was never interrupted, and the term survives to bear witness to this tradition; it will no doubt continue to do so whatever constitutional reforms the future may bring.

(*c*) *Ideas.* — The term *humour*, which English took over from Old French, is based on totally antiquated physiological conceptions: the theory of the 'four chief fluids (*cardinal humours*) of the body (blood, phlegm, choler, and melancholy or black choler), by the relative proportions of which a person's physical and mental qualities and disposition were formerly held to be determined' (*NED*). Subsequently these notions were forgotten and *humour* gradually developed into one of the key-terms of the British way of life; yet once again the word has been retained since there has been no break in continuity. A number of other modern terms — *choleric, melancholy, phlegmatic, sanguine, temperament* — have their roots in the same physiological theory.

(*d*) *Scientific concepts.* — While *humour* and its group were at one time scientific, or pseudo-scientific, terms they have long since ceased to be regarded as such and have passed into the category of general ideas. There are, however, many scientific concepts proper which have preserved their traditional names in spite of all the changes they have undergone. A glance at the etymology of some of these terms will show how completely they have outgrown their original meanings. *Electricity* comes from Greek ἤλεκτρον, Latin *ēlectrum*, 'amber'; *geometry* once meant 'the art of measuring ground'; more recently even the word *atom* has, as already noted (p. 56), become etymologically inappropriate since it meant 'indivisible' in Greek.

(3) *Social causes.* — When a word passes from ordinary language into

---

[1] Cf. W. D. Elcock, *The Romance Languages*, p. 183, and L. R. Palmer, *The Latin Language*, p. 53. Cf. also Bloch-Wartburg and Lewis and Short.
[2] See the *NED*; cf. above, p. 165.

O

a specialized nomenclature — the terminology of a trade, a craft, a profession or some other limited group — it tends to acquire a more restricted sense. Conversely, words borrowed from a group-language into common use are apt to widen their meaning. There are thus two socially conditioned tendencies working in opposite directions: specialization and generalization.

Specialization of meaning in a restricted social group is an extremely common process; it is, as we have seen (pp. 161 f.), one of the main sources of polysemy. In some cases, the specialized sense has completely superseded the more general one, and the range of the word has been considerably narrowed. This has happened in French to a number of ordinary verbs when they passed into the language of the farm-yard:[1]

Latin *cubare* 'to recline, to lie down'	>	French *couver* 'to hatch'
„ *mutare* 'to change'	>	„ *muer* 'to moult'
„ *ponere* 'to place'	>	„ *pondre* 'to lay eggs'
„ *trahere* 'to draw'	>	„ *traire* 'to milk'[2]

The converse process, *generalization*, is also very common. A number of terms from hunting and falconry, for example, have passed into ordinary language and have correspondingly widened their meaning.[3] *Haggard* originally referred to a hawk which was 'caught after having assumed the adult plumage' and was therefore wild and untamed (*NED*). *Lure*, and the verb *to allure*, are also derived from falconry: a *lure* was 'an apparatus used by falconers to recall their hawks, being a bunch of feathers attached to a cord, within which, during its training, the hawk finds its food' (*Shorter OED*). French *niais* 'foolish' comes from Vulgar Latin **nidax, *nidacem*, a derivative of *nidus* 'nest'; it originally denoted a 'nestling', a young falcon taken from the nest. Many idiomatic expressions — 'to be at bay', 'to beat about the bush', 'to be caught in the toils', and others — can also be traced back to various aspects of the chase.

To these three major factors established by Meillet one may add at least another three which are responsible for many changes of meaning.

(4) *Psychological causes.* — Semantic changes often have their roots in the speaker's state of mind or in some more permanent feature of his

---

[1] In some of these verbs, the restriction of meaning goes back to Latin times; in others it is a specifically French development (Bloch-Wartburg).

[2] *Traire*, as already mentioned (p. 187), replaced the verb *moudre* 'to milk', from Latin *mulgere*, after the latter had become homonymous with *moudre* 'to grind', from Latin *molere*.

[3] On hunting terms see N. Edgar, *Les Expressions figurées d'origine cynégétique en français*, Uppsala, 1906, and, more recently, the series of *Cynegetica* published by G. Tilander. Cf. also J. Vendryes, 'Sur quelques mots de la langue des chasseurs', *Archivum Linguisticum*, i (1949), pp. 23-9, and Weekley, *The Romance of Words*, pp. 107 f.

mental make-up. Some of the psychological factors involved are super-ficial or even trivial. A chance similarity which catches the eye, a humorous association which comes to the mind, may produce an image which, because of its appropriateness or its expressive quality, will pass from individual style into common usage. The idea that something has a vague resemblance to a horse — in shape, situation or character — has inspired many graphic or jocular metaphors and idioms: *clothes-horse*, *horse-fish*, *horse-tail*, *horse-play*, *horse-sense*, 'to flog a dead *horse*', 'to mount the high *horse*', 'to look a gift *horse* in the mouth', etc. Such metaphors will sometimes result in a permanent change of meaning: the painter's *easel*, for example, comes from the Dutch word *ezel* which means an 'ass' (cf. German *Esel*).

Psychologically more interesting are those changes of meaning which spring from some deep-seated feature or tendency in the speaker's mind. Two such causes in particular have been strongly emphasized in semantic studies: emotive factors and taboo.

(*a*) *Emotive factors*. — The part played by feeling in semantic change was explored in great detail by Professor H. Sperber in a book published in 1923,[1] which tried to apply a Freudian approach to these problems. Sperber argued that if we are intensely interested in a subject, we tend to talk frequently about it; we shall even refer to it when speaking of totally different matters. Such subjects are ever present to our minds and will therefore suggest similes and metaphors for the description of other experiences. In Sperber's terminology, they will become 'centres of *expansion*'. At the same time, these important spheres will also form 'centres of *attraction*': we shall enlist analogies from other fields in order to describe them with the maximum of precision, freshness and variety. There will thus be a twofold movement of metaphors from and towards these emotional centres. Sperber cites some striking examples to show the impact of certain awe-inspiring weapons during the First World War. In the slang of the *poilus*, people and objects were sometimes nicknamed after these weapons: thus beans were called 'shrapnels', and a woman with many children was referred to as a 'machine-gun' (*mitrailleuse à gosses*). Conversely, all kinds of picturesque and humorous metaphors were applied to the weapons themselves; in an attempt to rob them of some of their terror they were compared to familiar objects: a machine-gun became a 'coffee-mill' or a 'sewing-machine', and a tank was nicknamed 'rolling kitchen' (ibid., pp. 45 ff.).

Of the two emotional forces posited by Sperber, 'attraction' certainly

[1] Op. cit., chs. 4-10.

plays an important role, even though it will not always carry the far-reaching implications suggested by the theory. As we saw in an earlier chapter (pp. 149 f.), subjects in which a community is interested, which epitomize its fears, its aspirations or its ideals, will tend to attract synonyms from all directions, and many of these will be metaphorical since metaphor is the supreme source of expressiveness in language. The role of 'expansion' is less obvious and more problematical. There is certainly nothing like an automatic connexion between the interest which a subject commands and the number of metaphors inspired by it. If such a correlation did exist one would expect countless images from aviation in our air-minded age, whereas the actual number of such figures in ordinary language is quite small. On the other hand there are undoubtedly cases where the interests of a generation are reflected in its choice of metaphors. In sixteenth-century France, where religion was the most important of all public issues, a number of figurative expressions were derived from that field: *vray comme la messe* 'as true as mass'; *vray comme le patenôtre* 'as true as the Lord's prayer'; *se rendre au premier coup de matines* 'to go at the first stroke of the matins bell' (= as soon as one is summoned); *il faut laisser le moustier où il est* 'one should leave the monastery where it is' (= respect tradition), and many more.[1] At the time of the French Revolution, there was a plethora of metaphors from science and medicine, reflecting public interest in recent advances in these fields: people spoke of the 'centrifugal force' of the revolutionary spirit and of the 'refrangibility of its regenerative rays', of the 'electrifying' effect of public meetings, of the 'phosphorous globules' which Pitt was blowing in the eyes of the public, and of the need to 'phlebotomize' journalists.[2] In the nineteenth century the introduction of railways into France was followed by the appearance of all kinds of metaphors from that sphere.[3]

The theory of 'expansion' is of direct relevance to the study of literary style. If there is any truth in this theory, then one would expect the dominant interests and preoccupations of a writer to be mirrored in his imagery; one might even hope to use his similes and metaphors as a clue to his basic attitudes and mental processes. This is what Professor C. F. E. Spurgeon set out to do in her well-known book, *Shakespeare's Imagery and what it tells us* (Cambridge, 1935). There can be no doubt that some

---

[1] See E. Huguet, *Le Langage figuré au seizième siècle*, Paris, 1933, pp. 1-18.
[2] See F. Brunot, *Histoire de la langue française*, vol. X, part 1, pp. 64 ff.
[3] Cf. P. J. Wexler, *La Formation du vocabulaire des chemins de fer en France*, 1778-1842, pp. 130 f.; see also my *Style in the French Novel*, p. 32. The vogue of certain suffixes in our own time — *beatnik* formed on the model of *sputnik* — is a symptom of the same tendency.

of Miss Spurgeon's findings are significant. She was struck, for example, by the frequency of flood images in Shakespeare:

> my particular grief
> Is of so flood-gate and o'erbearing nature
> That it engluts and swallows other sorrows,
> And it is still itself.
> *Othello*, Act I, scene 3.

> Never came reformation in a flood,
> With such a heady currance, scouring faults.
> *King Henry the Fifth*, Act I, scene 1.

Now it is known that the river Avon was frequently in flood in Shakespeare's day, as it still is at the present time. It is therefore quite reasonable to assume that there is some connexion between the floods which Shakespeare must have watched at Stratford as a child, and the persistent recurrence of the flood motif in his imagery.[1]

Nevertheless, the 'theory of dominant metaphors', as it has been called, has been severely criticized and must be handled with extreme caution.[2] It is clear, first of all, that arguments *ex silentio* are of no value whatsoever; the fact that certain experiences do not occur in a writer's imagery does not mean in any way that he was unfamiliar with, or uninterested in, these matters. It is amusing to note, for example, that in Izaac Walton's *Life of Donne* there is not a single image derived from fishing; the passionate hobby which inspired the *Compleat Angler* has left the imagery of the other work totally unaffected. In the fictional writings of Albert Camus I have found only one, rather uninteresting image connected with tuberculosis, an illness which had played such a serious part in his life. At the same time, the presence of a particular group of metaphors need not be related to any intense personal experience. It would be naïve to attribute the numerous insect images found in various modern novelists to an absorbing interest in entomology, or to some traumatic shock connected with insects; more often than not, the determining factor was simply the expressive force of this imagery and its

---

[1] Spurgeon, op. cit., pp. 93 ff. On a similar case in Proust, the psychological significance of his metaphors from medicine and surgery, see my *Image in the Modern French Novel*, pp. 130 ff.

[2] Cf. L. H. Hornstein, 'Analysis of Imagery: a Critique of Literary Method', *Publications of the Modern Language Association of America*, lvii (1942), pp. 638-53; R. Wellek and A. Warren, *Theory of Literature*, London, 1954 impr., pp. 213 ff.; and my *Style in the French Novel*, pp. 31 ff.

unpleasant emotional overtones which fitted in with the whole atmosphere of the works concerned.[1]

It may also happen that a writer will try to achieve verisimilitude by adapting the style of his characters, including their imagery, to their personal interests and background. This is what Victor Hugo did with good effect at the end of his poem *Booz endormi* which is based on the Book of Ruth. After a day spent working on the land, Ruth is gazing up at the starry sky, her mind still full of the people and things she saw during the day:

> Ruth se demandait,
> Immobile, ouvrant l'œil à moitié sous ses voiles,
> Quel dieu, quel *moissonneur* de l'éternel été,
> Avait, en s'en allant, négligemment jeté
> Cette *faucille* d'or dans le *champ* des étoiles.[2]

(b) *Taboo*.[3] — *Taboo* is a Polynesian word which Captain Cook introduced into English whence it passed into other European languages. According to Captain Cook himself, the term 'has a very comprehensive meaning; but, in general, signifies that a thing is forbidden'.[4] In his book *Totem and Taboo*, Freud has given an interesting analysis of the meaning and implications of the word:

---

[1] Cf. G. O. Rees, 'Animal Imagery in the Novels of André Malraux', *French Studies*, ix (1955), pp. 129-42. In the case of Sartre, however, the obsessive recurrence of insect images seems to have a psychological motivation, judging by recent revelations in Simone de Beauvoir's *La Force de l'âge*. I am indebted to Madame Escoffier, of Lyons University, for drawing my attention to this point. On insect images in Sartre, see S. John, 'Sacrilege and Metamorphosis. Two Aspects of Sartre's Imagery', *Modern Language Quarterly*, xx (1959), pp. 57-66, and my *Style in the French Novel*, pp. 251 f.

[2] 'Motionless, half-opening her eyes beneath her veils, Ruth asked herself what god, what *harvester* of the eternal summer had, when leaving, casually thrown this golden *sickle* on the *field* of the stars.'

[3] A comprehensive account of linguistic taboos will be found in two monographs: W. Havers, *Neuere Literatur zum Sprachtabu*, Akademie der Wissenschaften in Wien, Phil.-Hist. Kl., Sitzungsber. 223, 5, 1946, and R. F. Mansur Guérios, *Tabus lingüísticos*, Rio de Janeiro, 1956. Of the vast literature on taboo and the related problem of euphemism, the following may be mentioned: G. Bonfante, 'Etudes sur le tabou dans les langues indo-européennes', *Mélanges Ch. Bally*, Geneva, 1939, pp. 195-207; Ch. Bruneau, 'Euphémie et euphémisme', *Festgabe E. Gamillscheg*, Tübingen, 1952, pp. 11-23; M. Cortelazzo, 'Valore attuale del tabu linguistico magico', *Rivista di Etnografia*, vii (1953), pp. 13-29; M. B. Emeneau, 'Taboos on Animal Names', *Language*, xxiv (1948), pp. 56-63; J. Marouzeau, 'Le Parler des gens moyens. Interdiction des convenances et tabou du sentiment', *Journal de Psychologie*, xxiv (1927), pp. 611-17; A. Meillet, 'Quelques hypothèses sur des interdictions de vocabulaire dans les langues indo-européennes', *Linguistique historique et linguistique générale*, vol. I, pp. 281-91; J. Orr, 'Le Rôle destructeur de l'euphémie', *Cahiers de l'Association Internationale des Etudes Françaises*, 1953, pp. 167-75. Cf. also Estrich-Sperber, op. cit., chs. 1-4; Gamillscheg, *Französische Bedeutungslehre*, ch. 35; Jespersen, *Mankind, Nation and Individual*, ch. 9; Nyrop, *Sémantique* VII.

[4] M. Guérios, op. cit., p. 8.

For us the meaning of taboo branches off into two opposite directions. On the one hand it means to us sacred, consecrated: but on the
other hand it means uncanny, dangerous, forbidden, and unclean. The
opposite for taboo is designated in Polynesian by the word *noa* and
signifies something ordinary and generally accessible. Thus something
like the concept of reserve inheres in taboo; taboo expresses itself
essentially in prohibitions and restrictions. Our combination of 'holy
dread' would often express the meaning of taboo.[1]

Taboo is of vital importance to the linguist because it imposes a ban
not only on certain persons, animals and things, but also on their names.
In most cases, though not in all, the tabooed word will be abandoned and
a harmless substitute, a *euphemism*,[2] will be introduced to fill the gap.
This will often involve an adjustment in the meaning of the substitute,
and in this way taboo is an important cause of semantic changes.

Language taboos fall into three more or less distinct groups according
to the psychological motivation behind them: some are due to fear, others
to a feeling of delicacy, others again to a sense of decency and propriety.

(i) *Taboo of fear.* — The awe in which supernatural beings are held
has often imposed taboo bans on their names. The Jews, as has already
been noted, were not allowed to refer directly to God; they used their
word for 'master' instead, and this circumlocution still survives in English
the Lord, French *Seigneur* and other modern forms (p. 166). The name of
the devil has given rise to countless euphemisms, including the curious
expression *l'Autre*, 'the Other One', in French. In his *Address to the Deil*
Burns has collected a whole series of friendly nicknames designed to
propitiate the devil and to show that one is on familiar terms with him:

> O thou! whatever title suit thee —
> Auld 'Hornie', 'Satan', 'Nick', or 'Clootie' ...
> Hear me, auld 'Hangie', for a wee ...
> But fare-you-weel, auld 'Nickie-ben'!

Names of evil spirits are tabooed in the same way. The attempt to
propitiate them can go to remarkable lengths: witness Greek Εὐμενίδες,
one of the names given to the Furies, which literally means 'well-disposed,
gracious'.

Ordinary creatures and things endowed with supernatural qualities can

---

[1] Pelican Books, London, 1940 impr., p. 37.
[2] From Greek *eu* 'well' + *phēmē* 'speaking'.

also become objects of fear and taboo. Particularly widespread are bans
on the names of animals. A recent book on the subject[1] cites no less than
twenty-four animals whose names are tabooed in different languages; they
range from ants, bees and worms to bears,[2] tigers and lions; even butter-
flies, rabbits and squirrels are included in the list. One of the most
intriguing cases is the well-known series of euphemistic names for the
weasel.[3] In the Romance languages there are only isolated survivals of
mustela, the Latin name of the animal. In French it has been replaced by
belette, a diminutive of *beau*, *belle*, which literally means 'beautiful little
woman'. Elsewhere, the euphemism has worked mainly by change of
meaning: the Italians and the Portuguese call the weasel 'little lady'
(*donnola*, *doninha*), the Spaniards 'gossip' (*comadreja*), whereas in Denmark it is known as 'beautiful' and 'bride', in Sweden as 'pretty little girl'
or 'young lady', in Greece and Albania as 'sister-in-law', etc. In English,
the weasel once had the by-name *fairy*, and Erasmus has recorded that it
was considered unlucky in England to mention the animal when one
went hunting.

Names of inanimate objects can also be struck by a taboo ban. Superstitions connected with the left hand have led to the creation of many
euphemisms in various languages. Latin *laevus* and *scaevus* have disappeared in Romance; *sinister* in the literal sense has survived in Italian
sinistro but has fallen elsewhere into disuse. Spanish has turned to Basque
for a replacement (*izquierdo*),[4] whereas French uses a Germanic term,
gauche, which originally meant 'the wrong way, clumsy' (Bloch-Wartburg). English *left* had the primary sense of 'weak, worthless' (*NED*),
and one of the Greek words for 'left', εὐώνυμος, is clearly a euphemism:
its original sense was 'of good name, honoured; of good omen, pros-
perous, fortunate' (Liddell and Scott).

(ii) *Taboo of delicacy.* — It is a general human tendency to avoid direct
reference to unpleasant subjects. We have already seen some of the
numerous euphemisms connected with illness and death (pp. 150 and
187). The history of words like *disease* and *undertaker* shows that
such substitutes can become so closely associated with the tabooed
idea that they lose all euphemistic value, and fresh replacements have to
be found to mitigate the unpleasantness.

---

[1] M. Guérios, op. cit., ch. 18.
[2] Cf. Meillet and Emeneau, loc. cit.
[3] See Guérios, op. cit., pp. 152 ff., with further references; cf. also Nyrop, *Sémantique*,
pp. 275 f., and Weekley, *The Romance of Words*, pp. 91 f.
[4] Cf. W. D. Elcock's remarks, op. cit., p. 178. Cf. also Entwistle, *The Spanish Language*,
p. 65.

Another group of words affected by this form of taboo are names of physical and mental defects. *Imbecile* comes via French from Latin *imbecillus*, or *imbecillis*, 'weak, feeble'. In the seventeenth century, Corneille could still refer to the 'gentle sex' as 'le sexe *imbécille*'; a century later, this usage had become so antiquated that Voltaire described it as a 'coarse and misplaced affront' (Nyrop, *Sémantique*, p. 22). Other words in the same sphere have developed on similar lines. French *crétin* is a dialectal form of *chrétien* 'Christian', borrowed in the eighteenth century from a Swiss French patois (Bloch-Wartburg). *Benêt* 'silly, stupid, simple-minded' comes from *benedictus* 'blessed' and is an obvious echo of the first beatitude: '*Blessed* are the poor in spirit: for theirs is the kingdom of heaven' (ibid.). It is quite probable that these uses were originally 'pseudo-euphemisms' rather than euphemisms proper: they were prompted by irony rather than by taboo. The same may be said of *idiot*, which goes back to a Greek word meaning 'private person, layman', and of *silly*, earlier *seely*, which once meant 'happy' and 'blessed' (cf. German *selig*).[1]

Yet another class of words which are often avoided for reasons of delicacy, or mock delicacy, are names of criminal actions such as cheating, stealing and killing. For 'cheating' there is in French a traditional periphrasis, *corriger la fortune*, which was made famous by a passage in Lessing's comedy, *Minna von Barnhelm* (Act IV, scene 2). 'Stealing' has given rise to numerous euphemisms in different languages; some of these have been noted in the chapter on synonymy (p. 151). An amusing example occurs in *The Merry Wives of Windsor*, Act I, scene 3:

NYM: The good humour is to steal at a minute's rest.
PISTOL: 'Convey' the wise it call. 'Steal' foh! A fico for the phrase!

In Nazi concentration camps, the verb *to organize* came to be used in many languages as a euphemism for 'procuring by illicit means' and thus for 'stealing'. This produced some curious combinations: 'Les magasins du camp sont pleins de tout ce que les S.S. ont *organisé* en France.'[2]

An example of a radical change of meaning due to this type of taboo is the French verb *tuer* 'to kill', which is derived from the Latin *tutari* 'to watch, to guard, to protect'. According to a recent inquiry, this usage seems to have 'originated as an ironic euphemism due ultimately to thieves' or soldiers' slang'.[3]

(iii) *Taboo of propriety*. — The three great spheres most directly

---

[1] Cf. Stern, op. cit., p. 403, and the *NED*.
[2] 'The camp stores are full of all the things the S.S. have *organized* in France' (see Amsler, *Le Français Moderne*, xiii, 1945, p. 248; cf. Y. Eyot, ibid., xiv, 1946, p. 167).
[3] B. Foster, *Essays Presented to C. M. Girdlestone*, pp. 109-21.

affected by this form of taboo are sex, certain parts and functions of the body, and swearing. There are extremely wide variations between the standards of decency obtaining in different periods: the bawdy of a Rabelais and the prudery of the Précieuses (cf. pp. 187 f.), the forthrightness with which Madame de Rambouliet in Sterne's *Sentimental Journey* refers to human physiology,[1] and the hypersensitivity of nineteenth-century American ladies who would speak of the *limbs* of a piano and of their own *benders* rather than mention *legs*, and would say *waist* rather than utter the word *body*.[2] Yet the sense of decency and propriety has been throughout the ages a rich source of taboos and euphemisms. A few expressions from the sphere of sexual relations will serve to illustrate this tendency.

The history of the French word *fille* shows that even one of the commonest words of a language can become tainted through euphemistic use. In the sense of 'daughter', *fille* is still perfectly respectable, but in the sense of 'girl, young woman' it is now necessary to say *jeune fille*, since *fille* by itself was so frequently used as a euphemism for 'prostitute' that this eventually became its ordinary meaning. A sentence like the following, which occurs in the eighteenth-century writer Marivaux, would be impossible today: 'Tu me dégoûtes de toutes les *filles* qu'on pourrait m'offrir pour mon fils.'[3] Other words in this sphere have had a similar fate: *garce*, the feminine form of *garçon*, has become a term of abuse, and the German *Dirne*, which was once applied to the Virgin Mary as the handmaid of God, has come to mean a 'drab' except in the South German dialects.[4]

Various terms connected with illicit love have deteriorated in meaning as a result of euphemistic use. When Alceste says to Célimène, in Molière's *Misanthrope*: 'Vous avez trop d'*amants* qu'on voit vous obséder' (Act II, scene 1),[5] this is far less insulting than it sounds to modern ears, for at that time *amant* merely meant 'someone in love with a woman'; it is only by euphemism that it gradually acquired the sense of 'lover', which is its sole meaning today. Similarly, there was nothing very shocking in Pauline's words in Corneille's *Polyeucte*: 'Mon père fut ravi qu'il me prît pour *maîtresse*' (Act I, scene 3); in the seventeenth century, *maîtresse* simply meant 'bride'.[6]

---

[1] In the chapter 'The Rose' (Penguin ed., p. 97); cf. Nyrop, *Sémantique*, pp. 303 f.
[2] Jespersen, *Growth and Structure*, p. 226.
[3] 'You make me feel disgusted with all the *girls* who might be offered to me for my son' (quoted by Gamillscheg, *Französische Bedeutungslehre*, p. 100).
[4] Priebsch-Collinson, op. cit., p. 304.
[5] 'You have too many *admirers* whom one sees besieging you.' This and the next example are quoted by Nyrop, *Sémantique*, p. 299.
[6] 'My father was delighted that he should have chosen me as his *bride*.'

Even the French word for 'kissing', *baiser*, has fallen victim to a taboo ban. Since it came to be used as a euphemism with obscene connotations it has been largely replaced in its original sense by *embrasser* 'to embrace', a derivative of *bras* 'arm'; hence such bizarre combinations as '*embrasser quelqu'un sur la joue*' 'to kiss someone on the cheek'.[1]

This small selection of examples will have shown that taboo and euphemism are important causes of semantic change. It should be noted, however, that this is only one of the ways in which a gap created by taboo can be filled. As we have seen, a tainted word is sometimes replaced by a new formation (*belette*) or by a term taken over from a foreign language (Spanish *izquierdo*). Bloomfield has drawn attention to the curious fact that the Russians took their word for 'moon', *luná*, from Latin whereas they have otherwise borrowed very little from that source, except some highly learned terms (*Language*, p. 400). Since every language is likely to have its own word for the moon, such a term would be imported from abroad only if the native name had been struck by a taboo ban. It can also happen that a tabooed word is not dropped altogether but is retained in a modified form. Archaic English *zounas* is a euphemistic variant of the oath *by God's wounds*, *drat* stands for *God rot!* and French *bougre*, though not as offensive as its English counterpart, becomes more respectable when it is changed to *bigre*.[2] A number of French oaths ending in *-bleu* — *corbleu, morbleu, parbleu, ventrebleu*, etc. — have nothing to do with the adjective *bleu* 'blue'; *bleu* is merely a modified form of *Dieu*. The swearing *palsambleu*, which belongs to the same family, is a well-camouflaged variant of the phrase *par le sang de Dieu* 'by God's blood'; cf. English '*sblood* and '*Od's blood*.

(5) *Foreign influence as a cause of semantic change.* — Many changes of meaning are due to the influence of some foreign model. To take an obvious example, the use of the word *bear* to denote two constellations, the *Great* and the *Lesser Bear*, is paralleled in many languages: French *Ourse*, Italian *Orsa*, Spanish *Osa*, German *Bär*, Hungarian *Medve*, etc. None of these is a spontaneous metaphor: they are all based on Latin *Ursa* and, beyond that, on Greek ἡ Ἄρκτος 'she-bear', both of which were already used in Classical Antiquity to denote the constellations.

The part played by foreign influence in semantic changes was discussed in some detail in the chapter on polysemy (pp. 165 ff. and 171); it is therefore unnecessary to cite further examples here.

(6) *The need for a new name as a cause of semantic change.* — Whenever

[1] See esp. J. Orr, 'Le Rôle destructeur de l'euphémie', loc. cit., pp. 170 ff.
[2] Cf. J. Orr, *Words and Sounds in English and French*, p. 227.

a new name is required to denote a new object or idea, we can do one of three things: form a new word from existing elements; borrow a term from a foreign language or some other source; lastly, alter the meaning of an old word. The need to find a new name is thus an extremely important cause of semantic changes.

The history of scientific and technological discoveries affords ample evidence of how such changes work. An interesting example is the use of the term *tank* to denote the armoured vehicle invented in the First World War. The new sense was added somewhat arbitrarily to the existing word in order to ensure secrecy during manufacture (*Shorter OED*). The name of an earlier weapon, the *torpedo*, also had an unusual origin. In Latin *torpedo*, which comes from the same root as *torpor*, meant 'stiffness, numbness' and, by transfer, the 'cramp-fish' or 'electric ray'. When, in the latter half of the eighteenth century, a new under-water weapon was invented, it was called, first in English and later in other languages, by the Latin name of the fish.[1] Another Latin word, *satelles*, *satellitis* 'attendant, life-guard', had a more complicated history. When Kepler needed a name to describe a smaller planet revolving round a larger one, he used the word *satellite* in this sense rather than coining a new term. In the course of time, *satellite* acquired several technical meanings in anatomy, zoology and town-planning; in the political sense it was first used by Frederick Naumann in his book *Mitteleuropa* (1915). During the last few years, the launching of the first *earth-satellites* has widened further the semantic range of the word. In all these cases, scientific discoveries and other developments made it necessary to find a new name, and the need was met by adding fresh meanings to the Latin term.[2]

The speed of scientific and technological progress in our time is making increasingly heavy demands on linguistic resources, and the possibilities of metaphor and other types of semantic change are being fully exploited. This can be seen, for example, in the rapidly changing nomenclature of the aircraft industry. First we had *flying-boats*, then *flying fortresses*; now we have *flying saucers* and even *flying bedsteads*. Many types of aircraft have expressive metaphorical names: *Hurricane, Spitfire, Comet, Constellation, Vampire*, and others. Among all the linguistic devices available, change of meaning is the simplest, the most discreet and perhaps the most elegant way of keeping pace with the progress of civilization.

[1] Migliorini, *The Contribution of the Individual to Language*, loc. cit., pp. 7 f.
[2] Ibid., pp. 9 f.

II. The Nature of Semantic Change

Leibniz's axiom: 'Natura non facit saltus' ('Nature makes no leaps'), is entirely applicable to semantic change. No matter what causes bring about the change, there must always be some connexion, some *association*, between the old meaning and the new. In some cases the association may be powerful enough to alter the meaning by itself; in others it will merely provide a vehicle for a change determined by other causes; but in one form or another, some kind of association will always underlie the process. In this sense association may be regarded as a necessary condition, a *sine qua non* of semantic change.

In the history of semantics, the associationist theory has appeared in two different forms. Some of the early semanticists professed a naïve associationism: they tried to explain changes of meaning as the products of associations between isolated words. In recent decades, a more sophisticated view, based on structural principles, has come to prevail; attention has shifted from single words to the wider units, the so-called 'associative fields', to which they belong. The difference between the two attitudes will be discussed more fully in the last chapter.

Several attempts have been made to classify semantic changes according to the associations underlying them. By an ingenious combination of Saussure's structural approach with some of the principles of Bergson's philosophy, the French linguist Léonce Roudet outlined, forty years ago, the first comprehensive classification of this kind, which was developed further by subsequent research.[1] Roudet's scheme has the immediate advantage of linking up with one of the basic definitions of meaning discussed in the third chapter of this book. It will be remembered that one school of thought regards meaning as a 'reciprocal and reversible relation between name and sense' (p. 57). If this formula is accepted as a working hypothesis, then semantic changes will fall naturally into two categories: those based on an association between the senses and those involving an association between the names. Each of these two categories can be further subdivided if we accept the customary distinction between

[1] See L. Roudet, 'Sur la classification psychologique des changements sémantiques', *Journal de Psychologie*, xviii (1921), pp. 676-92. Among Roudet's precursors, Wundt and Schuchardt were of particular importance. Roudet's scheme was adopted and perfected by the Hungarian linguist Z. Gombocz (see above, p. 57, n. 2). A discussion of the development of this theory, and a somewhat modified form of the scheme itself, will be found in my *Principles of Semantics*, pp. 213 ff.; cf. also Guiraud, *La Sémantique*, pp. 43 ff., and Ammer, op. cit., pp. 79 ff.

two kinds of association: similarity and contiguity.[1] These two pairs of criteria yield four cardinal types of semantic change, some of which can be broken down into further subdivisions.

1. Similarity of Senses (Metaphor)

The paramount significance of metaphor[2] as a creative force in language has always been recognized, and many extravagant claims have been made on its behalf. According to Aristotle, 'the greatest thing by far is to have a command of metaphor. This alone cannot be imparted by another; it is the mark of genius.'[3] In our own time Chesterton went so far as to assert that 'all metaphor is poetry',[4] while Sir Herbert Read has argued that 'we should always be prepared to judge a poet ... by the force and originality of his metaphors'.[5] Even more sweepingly, Proust declared in his article on the style of Flaubert: 'Je crois que la métaphore seule peut donner une sorte d'éternité au style.'[6] Even if one discounts some of these inflated claims, there can be no doubt about the crucial importance of metaphor in language and literature.

Metaphor is so closely intertwined with the very texture of human speech that we have already encountered it in various guises: as a major factor in motivation, as an expressive device, as a source of synonymy and polysemy, as an outlet for intense emotions, as a means of filling

---

[1] 'Contiguity' should be taken here in a broad sense: it includes any associative relations other than those based on similarity.

[2] Perhaps the most detailed treatise ever published on metaphor is C. F. P. Stutterheim's monumental *Het Begrip Metaphoor. Een taalkundig en wijsgerig onderzoek*, Amsterdam, 1941. Among the innumerable books and articles on the subject, the following may be noted here: H. Adank, *Essai sur les fondements psychologiques et linguistiques de la métaphore affective*, Geneva, 1939; C. Brooke-Rose, *A Grammar of Metaphor*, London, 1958; Ch. Bruneau, 'L'Image dans notre littérature', *Mélanges A. Dauzat*, Paris, 1951, pp. 55-67; E. Coseriu, *La Creación metafórica en el lenguaje*, Montevideo, 1956; G. Esnault, *Imagination populaire, métaphores occidentales*, Paris, 1925; P. Henle, 'Metaphor', *Language, Thought, and Culture*, ch. 7; L. G. Knights-B. Cottle (ed.), *Metaphor and Symbol* (Colston Research Society; Colston Papers 12), London, 1960; H. Konrad, *Etude sur la métaphore*, Paris, 1939; F. W. Leakey, 'Intention in Metaphor', *Essays in Criticism*, iv (1954), pp. 191-8; C. Day Lewis, *The Poetic Image*, London, 1947; J. Middleton Murry, 'Metaphor', *Countries of the Mind*, London, 1931; B. Migliorini, 'La Metafora reciproca', *Saggi linguistici*, pp. 23-30; L. Sainéan, *La Création métaphorique en français et en roman*, 2 vols., Halle a.S., 1905-7; M. Sala, 'Sur les métaphores réciproques', *Revue de Linguistique* (Bucharest), v (1960), pp. 311-17; W. B. Stanford, *Greek Metaphor*, Oxford, 1936; H. Werner, *Die Ursprünge der Metapher*, Leipzig, 1919. Cf. also Estrich-Sperber, op. cit., ch. 13 and *passim*; R. Jakobson-M. Halle, *Fundamentals of Language*, The Hague, 1956, pp. 76-82; E. Leisi, *Der Wortinhalt*, 2nd ed., Heidelberg, 1961; I. A. Richards, *The Philosophy of Rhetoric*, chs. 5-6; R. A. Sayce, *Style in French Prose*, Oxford, 1953, ch. 10; Wellek-Warren, *Theory of Literature*, ch. 15. Cf. also my *Style in the French Novel*, ch. 6, and *The Image in the Modern French Novel*, *passim*.

[3] Quoted by C. Day Lewis, op. cit., p. 17.

[4] *The Defendant. A Defence of Slang.* Cf. above, p. 151.

[5] Quoted by C. Day Lewis, loc. cit.

[6] 'I believe that metaphor alone can give style a kind of eternity' ('A propos du "style" de Flaubert', *Nouvelle Revue Française*, xiv, 1 (1920), pp. 72-90).

gaps in vocabulary, and in several other roles. It will thus be sufficient here to give a brief account of the psychological background of metaphor and to describe some of the characteristic forms which it assumes in language.

The basic structure of metaphor is very simple. There are always two terms present: the thing we are talking about and that to which we are comparing it. In Dr. Richards's terminology, the former is the *tenor*, the latter the *vehicle*, whereas the feature or features they have in common form the *ground* of the metaphor.[1] To take a concrete case, the Latin word *musculus* 'little mouse', a diminutive of *mus* 'mouse', was also used figuratively in the sense of 'muscle'; hence English *muscle* and other modern forms.[2] In this metaphor 'muscle' is the tenor, 'little mouse' is the vehicle, and the fancied similarity between the two forms the ground of the image, the common element underlying the transfer.[3] Instead of explicitly stating, in the form of a comparison, that a muscle *looks like* a little mouse, the tenor is identified with the vehicle by a kind of verbal shorthand. In this sense it is true to say that a metaphor is a 'condensed comparison positing an intuitive and concrete identity'.[4]

It should be noted that the similarity between tenor and vehicle may be of two kinds: objective and emotive. It is objective in the example just quoted or, for instance, when the ridge of a mountain is called a *crest* because it resembles the crest on an animal's head. It is emotive when we talk of a *bitter* disappointment because its effect is similar to that of a bitter taste. This is how the French word *déboire*, a derivative of *boire* 'to drink', which originally referred to the disagreeable after-taste of a drink, came to mean 'disappointment, blighted hope' (Bloch-Wartburg).

An important factor in the effectiveness of a metaphor is the distance between tenor and vehicle or, as Dr. Sayce calls it, the 'angle' of the image.[5] If the two terms are very close to each other — if, for example, one flower is likened to another — the metaphor will be appropriate but without any expressive quality. As Wordsworth strikingly put it:

> The song would speak
> Of that interminable building reared
> By observation of affinities
> In objects where no brotherhood exists
> To passive minds.[6]

---

[1] *The Philosophy of Rhetoric*, pp. 96 ff. and 117. French critics have an even simpler terminology: they call the vehicle *le comparant* and the tenor *le comparé*.
[2] The same metaphor is found in Greek where μῦς 'mouse' can also mean 'muscle'.
[3] The Greek word *metaphora* literally means 'transfer': *meta* 'trans-' + *pherein* 'to carry'.
[4] Esnault, *Imagination populaire*, p. 30. Cf. above, p. 136.
[5] *Style in French Prose*, pp. 62 f.   [6] Quoted by C. Day Lewis, op. cit., p. 36.

Modern writers are fond of producing surprise effects by drawing unexpected parallels between disparate objects. The French Surrealist poet André Breton has unequivocally stated: 'To compare two objects, as remote from one another in character as possible, or by any other method put them together in a sudden and striking fashion, this remains the highest task to which poetry can aspire.' In quoting this statement, Dr. Richards makes the pertinent comment: 'As the two things put together are more remote, the tension created is, of course, greater. That tension is the spring of the bow, the source of the energy of the shot, but we ought not to mistake the strength of the bow for the excellence of the shooting; or the strain for the aim.'[1]

Among the innumerable metaphors in which the image-making faculty of man has expressed itself, there are four major groups which recur in the most diverse languages and literary styles.

(i) *Anthropomorphic*[2] *metaphors.* — One of the first thinkers who noticed the extraordinary frequency of this type of transfer was the eighteenth-century Italian philosopher Giambattista Vico. 'In all languages,' he wrote in his *Scienza nuova*, 'the greater part of expressions referring to inanimate objects are taken by transfer from the human body and its parts, from human senses and human passions ... Ignorant man makes himself into the yardstick of the universe.'[3] This tendency is attested in the most different languages and civilizations, and lies at the root of countless expressions in current usage. In the chapter on polysemy (pp. 162 f.) we saw a small sample of the metaphors in which inanimate objects are compared to the human eye. In the same way we talk of the *brow* of a hill, the *ribs* of a vault, the *mouth* of a river, the *lungs* of a town, the *heart* of the matter, the *sinews* of war, the *hands* of a clock, and many more, whereas the metaphorical uses of other organs, such as the *foot* and the *leg*, are virtually unlimited.

Naturally there are also many transfers in the opposite direction, where parts of the body are named after animals or inanimate objects: *muscle, polypus, spine, Adam's apple, apple* of the eye, ear-*drum*, and various others. In Sperber's terminology, the human body is a powerful centre of metaphorical expansion as well as attraction (cf. p. 201); on the whole, however, metaphors *from* this sphere seem to be far more common than those directed *towards* it.

---

[1] Loc. cit., pp. 123 and 125.   [2] From Greek *anthrōpos* 'man'+*morphē* 'form'.
[3] Quoted by Gombocz, op. cit., p. 73. The most comprehensive monograph on anthropomorphic metaphors is J. J. De Witte, *De Betekeniswereld van het lichaam*, Nijmegen, 1948. See also Carnoy, op. cit., pp. 324-36, and E. Cassirer, *Philosophie der symbolischen Formen*, vol. I, Berlin, 1923, pp. 158 ff.

(ii) *Animal metaphors.* — Another perennial source of imagery is the animal kingdom. These metaphors, some specimens of which have already been quoted (cf. pp. 201, 209, 213, etc.), move in two main directions. Some of them are applied to plants or insentient objects. Many plants owe their name to some vague resemblance, often fanciful or jocular, to an animal: *goat's-beard, cock's-foot, dog's-tail,* etc. *Dandelion* comes from the French *dent de lion* 'lion's tooth'. There are even combinations of animal metaphors, as in the French *chiendent queue-de-renard* 'hunger-grass', which literally means 'dog's tooth foxtail'. A great many inanimate objects, including various instruments, machines and parts of machines, are also called after an animal: *cat, cat-head, cat-o'nine-tails, crab, crane, cock* of a gun, *cock* in the sense of 'tap', and countless others.

Another large group of animal images are transferred into the human sphere where they often acquire humorous, ironical, pejorative or even grotesque connotations. A human being can be likened to an inexhaustible variety of animals: a *dog,* a *cat,* a *pig,* an *ass,* a *mouse,* a *rat,* a *goose,* a *lion,* a *jackal,* etc.; he can look or behave in a *catty, dogged, sheepish, owlish, fishy* or *mulish* way; he can *dog* a criminal, *ape* or *lionize* those he admires, and even *parrot* their words. This abundant imagery springs from the same attitude as the numerous literary works, from Aesop to La Fontaine and from the Greek *Batrachomyomachia* (War of the Frogs and Mice) to Orwell's *Animal Farm,* where beasts are made to talk and act as human beings. Although animal images are among the oldest devices of literary style—Homer already calls the goddess Hera 'ox-eyed' — they have lost none of their expressive and evocative force: all readers of Proust will remember the terse and vivid caricature of M. de Palancy 'qui, avec sa grosse tête de carpe aux yeux ronds, se déplaçait lentement au milieu des fêtes en desserrant d'instant en instant ses mandibules comme pour chercher son orientation'.[1]

(iii) *From concrete to abstract.* — One of the basic tendencies in metaphor is to translate abstract experiences into concrete terms. In many cases, the transfer is still transparent, but in others some etymological probing will be necessary to recapture the concrete image underlying an abstract word: to discover the Latin *finis* 'limit, end' behind *define* and *finance, limen* 'threshold' behind *eliminate, sidus* 'star' behind *desire, velum* 'veil' behind *reveal,* or *volvere* 'roll' behind *involve.* Such transfers are going on all the time; in fact it would be impossible to discuss any abstract subject without them. Take for example the innumerable

---

[1] 'who, with his large carp's head and round eyes, moved about slowly in the midst of the party, opening and closing his mandibles as if to find his bearings' (*Du Côté de chez Swann,* vol. II, p. 143). Cf. my *Image in the Modern French Novel,* pp. 176 ff.

metaphors connected with *light*: to throw *light* on, to put in a favourable *light*, leading *lights*, to *enlighten*, *illuminating*, *brilliant*, *beaming*, *radiant*, *coruscating*, *dazzling*, etc. That this metaphorical vein is far from exhausted can be seen from such comparatively recent expressions as *in the limelight*, *to hold the spotlight*, or *high-lights* in the sense of 'a moment or detail of vivid interest' (*Shorter OED*).

Even such a highly abstract and elusive experience as time[1] can be made concrete and tangible by the creative writer. The age-old cliché of the 'flow' of time is rejuvenated in the hands of Sartre when, evoking the languid atmosphere of a hot summer day, he speaks of 'time flowing softly, like an infusion warmed up by the sun'.[2] Elsewhere time is visualized in novel and arresting images. To Shakespeare it appears as 'Old Time the clock-setter, that bald sexton Time' (*King John*, Act III, scene 1). Tennyson pictures it as a 'maniac scattering dust' (*In Memoriam*, L). In Proust, whose whole work is centred on the problem of time, there are endless variations on this theme, culminating, at the very end of the cycle, in the nightmarish vision of men mounted on the ever-growing stilts of time until finally they topple over.[3]

(iv) '*Synaesthetic*'[4] *metaphors*. – A very common type of metaphor is based on transpositions from one sense to another: from sound to sight, from touch to sound, etc. When we speak of a *warm* or a *cold* voice, we do so because we perceive some kind of similarity between warm or cold temperature and the quality of certain voices. In the same way we talk of *piercing* sounds, *loud* colours, *sweet* voices and odours, and many more. Synaesthetic associations lie also at the root of certain etymologies. The German adjective *hell* 'clear, bright' is related to the verb *hallen* 'to resound' (cf. p. 101). Greek *barytone* is based on βαρύς 'heavy', and *oxytone*, 'having the acute accent', on ὀξύς 'sharp'; similarly Latin *gravis* and *acutus*, which gave our *grave* and *acute* accent. Commenting on such transpositions in *De Anima*, Aristotle wrote: '*Acute* and *grave* are here metaphors transferred from their proper sphere, namely, that of touch ... There seems to be a sort of parallelism between what is acute or grave to hearing and what is *sharp* or *blunt* to touch.'[5]

The systematic exploitation of these resources in literary style began

---

[1] Cf. G. Poulet, *Etudes sur le temps humain*, Edinburgh, 1949.
[2] 'Le temps coulait doucement, tisane attiédie par le soleil' (*La Mort dans l'âme*, Paris, 1949, p. 70; cf. *Style in the French Novel*, p. 256).
[3] *Le Temps retrouvé*, Paris, 1949 ed., vol. II, p. 229. On Proust's time metaphors see my *Image in the Modern French Novel*, pp. 213-17.
[4] From Greek *syn* 'together'+*aisthēsis* 'perception'. A full discussion of this type of metaphor, together with detailed references, will be found in my *Principles of Semantics*, pp. 266 ff.   [5] Quoted by Stanford, *Greek Metaphor*, p. 49.

with the advent of Symbolism, but the device itself is of respectable ancestry. The synaesthetic combination 'lily-voiced' already occurs in the *Iliad*,[1] and in the *Aeneid*, the sky is said to be 'kindled with shouts'.[2] Shakespeare was sufficiently conscious of this technique to ridicule it in *A Midsummer Night's Dream*, Act V, scene 1:

> PYRAMUS: I see a voice; now will I to the chink,
> To spy an I can hear my Thisby's face.

Yet Shakespeare himself did not hesitate to use the device; in *The Tempest*, Act IV, scene 1, he speaks of 'smelling music', and *Twelfth Night* opens with a complex sequence of synaesthetic images:

> If music be the food of love, play on,
> Give me excess of it, that, surfeiting,
> The appetite may sicken and so die.
> That strain again! It had a dying fall;
> O, it came o'er my ear like the sweet sound
> That breathes upon a bank of violets,
> Stealing and giving odour.[3]

There are several synaesthetic metaphors in the poetry of the seventeenth century, such as Donne's 'loud perfume'. (*Elegy*, IV: 'The Perfume') and Milton's 'blind mouths' (*Lycidas*, l. 119). The Romantics were particularly fond of such combinations; Byron was criticized for writing: 'the Music breathing from her face' (*The Bride of Abydos*, I, 6),[4] but Keats went further and combined three different senses when he wrote in *Isabella*: 'And taste the music of that vision pale'. Among the French Romantics, Théophile Gautier, with his *Symphonie en blanc majeur*, played an important part in the vogue of such transpositions.

Synaesthesia was erected into an aesthetic doctrine in Baudelaire's sonnet *Correspondances*:

> Les parfums, les couleurs et les sons se répondent.
> Il est des parfums frais comme des chairs d'enfants,
> Doux comme les hautbois, verts comme les prairies.[5]

---

[1] Quoted ibid., p. 53, from *Iliad*, iii, 152 (ὅπα λειριόεσσαν).

[2] 'Clamore incendunt caelum' (*Aeneid*, x, 895). Cf. E. Struck, *Bedeutungslehre. Grundzüge einer lateinischen und griechischen Semasiologie*, 1st ed., p. 98.

[3] On the history of this passage see E. v. Siebold, 'Synästhesien in der englischen Dichtung des 19. Jahrhunderts', *Englische Studien*, liii (1919-20), pp. 1-157 and 196-334: p. 217, n. 1.

[4] See E. v. Erhardt-Siebold, 'Harmony of the Senses in English, German, and French Romanticism', *Publications of the Modern Language Association of America*, xlvii (1932), pp. 577-92: pp. 587 f.

[5] 'Perfumes, sounds, and colours answer each to each. There are perfumes fresh and cool as the bodies of children, mellow as oboes, green as fields' (Francis Scarfe's translation in *Baudelaire*, Penguin Books, 1961, p. 37).

From that time onwards, synaesthetic imagery has been fully exploited and even overworked in poetry as well as in prose. Attempts were even made to systematize correspondences between the various senses; the best known experiment of this kind was Rimbaud's sonnet on the colour of vowel sounds: 'A noir, E blanc, I rouge, U vert, O bleu ... ', which may have been suggested by memories of a spelling-book used in his childhood.[1] At the present time, such transpositions are so common that nobody is shocked when a novelist speaks of 'yellow taste' or of 'green and pointed smells'.[2]

2. Contiguity of Senses (Metonymy)

Metonymy[3] is intrinsically less interesting than metaphor since it does not discover new relations but arises between words already related to each other. The difference between the two processes has been aptly summarized by M. Esnault: 'La métonymie n'ouvre pas de chemins comme l'intuition métaphorique; mais brûlant les étapes de chemins trop connus, elle raccourcit des distances pour faciliter la rapide intuition de choses déjà connues.'[4] But if metonymy is of limited interest to the student of style,[5] it is an important factor in semantic change; we have already encountered it in the discussion of proper names (p. 78), motivation (pp. 91 f.), polysemy (pp. 163 f.), and elsewhere.

Metonymies can best be classified according to the associations under-lying them. Some metonymic transfers are based on *spatial* relations. The shift of meaning from Latin *coxa* 'hip' to French *cuisse* 'thigh' is explained by the fact that the hip and the thigh are two contiguous parts of our body, without any sharp boundaries between them (p. 125). As will be seen in the last chapter, this was not the ultimate cause of the change; it was merely the condition which made such a transfer possible. A similar metonymy lies at the root of the French word for 'strike', *grève*, which derives its name from the *Place de Grève*, now called *Place de l'Hôtel de*

[1] Cf. H. Héraut, 'Du nouveau sur Rimbaud', *Nouvelle Revue Française*, xliii (1934), pp. 602-8; R. Etiemble, 'Le Sonnet des Voyelles', *Revue de Littérature Comparée*, xix (1939), pp. 235-61; J.-F. Barrère, 'Rimbaud, l'apprenti sorcier', *Revue d'Histoire Littéraire de la France*, lvi (1956), pp. 50-64.

[2] 'Le jeune goût jaune de bois tendre' (Sartre, *La Mort dans l'âme*, p. 233); 'des odeurs vertes et gaies, encore pointues, encore acides' (ibid., p. 45).

[3] From Greek *meta* 'trans'+*onoma* 'name'. Many examples of metonymy will be found in Nyrop, *Sémantique*, Book V, and in E. Huguet, *L'Évolution du sens des mots depuis le XVIe siècle*, Paris, 1934, ch. 7.

[4] 'Metonymy does not open new paths like metaphorical intuition; but, taking too familiar paths in its stride, it shortens distances so as to facilitate the swift intuition of things already known' (*Imagination populaire*, p. 31).

[5] Cf. my *Style in the French Novel*, pp. 211 ff.

Ville, where Parisian labourers used to assemble when they were out of work (Bloch-Wartburg).

Another group of metonymies are based on *temporal* relations. The name of an action or event can be transferred to something immediately preceding or following it. We have already seen an example of this in the history of the word *collation* (p. 98). A similar association between successive events accounts in all probability for the sense-development of English *mass*, French *messe* and related terms which denote the Roman Catholic service in many languages. All these go back to Ecclesiastical Latin *missa*, feminine past participle of Latin *mittere* 'to send, to dismiss'. Since the service ended with the formula: 'Ite, *missa* est (contio)' 'Go now, the meeting is *dismissed*', the word *missa* eventually came to stand for the service itself (Bloch-Wartburg). A closely similar case is that of the French word *veille* 'vigil', which now chiefly means 'eve, preceding day'.

Among other relations which can result in a metonymic change, one type is so important that it is sometimes treated as a separate category: *pars pro toto* or 'part for the whole'.[1] A simple example is the use of *redbreast* for 'robin' (p. 92), naming the bird after the most conspicuous detail in its appearance. Similarly, human types and social classes are often called after some characteristic garment: *redcoat*, *redcap*, *blue-stocking*,[2] *Blackshirt*; French *la blouse* 'workman; working class, proletariat', and more recently *blouson noir*, the French equivalent of a 'teddy boy', nicknamed after the black jacket worn by these youths. The connexion has ceased to be transparent in French *grisette*, a derivative of *gris* 'grey', which originally meant a cheap grey dress-material and then came to designate, with pejorative overtones, the young working girls wearing this kind of dress (Bloch-Wartburg).

Other types of metonymy are so simple and so well known that they require no detailed discussion. As already mentioned, inventions and discoveries are often named after the person responsible for them; when a physicist says that one *ampère* is the current that one *volt* can send through one *ohm* (*NED*), he is commemorating three great pioneers of his science: the Frenchman André Ampère, the Italian Count Alessandro

---

[1] This is part of the traditional figure of *synecdoche* (from Greek *syn* 'together'+ *ekdekhesthai* 'to take, to take up'), where a 'more comprehensive term is used for a less comprehensive or vice versa' (*NED*).

[2] Translated into various languages: French *bas-bleu*, German *Blaustrumpf*, Swedish *blåstrumpa*, Hungarian *kékharisnya*, etc. The expression 'dates from the assemblies which met at Montagu House in London about 1750 in order to substitute for card-playing literary conversation, etc., etc. At these a principal attendant was Mr. Benjamin Stillingfleet, who habitually wore blue worsted instead of black silk stockings. In reference to this the coterie was dubbed by Admiral Boscawen "the Blue Stocking Society" ' (*Shorter OED*).

Volta, and the German Georg Simon Ohm. Similarly, foods and drinks are called after their place of origin (*gruyère*, *champagne*), the content after the container ('to drink a *glass*, a *bottle* of wine'), and many more.

An interesting feature of metonymy is that, unlike metaphor, it tends to give abstract words a concrete meaning: the name of an action will stand for its result, the name of a quality for a person or object exhibiting it, etc. Bréal has graphically described these changes as 'thickening of meaning' (épaississement de sens).[1] There are countless examples of this tendency in various languages: the act of *binding* and the *binding* of a book; the *performance* of one's duty and an operatic *performance*; to keep *guard* and the *Horse Guards*, etc. Qualities are treated in the same way: a thing whose *beauty* we admire is called a *beauty*; a person of whom his relations are proud is the *pride* of his family; *falsehood* means falsity in the abstract and also a particular falsehood, a lie. In some words this usage has led to a radical shift of meaning. French *addition* means not only the act of adding and its result, but also a bill in a restaurant. French *témoin*, which comes from Latin *testimonium* 'evidence, testimony', now signifies almost exclusively 'a person who testifies, a witness'; the abstract meaning still survives in the legal phrase *en témoin de quoi* 'in witness whereof'. The English word *witness* has had a closely parallel development. In other cases the abstract sense has been completely eclipsed. French *ivrogne* 'drunkard' is derived from Vulgar Latin **ebrionia* 'drunkenness' (Bloch-Wartburg), and *élite*, an old past participle of the verb *élire* 'to elect, to choose', still meant 'choice, choosing' in the sixteenth century when Montaigne spoke of '*eslite* entre le bien et le mal',[2] whereas now it refers only to the 'choice part' of a society.

3. *Similarity of Names (Popular Etymology)*

Popular etymology, it will be remembered, can change both the form and the meaning of a word by wrongly connecting it with another term to which it is similar in sound. The investigations of Gilliéron and other linguistic geographers have shown that this is a more common process than one might have thought; nevertheless, it is obviously not on a par with metaphor or metonymy as a factor in semantic change. It does, however, contain an important warning to the etymologist: before trying to reconstruct the semantic history of a word, he must first satisfy himself that the development has been spontaneous and not induced by a

---

[1] *Essai de sémantique*, ch. 13. See also Gamillscheg, *Französische Bedeutungslehre*, pp. 53-8 and 73-94; K. Baldinger, *Kollektivsuffixe und Kollektivbegriff*, Berlin, 1950, Part I, 1; R. Zindel, *Des Abstraits en français et de leur pluralisation*, Berne, 1958.

[2] 'Choice between good and evil' (quoted by Huguet, loc. cit., p. 235).

phonetically similar term. Without this precautionary measure, some of our most plausible reconstructions may be purely gratuitous: we may be setting up what Professor Orr has called a 'pseudo-semantic development'.[1]

In the chapter on popular etymology (pp. 101 ff.), several semantic changes due to phonetic similarity have been discussed (*sand-blind*, French *ouvrable*, German *Sündflut*). One or two more examples may be given here to show the nature of these processes.[2] Changes of meaning due to this factor fall into two groups. In the more deceptive of the two, the old sense and the new are fairly close to each other, so that the latter *could* have developed spontaneously from the former though in actual fact it did not. The French word *forain*, which has given the English *foreign*, is a clear example of this type. It comes from Low Latin *foranus*, a derivative of Latin *foris* 'abroad, without'; its original meaning was 'foreign', as it still is in English. In the phrase *marchand forain* 'itinerant merchant', the term became wrongly associated with *foire* 'fair' (from Latin *feria(e)* 'holiday(s)'), which is the same word as English *fair*, and this association has affected the whole meaning of *forain*. The semantic link between the ideas of 'itinerant merchant' and 'fair' no doubt facilitated the change, but the phonetic similarity with *foire* must have been the decisive factor. In some dialects there is a collateral form *foirain* where the connexion with *foire* is even more marked (Bloch-Wartburg).

Another example of this type is the English noun *boon* which has already been mentioned (p. 195). As we have seen, this noun first meant 'prayer, request', then 'the matter prayed for or asked'; its current sense is 'a blessing, an advantage, a thing to be thankful for'. The semantic development could again have been spontaneous, but it was probably influenced by the homonymous adjective *boon*, an Anglicized form of French *bon* (*NED*).

The situation is rather different in the second type where the two meanings are so diverse that there seems to be no connexion between them. Rather than positing a purely imaginary line of development, the trained semanticist will look for the influence of some phonetically similar word which may supply the missing link. Thus the French *gazouiller* 'to twitter, to warble, to babble' can mean in popular speech

---

[1] *Words and Sounds in English and French*, ch. 15.

[2] In addition to the works already mentioned in the chapter on popular etymology, the following monographs may be noted here: H. Ammann, 'Wortklang und Wortbedeutung', *Neue Jahrbücher für Wissenschaft und Jugendbildung*, i (1925), pp. 221-35; A. Ernout, *Philologica*, Paris, 1946; H. Hatzfeld, *Über Bedeutungsverschiebung durch Formähnlichkeit im Neufranzösischen*, Munich, 1924; E. Löfstedt, *Vermischte Studien zur lateinischen Sprachkunde und Syntax*, Acta Reg. Soc. Hum. Litt. Lundensis, XXIII, 1936. Further references will be found in my *Principles of Semantics*, p. 236, n. 1.

'to have an unpleasant smell'. It would of course be naïve to try to derive this new meaning from the old, since it is obviously a vulgar witticism suggested by the assonance of the initial syllable with the word *gaz*.[1] Far more complicated is the double meaning of French *essuyer*: 'to wipe, to dry' and 'to suffer, to endure'. Professor Orr has demonstrated that this is another case of 'pseudo-semantic development': the second sense did not grow organically out of the first but was due to confusion with *essayer* which now means 'to try' but which, as recently as the sixteenth century, could also mean 'to experience, to endure'.[2] The implications of such processes for structural semantics will be considered more closely in the next chapter.

4. Contiguity of Names (Ellipsis)

Words which often occur side by side are apt to have a semantic influence on each other. We have already seen an example of this in the history of negation in French (p. 198). The commonest form which this influence takes is *ellipsis*:[3] in a set phrase made up of two words, one of these is omitted and its meaning is transferred to its partner. This may have grammatical consequences: an adjective may be turned into a noun (*the main* for *the main sea, a daily* for *a daily paper*), and in some languages there may be anomalies of number or gender, as in French *le cinquième hussards*, where *régiment* is left out, or in *un première Lyon* which is a double ellipsis for 'un (billet de) première (classe)'.

In a number of cases, ellipses of this kind have led to drastic changes in meaning. Omission of the French word *carrosse* 'coach' explains two old terms of transport which have also passed into English: *diligence* is short for *carrosse de diligence*, and *coupé*, which is really the past participle of the verb *couper* 'to cut', stands for *carrosse coupé*, a carriage one of whose two compartments have been cut off (Bloch-Wartburg). In the same way, a *drawing-room* is really a *withdrawing-room*; French *bouclier* 'buckler, shield' was originally *escu boucler* 'a shield with a buckle' (Bloch-Wartburg); *piano*, from an Italian adjective and adverb meaning 'soft, softly', is a shortened form of *pianoforte* 'soft and strong', so called by Cristofori, its inventor, to express the gradation of tone of which it is capable,

---

[1] Cf. Nyrop, *Sémantique*, p. 328.

[2] *Words and Sounds in English and French*, pp. 157-60.

[3] The following special studies on ellipsis may be noted: K. Bergman, *Die Ellipse im Neufranzösischen*, Freiburg, 1908; W. Franz, 'Ellipse und Bedeutungswandel', *Englische Studien*, lxii (1927-28), pp. 25-34; W. Horn, *Sprachkörper und Sprachfunktion*, Palaestra, CXXXV; 2nd ed., Leipzig, 1923; R. E. Keller, *Die Ellipse in der neuenglischen Sprache als syntaktisch-semantisches Problem*, Zurich, 1944; Wellander, op. cit., Parts II and III. For further references, see my *Principles of Semantics*, p. 238, n. 1.

(*Shorter OED*). A curious example is *porter*, which is short for *porter's ale*, *porter's beer*, apparently because this drink was originally made for porters and other labourers (*Shorter OED*).

English compounds and phrases adopted into French have often been curtailed by ellipsis. This has produced some usages which sound curious to native ears. Thus 'smoking-jacket' has been reduced to *smoking*, which now means a 'dinner-jacket' in French and other Continental languages. Similarly, a 'cargo-boat' becomes *un cargo*, a 'midshipman' un *midship*, a 'sidecar' *un side*, and a 'pin-up girl' *une pin-up*. Such shortenings are common in sport where *un goal* can mean a 'goalkeeper', *le catch* stands for 'catch-as-catch-can', *le cross* for 'cross-country running', while even 'football' and 'basket-ball' can be mutilated: 'des joueurs de *foot*, de *basket*'.[1]

The above classification of semantic changes calls for the following general comments:

(1) The four cardinal types are very different in scope. Metaphor is by far the most important of the four, but metonymy too is an extremely common process. Ellipsis, though by no means infrequent, is on the whole of limited importance, whereas popular etymology, despite its great interest, is a marginal phenomenon. It would seem, then, that associations between senses are of incomparably greater significance than those between names. A language without ellipsis and popular etymology would be a perfectly adequate medium of communication, whereas a language without metaphor and metonymy is inconceivable: these two forces are inherent in the basic structure of human speech.

(2) There are many semantic changes which seem to fit into more than one category. One may wonder, for example, whether expressions like *a Picasso* for 'a painting by Picasso', or *burgundy* for 'wine from Burgundy', are metonymic or elliptical.[2] Perhaps it might be simplest to regard them as '*composite*' changes due to the interplay of two different types of association.

(3) The semantic development of many words consists of a series of successive changes which may sometimes take them very far from their original sense. Darmesteter coined the term '*concatenation*' (enchaînement) to describe these complex processes.[3] A good example is French *cadeau* which was borrowed from Provençal in the early fifteenth century in the sense of 'capital letter', and did not reach its modern meaning of 'present,

---

[1] All these examples are from Harmer, op. cit., pp. 118 f.

[2] For another example of ellipsis combined with metonymy, see the history of the word *mass* discussed on p. 219.

[3] *La vie des mots*, pp. 76 ff.

gift' until three and a half centuries later. The following were the main stages in the semantic history of the word: 1. 'capital letter'; 2. 'strokes of calligraphy'; 3. 'superfluous words used as mere ornaments'; 4. 'entertainment, amusement, especially when offered to a lady'; 5. 'present, gift' (Bloch-Wartburg). The student of meaning will of course have to examine each change separately and try to reconstruct its background. An etymologist who gave only the starting-point and the terminal point of such a chain of events would be, according to Gilliéron's amusing simile, comparable to a literary critic who summarized the life of Balzac in these two sentences: 'Balzac, sitting in the lap of his nurse, wore a blue dress with red stripes. He wrote the *Comédie humaine.*'[1]

(4) The question has often been asked whether semantic changes are entirely haphazard, or whether there is some kind of regularity or pattern behind them.[2] Ever since Bréal suggested that the new science of semantics should try to establish the 'laws governing changes in meaning' (cf. above, p. 6), the search for *'laws'* has been one of the main preoccupations of workers in this field. Some linguists were sceptical about the prospects of this quest. Commenting on the sense-change of French *poutre*, which originally meant a 'filly' and now denotes a 'beam' or 'girder', Saussure wrote: 'cela est dû à des causes particulières et ne dépend pas des autres changements qui ont pu se produire dans le même temps; ce n'est qu'un accident parmi tous ceux qu'enregistre l'histoire d'une langue'.[3] Nyrop was even more categorical: 'ici les conditions qui déterminent les changements sont tellement multiples et tellement complexes, que les résultats défient constamment toute prévision et offrent les plus grandes surprises'.[4] Yet, despite these and many other warnings, the quest went on and was not altogether barren of results. Even today there are linguists who firmly believe that the principal task of semantics is to study the 'specific laws of the development of language'.[5]

Perhaps the most ambitious attempt to formulate such a 'specific law' was the late Gustaf Stern's monograph on Middle English terms for 'swift' and 'swiftly' (cf. above, p. 144, n. 1). A thorough examination of

[1] Quoted by Wartburg, *Problèmes et méthodes*, p. 107. Cf. above, pp. 30 f.

[2] A detailed discussion of 'semantic laws', together with bibliographical references, will be found in my *Principles of Semantics*, ch. 4, section 3, and ch. 5. See now also Zvegintsev, *Semasiologija*, ch. 9, and Sauvageot's article referred to on p. 196, n. 4.

[3] 'This is due to particular causes and does not depend on other changes which may have taken place at the same time; it is a mere accident among all those recorded in the history of a language' (op. cit., p. 132).

[4] 'Here the conditions which determine the changes are so numerous and so complex that the results constantly defy any prediction and present the greatest surprises' (*Sémantique*, p. 79).

[5] Zvegintsev, op. cit., p. 46.

chronological data led Stern to the following, remarkably precise conclusion:

> English adverbs which have acquired the sense 'rapidly' before 1300, always develop the sense 'immediately'. This happens when the adverb is used to qualify a verb, the action of which may be apprehended as either imperfective or perfective, and when the meaning of the adverb consequently is equivocal: 'rapidly/immediately'. Exceptions are due to the influence of special factors. But when the sense 'rapidly' is acquired later than 1300, no such development takes place. There is no exception to this rule (*Meaning and Change of Meaning*, p. 190).

If Professor Stern's formula is really valid,[1] then he was right in claiming that it is on all fours with the phonetic laws of which nineteenth-century linguists were so proud: 'This "law" has the form of a sound-law: it gives the circumstances of the change and a chronological limit' (ibid.). One may wonder, however, whether this can be accepted as a genuine semantic law. The parallel sense-developments did not arise spontaneously: the various words must have influenced each other by a process of analogy or 'synonymic radiation' which was discussed in Chapter 6 (pp. 150 f.).

It is in a different direction that most linguists have looked for regular patterns in semantic change. They tried to collect instances of similar changes which had occurred, independently of each other, in different languages and periods, and which could therefore be regarded as symptoms of a common tendency, of a widespread and abiding feature of the human mind. Some linguists confined themselves to specific developments whereas others tried to formulate more general laws. Among the specific tendencies examined, parallel metaphors have yielded some remarkable results.[2] In many languages, for example, verbs meaning 'to catch' or 'to grasp' are used figuratively in the sense of 'to understand': English *catch*, *grasp*; French *comprendre* (from *prendre* 'to take'), *saisir*; Italian *capire*, from Latin *capere* 'to catch'; German *begreifen*, from *greifen* 'to grasp'; and there are similar formations in Russian, Finnish, Hungarian and Turkish.[3] The difficulty is of course to determine how far these various languages may have influenced each other. This difficulty can be eliminated if the examples are taken from widely different idioms and civilizations which have had little or no contact with one

---

[1] See E. Oksaar's reservations in op. cit., pp. 499 ff.
[2] See esp. Gombocz, op. cit., pp. 5 ff.; cf. also Sauvageot, loc. cit., and De Witte, op. cit., *passim*.
[3] See Gombocz, loc. cit.

another. Thus it is interesting to learn that the English expression *eye of a needle* has exact parallels in Eskimo and in Chuvash, a Turkish language spoken in Russia, and that the 'eyelid' is called 'skin' or 'rind' of the eye in Hungary and in the Marquesas Islands of Oceania as well as in some other areas.[1] Even more surprising is the case of *pupil* 'apple of the eye', which, as already noted (pp. 98 and 177 f.), is the same word as the other *pupil*. The Latin *pupilla* 'orphan girl, ward, minor' could also denote the apple of the eye, because of some vague similarity between a small girl and the minute figure reflected in the pupil (Bloch-Wartburg). Now it has been found that in more than thirty languages belonging to the most different groups, the apple of the eye is called metaphorically 'little girl' or, more rarely, 'little boy'.[2] Nor are such parallel developments confined to metaphor: metonymies can be just as widespread. The use of the word for 'tongue', organ of speech, in the sense of 'language' occurs not only in many European idioms which may have influenced each other, but is also found in various non-European languages.[3]

Some linguists have aimed even higher and have tried to identify certain broad tendencies governing semantic change. One of the first experiments of this kind was Bréal's 'law of differentiation between synonyms', which has already been mentioned (p. 141). Most of the later attempts have centred on metaphor, though metonymy has also received some attention. G. Esnault threw out some brief and provocative hints on the nature of both processes, such as, for example, that we tend to describe time by means of metaphors from space, but not space by means of metaphors from time.[4] Sperber has developed his theory of 'expansion' (cf. pp. 201 ff.) into a semantic 'law': 'If at a certain time a complex of ideas is so strongly charged with feeling that it causes *one* word to extend its sphere and change its meaning, we may confidently expect that other words belonging to the same emotional complex will also shift their meaning.'[5] Close study of anthropomorphic metaphors has convinced De Witte that transfers *from* the human body are more frequent than those directed *towards* that sphere (cf. p. 214). Bloomfield has plausibly suggested that 'refined and abstract meanings largely grow out of more concrete meanings'.[6] I myself have found certain common features in the

[1] Sauvageot, loc. cit., pp. 466 f.
[2] C. Tagliavini, 'Di alcune denominazioni della "pupilla"', *Annali dell'Istituto Universitario Orientale di Napoli*, N.S., iii (1949), pp. 341-78: pp. 363 ff.
[3] Gombocz, op. cit., p. 94; Révész, *The Origins and Prehistory of Language*, pp. 56 f.
[4] 'Lois sémantiques', in *Où en sont les études de français*, pp. 130-8.
[5] Op. cit., p. 67; English translation by Professor W. E. Collinson, *Modern Language Review*, xx (1925), p. 106.
[6] *Language*, p. 429; cf. G. Bonfante, *Word*, i (1945), p. 145.

synaesthetic images of various English, French and Hungarian writers; it seems, for example, that transfers from the lower and less differentiated senses to the higher and more differentiated ones are more common than those in the opposite direction: acoustic and visual impressions are more often transcribed in terms of touch or heat than vice versa.[1] Some of these 'laws' may well be confirmed, others contradicted by further research; what is needed for all of them is a far broader empirical basis, including statistical data from many different languages. In this sense Professor Spitzer was perfectly right when he declared in 1943 that 'no one has ever thought of offering a "semantic law" '.[2] In view of the scale of the investigations involved, these problems could best be tackled in the form of a series of international research projects. The results of such inquiries would be of great importance not only to linguistics, but also to psychology, to cultural anthropology and various other disciplines.

III. The Consequences of Semantic Change

Among the innumerable consequences which may result from semantic changes, two problems have received particular attention: the range and the emotive overtones of the new meaning as compared to the old.

1. *Changes in Range: Extension and Restriction of Meaning*

Many early writers on semantics divided changes of meaning into three categories: extension, restriction, and a miscellaneous third group which showed neither widening nor narrowing of range. This so-called 'logical classification',[3] though simple and easy to handle, had some serious weaknesses. It rested on purely formal criteria and threw no light either on the ultimate causes of a change or on its psychological background. Another disadvantage was that all three categories were heterogeneous: under the headings 'extension' and 'restriction' there appeared a wide variety of changes which had nothing in common beyond the superficial fact that the new sense was wider or narrower than the old; everything that was not amenable to this criterion was consigned indiscriminately to the miscellaneous group.

---

[1] *The Principles of Semantics*, pp. 277 ff. These findings seem to agree with the expectations of psychologists; cf. H. Werner, *Language*, xxviii (1952), p. 256. Cf. also A. H. Whitney, 'Synaesthesia in Twentieth-Century Hungarian Poetry', *The Slavonic and East European Review*, xxx (1951-52), pp. 444-64.

[2] 'Why Does Language Change?', *Modern Language Quarterly*, iv (1943), pp. 413-31: p. 427; cf. Bonfante, loc. cit., p. 146.

[3] For a more detailed discussion and bibliographical references, see my *Principles of Semantics*, pp. 203 ff.

The fact remains that many words have, for a variety of reasons, widened or narrowed their meaning and continue to do so all the time. Some terms have almost exactly doubled or halved their range. Our word *uncle*, for example, comes via French from the Latin *avunculus* which meant only one kind of uncle, namely, the mother's brother, whereas the father's brother was called *patruus*. Since the latter word fell into disuse, the descendants of *avunculus* have come to stand for both kinds of uncle, so that the range of the Latin term has been doubled. In most cases, however, extension and restriction have altered far more drastically the field of application of the words involved.

(1) *Restriction of meaning.*[1] — The mechanism at work can be demonstrated on a simple example. The English word *voyage* originally meant a 'journey', as the corresponding French term still does. In the course of time, its range was narrowed and it came to refer more specifically to a 'journey by sea or water'. The net result of the change was that the word is now applicable to fewer things but tells us more about them; its scope has been restricted but its meaning has been enriched with an additional feature: that of travel by *water*. As a logician would put it, its 'extension' has been reduced while its 'intension' has been correspondingly increased (cf. p. 119). A similar change has overtaken the French *viande*, from Vulgar Latin *vivenda*, a derivative of *vivere* 'to live'. Until the seventeenth century, *viande* meant 'food' in general; since then it has become specialized in the sense of 'meat'. Corresponding words in other languages — Italian *vivanda*, Spanish *vianda*, English *viand(s)* — have preserved the wider sense (Bloch-Wartburg).

The most frequent cause of restriction is specialization of meaning in a particular social group. More often than not this will merely give rise to polysemy (see above, pp. 161 f.), but it can also permanently reduce the range of the word as a whole. Several examples of this process were given earlier on in this chapter (pp. 199 f.), and there is no need to multiply them here. Another cause of restriction is euphemism, including the variety which is prompted by irony rather than by taboo (cf. p. 207). A famous case in point is *poison* which is historically the same word as *potion*. The most unpleasant aspect of the sense, the fact that the potion is a 'poisonous' one, was left unsaid, but when the word became closely associated with the tabooed meaning, it was gradually limited to denote this particular kind of potion and no other. The German word for 'poison', *Gift*, under-

---

[1] On this question see recently H. Schreuder, 'On Some Cases of Restriction of Meaning', *English Studies*, xxxvii (1956), pp. 117-24. Most of the English examples that follow are taken from this article. See also H. Werner, 'Change of Meaning', loc. cit., pp. 201 ff.

went an even more radical reduction: among all the possible 'gifts' one can bestow, it came to be applied to this single variety. Restriction of meaning can also result from ellipsis (*canine* for 'canine tooth'), from the need to fill a gap in vocabulary (*traire* 'to draw' replacing *moudre* in the sense of 'to milk'),[1] and from various other causes.[2]

Several names of animals have been restricted from genus to species or have suffered a more drastic reduction. *Deer* once meant a 'beast', *hound* a 'dog', and *fowl* a 'bird' in general: 'Behold the *fowls* of the air: for they sow not, neither do they reap, nor gather into barns' (*St. Matthew*, vi, 25). It is interesting to note that in all three cases the corresponding German word — *das Tier, der Hund, der Vogel* — has retained the wider sense. In the same way, French *oie*, Italian and Spanish *oca* 'goose', come from Vulgar Latin **avica*, derived from *avis* 'bird', as if the goose were regarded as the domestic bird *par excellence* (Bloch-Wartburg). By a different route, French *sanglier* 'wild boar' has evolved, through ellipsis, from Latin *singularis* 'single, solitary', in the phrase *singularis porcus* 'solitary pig' (ibid.). Some verbs have developed on similar lines: *to starve* once meant 'to die', as it still does in German *sterben*, and French *nover* 'to drown' goes back to Latin *necare* 'to kill' (cf. p. 185).

An interesting example of restriction is the English word *corn* which, in addition to its general meaning of 'seed of cereal plants', has come to denote the most important cereal crop produced in a particular area: wheat in England, oats in Scotland, maize in America.[3]

(2) *Extension of meaning.* — Several linguists have suggested that extension is a less common process than restriction,[4] and this has recently been borne out by experiments conducted by the psychologist Heinz Werner. According to Professor Werner himself, there are two main reasons for this tendency:

> One is that the predominant developmental trend is in the direction of differentiation rather than of synthesis. A second reason, related to the first, is that the formation of general concepts from specific terms is of lesser importance in non-scientific communication though it is rather a characteristic of scientific endeavour. In other words, language in everyday life is directed toward the concrete and specific rather than toward the abstract and general.[5]

[1] See above, pp. 187 and 200.
[2] Schreuder, loc. cit., pp. 118 ff., distinguishes six main causes of restriction: professional language, synonymity, middle terms, euphemism, substitution, and phrasal associations.
[3] See Schreuder, loc. cit., pp. 119 f.; cf. Weinreich, *Languages in Contact*, p. 49.
[4] Bréal, *Essai de sémantique*, p. 107; Vendryes, *Le Langage*, p. 237; Bloomfield, *Language*, p. 151; cf. Werner, loc. cit., p. 203.   [5] Loc. cit., ibid.

Nevertheless, cases of semantic widening are fairly frequent in various languages. From a purely logical point of view, they are the exact opposite of restriction: here we have an increase in 'extension', the word being applied to a wider variety of things; at the same time its 'intension' will decrease, it will tell us less about the things referred to. Thus the French *panier* 'basket' comes from the Latin *panarium* 'bread-basket', derived from *panis* 'bread'. When the connexion with 'bread' disappeared, the word could be applied to more objects than before, but its meaning had been impoverished as it had lost one distinctive trait. *Target*, a diminutive of *targe* 'shield', originally meant a 'light round shield or buckler', as well as a 'shield-like structure, marked with concentric circles, set up to be aimed at in shooting practice'; now it has a far wider and therefore less specific range of meaning (*NED*).

Extension, like restriction, is often due to social factors. As we have seen, a word passing from a limited milieu into common use will some-times widen its meaning and lose some of its distinctive features in the process (p. 200). An often quoted example is French *arriver*, English *arrive*, both of which once meant 'come to shore', as did their Vulgar Latin ancestor **arripare*, a derivative of *ripa* 'bank, shore'. From a related sphere we have our modern word *rival*, due to an extension of meaning which goes back to Roman times: the Latin *rivales*, from *rivus* 'brook, small stream', literally meant 'those who have or use the same brook, neighbours'; later on the 'rivalry' spread to love and other matters (Lewis and Short).

Another cause of extension is the need for 'omnibus words' with an extremely hazy and general meaning. Latin *causa* was a precise and well-defined term, whereas its Romance descendants, French *chose*, Italian and Spanish *cosa* 'thing', are now among the vaguest words in those languages; in French the combination *quelque chose* has actually become an indefinite pronoun meaning 'something' or 'anything'. Mean-while French *cause*, Italian and Spanish *causa*, which were borrowed directly from Latin, retain their pristine precision. The word *machine* has also become an omnibus word in French, in the sense of 'thing, gadget, contraption'; it has even given birth to a jocular masculine form *machin*.

Among words which have widened their meaning there are several names of animals and plants. A curious case is that of the word for 'rose' in some Southern Slav languages which use it in the generic sense of 'flower'. This usage has even affected some neighbouring German and Italian dialects (Vendryes, *Le Langage*, p. 237). In several cases a term which once meant a young animal or plant has come to stand for the whole species: French *pigeon* (cf. p. 94), *dindon* 'turkey-cock', and *hêtre* 'beech' acquired their present meanings in this way. At a more general level, *bird* comes from Old English *brid* 'young bird' (*NED*), and *plant*, French *plante*, from Latin *planta* 'sprout, slip, cutting' (cf. above, p. 119).

2. Changes in Evaluation: Pejorative and Ameliorative Developments

Pejorative developments[1] are so common in language that some early semanticists regarded them as a fundamental tendency, a symptom of a 'pessimistic streak' in the human mind. Bréal protested vigorously against this assumption. 'La prétendue tendance péjorative', he wrote, 'est l'effet d'une disposition très humaine qui nous porte à voiler, à déguiser les idées fâcheuses, blessantes ou repoussantes ... Il n'y a pas là autre chose qu'un besoin de ménagement, une précaution pour ne pas choquer, — précaution sincère ou feinte, et qui ne sert pas longtemps, car l'auditeur va chercher la chose derrière le mot et ne tarde pas à les mettre de niveau.'[2]

As Bréal rightly saw it, *euphemism*, or pseudo-euphemism, is the motive force behind many pejorative developments. If a euphemistic substitute ceases to be felt as such, if it becomes directly associated with the idea it was designed to veil, this will result in a permanent depreciation of its meaning. It is this factor which accounts for the deterioration of many of the words examined in the section on taboo: *disease, undertaker, tuer, fille, amant, maîtresse, imbecile, crétin, silly* and others.

A second factor leading to pejorative sense-change is the influence of certain *associations*. The semantic ramifications of Latin *captivus* may serve to illustrate this. Starting from the idea of captivity, this word has acquired unfavourable meanings in various languages though not in all: Spanish *cautivo* still means 'prisoner'. In French it has become *chétif* 'weak, sickly, poor, miserable'; the connecting link was the idea of a man dominated and weakened by his passions (Bloch-Wartburg). The same associations led to a different result in Italian where *cattivo* means 'bad'. Yet

---

[1] See esp. H. Schreuder, *Pejorative Sense-Development in English I*, Groningen, 1929, and K. Jaberg, 'Pejorative Bedeutungsentwicklung im Französischen', *Zeitschrift für Romanische Philologie*, xxv (1901), pp. 561-601; xxvii (1903), pp. 25-71; xxix (1905), pp. 57-71. Cf. also Nyrop, *Sémantique*, Book III; Huguet, *L'Evolution du sens des mots*, ch. 4; Gamillscheg, *Französische Bedeutungslehre*, pp. 94-115; G. Gougenheim, 'Adjectifs laudatifs et adjectifs dépréciatifs', *Le Français Moderne*, xxvi (1958), pp. 3-15.

[2] 'The alleged pejorative tendency is the result of a very human attitude which leads us to veil and disguise awkward, offensive or repulsive ideas ... It is no more than an effort to be tactful, to avoid shocking people — an effort which may be genuine or feigned and whose effects are short-lived since the hearer will look for the thing behind the word and will soon connect them with each other' (*Essai de sémantique*, pp. 100 f.; cf. Schreuder, loc. cit., ch. 11).

Q

another line of development is found in English *caitiff*, of Anglo-Norman origin, which is now archaic and poetical. This has evolved through three stages: 1. 'a captive, a prisoner'; 2. 'one in a piteous case'; 3. 'a base, mean, despicable wretch, a villain'. In Shakespeare's phrase: 'the wicked'st *caitiff* on the ground' (*Measure for Measure*, Act V, scene 1), the word has travelled very far from its origins.[1] A similar fate has befallen some other terms in the same sphere. English *wretch* once meant 'exile'; while its meaning has strongly deteriorated,[2] the corresponding German word, *Recke*, has risen in estimation and now means 'warrior, hero'. The German adjective *schlecht*, related to English *slight*, has had a similar history: it meant first 'straight', then 'smooth' (now *schlicht*), 'simple', 'plain', 'poor', and finally 'bad', 'wicked' (Priebsch-Collinson, op. cit., p. 305).

A third source of pejorative developments is human *prejudice* in its various forms. Xenophobia has, as already noted (p. 135), filled some foreign words with a derogatory sense:[3] German *Ross* 'charger, steed' has given the French *rosse* 'sorry steed, crock', and mediaeval Dutch *boeckin* 'little book' the French *bouquin* 'old book, book of no value', though in familiar speech this term is now free from any unfavourable connotations (Bloch-Wartburg). Portuguese *palavra* 'word' has become *palaver* in English (*NED*). The same anti-foreign bias is reflected in the strange vicissitudes of some ethnic names. English *slave*, French *esclave*, etc., are the same word as *Slav*, and *Bulgarus* 'Bulgarian' is the origin of French *bougre*, which has already been mentioned (p. 209), and its more disreputable English counterpart. *Bougre* was used in the Middle Ages in the sense of 'heretic' because the Bulgarians were members of the Eastern Church; it then came to mean 'sodomite' and eventually developed into a term of abuse which gave Sterne the idea for a coarse but amusing incident in *Tristram Shandy* (Book VII, chs. 20-5).[4]

Social prejudice against certain classes and occupations has also deformed the meaning of many words.[5] Terms like English *boor* and French *rustre* 'boor, churl, lout', from Latin *rusticus*, show the contempt in which peasants used to be held. Low Latin *villanus*, 'inhabitant of a farm (*villa*)', has given in English the historical term *villein* 'serf' and also the pejorative *villain*, while Modern French *vilain* means 'ugly' and

[1] See the *NED* and Schreuder, loc. cit., pp. 85 f.
[2] Ibid., pp. 82 f.
[3] Ibid., ch. 7.
[4] See Bloch-Wartburg and the *NED*; cf. also J. Orr, '*Bougre* as Expletive' *Romance Philology*, i (1947), pp. 71-4, and Estrich-Sperber, op. cit., pp. 26 f.
[5] Cf. Schreuder, loc. cit., ch. 6.

'nasty'. Other social groups have been the victims of similar prejudices. A *brigand* was originally a 'light-armed, irregular foot-soldier', and *knave* once meant a 'boy' (cf. German *Knabe*), and especially a boy employed as a servant (*NED*). French *coquin* 'rogue, rascal' had the earlier meaning of 'beggar', and *faquin* 'cad' that of 'porter' (Bloch-Wartburg). Nor have the higher reaches of the social hierarchy been spared by prejudice. A *pedant* was once a 'pedagogue' or 'schoolmaster',[1] and the ups and downs of the word *bourgeois* would form an interesting chapter of social history. This class has been the target of attacks not only by its superiors and inferiors, but also by artists and intellectuals. Théophile Gautier defined a *bourgeois* as a man who 'has no understanding for any of the arts, no sense of form or style, who is without enthusiasm and passion, and does not admire nature',[2] and Flaubert put the same views more tersely and cuttingly in his famous dictum: 'J'appelle *bourgeois* quiconque pense bassement.'[3]

While there are thus many words which have deteriorated in meaning, others have changed in the opposite direction. These so-called '*ameliorative*' developments have received less attention than pejorative ones,[4] and on the whole they seem to be less frequent. They fall into two categories. The first includes those cases where the improvement is purely *negative*: by a process of gradual weakening, a term with an unpleasant sense will lose much of its stigma and become only mildly unfavourable. Thus *to blame* is historically the same word as to *blaspheme*, and to *annoy*, French *ennuyer*, originated in the Latin phrase *in odio esse* 'to be the object of hatred' (*NED* and Bloch-Wartburg). French *regretter* once signified 'to lament over the dead', and *gêne* meant 'physical or moral torture' until the end of the seventeenth century whereas now it has the much weaker sense of 'discomfort, embarrassment' (Bloch-Wartburg). An extreme example of weakening is the English *pest* which once meant pestilence and in particular the bubonic plague (*NED*). The word *plague* has had a similar development.

In hyperbolical expressions, such weakening can completely cancel out the unpleasant meaning of a word. This has happened, as we have seen (p. 137), with a number of English adjectives: *awful, dreadful, frightful* and others. A more advanced stage of this development can be seen in

---

[1] Cf. ibid., pp. 91 f.; Jaberg, loc. cit., xvii, p. 51, n. 1; Nyrop, *Sémantique*, p. 126.
[2] Quoted by G. Matoré, *Le Vocabulaire et la société sous Louis-Philippe*, Geneva — Lille, 1951, p. 76; cf. ibid., p. 234.
[3] 'I call *bourgeois* whoever thinks meanly'; quoted by Nyrop, *Sémantique*, p. 130.
[4] See G. A. van Dongen, op. cit.; cf. Nyrop, *Sémantique*, pp. 138 ff., and Gamillscheg, *Französische Bedeutungslehre*, pp. 115 ff.

German *sehr* 'very' which is etymologically the same word as English *sore*.[1]

There are also various cases of *positive* improvement of meaning. These may come about by a simple association of ideas. The adjective *nice* is derived, via Old French, from Latin *nescius* 'ignorant', and in Shakespeare's time it had several unfavourable senses: it could mean 'wanton, lascivious':

'These are complements, these are humours; these betray *nice* wenches, that would be betrayed without these' (*Love's Labour's Lost*, Act III, scene 1),

and 'thin, unimportant, trivial':

... feed upon such *nice* and waterish diet.
Othello, Act III, scene 3.

In such a time as this it is not meet
That every *nice* offence should bear his comment.
Julius Caesar, Act IV, scene 3.

Gradually the word developed, through meanings like 'fastidious' and 'delicate', in an ameliorative direction; since the second half of the eighteenth century, it has the sense of 'agreeable, delightful', and since the early nineteenth, that of 'kind, considerate, pleasant to others'.[2]

Other ameliorative developments are due to *social* factors.[3] A modest or even a menial office may gradually rise in prestige and may even end up at the top of the hierarchy. *Chancellor*, French *chancelier*, is derived from Late Latin *cancellarius*, an 'usher who was stationed *ad cancellos* at the *bar* of a basilica or other law court. In the Eastern Empire this officer had risen to be a secretary or notary, and, later, had judicial functions. Edward the Confessor introduced the office into England, and its importance increased under the Norman Kings' (*Shorter OED*). *Ministers* too have risen to their present eminence from modest beginnings: the Latin *minister*, derived from *minus* 'less', meant 'attendant, servant' (*NED* and Lewis and Short).

As a result of movements up and down the social scale, the same word may appear at two widely different points in a particular hierarchy. *Marshal*, an old Germanic term compounded of the words for 'horse' (cf. *mare*) and 'servant', is now the title of several high-ranking officers and

[1] See Stern, *Meaning and Change of Meaning*, p. 393.
[2] See the *NED*, from where the above quotations are taken; cf. also G. L. Brook, *A History of the English Language*, London, 1958, p. 184.
[3] Cf. Van Dongen, op. cit., ch. 2.

functionaries in England, but in the French army there are two kinds of 'marshals': *maréchal* (*de France*) 'field-marshal', and *maréchal des logis* 'sergeant'; there is also the *maréchal ferrant* 'farrier, shoeing-smith', who has remained nearest to the etymological sense of the term (cf. *NED* and Bloch-Wartburg). A similar ambivalence is sometimes found in meanings of the same word in different languages, as for instance in English *knight* compared with German *Knecht* 'servant'.[1]

A special group of ameliorative and pejorative developments are those which affect the meaning of so-called '*middle terms*' (voces mediae): words which are intrinsically neutral and which will take on a favourable or unfavourable significance according to their context.[2] It sometimes happens that such words, or their derivatives, become fixed either in the positive or in the negative meaning. *Fortune* is such a middle term since it may be either good or bad; but it has an exclusively positive value in the adjective *fortunate* and also when used metonymically in the sense of 'wealth'. *Luck*, though ambivalent, tends to imply 'good luck' when there is no counter-indication, and the adjective *lucky* has only the latter meaning. Similarly the old French word *heur*, from Latin *augurium* 'augury', meant 'good or bad luck', *bonheur* or *malheur*, whereas the adjective *heureux* means only 'happy, lucky' (Bloch-Wartburg). *Chance*, from Vulgar Latin **cadentia* 'falling', originally referred to the way the dice fell; it then widened its meaning and, in phrases like 'to give, to stand a *chance*', it has come down on the favourable side (ibid.). While all these words have evolved in an optimistic sense, others have moved in the opposite direction. *Hazard*, an Arabic term which also referred to the game of dice, has come to mean 'risk of loss or harm, peril, jeopardy' (ibid. and *NED*). *Accident* in some of its uses shows the same tendency, though the adjective *accidental* is immune from it. From *fate*, a middle term leaning towards the pessimistic side, two adjectives are derived: *fatal*, which is almost entirely unfavourable, and *fateful*, which is more non-committal. A comparative study of the development of such expressions in various languages might throw an interesting sidelight on human psychology.

[1] On the semantic development of the German word, see Priebsch-Collinson, op. cit., p. 303. On the history of the English word, see Van Dongen, op. cit., pp. 17 ff.
[2] See esp. Schreuder, *Pejorative Sense-Development*, ch. 10, and Van Dongen, op. cit., chs. 3-4.

CHAPTER 9

THE STRUCTURE OF THE VOCABULARY

ACCORDING to a recent estimate, there are 44 or 45 phonemes in English while on the other hand the *Oxford Dictionary* contains nearly 415,000 words. The contrast between the phonological and the lexical resources of English is therefore of the order of roughly 1 to 10,000. Few languages have of course as extensive a vocabulary as English, but the odds are that in most cases there would also be fewer phonemes since we are told by the same authority that their number in different idioms varies approximately from 15 to 50.[1]

A comparison between the vocabulary and the grammar of a language would yield a somewhat different result, but the discrepancy would still remain very considerable. A complete inventory of all suffixes and prefixes, flexions, form-words, intonations, patterns of sentence-structure and kindred features would contain a larger number of items than the phonological system, but this total would still be very small when compared to the size of the vocabulary. It is common experience that the grammar of even a highly inflected language can be mastered in a comparatively short time and remembered without too much difficulty, whereas very few people will know more than 10% of the words of their mother tongue.[2]

The magnitude of this contrast has serious implications for the future of semantics. As already stated in the introductory chapter, modern linguistics is dominated by the idea of *structure*. Developing Saussure's conception of language as a *Gestalt*, a highly organized system of interdependent elements, it seeks to determine the unique structure of each idiom, the fundamental pattern which differs from one language to another and even from one period to another in the history of the same language. As one of the pioneers of structural linguistics, Edward Sapir, once wrote,

> it must be obvious to anyone who has thought about the question at all or who has felt something of the spirit of a foreign language that there is such a thing as a basic plan, a certain cut, to each language.

[1] S. Potter, *Modern Linguistics*, pp. 40 and 101. According to an unpublished paper by J. H. Greenberg, C. E. Osgood and J. J. Jenkins, 'for all languages the number of phonemes is not fewer than 10 or more than 70'.

[2] Cf. Jespersen, *Growth and Structure*, p. 196. Cf. above, p. 181.

This type or plan or structural 'genius' of the language is something much more fundamental, much more pervasive, than any single feature of it that we can mention, nor can we gain an adequate idea of its nature by a mere recital of the sundry facts that make up the grammar of a language.[1]

This approach has yielded spectacular results in phonology and morphology and, to a somewhat lesser extent, in syntax; the vital question which now arises is whether it is applicable to the vocabulary.

At first sight it would seem more than doubtful that the same methods which have proved their worth in phonology and grammar could be extended to the study of semantics. Not only does the latter have to deal with an infinitely larger number of units, but these units themselves are rather loosely organized; the most efficient way of arranging them is the purely mechanical form of an alphabetical dictionary. One or two attempts have been made, notably at the Eighth International Congress of Linguists held in Oslo in 1957, to introduce ordinary structural criteria into semantics,[2] but the results were inconclusive and not very encouraging. Most linguists are sceptical about the prospects of such experiments. In the words of Professor Martinet,

> as long as one deals with those meaningful units whose denotative value is imprecise and whose relational value is high, namely, grammatical morphemes, the structural parallelism of the two planes (viz. the planes of expression and content) can easily be maintained; but the lexicon proper seems far less easily reducible to structural patterning, once certain particularly favourable fields, such as kinship terms, numerals and a few others, have been dealt with.[3]

Other structuralists have gone considerably further and have suggested

---

[1] *Language*, p. 120.

[2] See the *Proceedings* of that congress, pp. 636-704. Cf. also the following: C. E. Bazell, 'La Sémantique structurale', *Dialogues*, ii (1953), pp. 120-32; Y. Bar-Hillel, 'Logical Syntax and Semantics', *Language*, xxx (1954), pp. 230-7, and N. Chomsky's reply, ibid., xxxi (1955), pp. 36-45; I. Coteanu, *Probleme de Lingvistică Generală*, vol. II, pp. 33-48; I. Rizescu, ibid., pp. 49-64; W. H. Goodenough, 'Componential Analysis and the Study of Meaning', *Language*, xxxii (1956), pp. 195-216; P. Diderichsen, 'Semantiske Problemer i logik og lingvistik', *Nordisk Sommer Universitet*, 1953, pp. 248-78; L. Hermodsson, 'Zur "glossematischen" Bedeutungsforschung', *Studia Neophilologica*, xxvi (1953-54), pp. 35-57, and G. Bech's rejoinder, ibid., xxvii (1955), pp. 108-25; J. Holt, *Rationel Semantik (Plerenik)*, *Acta Jutlandica*, xviii, 3, Aarhus — Copenhagen, 1946. These problems are also discussed in several articles in *Voprosy Jazykoznanija*, 1957; cf. also V. I. Grigorjev, ibid., 1958, no. 4, pp. 24-36, and Y. D. Apresyan, ibid., 1959, no. 2, pp. 139-45. There is a new chapter on 'Semantics and Structuralism' in the second ed. of E. Leisi's *Der Wortinhalt*; cf. also B. Carstensen's comments in *Die Neueren Sprachen*, N.F., vii (1961), pp. 334-9.

[3] 'Structural Linguistics', in *Anthropology Today*, ed. A. L. Kroeber, Chicago, 1953, pp. 574-86: p. 582.

that one ought to distinguish between the 'structural' and the 'semantic' side of language.[1] It is not usually very profitable to argue about terminology, but in this particular case the choice of terms is singularly unfortunate. To oppose the 'structural' side of a language to its 'semantic' side is to suggest that the latter has no structure at all, whereas what is really meant is simply that it does not have the same *kind* of structure as the phonological and grammatical system. In actual fact, no linguist would seriously argue that the vocabulary is completely amorphous, without any pattern or organization. Such an assumption would be unrealistic since it would run counter to the very nature of the human mind. 'I do not find language either systematic or wholly unsystematic', wrote the late Professor Entwistle, 'but impressed with patterns, generally incomplete, by our pattern-making minds.'[2] It is such incomplete patterns and half-finished designs that we are likely to encounter in the semantic structure of a language.

In recent years there have been a number of attempts to discover some of the principles on which the vocabulary is organized. These inquiries have moved on three different planes: that of single words, that of conceptual spheres, and lastly, that of the vocabulary as a whole. The results achieved so far are limited and tentative, but they must be recorded here because of their great potential interest, and because of the important role this approach is likely to play in the further development of semantic studies.

I. The Word and its Associative Field

Every word is, as we already know (p. 63), surrounded by a network of associations which connect it with other terms. Some of these associations are based on connexions between the senses, others are purely formal, while others again involve both form and meaning. In Saussure's graphic formula, 'un terme donné est comme le centre d'une constellation, le point où convergent d'autres termes coordonnés, dont la somme est indéfinie'.[3] Saussure tried to represent these associations in the form of a diagram:[4]

---

[1] See *Language in Culture*, pp. 95 and 156; cf. above, p. 55.

[2] *Aspects of Language*, p. viii. The same point is made more explicitly in a private letter dated November 20th, 1951: 'I do not know if I am a systematist or non-systematist. My view seems to be that we have pattern-forming minds and impress patterns on unorganized material. But we rarely complete a design before thinking of a new one.'

[3] 'A given term is like the centre of a constellation, the point where an indefinite number of coordinated terms converge' (op. cit., p. 174).

[4] Ibid., p. 175.

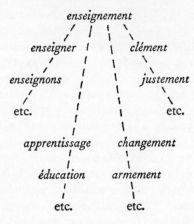

In this diagram, four lines of association radiate from the noun *enseignement* 'teaching': (1) it is connected with the verb *enseigner* 'to teach' by formal and semantic similarity based on the common stem; (2) with *apprentissage* 'apprenticeship' and *éducation* by semantic similarity; (3) with *changement* 'change' and *armement* 'armament' because they all have the suffix *-ment* forming abstract nouns from verbs; (4) with the adjective *clément* 'clement, merciful' and the adverb *justement* 'justly, precisely' by an accidental similarity in their endings.

Developing these ideas further, Saussure's disciple Bally introduced the useful concept of *associative fields* which he narrowed down, somewhat arbitrarily, to purely semantic associations, but analysed in greater detail:

> Le champ associatif est un halo qui entoure le signe et dont les franges extérieures se confondent avec leur ambiance ... Let mot *boeuf* fait penser: (1) à 'vache, taureau, veau, cornes, ruminer, beugler', etc.; (2) à 'labour, charrue, joug', etc.; enfin (3) il peut dégager, et dégage en français, des idées de force, d'endurance, de travail patient, mais aussi de lenteur, de lourdeur, de passivité.[1]

---

[1] 'The associative field is a halo which surrounds the sign and whose outer fringes merge into their environment ... The word *ox* makes one think (1) of "cow, bull, calf, horns, ruminating, bellowing", etc.; (2) of "tilling, plough, yoke", etc.; finally, (3) it can evoke, and does evoke in French, ideas of strength, endurance, patient work, but also of slowness, heaviness and passivity' ('L'Arbitraire du signe', *Le Français Moderne*, viii, 1940, pp. 193-206: pp. 195 f.). For further developments of this concept, see esp. H. Frei, 'Ramifications des signes dans la mémoire', *Cahiers Ferdinand de Saussure*, ii (1942), pp. 15-27; P. Guiraud, 'Les champs morpho-sémantiques', *Bulletin de la Société de Linguistique de Paris*, lii (1956), pp. 265-88; T. Cazacu, 'La "Structuration" dynamique des significations', *Mélanges linguistiques publiés à l'occasion du VIIIᵉ Congrès International des Linguistes*, pp. 113-27; O. Ducháček, 'Les Champs linguistiques', *Philologica Pragensia*, iii (1960), pp. 22-35.

As can be seen, the 'associative field' of a word is formed by an intricate network of associations, some based on similarity, others on contiguity, some arising between senses, others between names, others again between both. The field is by definition open, and some of the associations are bound to be subjective though the more central ones will be largely the same for most speakers. Attempts have been made to identify some of these central associations by psychological experiments,[1] but they can also be established by purely linguistic methods; by collecting the most obvious synonyms, antonyms[2] and homonyms of a word, as well as terms similar in sound or in sense, and those which enter into the same habitual combinations — the same 'consociations', to use Professor Sperber's term. Many of these associations are embodied in figurative language: metaphors, similes, proverbs, idioms and the like. Bally mentions for example 'un vent à décorner les *boeufs*' 'it is blowing great guns' for his first series; 'mettre la charrue devant les *boeufs*' 'to put the cart before the horse' for the second; and 'c'est un *boeuf* pour le travail' 'he is a glutton for work' for the third. The number of associations centred on one word will of course be extremely variable, and for some very common terms it may be very high. Professor Guiraud, who has fully investigated the associative field of the French word *chat* 'cat', was able to collect about 2000 terms which were related to it on formal or semantic grounds. By subjecting this vast material to structural and other criteria he was able to reduce it to about 300 words which form, so to speak, the minimum associative field of the term *chat* (loc. cit., p. 286).

Those who stand to benefit most directly from this new concept are the etymologist, the lexicographer, and the student of semantic change. As already mentioned in the last chapter (p. 211), the naïve associationism of earlier days, which was concerned with relations between particular words, has given way to a broader and more sophisticated approach which keeps its gaze firmly fixed on the associative field as a whole. This has completely revitalized the methods of etymological research and is of direct relevance to the reconstruction of Primitive Indo-European and other extinct languages (cf. p. 31). As a leading etymologist has put it:

Quiconque veut écrire aujourd'hui l'étymologie d'un mot ne doit pas se contenter de constater la disparition d'une signification ou l'adjonction d'une signification nouvelle. Il doit se demander encore

[1] Cazacu, loc. cit., pp. 120 ff.
[2] Cf. V. N. Komissarov, 'Problema opredelenija antonima', *Voprosy Jazykoznanija*, 1957, no. 2, pp. 49-58, and A. Rygaloff, 'A propos de l'antonymie: l'exemple du chinois', *Journal de Psychologie*, lv (1958), pp. 358-76. Cf. above, pp. 143 f.

quel mot est l'heureux concurrent, héritier de la signification disparue, ou à quel mot il a ravi sa nouvelle signification. La première condition pour effectuer cette recherche est une exacte compréhension de la sémantique et des conditions dans lesquelles se développe la vie des mots.[1]

The wider vistas opened up by the concept of associative fields will affect the study of *semantic changes* in three main ways: (1) they will provide a complete explanation of processes which could only be partially explained by traditional methods; (2) they will protect the linguist against certain pitfalls inherent in his material; (3) they will suggest a solution to problems which would otherwise have remained insoluble.

(1) In many cases the new approach will not invalidate earlier explanations but will merely *complete* them and place them in a broader perspective. Two of the examples discussed in the previous chapter will illustrate the difference between traditional and modern methods. The first is the case of French *viande* which, since the seventeenth century, has lost its wider sense of 'food' and has become limited to that of 'meat', a specialized meaning which it had developed as early as the fifteenth century. The orthodox semanticist would describe this as a case of restriction, and so it undoubtedly was. The question arises, however, *why* this restriction should have happened in French whereas it did not occur in Spanish, Italian or English, as we have already seen (p. 228). The answer lies in the associative field of the French word. *Viande* changed its meaning because it was needed to take the place of one of its neighbours, *chair* 'flesh', in the sense of 'meat'. But this is still not a complete answer since it prompts the question: why did *chair* fall into disuse in this meaning? A solution to this further problem will be found in the associative field of the word *chair*. This term, which comes from Latin *caro, carnem*, has a homonym in *chère*, from Late Latin *cara* 'face', which is the same word as the English *cheer*. *Chère* originally meant 'face' but subsequently developed other meanings some of which were very close to those of its homonym *chair*: it came to mean 'cheer, fare, living', as in *faire bonne*

---

[1] 'Whoever wishes to write today the etymology of a word must not be content to note the disappearance of a meaning or the addition of a new meaning. He must also ask himself which is the lucky rival, the heir to the meaning which has disappeared, or which is the word from which the term in question has taken its new meaning. The first condition for conducting this kind of research is an exact understanding of semantics and of the circumstances governing the life of words' (Wartburg, *Problèmes et méthodes de la linguistique*, p. 104). Cf. above, pp. 30 f..

chère 'to have a good feed, to do oneself well'. At this stage a homonymic clash occurred between *chair* and *chère*; confusion between the two would be particularly awkward during Lent, with its rules about fasting and especially about meat. As a result of this homonymic clash, *chair* in the sense of 'meat' dropped out of use, though it survives in many dialects and also in some set expressions such as *n'être ni chair ni poisson*, the equivalent of the English phrase 'to be neither fish nor fowl'. Ultimately, then, *viande* suffered a restriction of meaning because a word in its neighbourhood became involved in a homonymic clash (see Bloch-Wartburg, *s.v. viande, chair*, and *chère*).

The other example, which is more complex, is the change from Latin *coxa* 'hip' to French *cuisse*, Italian *coscia* 'thigh'. On p. 218 above, this was explained as a metonymic transfer facilitated by the fact that there is no sharp boundary between these two adjacent parts of the body. Once again this is true, but it is not the whole truth. An examination of what happened, in Vulgar Latin times, in the immediate vicinity of the word *coxa* reveals a complicated series of changes, a veritable chain-reaction, which Professor Wartburg has brilliantly reconstructed. There were four distinct phases in the process:

(*a*) Latin *fimus* 'dung, excrement' became *femus, femoris* under the influence of its synonym, *stercus, stercoris*.

(*b*) As a result, a homonymic clash occurred between *femus* and *femur, femoris* 'thigh', and the latter term was dropped.

(*c*) *Coxa* 'hip' changed its meaning to 'thigh' to replace *femur*.

(*d*) The gap created by the last change was filled by borrowing the Germanic word **hanka*: hence French *hanche*, Italian *anca* 'hip'. English *haunch* comes from the French *hanche*.[1]

One can see that the etymologist has to cast his net very wide to find a definitive explanation for an apparently simple shift of meaning.

(2) The new approach will put us on our guard against '*pseudo-semantic developments*': sense-changes which look spontaneous but are really due to the influence of another word. Several such cases were discussed in the last chapter (pp. 220 ff.), so that it will be sufficient here to give one more example. The French adjective *fruste*, which was taken over from Italian during the Renaissance, originally meant 'worn, defaced'; since the middle of the last century it has acquired the sense of 'rough, unpolished'. Rather than assuming a spurious connexion between

---

[1] *Problèmes et méthodes de la linguistique*, p. 106. See also Baldinger, *Cahiers de l'Association Internationale des Etudes Françaises*, xi (1959), pp. 242 f., and E. Gamillscheg, 'Sprach-geschichtlicher Kommentar zur Karte *anca* "Hüfte" des AIS', *Etymologica*, pp. 261-80.

the two meanings, one ought to look round in the associative field of the word for a clue which might explain the change. It is then found that *fruste* owes its new sense to the influence of the phonetically similar adjective *rustre* 'boorish, loutish, clownish' (cf. p. 232); the form *frustre*, attested as early as the fifteenth century, shows that the two terms have for a long time been associated in people's minds. It is also quite possible that other similar words (*brusque*, *robuste*) may have played some part in the change.[1] It should be emphasized that there is nothing very new or startling in such interferences; linguistic geographers and others have been familiar with them for many decades. But whereas in the past many linguists regarded them as mere accidents or freaks, they now take their place in the general theory of associative fields, and an etymologist imbued with the new approach will be less likely to fall into the trap of 'pseudo-semantic developments'.

(3) Associative fields can also provide an unexpected answer to baffling *etymological problems*. Professor Guiraud's studies on the field of French *chat* have enabled him, for example, to solve one such riddle: the connexion between *maroufle* 'rogue, scoundrel', which once also meant 'large cat', and another *maroufle* which means a 'strong paste for remounting pictures'. These words used to be recorded by the dictionaries as unconnected homonyms, but, as Guiraud rightly argues, their form is so distinctive that there must be some connexion between them. The connexion is found in the fact that *chat*, a synonym of the first *maroufle* in the sense of 'cat', has a homonym *chas* which means 'starch paste, dressing'. The use of *maroufle*, a synonym of *chat*, in the sense of *chas*, a homonym of the latter, must have started as a jocular pun, by a process which is very common in slang and in the jargon of trades and crafts (loc. cit., pp. 269 ff.; cf. also Bloch-Wartburg).

II. CONCEPTUAL SPHERES

It is in the study of conceptual spheres that structural semantics has achieved its most striking successes. Most of these are directly or indirectly connected with the theory of '*semantic fields*' which was first put forward thirty years ago by Professor Jost Trier of Munster, Westphalia.

The field theory has been described as 'Neo-Humboldtian',[2] and some of its ideas can in fact be traced back to Wilhelm von Humboldt's

[1] See Bloch-Wartburg and also J. Orr, *Revue de Linguistique Romane*, xviii (1954), p. 133.
[2] H. Basilius, 'Neo-Humboldtian Ethnolinguistics', *Word*, viii (1952), pp. 95-105.

linguistic doctrine. 'According to Humboldt, each separate language, even the most despised dialect, should be looked upon as an organic whole, different from all the rest and expressing the individuality of the people speaking it; it is characteristic of one nation's psyche, and indicates the peculiar way in which that nation attempts to realize the ideal of speech.'[1] The new theory also had some more immediate philosophical antecedents in phenomenology and in Cassirer's teaching about the influence of language upon thought. These ideas were blended in the field theory with some of Saussure's structuralist principles, in particular with his picture of language as an organized whole whose elements delimit each other and derive their significance, their 'value', from the general framework in which they are placed. Thus Saussure had argued that French *mouton* has a different value from English *sheep* since it covers the whole area which in English is divided between *sheep* and *mutton*. The same is true of synonyms: 'Dans l'intérieur d'une même langue, tous les mots qui expriment des idées voisines se limitent réciproquement: des synonymes comme *redouter*, *craindre*, *avoir peur* n'ont de valeur propre que par leur opposition; si *redouter* n'existait pas, tout son contenu irait à ses concurrents.'[2]

Some isolated attempts had been made from time to time to study the structure of certain conceptual spheres, such as the hierarchy of military ranks,[3] but, as is so often the case, linguists did not become fully aware of the problem until it was crystallized in a name. This happened in 1924 when the term 'semantic field' was introduced by G. Ipsen to denote such spheres.[4] In the years that followed, several fields were systematically explored. The champions of the new approach were at times openly hostile to orthodox semantics which one of them contemptuously dismissed as a 'false trail' in linguistic studies.[5] It was in this spiritual climate that Trier's monograph on intellectual terms in German was conceived.[6] In that book, which appeared in 1931, and in a series of important articles

[1] Jespersen, *Language*, p. 57.
[2] 'Within one language, all words which express neighbouring ideas delimit each other reciprocally: synonyms like *redouter* ('to dread'), *craindre* ('to fear'), *avoir peur* ('to be frightened' or 'afraid') have no real value except through their opposition to one another; if *redouter* did not exist, its whole content would go to its rivals' (op. cit., p. 160).
[3] R. M. Meyer, 'Bedeutungssysteme', *Zeitschrift für vergleichende Sprachforschung*, xliii (1910), pp. 352-68.
[4] G. Ipsen, 'Der alte Orient und die Indogermanen', in *Stand und Aufgaben der Sprachwissenschaft. Festschrift für Streitberg*, Heidelberg, 1924, pp. 200-37: p. 225. According to Ducháček, loc. cit., p. 26, the term had been used before Ipsen by A. Stöhr in his *Lehrbuch der Logik in psychologisierender Darstellung*, Leipzig – Vienna, 1910.
[5] L. Weisgerber, 'Die Bedeutungslehre – ein Irrweg der Sprachwissenschaft?', cited on p. 57, n. 2.
[6] See above, p. 7.

which followed,[1] Trier elaborated his conception of fields as closely-knit sectors of the vocabulary, in which a particular sphere is divided up, classified and organized in such a way that each element helps to delimit its neighbours and is delimited by them. In Ipsen's picturesque formula, their contours fit into each other like pieces of different shapes in a mosaic. In each field, the raw material of experience is analysed and elaborated in a unique way, differing from one language to another and often from one period to another in the history of the same idiom. In this way, the structure of semantic fields embodies a specific philosophy and a scale of values.

Trier's ideas, which were empirically tested in the researches of some of his pupils, gave rise to lively discussions in the course of which several rival definitions of semantic fields were put forward.[2] Some of these were interesting, but none has had the same influence as Trier's. In subsequent years, Trier turned to other problems, and the progress of the field theory was delayed by the war and its aftermath. In the 1950s, however, there was a considerable revival of interest in these questions, and at the present time this is one of the most active branches of semantics both on the theoretical and on the empirical plane.[3]

---

[1] See in particular: 'Die Idee der Klugheit in ihrer sprachlichen Entfaltung', *Zeitschrift für Deutschkunde*, xlvi (1932), pp. 625-35; 'Deutsche Bedeutungsforschung', *Germanische Philologie: Ergebnisse und Aufgaben. Festschrift für O. Behaghel*, Heidelberg, 1934, pp. 173-200; 'Das sprachliche Feld. Eine Auseinandersetzung', *Neue Jahrbücher für Wissenschaft und Jugendbildung*, x (1934), pp. 428-49.

[2] G. Ipsen, 'Der neue Sprachbegriff', *Zeitschrift für Deutschkunde*, xlvi (1932), pp. 1-18; A. Jolles, 'Antike Bedeutungsfelder', *Beiträge zur Geschichte der deutschen Sprache und Literatur*, lviii (1934), pp. 97-109; W. Porzig, 'Wesenhafte Bedeutungsbeziehungen', ibid., pp. 70-97. Porzig's ideas were subsequently modified in his book, *Das Wunder der Sprache*, 2nd ed., Berne, 1957. See also, on rather different lines, E. Leisi, *Der Wortinhalt*, which has already been mentioned.

[3] Among recent works on the field theory, those by L. Weisgerber occupy a prominent place; see especially the two volumes of his *Vom Weltbild der deutschen Sprache* (cf. above, p. 9, n. 2). A full list of Weisgerber's contributions will be found at the end of *Sprache — Schlüssel zur Welt. Festschrift für Leo Weisgerber*, Düsseldorf, 1959. Another valuable monograph is Suzanne Öhman's *Wortinhalt und Weltbild*, Stockholm, 1951. The following articles may also be noted: F. Hiorth, 'On the Relation between Field Research and Lexicography', *Studia Linguistica*, x (1956), pp. 57-66; B. von Lindheim, 'Neue Wege der Bedeutungsforschung', *Neuphilologische Zeitschrift*, iii (1951), pp. 101-15; G. Müller, 'Wortfeld und Sprachfeld', in *Beiträge zur Einheit von Bildung und Sprache im geistigen Sein. Festschrift E. Otto*, Berlin, 1957, pp. 155-63; S. Öhman, 'Theories of the "Linguistic Field" ', *Word*, ix (1953), pp. 123-34; H. Schwarz, 'Leitmerkmale sprachlicher Felder', in *Sprache — Schlüssel zur Welt*, pp. 245-55; N. Törnqvist, 'Gedanken zur Wortforschung', *Neuphilologische Mitteilungen*, lix (1958), pp. 197-211. Cf. also Kronasser, op. cit., pp. 133 ff.; Wartburg, *Problèmes et méthodes de la linguistique*, pp. 141 ff.; Zvegintsev, op. cit., pp. 266 ff., and my *Principles of Semantics*, ch. 3, section 2, and pp. 309 ff., and *Précis de sémantique française*, ch. 12 and pp. 331 f., where some empirical inquiries on semantic fields are listed. Several articles in *Sprache — Schlüssel zur Welt* deal with specific questions related to the field theory. A recent book by the philosopher A. P. Ushenko, *The Field Theory of Meaning*, Ann Arbor, 1958, bears no relation to what is meant in linguistics by that term.

A few examples will illustrate the role of semantic fields in the organizing of our experiences. The importance of this role will largely depend on the nature of the field itself, whether it is concrete or abstract, continuous or made up of discrete elements. An example of a *concrete* sphere where man is faced with a continuum which he has to divide up and arrange in some sort of orderly pattern, is the system of *colours*.[1] The spectrum is a continuous band (cf. p. 125), and the number and nature of the distinctions which we superimpose on it are of necessity arbitrary and variable. Each language may therefore classify colours in its own way. The Greek system was so different from ours that it was at one time seriously suggested that the Greeks must have been colourblind. The Latin nomenclature too differs on some essential points from our own; it has, for instance, no single term for 'brown' or 'grey': the French names of these colours, *brun* and *gris*, are borrowings from Germanic. In our own day, Lithuanian, which is in many ways an extraordinarily archaic language, has similarly no general word for 'grey': specific terms are used for the grey colour of wool, of a horse, a cow or human hair.[2] On the other hand, Russian has two adjectives for 'blue': *sinij* 'dark blue' and *goluboj* 'azure, sky-blue'. If we turn to languages outside Europe, the diversity becomes even more bewildering. The Navaho, an American Indian tribe, 'possess colour terms corresponding roughly to our "white", "red", and "yellow" but none which are equivalent to our "black", "grey", "brown", "blue", and "green". They have two terms corresponding to "black", one denoting the black of darkness, the other the black of such objects as coal. Our "grey" and "brown", however, correspond to a single term in their language and likewise our "blue" and "green".'[3] The relativity of colour distinctions helps to explain the behaviour of certain patients suffering from aphasia, whose reactions to colour tests were so erratic that they were at first diagnosed as colourblind. There was, in fact, nothing wrong with their sense of colour, but they had forgotten the *names* of colours and had thereby lost the ability to classify their sensations and arrange them in a meaningful pattern.[4]

[1] On this problem see esp. Weisgerber, *Vom Weltbild der deutschen Sprache*, vol. II, pp. 83 ff., and the volume *Problèmes de la couleur*, ed. I. Meyerson, Paris, 1957. Cf. also S. Skard's useful bibliographical survey, *The Use of Color in Literature, Proceedings of the American Philosophical Society*, XC, 1946, 3, and G. Matoré, 'A propos du vocabulaire des couleurs', *Annales de l'Université de Paris*, xxviii (1958), pp. 137-50.

[2] G. Bonfante, 'Semantics, Language', *Encyclopedia of Psychology*, ed. P. L. Harriman, New York, 1946, pp. 837-70: p. 852.   [3] P. Henle, *Language, Thought, and Culture*, p. 7.

[4] Stern, *Meaning and Change Meaning*, pp. 96 f.; Wartburg, *Problèmes et méthodes de la linguistique*, pp. 154 f. On connexions between semantic studies and research into aphasia, see recently Sir Russell Brain, 'The Semantic Aspect of Aphasia', *Archivum Linguisticum*, viii (1956), pp. 20-7.

In the case of colours we are faced with phenomena which nature has left undivided and which man has therefore had to analyse through the medium of language. But the role of semantic fields is by no means negligible even when a sphere of experience consists of distinct and separate units. The network of *kinship terms* may serve as an example. A few basic relations such as 'father', 'mother', 'son' and 'daughter' are probably semantic 'constants' which will somehow have to be expressed in any language, though even here there is room for diversity: in Latin, for example, there were two words for 'father', *pater* and *genitor*, the second of which referred to purely physiological fatherhood whereas the former could also carry social connotations.[1] But as soon as we step outside the close circle of basic relations, a number of different solutions become possible. Even words for 'brother' and 'sister' are not absolute necessities: there were no such terms in Hungarian until well into the nineteenth century. Instead there were, and still are, two pairs of words in which age is combined with sex: *bátya* 'elder brother', *öcs* 'younger brother', *néne* 'elder sister', and *hug* 'younger sister'.[2] In Malay, on the other hand, there is only one common word for 'brother' and 'sister', irrespective of sex. In his report to the Oslo congress, Professor Hjelmslev has represented the three systems in the following diagram:[3]

	Hungarian	English	Malay
'elder brother'	*bátya*	*brother*	*sudarā*
'younger brother'	*öcs*		
'elder sister'	*néne*	*sister*	
'younger sister'	*hug*		

[1] See Meillet, *Linguistique historique et linguistique générale*, vol. I, p. 41. On kinship terms see recently L. Dumont, 'The Dravidian Kinship Terminology as an Expression of Marriage', *Man*, liii (1953), pp. 34-9; H. Galton, 'The Indo-European Kinship Terminology', *Zeitschrift für Ethnologie*, lxxxii (1957), pp. 121-38; Goodenough, loc. cit.; F. G. Lounsbury, 'A Semantic Analysis of the Pawnee Kinship Usage', *Language*, XXXII (1956), pp. 158-94; Öhman, *Wortinhalt und Weltbild*, pp. 159 ff.; O. N. Trubachov, *Istorija slavianskich terminov rodstva*, Moscow, 1959; Weisgerber, *Vom Weltbild der deutschen Sprache*, vol. I, pp. 59 ff., and vol. II, pp. 81 f.

[2] The word *fivér* 'brother' is a neologism first attested in 1840-42, and the word for 'sister', *nővér*, appeared a year earlier. The noun *testvér*, a collective term for 'brother' and 'sister', was formed by ellipsis at the beginning of the nineteenth century (see Bárczi, *Magyar Szófejtő Szótár, s.v. fiú, nő, testvér*).

[3] 'Pour une sémantique structurale', reprinted in *Essais linguistiques*, pp. 96-113: p. 104. I have replaced the French terms by English ones. As Professor Harold C. Conklin, of Columbia University, kindly informs me, the Malay term is *saudara*, not *sudarā*, and it means 'sibling or cousin'. There are also separate terms for younger and elder sibling or cousin, the latter being further subdivided into male and female.

R

Terms for grandparents show the same diversity. In Swedish, for instance, there is no single word for either 'grandfather' or 'grandmother', but a distinction between *farfar* 'father's father' and *morfar* 'mother's father', *farmor* 'father's mother' and *mormor* 'mother's mother'. Similarly, there is in Latin, as we have seen (p. 228), no general term for 'uncle', nor is there one for 'aunt'; a distinction had to be made between the 'father's brother', *patruus*, and the 'mother's brother', *avunculus*, and between the 'father's sister', *amita*, and the 'mother's sister', *matertera*. French *oncle* and English *uncle* derive from *avunculus*, French *tante*[1] and English *aunt* from *amita*. For more distant relationships there is an even wider variety conditioned by the social organization of the community.

The importance of language as the organizer of experience can best be seen in the realm of *abstract* ideas, for example in the field of intellectual terms studied by Trier. In such spheres everything will depend on the number and nature of the concepts we have, on how we delimit them and how we classify them. Trier has shown this very convincingly by comparing the basic structure of the intellectual field in Middle High German around 1200 and a century later.[2] In the first period, the field was organized around three key-terms: *wîsheit*, *kunst* and *list*. In Modern German these mean respectively 'wisdom' 'art' and 'cunning, craft, trick', but to the contemporary speaker they had a totally different meaning and significance. They embodied two fundamental principles of mediaeval civilization: feudalism and universality. The feudal principle was expressed in the distinction between *kunst* and *list*: the former referred to courtly and chivalric attainments, the latter to skills which fell outside the courtly sphere. Universality was ensured by *wîsheit* which could act as an alternative for both *kunst* and *list* and also as a global term denoting human wisdom in all its aspects, theological as well as mundane.

A very different picture emerges from German mystical vocabulary around 1300, which was investigated by one of Trier's pupils. First of all, the terms themselves are different: *wîsheit*, *kunst*, and *wizzen*. *List* has dropped out of the intellectual sphere since the pejorative components of its meaning had cast a shadow on its more reputable uses; on the other hand, the substantivized infinitive *wizzen* has joined the key-terms of the

---

[1] French *tante* goes back to an earlier *ante* which survives in English *aunt*. The initial *t-* in the Modern French form is due to an alteration in child language (Bloch-Wartburg). See on the above terms Wartburg, *Problèmes et méthodes de la linguistique*, p. 141.

[2] See esp. Trier, 'Das sprachliche Feld', loc. cit., pp. 432 ff. Cf. also Weisgerber, *Vom Weltbild der deutschen Sprache*, vol. II, pp. 110 ff., and Wartburg, *Problèmes et méthodes de la linguistique*, pp. 142 ff.

field. But it is not simply a case of replacing one word by another: the structure of the field, and the whole philosophy behind it, have radically altered. The two pillars on which the earlier system rested have crumbled away. Feudalism has disintegrated, and the distinction between courtly and non-courtly attainments has become superfluous and even meaningless. The catholicity of the earlier outlook has also been lost: *wîsheit* is no longer a general term covering the whole range of human wisdom, but is now reserved for religious and mystical experiences. Meanwhile the pair *kunst — wizzen* shows an incipient distinction between knowledge and art. The contrast between the two systems may be summed up in the following diagram:[1]

The field theory has been strongly criticised from various quarters,[2] and some of the claims put forward by its champions are no doubt extravagant and unconvincing. The neatness with which words delimit each other and build up a kind of mosaic, without any gaps or overlaps, has been greatly exaggerated. This is true only of specialized and rigidly defined systems such as army ranks; in ordinary language, vagueness, synonymy, ambiguity and similar factors will produce a much less tidy picture. It is also unrealistic to claim that the entire vocabulary is covered by fields in the same organic way in which the fields themselves, or at least some of them, are built up. Quite apart from overlaps between the various conceptual spheres, it is clear that many of these have no systematic organization of any kind. The field theory has concentrated so far on the study of a few highly integrated sectors: colours, family relations,

---

[1] This diagram is taken from Guiraud, *La Sémantique*, p. 72.

[2] See especially F. Scheidweiler, 'Die Wortfeldtheorie', *Zeitschrift für deutsches Altertum*, lxxix (1942), pp. 249-72; W. Betz, 'Zur Überprüfung des Feldbegriffes', *Zeitschrift für vergleichende Sprachforschung*, lxxi (1954), pp. 189-98; M. Konradt-Hicking, 'Wortfeld oder Bedeutungsfeld (Sinnfeld)?', ibid., lxxiii (1956), pp. 222-34; G. Kandler, 'Die Lücke im sprachlichen Weltbilde', *Sprache — Schlüssel zur Welt*, pp. 256-70; W. Rothwell, 'Mediaeval French and Modern Semantics' (to appear in *Modern Language Review*); N. C. W. Spence, 'Linguistic Fields, Conceptual Systems and the *Weltbild*' (to appear in *Transactions of the Philological Society*, 1961).

intellectual qualities, ethical[1] and aesthetic[2] concepts, mental processes,[3] religious and mystical experiences;[4] and one may wonder whether there are many other closely organized spheres of this kind in everyday language. It is perhaps a sobering thought that a full-scale investigation published recently on words for 'swiftness' in German has failed to reveal anything in the nature of a semantic field.[5]

These limitations must not, however, be allowed to obscure the outstanding importance of the field theory. Its significance in the development of semantic studies is threefold. Firstly, it has succeeded in introducing a truly structural method into a branch of linguistics which, as we have seen, has been rather slow in admitting such an approach. The concept of associative fields was an important step in this direction, but it still remained centred on individual words, whereas for the Trier school words as such are of secondary importance: what matters is the structure of the semantic field as a whole. Another merit of the theory is that it enables one to formulate problems which would otherwise have passed unobserved. A traditional inquiry into the history of intellectual terms in German would have carefully plotted the evolution of each word, but it would have been unable to interpret, or even to notice, the transformation of the entire system between 1200 and 1300, with all the far-reaching implications involved in that process. Lastly, the field theory provides a valuable method of approach to an elusive but crucially important problem: the influence of language on thinking. A semantic field does not merely reflect the ideas, values and outlook of contemporary society, but it crystallizes and perpetuates them: it hands down to the oncoming generation a ready-made analysis of experience through which the world will be viewed until the analysis becomes so palpably inadequate and out-of-date that the whole field has to be recast.

At this point the field theory links up with another recent development

[1] Cf. J. Trier, 'Über die Herkunft einiger Wörter des sittlichen Bereichs', *Studium Generale*, i (1948), pp. 103-10; L. R. Palmer, 'The Concept of Social Obligation in Indo-European. A Study in Structural Semantics', *Hommages à M. Niedermann*, Brussels, 1956 pp. 258-69; H. Yamaguchi, 'The Image of Man and his Fortune. A Study of Semantic Fields' *Anglica* (Osaka), iii (1958), pp. 197-229.

[2] See O. Ducháček, *Le Champ conceptuel de la beauté en français moderne*, Prague, 1960; cf. Id., *Vox Romanica*, xviii (1959), pp. 297-323, and *Le Française Moderne*, xxix (1961), pp. 263-84.

[3] See H. Sckommodau, *Der französische psychologische Wortschatz der zweiten Hälfte des 18. Jh.*, Leipzig – Paris, 1933.

[4] See H. Hatzfeld, 'Linguistic Investigation of Old French High Spirituality', *Publications of the Modern Language Association of America*, lxi (1946), pp. 331-78; H. Rheinfelder, 'Semantik und Theologie', *Estudios ... Menéndez Pidal*, vol. II, Madrid, 1951, pp. 253-71 (cf. *Annales de l'Université de Paris*, 1956, pp. 486-504); Sr. L. Tinsley, *The French Expressions for Spirituality and Devotion*, Washington, 1953.

[5] Oksaar, op. cit., p. 509 and passim.

in linguistics: the so-called *Sapir-Whorf hypothesis* on the influence of language upon thought. That such an influence exists is not a new idea; we have seen Dickens talking about the 'tyranny of words' (p. 154), and long before him Bacon had written: 'Men imagine that their minds have command of language: but it often happens that language bears rule over their minds.'[1] Modern philosophers, 'linguistic analysts' and others, are deeply concerned about the possibility that some philosophical problems are pseudo-problems generated by the structure of our languages.[2] Following some brilliant suggestions by Edward Sapir, the late Benjamin Lee Whorf approached the question in a novel and fruitful way: by comparing our own European languages — 'Standard Average European', as he called them — with the totally different structure of American Indian idioms, he tried to determine what features in thought and culture could be traced back to linguistic influence. His researches convinced him that each language contains a 'hidden metaphysics', that it embodies a unique way of viewing the world and imposes this outlook on its speakers. 'The linguistic system of each language', he argued, 'is not merely a reproducing system for voicing ideas, but rather is itself the shaper of ideas, the program and guide for the individual's mental activity, for his analysis of impressions, for his synthesis of his mental stock-in-trade ... We dissect nature along lines laid down by our native languages.'[3]

The Sapir-Whorf hypothesis has aroused considerable interest in America and has been the subject of many searching debates.[4] Attention has so far been focused mainly on grammatical structure and its impact on thought, for example on the linguistic foundations of our conception of time; lexical problems, though not overlooked, have remained in the background. Close liaison between this approach and the field theory would therefore be particularly valuable, since it is in semantics that some of Whorf's assumptions could be most readily tested. Meanwhile it is not without interest that the two movements, which started from widely different premises and developed for a long time

[1] Quoted by S. Potter, *Language in the Modern World*, London, 1960, p. 19.

[2] See, e.g., A. H. Basson-D. J. O'Connor, 'Language and Philosophy. Some Suggestions for an Empirical Approach', *Philosophy*, xxii (1947), pp. 49-65, and A. Flew, 'Philosophy and Language', in *Essays in Conceptual Analysis*, ch. 1.

[3] *Language, Thought, and Reality. Selected Writings of Benjamin Lee Whorf*, ed. by J. B. Carroll, New York — London, 1956, pp. 212 f. On the whole theory see also J. B. Carroll, *The Study of Language. A Survey of Linguistics and Related Disciplines in America*, Cambridge, Mass., 1953, pp. 43 ff.

[4] See the volumes *Language in Culture*, ed. by H. Hoijer, and *Language, Thought, and Culture*, ed. by P. Henle, both of which have already been referred to.

independently of each other, should have led to closely parallel conclusions regarding the central problem.[1]

During the last few years, a new concept of semantic fields has been evolved by the French linguist Georges Matoré. Professor Matoré's fields are akin to those of the Trier school, but are distinguished from them by a strong emphasis on *social* criteria. He gave a practical demonstration of his method in his important monograph on *Le Vocabulaire et la Société sous Louis-Philippe* (1951); two years later, he outlined the general principles of his theory in another book, *La Méthode en lexicologie*. He made his position quite clear in the preface to the first work: 'Nous nous proposons de considérer le mot non plus comme un objet isolé, mais comme un élément à l'intérieur d'ensembles plus importants, que nous classons hiérarchiquement en partant d'une analyse des structures sociales.'[2] To this end he has investigated the vocabulary of various sectors of society in his chosen period: political and social life, journalism, the salons, trades and crafts, art and science, the law, sport, and other spheres. A lexicology conceived on such lines is bound to merge into sociology, and some linguists will feel that Professor Matoré has gone too far when he declared: 'c'est en partant de l'étude du vocabulaire que nous essaierons d'expliquer une société. Aussi pourrons-nous définir la lexicologie comme une discipline sociologique utilisant le matériel linguistique que sont les mots.'[3]

In order to describe the social structure of a given period through its vocabulary, Professor Matoré has introduced two useful concepts: 'witness-words' (mots-témoins) and 'key-words' (mots-clés). Witness-words are defined as 'des éléments particulièrement importants en fonction desquels la structure lexicologique se hiérarchise et se coordonne'.[4] Each major conceptual sphere will have its witness-words; in the period just before and just after the July Revolution of 1830, for example, the terms *magasin* 'large shop' and *négociant* 'merchant, trader' occupied such a privileged position in the world of commerce.[5] A key-word, on the other hand, is an 'unité lexicologique exprimant une société ... un être, un sentiment, une idée, vivants dans la mesure même où la société reconnaît

---

[1] Cf. Weisgerber, *Vom Weltbild der deutschen Sprache*, vol. II, pp. 255 ff.

[2] 'We intend to consider the word, no longer as an isolated object, but as an element within larger wholes which we class hierarchically by starting from an analysis of social structures.'

[3] 'It is by starting from the study of vocabulary that we shall try to explain a society. We could therefore define lexicology as a sociological discipline using linguistic material, namely, words' (*La Méthode en lexicologie*, p. 50).

[4] 'Particularly important elements which determine the hierarchy and organization of lexicological structure' (ibid., p. 65).

[5] Ibid., p. 66; cf. also *Le Vocabulaire et la Société sous Louis-Philippe*, pp. 30 f.

en eux son idéal'.[1] In the period around 1830, the two key-words which dominated the social scene were *individualisme* and *organisation*; among human types, *bourgeois* had undisputed primacy, with *prolétaire* and *artiste* as 'secondary key-terms'.[2] This concept of 'key-words' can also render useful services in stylistics; Corneille, for example, has been studied in the light of half a dozen crucial terms epitomizing his ideals: *mérite, estime, devoir, vertu, générosité* and *gloire*.[3]

Professor Matoré has given further illustrations of his method in a series of interesting articles.[4] His teaching and example have also stimulated a number of inquiries into specialized vocabularies, ranging from feudalism to railways and from fashion to medicine.[5] These investigations have found a focal point in the recently established centre of lexicological studies at Besançon, where large-scale research projects are being organized with the aid of modern mechanical devices.[6]

III. The Vocabulary

The general structure of the vocabulary can be studied by statistical and by purely linguistic methods. *Statistical* inquiries, inspired by the theory of information and helped by electronic computers, have already had some applications in semantics; as we have seen, these studies have thrown fresh light on such crucial problems as the nature of signs (p. 18), polysemy (p. 169), homonymy (p. 177), semantic change (p. 226 f.), and, most important of all, the concept of meaning itself (pp. 68 ff.). Stylistics may also stand to benefit by such experiments: questions such as the disputed authorship or unity of a literary work, or the chronology of writings by the same author, may be settled by so-called 'stylo-statistical'

[1] 'A lexicological unit expressing a society ... a person, a feeling, an idea which are alive in so far as society recognizes in them its ideal' (*La Méthode en lexicologie*, p. 68).

[2] Ibid., pp. 69 f. and Appendix I: 'Le Champ notionnel d'art et d'artiste entre 1827 et 1834' (pp. 99-117).

[3] O. Nadal, *De quelques mots de la langue cornélienne*, Paris, 1948.

[4] Cf., e.g., 'La Naissance du génie au XVIIIe siècle', *Le Français Moderne*, xxv (1957), pp. 256-72 (jointly with A.-J. Greimas); 'Vocabulaire et littérature', *Cahiers de l'Association Internationale des Études Françaises*, xi (1959), pp. 301-6; 'Le Mouvement et la communication dans le vocabulaire contemporain', *Journal de Psychologie*, lvi (1959), pp. 275-302.

[5] K. J. Hollyman, *Le Développement du vocabulaire féodal en France pendant le haut moyen âge*, Geneva — Paris, 1957; P. J. Wexler, op. cit.; A.-J. Greimas, *La Mode en 1830*, unpublished thesis summarized in Appendix II of Matoré's *La Méthode en lexicologie*; B. Quemada, *Introduction à l'étude du vocabulaire médical, 1600-1710*, Paris — Besançon, 1955.

[6] This centre, headed by Professor Quemada, publishes a series entitled *Cahiers de Lexicologie*, as well as a *Bulletin d'Information du Laboratoire d'Analyse Lexicologique*.

methods.[1] The champions of this approach may indeed be right in claiming that the theory of information is opening a new field for semantic studies.[2] It is to be feared, however, that comparatively few linguists will be able to follow the mathematical operations involved in these researches, while on the other hand the statisticians may not always have an adequate grasp of philological problems. As one of the advocates of this method rightly points out, 'both philology and mathematics are essentially esoteric subjects, the latter more so than the former. This means that the mathematics will not be intelligible to someone who is not a mathematician and the philology will, at the best, be difficult for someone who is not a philologist'.[3] Unfortunately the linguist's difficulties are not always taken into account by his scientific colleagues writing on these matters. They should ponder Professor Martinet's warning:

> Flaunting mathematical formulae before a linguistic audience or in a linguistic publication is either grossly misinterpreting the needs and capacities of one's audience or readers, or else trying to bully them into accepting one's views by claiming for these the support of a science they tend to respect as the most exact of all sciences, but whose data they are not in a position to verify. We need more and more rigour in linguistics, but our own brand.[4]

Among purely linguistic researches into the structure of the vocabulary, two lines of inquiry are being actively pursued at the present time: attempts are being made to devise a rational system of concepts, and also to evolve a 'semantic typology', a classification of languages on semantic grounds.

1. *How Concepts are Organized*

'Dictionaries, like electric lights and written constitutions, must be ranked among the basic facts of modern civilized life. Without them, our Western culture would no doubt survive, but only at the price of a notable increase in frustration, confusion and unhappiness.'[5] The out-

---

[1] See esp. G. U. Yule, *The Statistical Study of Literary Vocabulary*, London, 1944, and G. Herdan, *Language as Choice and Chance*, which has already been mentioned. Cf. also my *Style in the French Novel*, pp. 29 ff. and R.-L. Wagner-P. Guiraud, 'La Méthode statistique en lexicologie', *Revue de l'Enseignement Supérieur*, 1959, no. 1, pp. 154-9.

[2] Guiraud, *La Sémantique*, p. 100.

[3] A. S. C. Ross, 'Philologica Mathematica', *Časopis pro Moderní Filologii*, xxxi (1937): p. 16 of offprint.

[4] 'The Unity of Linguistics', *Word*, x (1954), pp. 121-5: p. 125.

[5] S. M. Kuhn, *Language*, xxx (1954), p. 551, quoted by S. Potter, *Modern Linguistics*, p. 156, n. 2.

standing importance of dictionaries in the modern world explains why some lexicographers are dissatisfied with the mechanical method of arranging words in alphabetical order, and would prefer to classify them according to the concepts which they express. Roget's *Thesaurus*, published over a century ago, was a valuable pioneering work in this field. In recent years several *conceptual dictionaries*, based on sound and scholarly methods, have appeared,[1] and it is an indication of the importance which modern linguists attach to this problem that it was fully discussed at one of their last international congresses.[2]

It would obviously be a great convenience if conceptual dictionaries of different languages, periods or single authors could conform to the same general pattern so that they could be readily compared with each other. To this end one would require a *conceptual framework* so comprehensive and yet so elastic that the most diverse languages and the most idiosyncratic writers would fit smoothly into it. Such a broad classification of concepts was put forward by R. Hallig and W. von Wartburg in 1952.[3] In constructing their scheme, the authors were guided by two principles. Firstly, they visualized the system of concepts as an 'intermediate world' (sprachliche Zwischenwelt) which language interposes between man and the universe, and sought to represent it as an integrated structure of interlocking elements. Secondly, they adopted a point of view described as 'naïve realism': their aim was to set forth 'the intelligent average individual's view of the world, based on pre-scientific general concepts made available by language' (p. xiv). They divided concepts into three broad categories, each of them comprising numerous subdivisions: 'the Universe', 'Man', and 'Man and the Universe'. When Professor Wartburg outlined the scheme at the London congress in 1952, he was gratified to find that another scholar who had also been working for a long time on this problem had arrived at a very similar conclusion.[4]

Long before it was published, the Hallig-Wartburg scheme had been used as a common framework for a number of monographs on the

---

[1] See esp. F. Dornseiff, *Der deutsche Wortschatz nach Sachgruppen*, which has already been mentioned. On conceptual dictionaries see K. Baldinger, 'Die Gestaltung des wissenschaftlichen Wörterbuchs', *Romanistisches Jahrbuch*, v (1952), pp. 65-94; Id., 'Grundsätzliches zur Gestaltung des wissenschaftlichen Wörterbuchs', *Deutsche Akademie der Wissenschaften zu Berlin, 1946-1956*, Berlin, 1956, pp. 379-88; Id., 'Alphabetisches oder begrifflich gegliedertes Wörterbuch?', *Zeitschrift für Romanische Philologie*, lxxvi (1960), pp. 521-36. Cf. also F. Hiorth, 'Zur Ordnung des Wortschatzes', *Studia Linguistica*, xiv (1960), pp. 65-84.

[2] See the *Proceedings of the Seventh International Congress of Linguists*, pp. 77-89 and 343-73.

[3] *Begriffssystem als Grundlage für die Lexikographie. Versuch eines Ordnungsschemas*, Abhandlungen der Deutschen Akademie der Wissenschaften zu Berlin, Klasse für Sprachen, Literatur und Kunst, Heft 4, 1952.

[4] *Proceedings*, p. 373. Cf. F. Mezger's report, ibid., pp. 77 ff.

history of the French vocabulary prepared under the direction of Professor Wartburg himself.[1] Since its publication, it has been, and is being, utilized in the same way in further lexicological studies.[2] Nearly all the work done so far has been on French material, but one or two inquiries have dealt with other Romance languages.[3] Needless to say, the Hallig-Wartburg system is only one of various possible ways in which concepts could be classified; the aim was not so much to devise an ideal scheme as to have a uniform basis for specific investigations. If this idea were to be widely adopted, a series of coordinated research projects could be planned, with sufficient flexibility to adapt the scheme to the material examined, and yet with enough common ground to make the results comparable.

It is perhaps in the field of historical semantics that such a programme would be most rewarding. Until recently, this branch of linguistics had been exclusively concerned with the evolution of single words. Trier took an important step forward when he tried to trace the development of an entire semantic field.[4] Now Professor Wartburg would go one step further and apply the same technique to the history of the vocabulary as a whole. This would lead, in Wartburg's own words, to a 'historico-structural' approach which he has long recognized as an urgent necessity in linguistics. 'Le but est clair:' he wrote many years ago, 'suivre la structure globale d'une langue dans son processus de transformation progressive. De cette manière la science du langage deviendra, dans une nouvelle phase de son évolution, une véritable histoire structurelle.'[5]

2. *Towards a Semantic Classification of Languages*

Like many other new ideas in modern linguistics, the possibility that languages could be classified on semantic grounds was first suggested by

---

[1] Listed in Wartburg, *Problèmes et méthodes de la linguistique*, p. 161, n. 1; cf. Baldinger, *Romanistisches Jahrbuch*, v, p. 93.

[2] See H. E. Keller, *Etude descriptive sur le vocabulaire de Wace*, Berlin, 1953.

[3] See M. H. J. Fermin, *Le Vocabulaire de Bifrun dans sa traduction des quatre Evangiles*, Amsterdam, 1954, where the Hallig-Wartburg scheme is applied, with some modifications, to the vocabulary of a sixteenth-century translation of the Gospels into Romansh. See also W. Runkewitz, 'Kritische Betracl. ungen zum Begriffssystem Hallig-v. Wartburg im Zusammenhang mit den Arbeiten am altgaskognischen Wörterbuch', *Forschungen und Fortschritte*, Band 33, Heft 1, Berlin, 1959, pp. 19-24; cf. K. Baldinger-W. Runkewitz, *Monatsberichte der Deutschen Akademie der Wissenschaften zu Berlin*, Sprachen und Literaturen, Band 1, Heft 1, 1959, pp. 73-9.

[4] See esp. *Der deutsche Wortschatz im Sinnbezirk des Verstandes*, p. 13.

[5] 'The aim is clear: to follow the global structure of a language in its process of gradual transformation. In this way the science of language will become, in a new phase of its development, a real structural history' (*Problèmes et méthodes de la linguistique*, p. 162). See already by the same author: 'Betrachtungen über die Gliederung des Wortschatzes und die Gestaltung des Wörterbuchs', *Zeitschrift für Romanische Philologie*, lvii (1937), pp. 296-312; cf. *Mélanges Bally*, pp. 3-18.

Saussure. We have seen (p. 105) that he divided them into two groups: 'lexicological' languages, which have a preference for opaque words, and 'grammatical' ones, where the transparent type predominates. These brief hints were developed by other linguists, especially by Charles Bally who, in his *Linguistique générale et linguistique française,* established a number of characteristic tendencies in contemporary French by systematically comparing it with German. Bally's study covered all levels of the linguistic system, phonology and grammar as well as vocabulary, and semantic features played, on the whole, a subsidiary role in his general conclusions.

In Chapters 4-7 of this book, I have tried to follow up these and other ideas and to identify certain *semantic tendencies* which may distinguish languages from each other and from earlier stages in their own history. By tabulating these general tendencies, one can obtain a set of criteria for what might become one day a semantic '*typology*' of languages:

(1) The relative frequency of opaque and transparent words and, among the latter, of the various types of motivation (onomatopoeia, derivation and composition, etc.).

(2) The relative frequency of particular and generic terms.

(3) Specific devices available for heightening the emotive effect of words (e.g. the emotional accent and the place of the adjective in French).

(4) Synonymic patterns (e.g. the double and triple scale of synonyms in English); concentrations of synonyms as symptoms of the predominant interests of a community.

(5) The relative frequency of polysemy; its characteristic forms (e.g. concentrations of metaphors as symptoms of interest in a particular sphere); specific safeguards available against ambiguity resulting from polysemy (e.g. grammatical gender).

(6) The relative frequency of homonymy; its connexions with word-length and word-structure; specific safeguards available against homonymic conflicts (e.g. gender, spelling, etc.).

To these six criteria a seventh may be added by combining numbers (2), (5) and (6). Generic meanings, polysemy and homonymy have this in common that they all tend to restrict the autonomy of the word and to increase the importance of context, to make individual terms more 'context-bound'. This gives us one more criterion:

(7) The relative independence of words, and the importance of context in determining their meaning.

It will not be necessary to discuss these criteria here since they have been fully examined in the appropriate chapters. I have also tried to apply them to a specific language, contemporary French, in my *Précis de sémantique française*.[1] The criteria can of course serve a dual purpose: they can be used in comparisons between different idioms and between successive phases in the history of one language. Thus Modern French and Modern English are not only less 'transparent' than Modern German; they are also a great deal less transparent than was the English of King Alfred or the French of the *Chanson de Roland*, and a structurally oriented semantics will seek to establish the various forces which led to this loss of transparency.[2]

It will have been noted that four of the six basic criteria concern relative frequencies. This does not mean that they are all amenable to statistical formulation.[3] Some of the features involved, such as for instance homonymy, are so precise that they will naturally invite this kind of treatment; other tendencies, however obvious they may be, are too fluid and subjective to lend themselves to numerical counts. Thus it will be clear to even the most casual observer that German is richer than French in onomatopoeic words; yet the nature of onomatopoeia is such that it would be difficult to subject it to mathematical analysis. Statistics is a valuable tool, but it must not be allowed to become a fetish, and it is often too crude to catch the finer nuances of semantic phenomena.

[1] See esp. pp. 316 f.; cf. also my two articles: 'Les Tâches de la sémantique descriptive en français', *Bulletin de la Société de Linguistique de Paris*, xlviii (1952), pp. 14-32, and 'Descriptive Semantics and Linguistic Typology', *Word*, ix (1953), pp. 225-40.

[2] Cf. my article, 'Historical Semantics and the Structure of the Vocabulary', *Miscelánea Homenaje a André Martinet: 'Estructuralismo e Historia'*, vol. I, La Laguna, 1957, pp. 289-303: pp. 300 f.

[3] Cf. U. Weinreich's review of my *Précis de sémantique française* in *Language*, xxxi (1955), pp. 537-43, and D. H. Hymes, 'On Typology of Cognitive Styles in Language', *Anthropological Linguistics*, III (1961), pp. 22-54; p. 27. Cf. above, p. 106, n. 1.

CONCLUSION

THE main purpose of this book was not so much to present an established body of facts and doctrine, but rather to submit an interim report on a new and vigorous science; to record past achievements, but also to formulate problems, to suggest fresh lines of inquiry, and to speculate upon the future. The most encouraging feature in the present state of semantic studies is the considerable quickening of interest in these matters, both inside and outside linguistics, during the last decade or so. This is reflected first of all in the greatly increased volume of publications on the subject. It is also shown in the prominence which problems of meaning are given at congresses and conferences,[1] and in the many forms of fruitful co-operation which have developed between semanticists and others interested in these matters.[2] During the last few years, semantics has become an integral part of the linguistic curriculum in a number of universities, and a popular subject for postgraduate research. At the same time there still remain some unsolved problems regarding the aims, methods and general status of semantic studies. The following factors seem to me of decisive importance for the future of this discipline:

(1) It is essential that research in semantics should develop in a *balanced* way. While it is both right and natural that young research-workers should be attracted to the more modern and experimental side of the subject, it would be a pity if this led to a neglect of the older branches of semantics. As I have tried to show in the chapter on change of meaning, there are still many important questions here which await solution and which could be profitably attacked with the aid of up-to-date methods. There should also be a reasonable balance between theory and practice. Looking back on the history of semantics it is perfectly clear that nearly all important advances have come from empirical studies, but only when these were conducted with a firm grasp of theory and method. There are many branches of linguistics and other sciences where valuable

---

[1] There has even been a special conference on semantics, held in Nice in March 1951; cf. above, p. 58. A conference on lexicology — with special reference to plans for a new historical dictionary of the French language — was held in Strasbourg in November 1957; see now the volume, *Lexicologie et lexicographie françaises et romanes*, Paris, 1960.

[2] To mention but one of these, at the 1955 conference of the British Association there was a symposium on semantics in which a psychologist, a neurologist, a linguist and a logician took part. A summary of this symposium will be found in G. P. Meredith, 'Language, Meaning and Mind', *Nature*, clxxvi (1955), pp. 673-4. Three of the contributions have been published in *Archivum Linguisticum*, viii (1956), pp. 1-27, under the title: 'Semantics: A Symposium'.

work can be done without any interest in general principles; in semantics, however, the nature of the subject makes it imperative for theory and practice to proceed *pari passu*.

(2) As mentioned at several points in this book, there are in semantics certain highly important problems, some very old, others entirely new, which could be solved only if they were tackled on a vast scale, in the form of a series of closely planned and coordinated *research projects*. An obvious example is the question of so-called 'universals': semantic 'laws' and other general tendencies which are inherent in the structure of language and perhaps in that of the human mind. Only inquiries conducted at a truly international level could conclusively show whether such universals really exist and, if so, how regular they are, what forms they take, under what conditions they operate, etc. Given the exceptional importance of such problems for linguists and non-linguists alike, it is to be hoped that ways and means will be found to organize long-term research programmes on these and similar themes.[1]

(3) The future of semantics will largely depend on its *status* within linguistics. There is no doubt at all that progress in this field was retarded, and at times almost brought to a standstill, by the climate of linguistic opinion in the late 1930s and in the 1940s, when anything connected with meaning was frowned upon, or looked at askance, by many leading structuralists. This was the attitude of which an eminent American linguist once said, in a passage already quoted: 'For many linguistic students the word *meaning* itself has become almost anathema.'[2] This taboo has now been considerably relaxed, but there is still a marked reluctance in some quarters to handle problems of meaning. Discussions on the Sapir-Whorf theory for example have, as already noted (p. 251), been cramped by the paradoxical fact that although it is crying out for a semantic approach, it has scarcely been examined so far from that point of view.[3]

On a more theoretical plane, the same bias is seen in the marginal place which some linguists would assign to semantic studies. One of the latest textbooks, Professor C. F. Hockett's valuable *Course in Modern Linguistics*, is symptomatic in this respect. Hockett distinguishes between

---

[1] At a conference on 'Language Universals', held at Dobbs Ferry, New York, in April 1961 under the auspices of the American Social Science Research Council, there were two papers on 'Semantic Universals', one by Professor Uriel Weinreich, the other by myself. These papers will be published in the proceedings of the conference.

[2] C. C. Fries in *Language*, xxx (1954), p. 58; cf. above, p. 71. On these matters, see the Supplement to the second edition of my *Principles of Semantics*, pp. 317 ff.

[3] Cf. my review of the volume *Language in Culture* in *Romance Philology*, x (1957), pp. 225-32.

'five principal subsystems' in language, of which three are 'central' and two 'peripheral'. The three central ones are the grammatical, the phonological and the 'morphophonemic' system, the last one being 'the code which ties together' the phonology and grammar of a language. The two 'peripheral' ones are the semantic and the phonetic system. On the respective status of the two groups Professor Hockett writes:

> Linguistics has always concentrated on the three central subsystems, without much concern with the peripheral systems. Some scholars, indeed, prefer to define 'language' so as to include only the central subsystems, regarding problems of meaning and of articulatory and acoustic phonetics as belonging to sister sciences rather than to linguistics. The choice of broader or narrower definition of the term is a matter of personal taste, and not important. Likewise, anyone is free to focus on the central subsystems or to invade the peripheral ones as he pleases. The peripheral systems are just as important as the central ones; the fact is, however, that they are much harder to study and that, so far, less has been learned about them (pp. 137 f.).

I have quoted Professor Hockett's views in full because they are typical of an attitude towards semantics which is still prevalent in many influential circles. Clearly this is not a terminological issue of minor importance, as Hockett suggests; the distinction between central and peripheral subsystems, and the relegation of meaning to a marginal position, implies an order of priorities, of 'first things first'. Most structuralists will naturally start with the 'central' problems and will become so engrossed in them that they will never reach the 'peripheral' ones. The situation has been aptly summed up by a well-known American anthropologist: 'If for a time at least — and that may be a lifetime — we concentrate on structure, we will really find out more about structure than if we constantly mingle that with matters of content.'[1] As for the suggestion that linguistics, and language itself, can be so defined as to exclude problems of meaning,[2] this is an extreme position which would be acceptable to no linguist who takes a broad and realistic view of his subject, and would certainly be incomprehensible to the non-specialist who rightly regards meaning as one of the basic elements in any language. As Professor W. S. Allen has recently reminded us, 'without meaning linguistics cannot exist'.[3]

The reservations which many structuralists still have about semantics

[1] A. L. Kroeber, *Language in Culture*, pp. 157 f.
[2] Cf. Hockett, ibid., p. 152.
[3] *On the Linguistic Study of Languages*, p. 22 (cf. above, p. 71).

can be traced back to two main causes. One is the strong emphasis in modern linguistics on the need for scientific rigour, coupled with the assumption that such rigour is impossible in semantics. Even if this were true it would not justify us in excluding meaning from linguistics; it would be far more logical to admit that in this part of language study rigorously scientific methods cannot be applied. Actually, however, the assumption is not borne out by the facts. As we have seen, there are many semantic phenomena which can be formulated with the utmost precision; what could be more rigorously scientific than the reconstruction of homonymic clashes with the aid of linguistic atlases? Some semantic tendencies can even be stated in statistical terms; as regards others, it will be the semanticist's duty to define them with the maximum of rigour allowed by his subject-matter.

The other reason why structuralists are sometimes hesitant about semantics is, on the face of it, more respectable. The new conception of language as a highly integrated structure produced, as we have seen, quick and spectacular results in phonology and grammar, but seemed at first inapplicable to semantics. The situation has, however, changed radically since the field theory and other experiments have shown that the vocabulary has an organization of its own which can be described in structural terms. This approach has already revitalized semantic studies and is likely to yield further valuable results in the years to come. As a recent article from New Zealand rightly claimed, semantics has 'come of age',[1] and it is to be hoped that any lingering prejudice against it will now speedily disappear. This is all the more important as such preconceptions are bound to affect the morale of semanticists and the recruitment of future research-workers.

(4) At a time when some linguists would like to turn their discipline into an 'immanent' study having 'nothing to do, directly, with the non-speech world in which speaking takes place',[2] semanticists are anxious to foster their manifold *contacts* with neighbouring sciences. Some of these contacts are of old standing; others are only just beginning to take shape. Since the inception of semantic studies, there has been close liaison with philosophers, psychologists and historians; somewhat later, fruitful relations were established with sociology. The study of connexions between language and culture has brought semanticists into contact with anthropologists; the work of neurologists on aphasia has thrown fresh

[1] K. J. Hollyman, 'Semantics Comes of Age', *Journal of the Australasian Modern Language Association*, iv (May 1957), pp. 70-3.
[2] Hockett, op. cit., p. 137. On this approach see especially K. Togeby, *Structure immanente de la langue française*, Travaux du Cercle Linguistique de Copenhague, vi, 1951.

light on normal semantic processes; recent progress in stylistics has deepened our understanding of metaphor, ambiguity, emotive overtones and similar features. During the last few years, the semanticist has found unexpected partners in the statistician and the communication engineer. In fact, language is such a central force in human life, and meaning such a central factor in language, that the ramifications of semantics are virtually unlimited; they may even extend to such remote subjects as symbolism in music and in the visual arts. Without becoming the Jack of all trades of the humanities and losing its identity in the process, semantics has something to offer to, and something to learn from, all of them. It is this universality which gives the study of meaning its outstanding educational value.

S

SELECT BIBLIOGRAPHY

H. ADANK, *Essai sur les fondements psychologiques et linguistiques de la métaphore affective* (Geneva, 1939).

W. S. ALLEN, *On the Linguistic Study of Languages* (Cambridge, 1957).

H. AMMANN, *Die menschliche Rede* (2 vols., Lahr i.B., 1925-28).

K. AMMER, *Einführung in die Sprachwissenschaft I* (Halle a.S., 1958).

A. BACHMANN, *Zur psychologischen Theorie des sprachlichen Bedeutungswandels* (Munich, 1935).

K. BALDINGER, *Die Semasiologie. Versuch eines Überblicks* (Deutsche Akademie der Wissenschaften zu Berlin, Vorträge und Schriften, Heft 61, 1957).

CH. BALLY, *Linguistique générale et linguistique française* (3rd ed., Berne, 1950).

—— *Traité de stylistique française* (2 vols., 3rd ed., Geneva – Paris, 1951).

—— *Le Langage et la vie* (3rd ed. revised, Geneva – Lille, 1952).

L. BLOOMFIELD, *Language* (New York, 1933).

N. BØGHOLM, *Engelsk Betydningslaere* (Copenhagen, 1922).

M. BRÉAL, *Essai de sémantique. Science des significations* (5th ed., Paris, 1921).

V. BRØNDAL, *Le Français, langue abstraite* (Copenhagen, 1936).

—— *Essais de linguistique générale* (Copenhagen, 1943).

C. BROOKE-ROSE, *A Grammar of Metaphor* (London, 1958).

F. BRUNOT, *La Pensée et la langue* (3rd ed., Paris, 1936).

C. D. BUCK, *A Dictionary of Selected Synonyms in the Principal Indo-European Languages* (Chicago, 1949).

K. BÜHLER, *Sprachtheorie. Die Darstellungsfunktion der Sprache* (Jena, 1934).

E. BUYSSENS, *Les Langages et le discours* (Brussels, 1943).

R. CARNAP, *Introduction to Semantics* (Cambridge, Mass., 1942).

A. CARNOY, *La Science du mot. Traité de sémantique* (Louvain, 1927).

J. B. CARROLL, *The Study of Language. A Survey of Linguistics and Related Disciplines in America* (Cambridge, Mass., 1953).

J. CASARES, *Introducción a la lexicografía moderna* (Madrid, 1950).

E. CASSIRER, *Philosophie der symbolischen Formen* (3 vols., Berlin, 1923-29).

S. CHASE, *The Tyranny of Words* (London ed., 1938).

—— *The Power of Words* (London ed., 1955).

C. CHERRY (Ed.), *Information Theory* (London, 1956).

—— *On Human Communication* (New York – London, 1957).

N. CHOMSKY, *Syntactic Structures* (The Hague, 1957).

M. COHEN, *Pour une sociologie du langage* (Paris, 1956).

C. S. R. COLLIN, *A Bibliographical Guide to Sematology* (Lund, 1914).

E. COSERIU, *La Creación metafórica en el lenguaje* (Montevideo, 1956).

—— *Sincronía, diacronía e historia. El problema del cambio lingüístico* (Montevideo, 1958).

M. Cressot, *Le Style et ses techniques* (Paris, 1947).

A. Darmesteter, *La Vie des mots étudiée dans leurs significations* (Paris, 1946 ed.)

A. Dauzat, *Etudes de linguistique française* (2nd ed., Paris, 1946).

—— *Précis d'histoire de la langue et du vocabulaire français* (Paris, 1949).

A. Dauzat (Ed.), *Où en sont les études de français* (2nd ed., Paris, 1949).

H. Delacroix, *Le Langage et la pensée* (Paris, 1924).

L. Deroy, *L'Emprunt linguistique* (Paris, 1956).

G. Devoto, *I Fondamenti della storia linguistica* (Florence, 1951).

G. A. van Dongen, *Amelioratives in English I* (Rotterdam, 1933).

F. Dornseiff, *Der deutsche Wortschatz nach Sachgruppen* (5th ed., Berlin 1959).

O. Ducháček, *Le Champ conceptuel de la beauté en français moderne* (Prague, 1960).

C. L. Ebeling, *Linguistic Units* (The Hague, 1960).

W. Empson, *Seven Types of Ambiguity* (2nd ed., London, 1949).

—— *The Structure of Complex Words* (London, 1951).

W. J. Entwistle, *Aspects of Language* (London, 1953).

K. O. Erdmann, *Die Bedeutung des Wortes* (4th ed., Leipzig, 1925).

A. Ernout, *Philologica* (Paris, 1946).

G. Esnault, *Imagination populaire, métaphores occidentales* (Paris, 1925).

S. M. Estrich-H. Sperber, *Three Keys to Language* (New York, 1952).

H. Falk, *Betydningslaere* (Oslo, 1920).

J. R. Firth, *The Tongues of Men* (London, 1937).

—— *Papers in Linguistics, 1934-1951* (London — New York — Toronto, 1957).

A. Flew (Ed.), *Essays in Conceptual Analysis* (London, 1955).

O. Funke, *Innere Sprachform. Eine Einführung in A. Martys Sprachphilosophie* (Reichenberg, 1924).

E. Gamillscheg, *Französische Bedeutungslehre* (Tübingen, 1951).

Sir Alan Gardiner, *The Theory of Speech and Language* (2nd ed., Oxford, 1951).

—— *The Theory of Proper Names* (2nd ed., London — New York — Toronto, 1954).

J. Gilliéron, *Généalogie des mots qui désignent l'abeille* (Paris, 1918).

—— *Pathologie et thérapeutique verbales* (Paris, 1921).

J. Gilliéron-M. Roques, *Etudes de géographie linguistique* (Paris, 1912).

K. Goldstein, *Language and Language Disturbances* (New York, 1948).

Z. Gombocz, *Jelentéstan* (Pécs, 1926).

W. L. Graff, *Language and Languages. An Introduction to Linguistics* (New York — London, 1932).

R. de la Grasserie, *Essai d'une sémantique intégrale* (Paris, 1908).

L. H. Gray, *Foundations of Language* (New York, 1939).

J. H. Greenberg, *Essays in Linguistics* (Chicago, 1957).

J. B. Greenough-G. L. Kittredge, *Words and their Ways in English Speech* (London ed., 1902).

V. Grove, *The Language Bar* (London, 1949).

R. F. M. Guérios, *Tabus lingüísticos* (Rio de Janeiro, 1956).

P. Guiraud, *Les Caractères statistiques du vocabulaire* (Paris, 1954).

—— *La Sémantique* (Paris, 1955).

—— *La Grammaire* (Paris, 1958).

—— *Problèmes et méthodes de la statistique linguistique* (Paris, 1959).

—— *Les Locutions françaises* (Paris, 1961).

H. Güntert, *Grundfragen der Sprachwissenschaft* (2nd ed., Heidelberg, 1956).

R. Hallig-W. von Wartburg, *Begriffssystem als Grundlage für die Lexikographie. Versuch eines Ordnungsschemas* (Abhandlungen der deutschen Akademie der Wissenschaften zu Berlin, Klasse für Sprachen, Literatur und Kunst, Heft 4, 1952).

E. P. Hamp, *A Glossary of American Technical Linguistic Usage, 1925-1950* (Utrecht — Antwerp, 1957).

L. C. Harmer, *The French Language Today. Its Characteristics and Tendencies* (London, 1954).

Z. S. Harris, *Methods in Structural Linguistics* (Chicago, 1951).

H. Hatzfeld, *Leitfaden der vergleichenden Bedeutungslehre* (Munich, 1924).

—— *Über Bedeutungsverschiebung durch Formähnlichkeit im Neufranzösischen* (Munich, 1924).

—— *A Critical Bibliography of the New Stylistics Applied to the Romance Literatures, 1900-1952* (Chapel Hill, 1953).

W. Havers, *Neuere Literatur zum Sprachtabu* (Akademie der Wissenschaften in Wien, Phil.-Hist. Klasse, Sitzungsberichte 223, 5, 1946).

P. Henle (Ed.), *Language, Thought, and Culture* (Ann Arbor, 1958).

G. Herdan, *Language as Choice and Chance* (Groningen, 1956).

—— *Type-Token Mathematics* (The Hague, 1960).

L. Hjelmslev, *Prolegomena to a Theory of Language* (transl. by F. J. Whitfield, Baltimore, 1953).

—— *Essais linguistiques* (Copenhagen, 1959).

C. F. Hockett, *A Course in Modern Linguistics* (New York, 1958).

H. M. Hoenigswald, *Language Change and Linguistic Reconstruction* (Chicago, 1960).

H. Hoijer (Ed.), *Language in Culture. Conference on the Interrelations of Language and other Aspects of Culture* (Chicago, 1954).

K. J. Hollyman, *Le Développement du vocabulaire féodal en France pendant le haut moyen âge (Étude sémantique)* (Geneva — Paris, 1957).

J. Holt, *Rationel Semantik (Pleremik)* (Acta Jutlandica XVIII, 3; Aarhus — Copenhagen, 1946).

E. Huguet, *Le Langage figuré au XVIe siècle* (Paris, 1933).

—— *L'Evolution du sens des mots depuis le XVIe siècle* (Paris, 1934).

—— *Mots disparus ou vieillis depuis le XVIe siècle* (Paris, 1935).

I. IORDAN-J. ORR, *An Introduction to Romance Linguistics. Its Schools and Scholars* (London, 1937).

K. JABERG, *Aspects géographiques du langage* (Paris, 1936).

—— *Sprachwissenschaftliche Forschungen und Erlebnisse* (Paris — Zurich — Leipzig, 1937).

R. JAKOBSON-M. HALLE, *Fundamentals of Language* (The Hague, 1956).

O. JESPERSEN, *Mankind, Nation and Individual from a Linguistic Point of View* (Oslo, etc., 1925).

—— *The Philosophy of Grammar* (London — New York, repr. 1929).

—— *Growth and Structure of the English Language* (6th ed., Leipzig, 1930).

—— *Linguistica* (Copenhagen — London, 1933).

—— *Language: its Nature, Development and Origin* (London — New York, repr. 1934).

F. KAINZ, *Psychologie der Sprache* (4 vols., Vienna, 1954-56).

R. E. KELLER, *Die Ellipse in der neuenglischen Sprache als syntaktisch-semantisches Problem* (Zurich, 1944).

K. KNAUER, *Grenzen der Wissenschaft vom Wort* (Akademie der Wissenschaften und der Literatur, Abhandlungen der Geistes- und Sozialwissenschaften, Klasse 13, Mainz, 1950).

L. G. KNIGHTS-B. COTTLE (Ed.), *Metaphor and Symbol* (London, 1960).

H. KONRAD, *Etude sur la métaphore* (Paris, 1939).

A. KORZYBSKI, *Science and Sanity. An Introduction to Non-Aristotelian Systems and General Semantics* (3rd ed., Lakeville, Conn., 1948).

H. KRONASSER, *Handbuch der Semasiologie. Kurze Einführung in die Geschichte, Problematik und Terminologie der Bedeutungslehre* (Heidelberg, 1952).

L. LANDGREBE, *Nennfunktion und Wortbedeutung. Eine Studie über Martys Sprachphilosophie* (Halle a.S., 1934).

R. LEHMANN, *Le Sémantisme des mots expressifs en Suisse Romande* (Romanica Helvetica XXXIV; Berne, 1949).

E. LEISI, *Der Wortinhalt. Seine Struktur im Deutschen und Englischen* (2nd ed., Heidelberg, 1961).

—— *Das heutige Englisch. Wesenszüge und Probleme* (2nd ed., Heidelberg, 1960).

C. DAY LEWIS, *The Poetic Image* (London, 1947).

C. S. LEWIS, *Studies in Words* (Cambridge, 1960).

Lexicologie et lexicographie françaises et romanes. Orientations et exigences actuelles (Colloques Internationaux du Centre National de la Recherche Scientifique, Sciences Humaines; Paris, 1960).

L. LINSKY (Ed.), *Semantics and the Philosophy of Language* (Urbana, 1952).

E. LÖFSTEDT, *Syntactica II* (Lund, 1933).

J. MAROUZEAU, *La Linguistique ou science du langage* (2nd ed., Paris, 1944).

—— *Précis de stylistique française* (3rd ed., Paris, 1950).

—— *Lexique de la terminologie linguistique* (3rd ed., Paris, 1951).

A. MARTINET, *Eléments de linguistique générale* (Paris, 1960).

A. MARTY, *Untersuchungen zur Grundlegung der allgemeinen Grammatik und Sprachphilosophie* (Halle a.S., 1908).

—— *Über Wert und Methode einer allgemeinen beschreibenden Bedeutungslehre* (ed. O. Funke; 2nd ed., Berne, 1950).

G. MATORÉ, *Le Vocabulaire et la société sous Louis-Philippe* (Geneva — Lille, 1951).

—— *La Méthode en lexicologie. Domaine français* (Paris, 1953).

A. MEILLET, *Linguistique historique et linguistique générale* (2 vols., Paris, repr. 1948-52).

J. MELICH, *Jelentéstani kérdések* (A Magyar Nyelvtudományi Intézet Kiadványai XLII; Budapest, 1938).

D. CATALÁN MENÉNDEZ PIDAL, *La Escuela lingüistica española y su concepción del lenguaje* (Madrid, 1955).

B. MIGLIORINI, *Dal Nome proprio al nome comune* (Geneva, 1927).

—— *Lingua e cultura* (Rome, 1948).

—— *Che cos'è un vocabolario?* (2nd ed., Florence, 1951).

—— *The Contribution of the Individual to Language* (Oxford, 1952).

—— *Saggi linguistici* (Florence, 1957).

—— *Linguistica* (3rd ed., Florence, 1959).

G. A. MILLER, *Language and Communication* (New York — Toronto — London, 1951).

C. MORRIS, *Signs, Language and Behavior* (New York, 1946).

K. NYROP, *Grammaire historique de la langue française. IV: Sémantique* (Copenhagen, etc., 1913).

—— *Linguistique et histoire des mœurs* (Paris, 1934).

C. K. OGDEN-I. A. RICHARDS, *The Meaning of Meaning* (4th ed., London, 1936).

S. ÖHMAN, *Wortinhalt und Weltbild. Vergleichende und methodologische Studien zu Bedeutungslehre und Wortfeldtheorie* (Stockholm, 1951).

E. OKSAAR, *Semantische Studien im Sinnbereich der Schnelligkeit. 'Plötzlich, schnell' und ihre Synonymik im Deutsch der Gegenwart und des Früh-, Hoch- und Spätmittelalters* (Stockholm, 1958).

J. ORR, *Words and Sounds in English and French* (Oxford, 1953).

C. E. OSGOOD, G. J. SUCI, P. H. TANNENBAUM, *The Measurement of Meaning* (Urbana, 1957).

E. OTTO, *Stand und Aufgabe der allgemeinen Sprachwissenschaft* (Berlin, 1954).

L. R. PALMER, *An Introduction to Modern Linguistics* (London, 1936).

H. PAUL, *Prinzipien der Sprachgeschichte* (5th ed., Halle a.S., 1920).

J. PERROT, *La Linguistique* (2nd ed., Paris, 1957).

K. L. PIKE, *Language in Relation to a Unified Theory of the Structure of Human Behavior*, 3 parts (Glendale, 1954-60).

I. DE SOLA POOL (Ed.), *Trends in Content Analysis* (Urbana, 1959).

P. PORTEAU, *Deux études de sémantique française* (Paris, 1961).

W. Porzig, *Das Wunder der Sprache* (2nd ed., Berne, 1957).

S. Potter, *Modern Linguistics* (London, 1957).

—— *Language in the Modern World* (London, 1960).

Proceedings of the Seventh International Congress of Linguists (London, 1956).

Proceedings of the Eighth International Congress of Linguists (Oslo, 1958).

B. Quadri, *Aufgaben und Methoden der onomasiologischen Forschung* (Romanica Helvetica XXXVII; Berne, 1952).

B. Quemada, *Introduction à l'étude du vocabulaire médical (1600 à 1710)* (Paris — Besançon, 1955).

N. Rayevskaya, *English Lexicology* (Kiev, 1957)

H. Regnéll, *Semantik. Filosofiska och språkvetenskapliga grundfrågor inom betydelseläran* (Stockholm, 1958).

A. J. B. N. Reichling, *Het Woord. Een studie omtrent de grondslag van taal en taalgebruik* (Nijmegen, 1935).

T. B. W. Reid, *Historical Philology and Linguistic Science* (Oxford, 1960).

W. O. Renkonen, *Sur l'origine des gallicismes. Etude sémantique* (Turku, 1948).

P. F. Restrepo, *Diseño de semántica general* (2nd ed., Mexico, 1952).

G. Révész, *The Origins and Prehistory of Language* (transl. by J. Butler, London, 1956).

I. A. Richards, *Practical Criticism* (London, 1935 ed.).

—— *The Philosophy of Rhetoric* (New York — London, 1936).

—— *Principles of Literary Criticism* (2nd ed., London, 1938).

—— *How to Read a Page* (London, 1943).

—— *Speculative Instruments* (London, 1955).

J. Ries, *Was is Syntax?* (Beiträge zur Grundlegung der Syntax I; 2nd ed., Prague, 1927).

R. H. Robins, *Ancient and Mediaeval Grammatical Theory in Europe with Particular Reference to Modern Linguistic Doctrine* (London, 1951).

R. Robinson, *Definition* (Oxford, 1950).

A. Rosetti, *Le Mot. Esquisse d'une théorie générale* (2nd ed., Copenhagen — Bucharest, 1947).

A. S. C. Ross, *Etymology. With Especial Reference to English* (London, 1958).

J. von Rozwadowski, *Wortbildung und Wortbedeutung* (Heidelberg, 1904).

A. Rudskoger, *'Fair, Foul, Nice, Proper': a Contribution to the Study of Polysemy* (Stockholm, 1952).

B. Russell, *An Inquiry into Meaning and Truth* (London, 1940).

K. Sandfeld-Jensen, *Die Sprachwissenschaft* (2nd ed., Leipzig — Berlin, 1923).

M. Sandmann, *Subject and Predicate. A Contribution to the Theory of Syntax* (Edinburgh, 1954).

E. Sapir, *Language. An Introduction to the Study of Speech* (New York, repr. 1949).

—— *Selected Writings in Language, Culture and Personality* (ed. D. G. Mandelbaum; Berkeley — Los Angeles, 1949).

F. DE SAUSSURE, *Cours de linguistique générale* (5th ed., Paris, 1955).

R. A. SAYCE, *Style in French Prose. A Method of Analysis* (Oxford, 1953).

C. SCHICK, *Il Linguaggio. Natura, struttura, storicità del fatto linguistico* (Turin, 1960).

M. SCHLAUCH, *The Gift of Language* (New York, 1955).

M. SCHÖNE, *Vie et mort des mots* (Paris, 1947).

H. SCHREUDER, *Pejorative Sense-Development in English I* (Groningen, 1929).

H. Schuchardt-Brevier. Ein Vademecum der allgemeinen Sprachwissenschaft (ed. L. Spitzer; 2nd ed., Halle a.S., 1928).

H. SCKOMMODAU, *Der französische psychologische Wortschatz der zweiten Hälfte des 18. Jh.* (Leipzig — Paris, 1933).

T. A. SEBEOK (Ed.), *Style in Language* (New York — London, 1960).

T. T. SEGERSTEDT, *Die Macht des Wortes. Eine Sprachsoziologie* (German transl., Zurich, 1947).

I. SEIDEL-SLOTTY, *Die Bedeutung der Wörter* (Halle a.S., 1960).

CH. SERRUS, *Le Parallélisme logico-grammatical* (Paris, 1933).

—— *La Langue, le sens, la pensée* (Paris, 1941).

T. SLAMA-CAZACU, *Langage et contexte* (The Hague, 1961).

A. I. SMIRNITSKIJ, *Leksikologija anglijskovo jazyka* (Moscow, 1956).

H. S. SØRENSEN, *Word-Classes in Modern English, with Special Reference to Proper Names, with an Introductory Theory of Grammar, Meaning and Reference* (Copenhagen, 1958).

H. SPANG-HANNSEN, *Recent Theories on the Nature of the Language Sign* (Copenhagen, 1954).

C. SPEARMAN, *The Nature of 'Intelligence' and the Principles of Cognition* (London, 1923).

H. SPERBER, *Einführung in die Bedeutungslehre* (2nd ed., Leipzig, 1930).

L. SPITZER, *Essays in Historical Semantics* (New York, 1948).

Sprache — Schlüssel zur Welt. Festschrift für Leo Weisgerber (Düsseldorf, 1959).

W. B. STANFORD, *Greek Metaphor* (Oxford, 1936).

—— *Ambiguity in Greek Literature* (Oxford, 1939).

L. S. STEBBING, *A Modern Introduction to Logic* (3rd ed., London, 1933).

G. STERN, *'Swift, Swiftly', and their Synonyms. A Contribution to Semantic Analysis and Theory* (Göteborgs Högskolas Årsskrift XXVII; Gothenburg, 1921).

—— *Meaning and Change of Meaning. With Special Reference to the English Language* (Göteborgs Högskolas Årsskrift XXXVIII; Gothenburg, 1931).

J. STÖCKLEIN, *Bedeutungswandel der Wörter* (Munich, 1898).

E. STRUCK, *Bedeutungslehre. Grundzüge einer lateinischen und griechischen Semasiologie mit deutschen, französischen und englischen Parallelen* (2nd ed., Stuttgart, 1954).

S. STUBELIUS, *Airship, Aeroplane, Aircraft. Studies in the History of Terms for Aircraft in English* (Gothenburg, 1958).

—— *Balloon, Flying-Machine, Helicopter. Further Studies in the History of Terms for Aircraft in English* (Gothenburg, 1960).

E. H. Sturtevant, *An Introduction to Linguistic Science* (New Haven, 1947).

C. F. P. Stutterheim, *Het Begrip Metaphoor. Een taalkundig en wijsgerig onderzoek* (Amsterdam, 1941).

B. A. Terracini, *Conflitti di lingue e di cultura* (Venice, 1957).

L. Tinsley, *The French Expressions for Spirituality and Devotion. A Semantic Study* (Washington, D.C., 1953).

J. Trier, *Der deutsche Wortschatz im Sinnbezirk des Verstandes. Die Geschichte eines sprachlichen Feldes. I: Von den Anfängen bis zum Beginn des 13. Jh.* (Heidelberg, 1931).

S. Ullmann, *Style in the French Novel* (Cambridge, 1957).

—— *The Principles of Semantics* (2nd ed., Glasgow — Oxford, repr. 1959).

—— *Précis de sémantique française* (2nd ed., Berne, 1959).

—— *The Image in the Modern French Novel* (Cambridge, 1960).

W. M. Urban, *Language and Reality* (London, 1939).

A. P. Ushenko, *The Field Theory of Meaning* (Ann Arbor, 1958).

J. Vendryes, *Le Langage. Introduction linguistique à l'histoire* (Paris, 1950 ed.).

C. de Vooys, *Inleiding tot de Studie van de Woordbetekenis* (Groningen — Batavia, 1938).

A. Waag, *Bedeutungsentwicklung unseres Wortschatzes* (4th ed., Lahr i.B., 1921).

H. R. Walpole, *Semantics. The Nature of Words and their Meanings* (New York, 1941).

M. Wandruszka, *Der Geist der französischen Sprache* (Hamburg, 1959).

W. von Wartburg, *La Posizione della lingua italiana* (Florence, 1940).

—— *Problèmes et méthodes de la linguistique* (French transl., Paris, 1946).

—— *Von Sprache und Mensch. Gesammelte Aufsätze* (Berne, 1956).

—— *Evolution et structure de la langue française* (5th ed., Berne, 1958).

E. Weekley, *The Romance of Words* (London, 1917 ed.).

U. Weinreich, *Languages in Contact. Findings and Problems* (New York, 1953).

L. Weisgerber, *Muttersprache und Geistesbildung* (Göttingen, 1929).

—— *Vom Weltbild der deutschen Sprache. I: Die inhaltbezogene Grammatik; II: Die sprachliche Erschliessung der Welt* (2nd ed., Düsseldorf, 1953-54).

T. D. Weldon, *The Vocabulary of Politics* (London, repr. 1955).

E. Wellander, *Studien zum Bedeutungswandel im Deutschen* (3 parts; Uppsala, 1917-28).

R. Wellek-A. Warren, *Theory of Literature* (London ed., repr. 1954).

H. Werner, *Die Ursprünge der Metapher* (Leipzig, 1919).

H. Werner-E. Kaplan, *The Acquisition of Word Meanings: a Developmental Study* (Child Development Publications; Evanston, Ill., 1952).

P. J. Wexler, *La Formation du vocabulaire des chemins de fer en France (1778-1842)* (Geneva-Lille, 1955).

J. WHATMOUGH, *Language. A Modern Synthesis* (London ed., 1956).

B. L. WHORF, *Language, Thought, and Reality. Selected Writings of Benjamin Lee Whorf* (ed. J. B. Carroll; New York — London, 1956).

E. R. WILLIAMS, *The Conflict of Homonyms in English* (Yale Studies in English 100, 1944).

H. WISSEMANN, *Untersuchungen zur Onomatopoiie. I: Die sprachpsychologischen Versuche* (Heidelberg, 1954).

J. J. DE WITTE, *De Betekeniswereld van het Lichaam* (Nijmegen, 1948).

L. WITTGENSTEIN, *Philosophical Investigations* (Oxford, 1953).

W. WUNDT, *Völkerpsychologie. I: Die Sprache* (2 vols., Leipzig, 1900).

H. YAMAGUCHI, *Essays towards English Semantics* (Tokyo, 1961).

G. U. YULE, *The Statistical Study of Literary Vocabulary* (Cambridge, 1944).

P. ZIFF, *Semantic Analysis* (Ithaca, 1960).

R. ZINDEL, *Des Abstraits en français et de leur pluralisation* (Romanica Helvetica LXIV; Berne, 1958).

G. K. ZIPF, *Human Behavior and the Principle of Least Effort* (Cambridge, Mass., 1949).

V. A. ZVEGINTSEV, *Semasiologija* (Moscow, 1957)

SUBJECT INDEX

abbreviation, 29
abstract and concrete, 43–4, 119–26, 145, 148, 169, 189, 195, 215–16, 220, 226, 246
abstraction, 10, 39, 59, 111, 163, 239, 248
accent, 24–5, 32, 40, 42–3, 46, 135–6, 180, 185, 193, 216, 257
acquisition of language, 193–4
adjective, place of, 137–8, 170, 257
 polysemy of, 160–1, 173–5
agglutination, 43
agreement, 32, 34, 48
alliteration, 83
allomorph, 34
allophone, 24–5, 34, 126
alternation, 33–4, 84–5
ambiguity, 40, 52–4, 74, 79, 142, 151–2, ch. 7, 195, 249, 257, 263; see also homonyms, polysemy
 explicit and implicit, 188–92
 grammatical, 156–8
 lexical, 158–92
 phonetic, 40, 156
 stylistic, 188–92
ambivalence, 137, 168, 234–5
ameliorative sense-development, 231–5
amphibology, 158
amphiboly, see amphibology
analogy, 150, 157, 163, 185, 225
analytical and synthetic languages, 137
 theories of meaning, see referential
Anglicism, 130, 133–5, 139, 149, 165–6, 223
anthropology, 14, 50, 120, 227, 261–2
anthroponymy, 77
antiphony, 84
antithesis, 112
antonym, 133, 143–4, 240
aphasia, 7, 246, 262–3
arbitrary word, see word, opaque and transparent
archaism, 3, 133, 143
article, 35, 40–1, 44–7, 76, 183
association, 39, 48, 63, 65, 67, 84, 86, 90, 92, 101–5, 115, 129, 132–5, 147, 151, 194, 198, 201, 206, 211–24, 228, 231–2, 238–43, 250
 by contiguity, 212, 218–20, 222–3, 240
 by similarity, 212–18, 220–2, 240
associationism, 211, 240
associative etymology, 101; see also popular etymology
 fields, see fields, associative

attraction, see metaphorical attraction, synonyms
autosemantic and synsemantic words, 44

back-formation, 29
behaviourism, 11–13, 18, 20, 60, 70
blends, 29
borrowing, 42, 89, 103, 112–13, 127, 129–30, 133–5, 139, 145–9, 159, 165–7, 171, 180, 187, 206, 209–10, 221, 223, 225–6, 232, 242; see also semantic borrowing
bound and free forms, see free and bound forms
breath-group, 40–1, 156

case, 34, 157, 167, 171; see also inflexion
chain-reaction, 125, 242
chauvinism, 78, 112–13, 135, 232
chiasmus, 138, 170
cliché, 112, 136, 139, 216
code, 15, 17–19, 21, 261
collocation, 152–5, 198, 240
colour, 125, 246–7, 250
 local, 133–4
communication, 12–20, 116, 119, 128, 223, 253–4, 263
comparative linguistics, 3, 30–1, 81–2, 86, 235, 240, 257–8
comparison, 36, 62, 65, 73–4, 136, 139, 152, 201–2, 213, 240
compensatory lengthening, 42
compound, 28–9, 32, 68, 91–3, 96–7, 102–3, 106–13, 122, 153, 170, 183, 194, 223, 257
concatenation, 223–4
concept, 13, 63–4, 117–18, 126–7, 165–6, 171–3, 198–9, 243–56
conceptual dictionary, see dictionary
 sphere, 149, 187, 238, 243–53
concord, see agreement
concrete, see abstract and concrete
conjunction, 44–6
connotation and denotation, 74
consociation, 240
contagion, 198
content, see expression and content
context, 32, 34, 39–40, 48–54, 61, 64–8, 74, 77, 87–9, 99, 121, 123–4, 129–31, 135, 138, 142–3, 151, 157–60, 168, 174–5, 181–2, 188–90, 195, 198, 235, 257
 of situation, 32, 50–1, 59, 87–8, 124

273

contextual meaning, *see* meaning
theories of meaning, *see* operational
contiguity, *see* association by contiguity
continuum, 125, 246
conventional word, *see* word, opaque and
transparent
conversion, 52–3
critique of language, 10, 39, 116–19, 167

definition, 57, 62, 118, 126–7, 172, 184;
see also meaning, definition of, and
word, definition of
delimitation of concepts, 125–7, 194, 218,
242, 244–5, 248–9
delimitative signs, 42–3
denotation, *see* connotation and denotation
derivative, 26–7, 29, 35, 92–3, 96–7, 102,
106–13, 122, 132, 138, 186, 209–10,
230, 235, 257
descriptive linguistics, *see* synchronic and
diachronic linguistics
designation, 64
diachronic linguistics, *see* synchronic and
diachronic linguistics
dialect, 3, 88, 133, 143, 147, 150, 175, 182,
184–6, 221, 242
dictionary, 11, 30, 39, 43, 49, 61, 63–4, 67,
69, 103, 126, 144–5, 160–3, 168–9, 178,
236–7, 243, 254–6, 259; *see also* lexicography
conceptual, 63–4, 67, 254–6
differentiation, orthographic, 170–1, 179
phonetic, 170–1, 175, 184–5, 209
diminutive, 101, 108, 132, 138, 206, 230
displaced speech, 59
distinctive features, 24–5, 58, 65, 74–5, 77,
118, 127, 228, 230
distribution, 61, 66, 149–50
law of, 141, 226
drift, 193

echoism, 82; *see also* onomatopoeia
elementary affinity, 86
elision, 41, 45
ellipsis, 32, 46, 49, 161–2, 219, 222–3, 229
emotive values, 9, 22, 25, 52, 59–60, 70, 79,
88, 128–40, 142–9, 151–3, 162, 174–5,
188, 201–4, 212–3, 215, 226–7, 231–5,
257, 263
devices for expressing, 135–8, 257
loss of, 138–40
sources of, 129–35
engram, 20
ethnolinguistics, 243
etymology, 1, 5, 30–1, 56, 77, 96–105, 109–10,
145, 164, 176, 178, 194, 199, 215–16,
202–2, 224, 240–3; *see also* associative
etymology, popular etymology
euphemism, 2, 150–1, 187, 204–9, 228,
231; *see also* taboo

pseudo-, 207, 228, 231
euphony, 130
evaluative words, 132–3, 231–5
evocative effects, 9, 82–4, 117, 133–5,
139–40, 142–3, 215
primary and secondary, 133–4
expansion, *see* metaphorical expansion
expression and content, 57, 237
expressiveness, 9, 15, 85–90, 94–5, 98, 112,
123, 129, 133, 136–40, 163, 202–3,
212–13
extension, 2, 79, 119, 125, 200, 227–31

factor analysis, 68–9
feeling-tone, 128–9, 142; *see also* emotive
values
fields, associative, 211, 238–43, 250
morpho-semantic, 239
semantic, 7–8, 64, 67, 243–53, 256, 262
figurative language, *see* metaphor, metonymy
foreign words, *see* borrowing
free and bound forms, 28, 32, 46, 156
frequency, *see* statistics
functional theory of meaning, 66; *see also*
operational

gender, 34, 48, 169, 183, 222, 230, 257
generalization of meaning, 200; *see also*
extension
generic terms, 58, 73, 118–23, 142, 169, 194,
229–30, 257
glossematics, 57, 237
government, 32
grammar, 1, 3, 5, 9, 11, 19–21, 24, 27–9,
34–5, 40, 43–5, 54–5, 75–7, 105, 133,
156–9, 167, 169–70, 183–5, 193, 195,
222, 236–8, 251, 261–2
'grammatical' and 'lexicological' languages,
105, 257

'hard' words, 115, 130
historical linguistics, *see* synchronic and
diachronic linguistics
holophrase, 32
homonymic clash, 156, 175, 180–8, 200,
241–2, 257, 262
homonymics, 181
homonyms, 24, 41, 53, 63, 75, 78–9, 81, 87,
98, 104, 156–9, 164–5, 167, 175–88,
190–2, 200, 221, 240–3, 253, 257, 262;
see also loan-homonymy
and polysemy, 164, 177–80
effective, 182
grammatical, 156–7, 184
reinterpretation of, 164, 167
safeguards against, 181–5, 257
secondary, 178
sources of, 176–80
stylistic uses of, 190–2
substitutes for, 186–8

hyperbole, 136–7, 139, 233
hypertrophy of meaning, 168, 175

iconic signs, 17, 25
identification, 73–5, 77, 79
ideophone, 84; see also onomatopoeia
idiolect, 22–3
immanent linguistics, 262
incorporating languages, see polysynthetic
    languages
individual language, see idiolect
infix, 29
inflexion, 26–7, 32, 35, 43–8, 157, 169–70,
    183, 236
information theory, 18, 253–4
initial sounds, 40–2, 45–6
intellectual terms, 7, 244, 248–50
intension, 119, 163, 228, 230
intention, 128, 212
interjection, 85–6
intonation, 25–7, 136, 158, 236
introspection, 58, 67, 70
isogloss, 185–6

juncture, 42

key-words, see words
kinship terms, 228, 237, 247–8, 250

language and speech, 19–23, 67, 74, 195
    bar, 114–15, 127
    units of, 23–35, 39–53, 123
law of diminishing returns, 139
    of distribution, see distribution
    semantic laws, see semantic
learned terms, 42, 95, 97, 106–15, 127, 142,
    145–9, 155, 187
learning, 18, 113
lexicography, 20, 30, 49, 54, 66–7, 69, 71,
    144, 169, 178, 195, 240, 254–6; see also
    dictionary
'lexicological' languages, see 'grammatical'
    and 'lexicological' languages
lexicology, 29–35, 48, 252–3, 255–6, 259
lexicon, see vocabulary
liaison, 41
linguistic geography, 63, 67, 103, 168, 175,
    181–2, 185–6, 220, 243, 262
loan-homonymy, 180
    -translation, 112
    -word, see borrowing
locution, see phrase
logic and language, 73–4, 79, 116–28, 173,
    227–8, 230, 259; see also philosophy
    and language

malapropism, 114–15
meaning, passim, esp. ch. 3
    ambiguity of term, 54–5, 172
    applied, 129

central, 129
change of, see semantic change
components of, 54–5, 70, 128–9, 237, 249
contextual, 129
definition of, 54–67, 211
essential, 129
grammatical, 55
importance of — in linguistics, 71, 260–2
lexical, 55
measurement of, 68–71, 164, 178, 253
multiple, 62–3, 67; see also homonyms,
    polysemy, synonyms
structural, 55
theories of, see operational, referential
units of, 26–31, 40, 48–53
mentalistic theories of language, 58–62, 66,
    70
metanalysis, see reshaping
metaphor, 2–3, 36–8, 61–2, 65, 78–9, 92–3,
    95, 97–8, 104, 106, 116, 130, 136, 138–9,
    149–51, 160–3, 166–7, 189–90, 192,
    195, 201–4, 209–10, 212–18, 220, 223,
    225–7, 240, 257, 263
    angle of, 213–14
    animal, 37–8, 136, 201, 203–4, 209, 213–15
    anthropomorphic, 37–8, 214, 226
    concentrations of, see metaphorical attrac-
    tion and expansion
    dominant, 201–4
    from concrete to abstract, 215–16, 220, 226
    ground of, 213
    parallel metaphors, 150–1, 225–6
    radiation of metaphors, 162
    reciprocal, 212
    revitalized, see revitalization
    synaesthetic, 36–7, 216–18, 226–7
    tenor of, 213
    vehicle of, 213
metaphorical attraction, 149–50, 201–2, 214
    expansion, 201–4, 214, 226, 257
metaphysics, 61, 251; see also philosophy
    and language, thought and language
metonymy, 78, 91–2, 163–4, 218–20, 223,
    226, 235, 242
middle terms, 235
moneme, 26
monosyllabism, 177, 183
morpheme, 26–9, 33–4, 54, 84, 91, 96, 237
morphology, 1, 6, 29, 32–3, 44–8, 91–3,
    96–115, 142, 194, 237
morphophonemics, 261
morpho-semantic fields, see fields
motivation, 1, 13, 17, 25, 77–8, ch. 4, 129,
    138, 162, 194, 205, 212, 218, 257–8
    absolute and relative, 92
    acquisition of, 94, 101–5
    loss of, 93–101, 138, 194
    morphological, 91–3, 96–115, 138, 257
    phonetic, see onomatopoeia
    semantic, 91–3, 96–106, 138, 162, 212, 218

name, *passim*, esp. 57, 61–4, 67, 80–1, 86–7, 129, 138, 158, 211–24, 238–40, 246; *see also* proper name
negation, 45, 156–7, 179, 182, 198, 222
neologism, 6, 129–30, 139, 173, 195, 209–10, 212–13
noa words, 205; *see also* euphemism, taboo
nominal syntax, 123
number, 34, 48, 76–7, 157–8, 169–70, 183, 222, 237

oaths, 208–9
obsolescence, 2, 6, 87, 97–8, 102, 156, 173–6, 185–8, 195, 241–2
omnibus words, 230
onomasiology, 64, 67
onomastics, 77
onomatopoeia, 1, 17, 25, 80, 82–92, 94–6, 101, 106, 129, 138, 257–8; *see also* motivation
    primary and secondary, 84
opaque words, *see* word, opaque and transparent
operational theories of meaning, 55, 64–7
overload of meaning, 168

padding, 154
part for the whole, 92, 219
pejorative sense-development, 1–2, 135, 147, 174–5, 203–4, 208–9, 215, 219, 231–5, 249
personification, 37–8
philosophy and language, 1, 3–4, 7, 9–10, 14–15, 30, 39, 44, 58, 64–7, 73–4, 79, 100–1, 112, 116–19, 126, 138, 151, 163, 167, 172–3, 227–8, 230, 244–5, 249, 251, 259, 262
phonaesthetic function, 82, 129–30
phoneme, 24–6, 33–4, 65, 75, 126, 141, 172, 184, 195, 236
    prosodic, 24
    suprasegmental, 24
phonemics, 26; *see also* phonology
phonetic change, 3, 21, 94–7, 101, 110, 145, 148, 176–7, 180, 194
    convergence, 176–7, 180
    laws, *see* sound-laws
phonetics, 6, 23–4, 26, 31, 40–1, 43, 54, 142, 261
phonology, 26, 29, 33, 35, 40–6, 236–8, 257, 261–2
phonostylistics, 135
phrase, 28–9, 32–3, 41, 44, 98, 107–18, 123, 132, 142, 153, 158, 170, 183, 195, 200–1, 209, 221–3, 229, 235, 242
plethora of meaning, 168
plural, *see* number
politics, 1–2, 20, 49–50, 77, 112–3, 126, 131–2, 135, 138–9, 173, 198–9, 232, 234, 252–3

polysemy, 3, 52, 62, 104, 137, 159–82, 185, 188–90, 195, 200, 209, 212, 214, 218, 228, 253, 257
    and homonymy, *see* homonyms
    conflicts caused by, 171–6
    of adjectives, *see* adjective
    safeguards against, 167–71, 257
    sources of, 159–67
    stylistic uses of, 188–90
polysynthetic languages, 32
polyvalency, 159
popular etymology, 101–5, 164, 220–3
portmanteau words, *see* blends
pragmatics, 15
prefix, 27, 29–30, 35, 46–7, 75, 97, 107–8, 122, 156–7, 236
preposition, 32, 35, 44–8, 108, 111, 122, 183
pronoun, 26, 28, 34–5, 44–7, 68, 85, 158, 198, 230
proper name, 52, 68, 71–9, 89–91, 101, 118, 129–30, 162, 218–20, 232
psychiatry, 69, 126
psychoanalysis, 14, 172, 201, 204–5
psycholinguistics, 68
psychology and language, 6–7, 12, 14–15, 20–3, 40, 57–62, 69–70, 120, 146, 164, 200–9, 213, 227, 229, 235, 240, 244, 250–1, 259–60, 262
psycho-physical parallelism, 61
puns, 40, 42, 124, 164–5, 179, 188–92, 243
purism, 111–13, 139, 149, 171

quid pro quo, 189, 191

reconstruction, 30–1, 140, 175, 185, 197, 221, 240, 242, 262
reduction, etymological, 100–1
    semantic, 92–3
reduplication, 29, 84, 94
referent, 49, 55–60
referential theories of meaning, 55–64, 66–8, 70
    use of words, 128
repetition, 152–4, 179, 189, 191
reshaping, 40–1
restriction, 2, 79, 200, 227–30, 241
revitalization, 99–101, 216
rhetoric, 3, 7, 88, 151
rhyme, 83, 134, 179, 181
rhythm, 83, 134

sandhi, 41
satellite words, 186
'Saxonisms', 111, 145
science and language, 20, 58–60, 64, 70–1, 88, 107, 111, 113–14, 118–19, 126–7, 141–2, 148–9, 171–3, 198–9, 202–3, 210, 219–20, 229, 252–5, 262–3
semanteme, 27

semantic borrowing, 165–7, 171, 180, 209, 225–6

change, *passim*, esp. ch. 8; causes of, 6, 197–210, 227; classification of, 6–7, 196, 211–23, 227; composite, 223; consequences of, 227–35; factors facilitating, 193–5; nature and conditions of, 211–27

constants, 209, 247

differential, 68–70

divergence, 177–80

laws, 6, 141, 196, 224–7, 260

pseudo-semantic developments, 221–2, 242–3

space, 69

semantics, ambiguity of term, 10, 29–30, 32–3, 172

'anecdotal', 197

'atomistic', 197

'crypto-', 71

experimental, 69

history of, 1–10

philosophical, 10, 15

place of — in linguistics, 29–30, 32–3, 71, 260–2

structural, 8, 222, ch. 9, 262

syntactical, 32–3, 48

semasiology, 5, 142

sememe, *see* semanteme

semiology, 15; *see also* signs, theory of

semiotic, 14, 54; *see also* signs, theory of

sense, *passim*, esp. 1, 57, 61–4, 67, 80, 86–7, 102, 128–9, 138, 158, 173, 185, 195, 211–24, 238–40

sentence, 28, 31–2, 34–5, 44, 46, 49, 123, 141, 156, 158, 172, 182, 195, 198, 236

shifts in application, 124–5, 159–61, 167, 194–5

signal, 12–13, 17

'significs', 14

signs and symbols, 10, 12–19, 54–6, 61–2, 70, 79, 91, 163, 253, 263

theory of, 10, 14–19, 54

similarity, *see* association by similarity

simile, *see* comparison

slang, 3, 88, 133, 140, 143, 150–1, 207

slogans, 131–2, 138, 148

social factors in language, 7, 15, 20–2, 60, 77, 113–15, 119, 128, 133, 140, 146, 161–2, 179, 195, 199–200, 219, 228, 230, 232–4, 247–8, 252–3, 262

sounds, 1, 21, 23–6, 29, 31, 40–3, 57, 63, 74–5, 77–8, 80–91, 94–7, 101–5, 109–10, 123, 129–30, 133, 135–6, 138, 145, 151, 156, 170–1, 176–7, 180, 184, 188, 191, 193–4, 199, 220–2, 240, 243; *see also* name, onomatopoeia, phonetic change, phonetics

-laws, 94–6, 225; *see a so* phonetic change

symbolism, *see* onomatopoeia

specialization of meaning, 161–2, 167, 195, 200, 228–9; *see also* restriction

speech, act of, 11–13, 20, 22–3

and language, *see* language and speech

spelling, *see* writing

pronunciation, 103

reform, 184

split infinitive, 158

statistics, 9, 18, 22, 43, 68–71, 89, 93, 104, 106–7, 149–50, 164, 168–9, 175–7, 179–81, 195, 227, 236, 240, 253–4, 257–8, 262–3

structuralism, 8, 10, 26, 55, 58, 63, 71, 79, 172, 195–6, 211, 222, ch. 9, 260–2; *see also* semantics, vocabulary

style, 8–9, 22–3, 45, 49–50, 53, 82–3, 85, 88–91, 123–5, 128, 133–40, 142–3, 151–5, 159, 161, 172, 188–92, 201–4, 212–18, 253–4, 263

stylistics, 8–9, 49–50, 128, 151, 172, 253–4, 253–4,263

stylo-statistics, 253–4

substitution test, 65–6, 84, 141, 143

suffix, 26–30, 35, 43, 46, 91–2, 97, 107–9, 132, 156, 236, 240

suppletion, 43

symbol, *see* signs and symbols

symbolic use of words, *see* referential

synaesthesia, *see* metaphor, synaesthetic

synchronic and diachronic linguistics, 7–8, 10, 79, 81, 101, 103–4, 109, 164, 178, 186, 196, 256

synecdoche, 92, 219

synonyms, 3, 62, 72, 79, 81, 87, 98, ch. 6, 186, 202, 207, 212, 226, 240, 242–4, 249, 257

attraction of, 149–50, 202

choice between, 151–2, 155

collocation of, 152–5; *see also* collocation

combination of, 152–5

concentrations of, 149–50, 257

delimitation of, 43–5

differences between, 141–5

distribution of, 141, 149–50, 226

integral, 142

patterns of, 145–51, 257

radiation of, 150–1, 225

scales of, 145–9, 257

stylistic uses of, 151–5

variation of, 152, 155

synsemantic words, *see* autosemantic and synsemantic words

syntactics, 15

syntax, 1, 5, 19, 31–5, 48, 76, 123, 135, 137–8, 158–9, 194, 236–7

synthetic languages, *see* analytical and synthetic languages

taboo, 39, 71–2, 187–8, 204–9, 228, 231, 260; *see also* euphemism

(taboo, cont.)
  of delicacy, 205–7
  of fear, 205–6
  of propriety, 187–8, 205, 207–9
  on animals, 206
  on proper names, 71–2
tautology, 153–4
thought and language, 9, 59, 116–21, 171–3, 190, 243–53, 255, 260
time, 216, 219, 226, 251
toponymy, 77
translation, 49, 53, 107, 112–13, 132, 137, 165–7, 171, 173, 180, 209, 225–6; *see also* loan-translation, semantic borrowing
transparent words, *see* word, opaque and transparent
typology, 9, 105, 254, 256–8

universals, 209, 224–7, 247, 254–6, 260; *see also* semantic constants, semantic laws

vagueness, 3, 52, 74, 116–28, 142, 160, 194, 230, 249
variation, elegant; *see* synonyms, variation of
verbicide, 131
vocabulary, 8–10, 16, 21, 35, 39, 46, 55, 63–4, 69, 79, 92, 105–15, 120–3, 126, 133, 149–50, 181, 195, 213, 229, ch. 9, 262

vowel harmony, 43, 46
whistle languages, 17–18
word, *passim*, esp. chs. 2 and 4
  apotheosis of the, 38, 173
  -classes, 34–5, 44, 48, 52–3, 159, 161, 174, 182–3, 222
  definition of the, 3, 26–8, 34–5, 39, 46, 65
  form-words and full words, 3, 35, 43–8, 157–8, 236–7
  images of the, 4, 13, 20, 30, 36–8, 61–2, 65, 116
  independence of the, ch. 2, 123, 257
  key-words, 50–1, 126, 138, 172, 248–9, 252–3
  -limits, 42–3
  opaque and transparent, *passim*, esp. ch. 4, 257–8; *see also* motivation
  -order, 32, 35, 45, 47, 137–8, 170, 257
  power of the, 3–4, 36–9
  pseudo-, 47
  -structure, 42–3, 45–6, ch. 4, 177, 257
  transparent, *see* opaque and transparent
  tyranny of the, 39, 154, 251
  witness-words, 252
words and things, 197
writing, 15, 17, 39, 42, 46, 72, 91, 96, 98–9, 103, 159, 170–1, 176, 179, 183–4, 257

xenophobia, 135, 232